SWITCHBACK TRAILS ACROSS THE SIERRA

THE STORY OF COMMERCIAL PACKING IN THE SIERRA NEVADA MOUNTAIN RANGE OF CALIFORNIA

Happy Trails! Marye Roeser

BY

MARYE ROESER
COLEVILLE, CA

Pack String – Drawing by Leslie Engelhart.

ISBN: 978-0-578-79452-5

Silhouette of Lou Roeser and string. (Steve Lucasik)

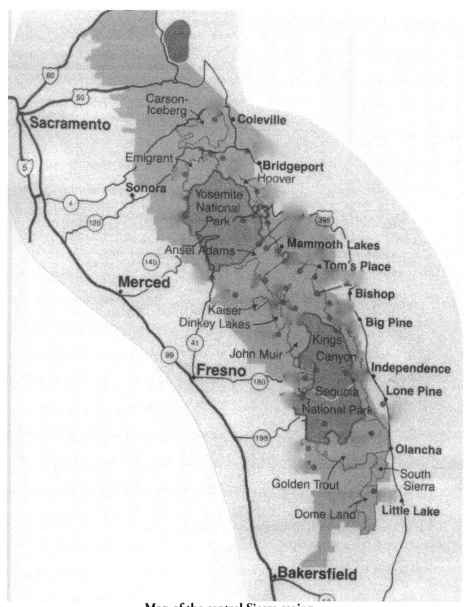

Map of the central Sierra region.

TABLE OF CONTENTS

Chapter   **Page**

TABLE OF CONTENTS

Chapter   **Page**

APPENDIX

EASTERN HIGH SIERRA PACK STATIONS - Page 173
Histories of individual pack stations and the geographical area from Little Lake following Highway 395 to Coleville at the Nevada State border on the east.

WESTERN HIGH SIERRA PACK STATIONS - Page 249
Histories of individual pack stations and the geographical areas from Walker Pass near Lake Isabella northward to Sonora Pass on the west.

Packing In – Drawing by Leslie Engelhart.

ACKNOWLEDGMENTS

My husband, Lou Roeser, and I have lived in the eastern Sierra of California since our marriage and have known and been friends with a vast number of wonderful people. I can't begin to acknowledge all the many conversations over the years, but I want to give thanks and recognition to these influences. In this book project, all of these people contributed and encouraged me in unseen ways they probably weren't even aware of.

The hard-working owners of pack stations where we worked taught and mentored us with incredible patience, sharing their knowledge. We owned and operated the Mammoth Lakes Pack Outfit, Sierra Meadows Equestrian and Ski Touring Center, and Mammoth Snowmobile Tours for many years, and we had the most amazing employees who taught me more than they will ever know. Deep gratitude goes to my superb co-workers, as well as to my many memorable students, at Antelope Elementary and Coleville High School, where I taught for twenty years.

In a project such as this, the legions of people from the past who wrote books, articles, diaries, and letters saved important details of the rich past that could have been lost to the dust of time. Thanks to the incredible museums of the region, including the Hayden Cabin Museum, the Laws Museum, and the Eastern California Museum, and their mostly volunteer staff. County Archives and library staff who make this material available to the curious public are highly commended from my ever-appreciative heart.

To my late sister Dorothy, a history and elementary teacher and deeply missed, and brother-in-law, Louie Fitzhugh, who shared so much of our mutual history, you are part of this story. A special thanks to the late Genny Smith, historian and a special friend, and to Jane Fisher, editor of The Album, published by Chalfant Press, both of whom encouraged me to write historical remembrances for their excellent books. Also, thank you to the editors of Mammoth Lakes and Bishop newspapers—including the Mammoth Lakes Herald, Mammoth Times, and Inyo Register—as well as to the editors of various area magazines, who encouraged and published my articles, giving me the courage to attempt this book.

I am deeply indebted to late Gary Nickell, who did the first proofreading of my manuscript and passed away before the book was completed. I had many conversations with Jack Fisher, author of *Stopping the Road*, a very well-researched historical account, concerning researching and self-publishing books. To Paul Verdugo, I give my heart-felt thanks for not only teaching me much about computer and Photoshop skills, but for also producing giclee prints of my art and Lou's photography. He is currently working on our oral history video, has read this manuscript, and has made suggestions on specific areas to rewrite and flesh out. I am honored to include some photographs taken by talented photographer, Sandy Powell, who is publishing her own gorgeous coffee table book on western lifestyles. A very special thank you to David Woodruff, my production assistant, for design, formatting, and publishing expertise. I couldn't possibly have completed this project without his irreplaceable help, guidance, and encouragement.

Last but not least, I owe my deepest gratitude to my incredible husband and remarkable family, without whom this book could not have been written. Our children grew up in the pack station lifestyle. We worked as a family, and they always "rode for the brand." My husband Lou is an endless well of information and support, and has patiently critiqued my manuscript. My son Lee and daughter-in-law Jennifer Roeser contributed their packing expertise and photos, and they work to carry on excellence in the packing and mule industry, mentoring others and always offering unlimited help. My daughter Kerry Roeser and son-in-law Mike Elam, also with so much knowledge of the packing business, geology, flora, fauna, etc., are essential to this project. Daughter Leslie and son-in-law Matt Engelhart are excellent horsemen who know the cattle ranching business like few others, and their three young adult children, Addie, Rial, and Zack are our future rodeo stars and ranchers. My gratitude goes to Leslie for allowing me to include some of her incredible pencil drawings depicting packing scenes. Thanks to beloved daughter Maryl Roeser, who loves the horses and mules and keeps my attitude centered and optimistic. Special blessings and my endless thanks go to my patient daughter Kerry (a fellow teacher) and to my talented granddaughter Kiera (for her exceptional writing and editing expertise) who took on the huge job of the final proofreading and corrections with dedication for a much improved document. Kiera became Chief Editor guiding the editing process, performing the final edit, and crafting a polished manuscript.

Jill – Drawing by Leslie Engelhart (at Mammoth Lakes Pack Outfit).

PREFACE

For a lengthy part of my life, this manuscript has been brewing in the back pages of my thoughts. I was first exposed to High Sierra pack stations as a young girl, when my family vacationed at Camp High Sierra in Mammoth Lakes, California. During my college years at UCLA, I worked on staff there during the summer, and also guided horseback rides at the Mammoth Lakes Pack Outfit for our guests. There, I met my future husband, a young summer packer from Arizona.

Pack stations became our lifestyle and livelihood for the next fifty years. After working at McGee Creek Pack Station and Rainbow Pack Outfit, we purchased the Mammoth Lakes Pack Outfit in 1960. We raised our family of four children in that life, and they have been an essential part of it, valuing it as we have. We are very aware that we enjoyed the rare opportunity to be an integral part of this particular cultural and historical aspect of the Old West. We have lived during a colorful part of a very unique history.

For many years, I have been wholly fascinated with the Sierra Nevada, its natural history, geography, geology, and history. I fervently studied, read, and took classes that were offered. When I was teaching elementary school in Coleville, California, I included the geology and plant and animal communities of the eastern Sierra in our science program.

My husband Lou and I listened ardently to old stories told by packers and always reflected that this heritage and history should somehow be preserved. Discovering that there was almost nothing written about Sierra pack stations, I began making notes and collecting photographs, stories, and bits and pieces of information. I started writing short stories and histories about packing and pack stations. After these were published, I considered a book.

The history of packing does not begin with packing in the Sierra, but is a very old tradition from early in the story of civilization. I have endeavored to thread together various traditions that connected in the story of westward movement, crossing the Sierra, and settlement in California. I culminated this by piecing together the development of commercial packing in the Sierra. In the Appendix section, I have summarized historical information on the individual pack stations located on both the east and west sides of the central part of this great mountain range, the Sierra Nevada.

The story can never be fully complete, but my hope is that this book will further inspire others to write about this rich historic record and legacy. My goal for this book is to portray some fresh insights into a distinctive past, describe the spectacular mountain country of the Sierra, and pique your interest in the exceptional people who have lived and worked here, and continue to do so.

Marye Russell Roeser-2020

Lou and Marye Roeser at corrals in 1965.

INTRODUCTION

Stretching northwesterly for 400 miles across California between the Great Central Valley and the mountainous deserts of the Great Basin, lies the grand Sierra Nevada Mountain Range. An early Spanish missionary, Fray Pedro Font, first saw the snow covered peaks from the west and called the range, "una gran Sierra Nevada." Sierra Nevada is translated from Spanish to mean "snow-covered mountains."

While winding roads lead into the mountains, only a few highways actually penetrate and cross this vast mountain range. In the central Sierra, this leaves a massive area of roadless backcountry located in national parks, national forests, state parks, and wilderness areas.

The Sierra Nevada granitic base rock has been uplifted along major fault systems tilting to the west. From Tehachapi Pass in the south to Fredonyer Pass just southeast of Mt. Lassen in the north, this mighty fault block mountain range varies from a little above sea level on the western slope as it rises out of the great Central Valley, to Mt. Whitney at 14,505 feet elevation on the eastern escarpment. Mt Whitney can be clearly seen looming above the town of Lone Pine. The Owens Valley, where Lone Pine is located, is a "rift valley," rimmed on the east by another fault block mountain system, the White Mountains and adjoining Inyo Mountains.

The work of glaciers and violent volcanic action modified the geography of the mountains. On a drive along Highway 395 through the Owens Valley on the east side of the range, the towering glaciated crest of the Sierra outlines the range, while glacial moraines are clearly visible at the mouths of many canyons. The gradual western slope, home of ancient sequoias, is blanketed in thick green forests marching up to the giant glaciated rock spires along the main crest, while the precipitous eastern face plunges abruptly to the arid Owens Valley floor. Driving across Highway 88 and Carson Pass or Highway 120 through Yosemite to Tioga Pass illustrate well the phenomena of a fault block mountain range.

The "Little Ice Age," referred to as a Climate Minima period, from around 1300 to 1870 was in place when the United States was settled. The Little Ice Age is identified as a period of cooling after a warmer period known as the Medieval Climate Optimum, lasting from approximately 900 to 1300 AD. Glaciers covered the higher elevations in the Sierra. The remnant glaciers, seen today on peaks of the Sierra, were formed during this period and are not remnants from the last major glaciation. Temperatures gradually increased, and the many small glaciers in the Sierra began to retreat.

This, then, was the geography of the Sierra Nevada when the first packers and their pack mules explored this vast region. It is in this rugged land of past glacial, tectonic, and volcanic activity that the packing industry evolved in the 1840s and still functions today in similar fashion. It is a backcountry where the only tracks on the trail are from hoofs, feet, and paws. In this remote range, packers with their horses and mules are still an integral part of the mountain scene.

Roesers and Fitzhughs in corrals at Mammoth Lakes Pack Outfit.

Roeser Family at horse drive. (Michael Cooke Photography)

CHAPTER ONE

EARLY PACKING TRADITIONS

Downward and around a narrow, rocky switchback trail, a Sierra mule packer vigilantly leads his string of dependable mules. He glances back over his shoulder frequently to ascertain that all the animals are following easily, and there is slack in the lead ropes. If one animal were to set back or stumble, it could cause a chain reaction along the string. Often with a steep precipice on one side of the trail and a rock wall on the other, options are limited. The surefooted, athletic mules steadily pick their way over rocks and rough terrain with loads of 150 pounds and up, avoiding scraping their well-balanced loads against trees when possible.

Mule packers in the High Sierra have been traveling these same narrow and precipitous trails throughout the mountains for over 150 years. Once, these pack trains supplied gold-mining settlements with equipment and provisions. Now, they provide vacationers with pack trips into the scenic wilderness areas of this vast roadless backcountry. The mules, horses, equipment, and packers are little changed from 1849.

Horses and mules are remarkable creatures. They are strong, fast, able to be domesticated, and are just the right size to adapt to humanity's usage. Man has never designed anything quite so functional and economical, and has always been enthralled with the beautiful mystique of the equine. World history itself would have been totally different without the priceless advantage of domesticated horses and mules. Land transport might have been greatly limited, and seafaring cultures may have dominated more. Land transportation of goods and persons was dependent on the equine. Saddle and pack animals have been utilized since man first domesticated them, and equines have pulled wheeled vehicles since the wheel was invented.

Mules are hybrid animals, a cross between a male "jack" donkey and a female "mare" horse. They have been serving mankind for over 4,000 years and are portrayed in Egyptian scrolls, the Bible, and by Homer in his writings. During the dawn of civilization in the Middle East, donkeys served as pack and riding animals and still are an important means of transportation in that region.

The horse has traditionally enabled man to access and travel throughout the land, and it is difficult to imagine the story of the West without these animals. People rode horseback or traveled in wagons and carriages, as walking was seldom the preferred mode of travel. The westward settlement of the United States was made possible on the backs of horses and mules, and historical dependence on the horse and mule is a vital part of our cultural heritage. An

1

important element of our pioneer and western cultural heritage lies in the humble hoof prints of horses and mules. Throughout the early history of the United States, California, and the Sierra Nevada Mountain Range, goods and provisions were transported by pack animals and freight wagons.

George Washington, the first president of the United States, raised mules on his farm at Mount Vernon. He was presented two Spanish jacks by King Charles III of Spain in 1785. One was appropriately named Royal Gift. Washington advertised these jacks at stud and took great pride in the quality mules he produced. Mules were highly valued in colonial America. The Quarter Horse also developed in colonial times and became the most versatile horse in the West.

Native American tribes recognized the immeasurable value of the equines brought in by the Spanish and quickly adapted their cultures to the use of the horse. The Great North American Plains were settled by formerly forest tribes only after their culture had mastered the use of the horse. Lewis and Clark, on their well-documented westward journey, discovered that a Shoshone tribe had acquired mules that were highly valued in what is now Idaho/Montana. They gifted Lewis with a riding mule and Spanish riding saddle. This tribe, as well as the Nez Perce in Oregon, probably acquired these animals through raiding and trading.

Mules have been valuable pack animals in all of our major conflicts, from the Revolutionary War, through the Civil War and the Indian Wars. The U.S. Army employed large numbers of mules and packers to move troops around the West during the Indian campaigns, and many soldiers soon became experienced mule packers. The U.S. Army utilized the largest pack trains in the country and printed a manual of pack transportation that is still a classic treatise on packing mules today.

THE FUR TRADE

The fur trade in the American West flourished and declined between 1820 and 1840. Fur trappers and traders trapped mostly beaver, while exploring the North American continent from coast to coast with horses and mules. The packing traditions of these men and the Army packers blended with Southwestern traditions of the Mexican arrieros (packers) to establish the packing techniques and gear used today.

In *This Reckless Breed of Men: The Trappers and Fur Traders of the Southwest,* Robert Glass Cleland observed:

> *This lack of navigable rivers compelled the fur traders of the Southwest to rely almost entirely upon the caravan or pack train for transportation. For such overland travel each trapper had one or more riding animals equipped with saddles usually of the Mexican type, and two pack mules or horses. The pack animals were equipped and packed after the Mexican fashion and usually carried a load of from two hundred to two hundred and fifty pounds. The stock foraged for itself the year round, and when grass and bushes failed, the inner bark of the quaking aspen or sweet cottonwood furnished a satisfactory substitute.*

Pack and riding animals included both mules and horses. The large companies of forty to sixty men also drove extra horses and mules. Each year, an annual Rendezvous drew trappers and traders from all over the West to the

Green River or Pierre's Hole in Idaho/Wyoming with well-laden pack animals, trading furs for supplies and additional goods for trading.

Jedediah Smith, a fur trapper, crossed the Sierra Nevada eastward from the Central Valley in California during late winter in 1827 with two other men, seven horses, and two mules. They crossed the crest in the vicinity of present day Ebbetts Pass with five surviving horses and one mule after a difficult journey of eight days. Smith had left the remainder of his exploratory expedition in the San Joaquin Valley of California, and his small contingent was traveling to reach the Rendezvous and resupply his party.

Joseph R. Walker led a party of fur traders to California in 1833, traversing the Sierra in what is now northeastern Yosemite National Park. They struggled through the myriad of canyons over Virginia Pass, found a Native American path near the present location of the Tioga Pass Road, and followed this route across the Sierra to the San Joaquin Valley. Their party was the first American group to view Yosemite Valley and the giant sequoias. Walker discovered the Walker Pass route on his return trip and crossed the Sierra many more times in his life. In later years, he purchased horses and mules in California and drove them through Walker Pass or Cajon Pass to access the Old Spanish Trail and Santa Fe Trail, then onward to Missouri to trade.

Ewing Young was a fur trapper and former Santa Fe trader who trapped extensively along the Sacramento and San Joaquin Rivers. After 1834, he became a regular dealer in mules and drove them between California and the Columbia River in Oregon, as well as to the Missouri River settlements.

THE SANTA FE AND OLD SPANISH TRAILS

The Santa Fe Trail, originating from first Franklin and then Independence, Missouri, to Spanish Santa Fe, New Mexico, was underway in 1821 and, by 1824, was a well-established route. It began largely as a pack train route and evolved into a wagon trail with the wagons pulled by mules or oxen. Yankee traders with their caravans left Independence and journeyed to Santa Fe with trade goods desired by the Southwest peoples. After weeks of trading in Santa Fe, the massive wagons turned around, and most traders accompanied the return trip to Independence.

Some traders, however, continued on to Los Angeles with huge pack mule trains. The California traders from Southern California, called Alta California, brought mules and horses to trade, along with exotic silks from China and other desired products. There was a considerable demand for mules and horses in the Spanish settlements in the Rio Grande Valley and farther east in Missouri. The pack mules leaving Santa Fe for the return trip to California were laden with woolen fabrics and large covers called serapes, jerzas, and cobertones. These blankets were exchanged for mules and horses, usually at the rate of one animal for two or three serapes.

The California traders had to depart from Los Angeles by April in order to navigate river crossings before the substantial spring run-off made the rivers too dangerous. The Old Spanish Trail crossed the Mojave Desert and then, by a very roundabout route, veered north into Utah and Colorado to avoid the difficult maze of deep canyons and the swift, treacherous crossings on the Green and Colorado Rivers. The Spanish Trail then headed southeast from Colorado into New Mexico and thence to Santa Fe. The Old Spanish

Pack Trail was the longest commercial pack animal trail in the United States, at 1,200 miles across wildly forbidding territory, where attacks by Native American tribes and lack of waterholes were a continuous threat.

The California packers were sometimes Mexican (arrieros) and American, but more often Californios (citizens of Alta California), and their riding gear and pack equipment were Mexican in origin. Some of the Americans had previously been fur trappers, such as Kit Carson. A typical caravan consisted of about 200 people (traders, packers, personal servants, and a few wives), saddle animals, and 1,000 mules. The traders banded together in a caravan for safety from attacks. The trip took two and a half months from Los Angeles to Santa Fe.

After meeting the west-bound wagons in Santa Fe, the two groups spent several weeks recuperating from their strenuous and difficult journeys, trading and provisioning for their return trips. By late August, the California traders were back on the Spanish Trail for the return trip to Los Angeles. They had to avoid high spring run-off waters in the rivers and also early snow in the mountains.

On the trail, mules were belled with different-sounding bells, enabling traders to identify their pack animals apart from other traders. The pack mules were not strung together but were loose herded by the arrieros. Mexican "mule skinners" packed animals with loads of up to 320 pounds. The mules were packed each morning, unloaded at the "nooning" rest stop, repacked, and unloaded again at night. At night, each mule was picketed by a reata, a braided rawhide rope, separately for grazing on whatever grass was available. The early California vaqueros were not familiar with shoeing horses and mules and learned that trade from the American "gringos" who came from a blacksmith heritage. Over the Spanish Trail, these mules were not shod.

ARRIEROS AND VAQUEROS

For 400 years, the mule served as the most important work animal in Mexico and Central and South America. Sebastian Aparicio established the freight-hauling industry called Arriero. He taught the Native American and Spanish methods of packing goods on mules. The business of hauling freight with trains of pack mules still continues throughout Central and South America, as it does in the Sierra, to this day.

According to Arnold R. Rojas in *These Were the Vaqueros,* Don Luis de Velasco, Viceroy of New Spain in 1555, remodeled the saddle brought to the New World by the Spaniards, creating the type of Western saddle in use today, and also created many new types of bits.

In Alta California during the Rancho Period, most travel throughout Spanish California between ranchos, missions, and villages was by horseback and pack train. There were very few roads suitable for wagon travel. The early Californios used some two-wheeled carts but did not use wagons extensively, so most travel was via a pack trail system. The Californios were expert horsemen, and traditionally everyone rode horses.

California ranchos were ideally suited for raising mules and horses. The climate and terrain favored literally "grass on a thousand hills," and provided grazing for multitudes of cattle, horses, mules, and burros or donkeys on the huge Spanish, and later Mexican, land grant ranchos. The Californios did not raise hay, so their herds of horses and mules subsisted on the rich grasslands available to them. The small, dusty town of Los Angeles became a renowned center for obtaining good mules and horses. This continued long after the Gold Rush, with mules bringing a premium price.

Other associated industries developed in California. The ranchos raised thousands of cattle for hides, and leather was used for harnesses, gear, saddles, and all manner of livestock equipment. Oak trees were plentiful for building wooden packsaddles, and tanbark was used for tanning leather. The rawhide reata was developed in those regions of Alta California where the maguey plant for making fiber ropes did not grow, but hides for rawhide were abundant. Ropes were also braided from horsehair, as horses were numerous, and mane and tail hair was readily available. Braiding rawhide reatas and horsehair ropes became a finely tuned art, and braiders were renowned for their skills.

THE AMERICAN EXPLORERS AND EMIGRANTS

Outfitting, packing, and guiding are ancient, historical professions the world over. In North America, the Hudson's Bay Company, Lewis and Clark, John Wesley Powell, Jedediah Smith, Joseph Walker, John Fremont, Kit Carson, Joseph Chiles, and many, many others were part of the outfitter-guide tradition. President Theodore Roosevelt frequently employed outfitter-guides to lead him on trips out West.

Emigrant trains crossing from the Midwest over the plains and deserts to California included pack animal trains as well as wagons. Pack trains moved along faster on the trail than the slower moving, cumbersome wagons pulled by ox teams. Mules were also considered tougher than the oxen or horses and survived the hardships of the trail better.

The Bartleson-Bidwell Emigrant Party of 1841 was the first overland party to attempt to take wagons across the plains to California. The larger party had split in Utah Territory, with half the party traveling to Oregon and the other half splitting off north of the Great Salt Lake, bound for California. A member of the party later said that, "We had no guide and no compass." They relied on a letter about California from John Marsh. However, they did not know that Marsh had never seen this country that he wrote about.

After struggling across the desert, the party was forced to abandon their wagons in eastern Nevada. They built packsaddles and equipment with the lumber of their wagons, and packed their remaining animals. They continued on as a pack train to California with the members riding horseback. They traversed the Sierra by way of the West Walker River and crossed over Sonora Pass to the Central Valley, accomplishing this without experienced guides or maps. Nancy Kelsey, at age seventeen, accompanied her husband, Ben, with their small one-year-old daughter, Martha Ann. As they were clambering down through the rocks on Sonora Pass, a member of the party looked back, observed that Nancy was walking barefoot (her shoes had worn out), carrying her child and leading her worn out horse without a single complaint and still smiling.

Many individuals in that party became prominent figures in California and its history. Nancy became the first woman to complete the overland journey to

California, and she was later remembered as being one of the women who sewed the first "bear flag" for the Bear Flag Revolt.

More emigrant pack horse and mule trains, as well as wagon trains, continued on the trail to California. They were not the later gold seekers, but primarily men and women seeking "free" land to farm and a new way of life in California. Most sought the Sacramento area and Sutter's Fort as their first destination. Some, like the well-documented Donner Party, suffered great tragedy, but most safely reached California.

Packer, Lou Roeser, rests his stock and party while all admire the view from Duck Pass to Mammoth Mountain, with a sparkling Barney Lake below.

CHAPTER 2

GOLD SEEKERS
EXPLORE THE
SIERRA NEVADA

Gold was discovered on the American River near Sutter's Fort in California in 1848, and the news spread quickly to the Eastern States. This was the spark that caused the large migration of people to this sparsely settled, pastoral land. With the advent of the Gold Rush in the Sierra Nevada, men from all over the world swarmed to California and the mountain gold fields seeking their fortune. Wagon trains were quickly put together, setting out from Independence, Missouri for California through largely unknown territory. Ships set sail for the West Coast, taking the long ocean journey around the horn of South America. San Francisco, then a small town, was the goal for the sea routes, while Sacramento was the aim of the wagon trains.

As the miners prospected across the Sierra hoping to strike it rich, pack trails accessing the area developed, often following original Native American footpaths. The colder and wetter climate that was present during the 1849 Gold Rush era made travel and prospecting in the Sierra much more difficult than the current climate does. In the mountains, glaciated valleys are U-shaped and can provide natural routes for trails. Native Americans residing near and in the Sierra followed these geographical features in their trading travels. Trails also followed rivers through valleys and canyons. These trails and routes were soon modified to suit the needs of miners, as well as packers with their animals. Among the passes used by indigenous peoples, and later by explorers and settlers, were Bloody Canyon to Mono Pass, Mammoth Pass, Paiute Pass, Kearsarge Pass, Hockett Pass, and Walker Pass. Numerous trails were improved, and new ones built by individuals, groups, or local towns, and financed by toll charges. As the miners prospected and explored, gold and silver mining towns sprang up.

During the California Gold Rush period, an important pack trail crossed the Isthmus of Panama. Ships carried gold seekers from the Atlantic Coast or New Orleans to Panama. There, skilled arrieros, with their horses and mule trains, met travelers at the seaport and packed them across Central America to the Pacific West Coast. Some sailing ships from California plied the Pacific Ocean from San Francisco to the Isthmus and back again, transporting travelers to the docks at San Francisco.

Throughout the 1850s, the transportation of merchandise by commercial pack train was a large and flourishing business. Although horses were also packed, the sturdy, dependable mule was the preferred pack animal. Mules were also considered smoother riding animals and were much sought after, often demanding higher prices. Southern California produced many mules, and large numbers of mules were also imported from Mexico, along with their arrieros.

The packing operations were most often owned or organized by storekeepers in the mountain communities, in order to keep their stores stocked with merchandise. They were conducted by, and frequently owned by, independent, professional, and mostly American packers who employed arrieros. These pack trains made regular trips over specified routes. Travelers also joined these pack trains, and were referred to as passengers or tourists. Packing companies or individuals transported merchandise, mail, and passengers, and served numerous customers along the way.

A typical pack train consisted of twenty-five to forty head of pack and riding animals. One specific train was composed of thirty-five mules, of which six were riding animals, while the rest carried freight. Some trains used a white mare with a bell around her neck to lead the train. The cook often rode a belled white mare and led a pack animal carrying food and camp equipment for the crew. The "cargadore" was the supervisor or foreman, and there were usually four arrieros. The mules were packed with 300 to 425 pounds of freight, including feed (barley) for the animals.

The aparejo packsaddle, of Spanish origin, was used extensively on many types of loads. Resembling a large envelope, the pad was constructed of leather with an inside frame of green willow sticks. It was stuffed with grass and was about six inches thick. The green willows dried to conform to the back of each pack mule. The packsaddle was fitted individually to each mule so as not to make them sore. A leather strap was used as a cinch. A crupper (a padded strap which passed under the mule's tail) was fastened to the saddle to prevent the load from shifting forward. Over the top, the packer slung two leather straps with large hooks on each end. Ore sacks were loaded between the hooks on each side. Then a diamond hitch was thrown by a rope with a lash cinch to tie the whole load together. A bulky load could require a double or even a triple diamond hitch.

The trains traveled from dawn to sunset, covering about fifteen to twenty-five miles per day, depending on the terrain and trail conditions. Where possible, stops were made each night for grazing, water, and rest for the animals and crew. When reaching the night camp, the goods were unloaded from the mules and the animals were turned out to graze.

In *Gold is the Cornerstone*, John Walton Caughey, highly acclaimed history professor at UCLA, discusses California pack trains:

Arrieros were Mexican packers following the vaquero traditions of Mexico and Alta California. Mexican in its genre, the pack train was most picturesque. Several graphic descriptions exist, notably that by Carl Meyer in Nach dem Sacramento. Enroute from Monterey to the mines, he joined a 150-mule train to which he allots several pages. After tributes to the short-coupled Mexican horse, now better known as the western pony, and to the more humble but durable mule, he sketches the events of a day on the trail.

Carl Meyer described the packers' breakfast of beans and tortillas, after which the night herders brought in the stock, and the animals were saddled:

The arrieros affix a balanced load, lashing everything securely in place. If they are expert, the procession is soon ready for the trail and troops off after the bell mare. If a pack slips, an arriero quickly lassos the mule, slips a tapaojos or hood over its eyes. The animal is repacked and moved back in line. The lunch stop is short and the packs are not removed. On, then, for the afternoon march, until the night camp is reached. Packs, aparejos, and saddles are pulled off and neatly piled. If a saddle sore is detected on one of the mules, it is cared for and the animals are turned out to graze. Only then, did the arrieros have supper and finally roll up in a blanket for the night.

Caughey continues:

In the mines, the meals of the packers were soon anglicized and the vocabulary partly so. Yet, many of the features that Meyer most praised – the nimbleness of the mules, their ability to follow a shelving trail over mountain and chasm, and the sound engineering of the aparejo – continued to be the justifying factors for packing. Packing reached its zenith in the upper reaches of the Sierra mining country and its less accessible parts.

Early packers depended on sturdy mules to carry heavy loads of equipment and supplies over narrow, rocky, mountain trails and high passes. The agility of mules enabled them to wind their way through thick forests without touching the trees on either side of their loads. Devoted mule packers claim mules are more efficient than a horse, can do three times as much work on one third of the feed, and graze on forage that horses will refuse. Mules take better care of themselves, and are careful where they place their hoofs.

The tough, hard hoofs mules inherited from the donkey side of the family endure the granite and volcanic rocks of the trails much better than the horse. Mules' feet are more straight walled than a horse and are generally smaller. In the early years, Californio traders and packers did not shoe their mules. Americans came from a background of blacksmiths and shod their horses and mules, knowing that their feet would hold up in the rocky terrain better and longer if they were properly shod.

During snowy winter months, some packers used snowshoes for their horses and mules when necessary. The snowshoes were about eleven inches square and were fastened on with turnbuckles. The animals took to the snowshoes almost instinctively, willingly plodding over the snow-covered trails.

Sometimes heavy snows closed trails for weeks. Over the Nevada Trail from Placerville to Genoa, needed supplies were finally broken through one year by laying blankets on top of the snow for the pack animals to struggle over.

Pack trains packed equipment and supplies to the mines and hauled ore out. Wood was needed at the mines for cook fires and warmth, since mines were usually located at higher elevations with cooler temperatures. Men cut wood and packed it on mule or burro trains to the mining settlements. As game was plentiful, others worked as hunters and packed wild game to town hotels and markets, as well as selling directly from the backs of their animals.

Miners and merchants lived in isolated mining camps and communities, and numbered in the thousands. Every pound of food and supplies was packed there by pack trains over often-hazardous trails. William Swain, a 49er, wrote home to his wife, brother George, and family from his camp on the South Fork of the Feather River. These letters were published in a book titled *The World*

Rushed In by James S. Holliday. The following excerpt describes how the miners at the "diggins" obtained needed supplies:

Supplies—everything from sandbag cloth and shovels to whiskey and barrels of flour—are packed in on mules. When mules can get no further, cargoes are transferred to the backs of men.There are many Mexicans here with pack mules... some of them with three hundred pounds on them... Whole barrels of pork are frequently mule-packed by the Mexicans. In fact, there is nothing, which they cannot carry on a mule. The best loading is one-hundred-pound sacks of flour, two or three of them according to the strength of the mules. According to an American packer, mules are rarely lazy and will travel the most dangerous mountain paths just as easily and unafraid as a somnambulist.

MINING DISCOVERIES EAST OF THE SIERRA CREST

Miners from the Mother Lode Country on the west side of the Sierra gradually worked their way over the crest to the eastern Sierra country. Prospectors soon discovered gold in Monoville and the East Walker River area near stark Mono Lake. This discovery led to the founding of mining towns Aurora and Bodie. The Sonora Pass Trail became an important west to east trail in 1859 as the most direct route. Sol Carter operated pack trains from Sonora over the old Sonora Trail, and transported supplies and passengers who rode horseback to the mining strikes in 1859. Terence Brodigan, owner of Sonora House and Livery Stable, was a friend of William Bodey, the discoverer of Bodie. Brodigan's pack trains also regularly crossed over Sonora Pass to the gold strikes in the eastern Sierra.

The Sonora-Mono Wagon Road from Sonora to Bridgeport, constructed by Mono County, was begun in 1863 and required five years to complete. The completion of this road greatly facilitated travel to the new mining claims from the western communities. Aurora became an important mining boomtown, followed by Bodie.

In the late 1870s, discoveries in Lundy Canyon, Lake Canyon, and Tioga Hill prompted the mining boomtowns of Lundy and Bennettville. The mines and towns were originally accessed by pack trails until, eventually, toll roads were constructed. The May Lundy mine was located at over 11,000 feet elevation on an almost inaccessible slope of Mt. Scowden. Ore had to be laboriously packed down to the mill in Lundy Canyon by strings of mules and horses. The hard working animals had to climb 4,500 feet from Mill Creek to the mine site.

The *Homer Mining Index*, a newspaper located in Lundy, reported the following information:

Onofre Moreno, the well-known Mexican packer, has entered into a contract with the Great Sierra Mining Company to pack 35 tons of freight from King's Ranch... up through Bloody Canyon and to the company's building on Tioga Hill. The freight will consist of provisions and machinery... Moreno left for Bodie on Wednesday to put twenty pack mules on the road.

In 1881, a pack trail was built from Lake Canyon to Tioga Hill. It was said to be an improvement over the Bloody Canyon route. However, this trail could not handle the large machinery needed at the Bennettville mines.

The Great Sierra Wagon Road started at Crocker's Station on the westside, which later became Crocker's Sierra Resort on the Big Oak Flat Road, and crossed the Sierra to Bennettville, above Tuolumne Meadows. The road was constructed mostly following the old Mono Trail that later became the Tioga Road. The planned road extension over the pack trail in Lake Canyon never extended to Lundy, because, by the middle 1880s, the mines had ceased operation.

In *Sierra Crossing: First Roads to California* by Thomas Frederick Howard, he states:

> *Though the Sierra Nevada today retains many officially recognized wilderness areas and has been less obviously altered by human activity than the adjacent Central Valley, the human imprint is nevertheless pervasive. In recent years, investigations by geographers have tended to remove the notion of a pristine pre-Columbian America, unaltered by human hands or feet, into the realm of myth. Aboriginal populations were substantial, and their actions, particularly the setting of fires, must have been a major determinant in the distribution of plant communities. Even so, the Indian impact was relatively slight compared with what began with the gold rush.*

The increase in activity was almost explosive after 1849. With mining, logging, ranching, and water development, the population of the Sierra rose to much higher densities than prevailed before, in many places higher than today. Great flows of people and goods throughout the mountains created a volume of traffic vastly larger and more environmentally altering than the Indian trade in back-packed food items and decorative objects.

A popular multi-day trail ride to the old mining town of Bodie where riders relive "Old West" history.

For a 1995 commercial film shoot, Lou Roeser assembled wagons, stock, and crew, replicating an 1849 wagon train in Death Valley.

CHAPTER THREE

TOURISM IN YOSEMITE

"Everybody needs beauty as well as bread, places to play and pray in, where Nature may heal and cheer and give strength to body and soul alike."
—John Muir, *The Yosemite*, 1912

Tourism to Yosemite commenced soon after the remarkable Yosemite Valley was discovered, when rumors of its spectacular beauty reached San Francisco and beyond. The deep, glacially carved valley is seven miles long and only one-and-a-half miles wide. At the time, there were no roads, only indigenous trails.

Would-be tourists had to make arrangements to hire guides, camp outfits, horses, and mules. Many of the first trail guides were young Native Americans. No maps or informative guide books were available. For twenty-three years after its discovery, Yosemite was only accessible by mule or horse. Riding horseback with gear packed on mules was regarded by California pioneers of the time as a commonplace travel mode. By the end of 1855, forty-two tourists had accomplished the difficult pack trip into Yosemite Valley. Enterprising citizens soon organized livery stables, camps, and hotels to accommodate the visitors.

In 1855, two brothers, Milton and Houston Mann, who owned a livery stable in Mariposa, began construction of a pack trail from Mariposa. The trail followed the South Fork of the Merced River to Clark's Station (now called Wawona) and on to Yosemite Valley. The brothers completed the fifty-mile-long trail in 1856 and did a "brisk business," renting pack animals and guides to tourists as well as charging a toll for using the trail. L. H. Bunnell and George W. Coulter, as well as others, constructed a second, more-direct trail from Coulterville and Bull Creek. This new competing trail opened in 1858, and a number of visitors began using it. The Manns then sold their pack trail to Mariposa County, and the trail became toll-free.

James Mason Hutchings, an English born journalist, was editor of a monthly periodical, *Hutchings' Illustrated California Magazine*. Hearing of the wonders of Yosemite Valley, he sought to explore the Valley for himself, and to accurately describe and promote the beauty to his readers. He organized one of the first tourist parties from San Francisco to visit Yosemite in 1855 and obtained a complete pack outfit with "two reliable Indian guides in Mariposa," as quoted by Francis P. Farquhar in *History of the Sierra Nevada*. The party followed the Mariposa trail route. Walter Millard and Alexander Stair, friends of Hutchings, and Thomas Ayers, a well-known landscape painter hired to make drawings for the magazine, were on that trip. While there, Ayers made many drawings and sketches, and was so impressed with the beauty of the Valley that he returned again in 1856.

Hutchings was so enchanted with Yosemite Valley that he purchased and enhanced the Upper Hotel for tourist parties in 1864. He and his family ran this hotel, called the Hutchings House, from 1864 to 1874. He began a saddle train business in 1866, building a barn and corrals. His livery operation met stages with Yosemite-bound visitors wherever the current wagon road ended. He guided tourist parties around Yosemite, showing them the sights. Early visitors hunted for their food, which consisted of deer and ducks. They also fished the Merced River, which provided native rainbow trout and sacramento perch. Some vegetables were also grown by the hotel.

Hutchings sold his saddle train business to William F. Coffman in 1874, just when the Big Oak Flat Road reached Yosemite Valley. When the State of California closed out the hotels and camps in the Valley in 1874, Hutchings fought this eviction in the courts for many years, but eventually lost. However, he was appointed Guardian of the Grant—caretaker of the Valley—in 1880 and was able to live in his cabin until 1884. California issued new ten-year leases for visitor services.

Coffman merged his saddle train business with the stable business of George Kenney to form Coffman and Kenney Yosemite Stables, located at an area called Kenneyville. Their barn was located on the site now occupied by the Ahwahnee Hotel. By 1888, the telegraph had reached Yosemite Valley. Visitors would telegraph Coffman and Kenney ahead of their visit and arrange for saddle horses or carriages, drivers, and guides to be at their hotel at an assigned time. The company provided all types of transportation, services, pack trips, and horseback trips for visitors until 1916, when the business was sold to Joe Desmond. Desmond had been awarded the Yosemite concession for visitor services by the newly organized National Park Service Agency, which he called the Desmond Park Service Co.

From 1855 on, many famous and affluent people with large parties visited Yosemite Valley from cities. They needed to be completely outfitted for their trips in the Valley and surrounding backcountry. This outfitting business included not just saddle horses, but pack mules, complete camping gear, packers and guides, cooks, and provisions.

Galen Clark was a 49er, professional packer, and a member of the Mariposa party in 1855, one of first two American tourist parties to actually see Yosemite Valley. He moved to what is now called Wawona, a Sierra Miwok campsite, at Yosemite's south entrance, to regain his failing health. He filed a preemption claim on 160 acres along the South Fork of the Merced River in 1856. He built a way station known as Clark's Station that offered meals and primitive lodging to travelers. When President Abraham Lincoln signed the Yosemite State Park Bill in 1864, Clark was appointed Guardian of Yosemite Park. In 1869, he took in a partner, Edwin Moore, and his station was then referred to as Clark and Moore's Station, or the Big Tree Station. Yosemite's wonderful mountain climate seemed to have cured Clark's health problems, as he lived in Yosemite until his death at age ninety-six.

In 1874, he sold his enterprise to Henry Washburn and two partners. Those partners dropped out, and Washburn and his two brothers, Ed and John, developed the resort venture into what it is today. Henry's wife, Jean, renamed it Wawona after the Miwok word woh-woh'-nau, which meant "big tree" and imitated the hoot of an owl, the guardian of the forest. Being very isolated, the Washburn ranch had to be self-sufficient, producing the food necessary for the hotel. The first recorded fish planting began in Yosemite in 1879. The hotel burned down in 1878, but was rebuilt in 1879 in time for the visit by President

Ulysses S. Grant. The Washburn's Yosemite Stage and Turnpike Co. provided transportation and livery services for visitors and met stages at Raymond. The barn and stables held over 100 animals. The Wawona Hotel Co. was eventually purchased by Yosemite National Park in 1932.

MONO PASS TRAIL/TIOGA PASS TRAIL

The Mono Pass-Bloody Canyon Trail was a well-traveled Indian route used by both eastern Paiute and western Miwok tribes. There were two branches of the trail. The northern branch, called "the Mono Indian trail" in Francis P. Farquhar's *History of the Sierra Nevada*, passed by Tenaya Lake, continuing to Tuolumne Meadows, and thence over Tioga Pass to Mono Lake. The southern branch traveled through Little Yosemite Valley and climbed over Cathedral Pass to Tuolumne Meadows, and then veered east over Mono Pass, where it descended through treacherous Bloody Canyon to Mono Lake. Mono Pass is 10,604 feet in elevation, and it is approximately five miles from the pass to Walker Lake, a small lake at 7,935 feet in elevation on the eastern side.

In 1853 and 1854, Tom McGee cleared a rough horse trail from Big Oak Flat to Cascade Flat on the western side of Yosemite Valley, and then continued on the northern branch to Tuolumne Meadows, Mono Pass, and Bloody Canyon on the Sierra Crest. The pack trail descends 3,000 feet in about four miles from the summit of the pass. Mono Pass was the principal east/west Sierra pack route for miners.

William Brewer and Charles Hoffman of the California Geological Survey, as part of their survey work, crossed on the Mono Pass Trail from Tuolumne Meadows in 1863. The trail had achieved a notorious reputation through Bloody Canyon, and to the survey team it appeared inaccessible to horses. Brewer called it a terrible trail, and related that commercial pack trains crossed the Sierra over the Tioga Road and Mono Pass through Bloody Canyon to the eastside gold discoveries weekly. He reported that supplies for Esmeralda in the Aurora region were packed on mules during the summer months from Mariposa, Coulterville, or Big Oak Flat.

J. Ross Browne, author of *Mining Adventures, California and Nevada 1863 to 1865*, stated:

> Within a year or two, when the facilities for crossing the Sierra Nevada are increased, visitors from the Yo Semite Falls will doubtless pay their respects to Mono Lake by way of the Bloody Canyon. A rough trail now crosses from that point by which the Falls of Yo Semite may be reached in something less than two days. I have known the trip to be made in thirty hours on a good mule.

EARLY ARTISTS

From the first tourist party, artists were drawn to Yosemite. These artists helped publicize the scenic attractions of Yosemite to the world with their many fine paintings.

Albert Bierstadt, a famous landscape painter, with Fitz Hugh Ludlow, art critic and author for the *Atlantic Monthly* tasked to write a series of articles and a book describing California, along with their party, traveled to Yosemite Valley in the spring of 1863. They purchased horses and saddles in San Francisco for their adventurous trip. Ludlow wrote that the saddles were "Californian" and that, "if there were a more perfect saddle than the Californian, I would ride bareback a good way to get it," as quoted in *Yosemite* by Margaret Sanborn. In Mariposa, they hired pack animals and a fifteen-year-old guide and packer. When they reached Yosemite, there were three or four other tourist parties in the Valley.

Several girls visiting there were wearing what they termed "informal mountain dress." The men denounced the huge hoop skirts then in fashion and approved the mountain attire of these young women in Yosemite. Several of the early travelers also commented on the characteristics of the first women visitors in Yosemite Valley. They were described as "strong-minded women who rode astride wearing bloomer suits."

Within the next eight years, Bierstadt painted fifteen paintings of Yosemite. He was originally from Germany but made America his home, and was the most sought-after landscape artist at that time. Bierstadt made other trips out to California from his East Coast headquarters from 1871 to 1873. In 1871, he visited Lake Tahoe and Donner Lake, making sketches, studies, and small paintings. In February of 1872, he again visited Yosemite Valley, seeing its scenic wonders in winter, and returned again in May for six weeks. He then took a pack trip to Hetch Hetchy Valley, and, later in his studio, painted four large oil paintings of Hetch Hetchy Valley. In 1880, he once again visited Yosemite Valley, which was to be his last visit there.

Thomas Hill was another well-known landscape painter who first visited Yosemite in 1862. He built a studio in Yosemite Valley but later moved to Wawona, where he became the most prolific of the Yosemite painters. His daughter, Estrella, married John Washburn, and Hill had his studio on the hotel grounds. Hill made many sketches and color studies on-site and then developed them in his studio into huge oil paintings. His painting, Yosemite, 1889, is very well known. These paintings magnificently advertised the beauties of Yosemite to the American public.

William Keith, who became one of the leading Western landscape painters during this time, first visited Yosemite Valley in 1868. He returned in 1872 with a letter of introduction to John Muir. They discovered their mutual Scottish heritage and became fast friends for life. Keith made many Sierra trips with Muir, including one to Mt. Whitney, and became an early Sierra Club member. His paintings of Yosemite grace many museum collections.

Chris Jorgenson built an art studio in Yosemite Valley in 1893 and remained in the Valley for many years. Thomas Moran, another famous painter, visited the area many times and produced a body of Yosemite work.

JOHN MUIR

John Muir was a Scottish immigrant whose family settled on a farm in Wisconsin. After a stint at the University of Wisconsin, Muir embarked on a foot journey in 1867 to see his adopted country, working along the way. In 1868, he sailed to San Francisco by way of the Isthmus of Panama. There he learned of the splendid scenery of Yosemite Valley. Muir, with a friend, arrived in Yosemite Valley on a ten day camping and exploring trip, having read about the wonders of the Valley.

After running out of money, Muir traveled down to the San Joaquin Valley and went to work for a rancher in Hopeton, breaking mustangs and assisting with the harvest. He also operated a ferry in Knight's Ferry. In 1869, he was hired by a neighboring rancher, Pat Delaney, to shear sheep. In the spring, Delaney hired him as a sheepherder, along with several other herders, to accompany Delaney's flock of 2,050 sheep to the headwaters of the Merced River in Tuolumne Meadows for the summer grazing in the high mountains.

Muir was the overseer of the flock, and his job was to gradually move the sheep higher through successive belts of forest and meadow as the snow melted. The herders traveled by horseback, with their camp and provisions packed on mules. Muir had an assistant herder and several protective dogs, and they sometimes camped for several weeks on the better meadows. Delaney packed in provisions to the camp throughout the season.

As the flock grazed its way to Tenaya Lake and Tuolumne Meadows, Muir recorded this experience in his journal. He gloried in exploring this high country. It was while working as a sheepherder in Yosemite that Muir explored and first conceived his glacial origin theories of Yosemite Valley and the Sierra Nevada Mountain Range. Observing and studying the Sierra landscape, he concluded that this scene was created by glacial action and that glaciers still existed there.

After the sheep flocks returned to the Central Valley, John Muir pined for the Yosemite he had come to love. That fall, with a ranch hand friend, Harry Randal, Muir returned to Yosemite Valley. They went to work for James Hutchings at his hotel in the Valley, spending a snowbound winter with the Hutchings family. Muir built and operated a sawmill for Hutchings, and created lumber to build more cabins for the resort. He also worked on the cabins and constructed one for himself. There had been about 1,000 tourists visiting Yosemite that year and more accommodations for visitors were sorely needed.

Hutchings had also established a stable with horses and mules to accommodate these tourist parties. When spring arrived, Muir occasionally served as a guide for tourist parties on sightseeing trips around the Valley and pack trips to further locations.

In 1870, the University Excursion Party arrived in Yosemite Valley for a long summer stay. This was a group of eight young men from the University of California, Berkeley, and their two professors. Joseph LeConte, Professor of Geology, was one of the teachers, and this was his first of many visits to Yosemite. The group rode their horses from Berkeley through the hot Central Valley and finally reached Yosemite Valley. John Muir joined the party for several weeks of traveling through Yosemite and on to Mono Lake. Muir revealed his glacial origin theory and won LeConte to his conclusions.

Muir, LeConte, and the party traveled over Mono Pass and down through Bloody Canyon, from Yosemite to the Mono Basin. The animals on the trip were driven loose down the pass because it was too treacherous to lead them. In *My First Summer in the Sierra,* he commented that all their animals were wounded on the trail:

> *I have never known an animal, either mule or horse, to make its way through the canyon, either in going up or down, without losing more or less blood from wounds on the legs. Occasionally one is killed outright—falling headlong and rolling over precipices like a boulder. But such accidents are rarer than from the terrible appearance of the trail one would be led to expect; the more experienced when*

driven loose find their way over the dangerous places with a caution and sagacity that is truly wonderful. During the gold excitement it was at times a matter of considerable pecuniary importance to force a way through the canyon with pack trains early in the spring while it was yet heavily blocked with snow; and then the mules with their load had sometimes to be let down over the steepest drifts and avalanche beds by means of ropes.

During a trip to San Francisco, Ralph Waldo Emerson—the famous writer—along with his wife, daughter, and son-in-law, traveled to Yosemite in 1871. They hired a pack train and used the Coulterville Trail. The trip required three and a half days to reach Yosemite Valley. John Muir was operating the sawmill for Hutchings at the time and often carried a book of Emerson's essays with him, reading them by firelight. Emerson eventually met John Muir in the Valley. Muir guided the horseback party around Yosemite Valley for several days, admiring the outstanding scenery. The party was then scheduled to pack out of the Valley for their return trip to San Francisco and the East Coast. Young Muir strongly urged Emerson to remain longer and take a pack trip with him, away from civilization. Muir had little patience with the demands of the outside world that commanded the much older Emerson's return to the East Coast schedule.

From 1871 to 1875, Muir guided a number of long, well-outfitted traveling pack trips throughout the Sierra, often riding his favorite mule, Brownie. Muir and Brownie took an extensive, three-month-long trip, alone and with minimal provisions, in 1875. He traveled through the giant sequoia belt and became intensely interested in preserving the Sierra forests. The surefooted mule learned to be extremely agile on Muir's cross-country travels. During the winters, Muir pastured Brownie in the San Joaquin Valley.

Muir further honed his oratory skills around many a blazing campfire, sharing his knowledge of natural history and explaining his theories of the glacial origin of Yosemite Valley. He stated his resolve to "lead men back to the healing powers of nature."

After these early years, Muir spent less time in Yosemite. Upon his marriage to his wife Louie in 1880, he managed her family's fruit ranch in Martinez. In 1894, he returned to the Valley after an absence of six years and noted sweeping changes during those intervening years. Many small visitor businesses (some he described as shanties) with ten-year leases covered the valley floor. There were barns and farm animals; 300 head of horses and mules grazed the meadows at night, and other meadows were cut for hay. Muir came to believe that the State of California was mismanaging the Valley.

MUIR GUIDES PRESIDENTS

President Theodore Roosevelt arranged for a Yosemite pack trip, to be guided by John Muir, in 1903. Roosevelt wrote to Muir, "I do not want anyone with me but you, and I want to drop politics absolutely for four days and just be out in the open with you."

Muir boarded the presidential Pullman railroad car in Oakland, California in May. The immediate party consisted of President Roosevelt, California Governor George Pardee, John Muir, and other officials. The party traveled by train overnight through the San Joaquin Valley and arrived at a terminus in Raymond. From here they rode in a stagecoach to Wawona, accompanied by a cavalry detail. On this long, jolting journey, they discussed the problems of Yosemite Valley. Muir urged the recession of the grant given to California by President Abraham Lincoln's proclamation back to the federal government.

At Wawona, a large party set out on horseback and visited the Mariposa Grove of sequoia trees. The larger party returned to Wawona unaware that the small party of Roosevelt, Muir, and two Yosemite rangers, Archie Leonard and Charles Leidig, had remained behind. The two rangers were well-qualified guides, as they were the first two appointed Yosemite park rangers. Archie Leonard had run a pack train business from Yosemite to Lundy, and Charles Leidig, son of George Leidig, an innkeeper in Yosemite Valley, had grown up in the Valley. They set up a comfortable camp in the grove and spent the first night amid the soaring trees of the Mariposa Grove. Leidig, who was an excellent backcountry cook, prepared the meals.

From there, the party rode to Glacier Point, followed by an Army packer with three pack mules, and camped in a nearby meadow. Another lengthy campfire followed, with in-depth conversation between Roosevelt and Muir. The party awoke in the morning to a four-inch dusting of snow. That day they rode down the steep trail into the Valley and camped in Bridalveil Meadows. The crowds of people were kept away by troopers, allowing Roosevelt seclusion to enjoy the beauty of the Valley. He exulted over the spectacular scenery, exploring and enjoying being "away from civilization." A larger support staff remained at Wawona, giving the President the privacy with John Muir he requested.

At the Yosemite Valley studio of well-known artist Thomas Hill, Roosevelt greatly admired a Yosemite painting and was presented that painting by the artist. A stagecoach arrived and transported Roosevelt and Muir back to Wawona, and eventually to Raymond and the awaiting train. As a result of this trip, Yosemite Valley and Mariposa Grove were joined to the park two years later.

Muir again toured Yosemite with a president. This time it was with President Taft in 1909. The presidential party traveled around the Valley by stagecoach and went up to Glacier Point. President Taft was too large a man to ride the available horses, weighing over 300 pounds. However, he desired to take the trail down into the Valley from the Point, so he and John Muir hiked the trail down to the valley floor while the rest of the party rode horses and mules. The two men talked, and Taft agreed with Muir that Hetch Hetchy Valley was a national treasure and should not be dammed for a reservoir. During Taft's tenure in the White House, he prevented the construction of the dam, and Hetch Hetchy remained a valley. The Congressional Raker Bill to build the O'Shaughnessy Dam and Hetch Hetchy Reservoir was signed by President Wilson in 1914. John Muir died on December 24, 1914.

ROADS

Gradually, some trails were widened and improved to accommodate wagon traffic. The Big Oak Flat Wagon Road began at Knights Ferry. A road was extended beyond Big Oak Flat in 1869, and finally reached Yosemite Valley in 1874. This was approximately the route of the ancient Mono Indian Trail. The Coulterville Road was also improved and reached Yosemite Valley in 1874, permitting transportation into the Valley by stagecoach.

By 1888, there were three stage or saddle horse roads into Yosemite. Stages met passengers at the railroad terminus or another stage line and drove them to Yosemite. The Raymond Route had a terminus of the Yosemite branch of the Southern Pacific Railroad. Stages met the trains and proceeded to Wawona, where visitors could stay overnight at the hotel. The Big Oak Flat Road had a terminus of the Stockton Copperopolis Railroad at Milton. Stages met the train, then transported visitors to Yosemite Valley. The third road also began at the Milton terminus, but traveled a more northern route to Yosemite Valley. Automobiles were banned from Yosemite Valley until 1913.

In 1881, Archie Leonard, who later became Yosemite's first ranger, had a ten-horse saddle train running between Yosemite and the town of Lundy. It took a day and a half, and Leonard charged eight dollars for a one-way trip. Leonard used Tioga Pass, which was a major pack trail across the Sierra.

A mining company, the Great Sierra Consolidated Silver Company, built the Great Sierra Wagon Road in 1882-1883 using Chinese labor. This road accessed the new mining town of Bennettville near Tioga Pass. The road from Groveland to Bennettville was a hundred miles long and was a toll road, with William Priest, builder of the Priest Grade above Groveland, authorized to collect the tolls. But, when the mines ceased through neglect, it again became a pack trail.

The Tioga Road was extended over Tioga Pass to Mono Lake in 1909 and was still a private road. Transportation was largely by wagons, saddle horses, and mule trains until World War I, when the automobile became more common. By 1914, with erosion gullies, fallen logs, and boulders, the old road was nearly impassable for early automobile travel. Stephan Mather, founder of the National Park Service and appointed its first director in 1916, wanted to repair it, but for the government to begin repairs, they needed to own the road. He raised about half of the purchase price of $15,500 from wealthy friends and paid for the remainder out of his own funds, then donated it to the park. Repairs to make it into a better automobile road began after Yosemite acquired it. Four years later, it was opened with ceremony, linking the east side of the Sierra to the San Joaquin Valley. In 1937, the National Park Service paved the road.

In 1901, the first Sierra Club Outing Trip traveled in Yosemite Valley and Tuolumne Meadows. (Laws Museum)

John Muir spent his early years working, exploring, and developing his glacial theory on the formation of Yosemite Valley. (Laws Museum)

A mule ride to Inspiration Point in Yosemite in 1891. Note the ladies' fashionable attire while riding side saddle. (Laws Museum)

Trail riders in Yosemite Valley 1891, ready to ride to Inspiration Point.
The ladies exhibit a variety of styles.   (Laws Museum)

These loose packed mules cross a dangerous snow bank on the trail at Army Pass
in 1912 on a Sierra Club Trip. (Laws Museum)

CHAPTER FOUR

EXPLORING THE SIERRA BACKCOUNTRY

THE HOCKETT TRAIL

Local communities along the western foothills realized they needed trails to access the Sierra regions to the east. The Cerro Gordo Mines had opened in the eastern Sierra near Owens Lake and reports of their richness quickly reached the towns.

John Jordan and his partner, Alney T. McGee, with both their families, joined a large wagon train leaving Texas and bound for California. Jordan was voted captain, and McGee, the wagon master of the train. They crossed the southern plains in 1850 and eventually reached Tulare County in California. Jordan and his family eventually settled in Yokohl Valley, about ten miles east of Visalia, and raised cattle on their ranch. Alney T. McGee settled and ranched in Tulare. In 1861, Alney T. McGee and his son, Alney Lee McGee, drove a herd of cattle to the Owens Valley from Tulare, and settled in Inyo and Mono Counties with their families, on the east side of the range.

After realizing the need for a trans-Sierra pack trail, Jordan mapped out a route, and obtained permission from Tulare County to construct a pack trail from Visalia to Owens Lake. This would provide a link to the Cerro Gordo Mines from the Central Valley. The trail began in Yokohl Valley, and he and two of his sons constructed the trail as far east as the Kern River in 1861. During spring construction in 1862, sadly, Jordan accidentally drowned in the Kern River while attempting to cross it in a raft. His sons decided not to pursue building the trail.

John B. Hockett was twenty-two when, along with his father, he joined a wagon train to California in 1849, becoming a 49er. John tried mining first and did not find it very lucrative. However, he was able to buy a pack outfit and packed supplies to mining communities. The supply business was lucrative, and he packed goods for miners from Stockton to Porterville. Settling in Porterville in 1859, Hockett purchased farm land, ran cattle, and married Margaret McGee, Alney T. McGee's daughter.

After Jordan's death, Hockett took over the Jordan trail project and completed the trail to the Owens River in December of 1863. The Hockett Trail, as it was then called, commenced at Three Rivers, proceeded up the South Fork of the Kaweah River, passed Hockett Lakes and Meadows, and joined the previous Jordan Trail, continuing on its route to the Kern River. It ascended the steep wall of Kern Canyon and made its way via Whitney Meadows to the crossing at Cottonwood Creek near Cottonwood Lakes, and thence down to the town of Lone Pine. It was a toll trail charging fifty cents for a mounted rider, twenty-five cents for a person on foot, and fifty cents for a packed animal. The Jordan/Hockett Trail in the southern Sierra became a very important access route across the mountains beginning in 1864.

CALIFORNIA STATE GEOLOGICAL SURVEY

The Gold Rush had created much interest in minerals and mining in California. Since there had never been a comprehensive geological survey done of the state's resources, in 1860, the California State Legislature passed an act establishing the California Geological Survey. They appointed Josiah D. Whitney as the state geologist, directing him, "with the aid of such assistants as he may appoint, to make an accurate and complete Survey of the State." He was directed to supply maps, diagrams, and complete descriptions of the rocks, fossils, soils, minerals, and botanical and zoological specimens.

The first person Whitney selected for his staff, to be the field head, was William H. Brewer. At the time, Sierra historian Francis P. Farquhar described Brewer as possessing, "the strongest fiber, unflagging energy, the soundest judgement, the utmost tact, and unequivocal honesty and loyalty." Brewer was a well-educated young professor from New York and came extremely well recommended. His primary education was in the sciences of agriculture, and he had learned scientific methods that were applicable to the study of all natural sciences. Brewer had recently lost his young wife and baby after childbirth. This job offer arrived just as he was wanting to make a change in his location and activities.

Brewer began his work with the California State Geological Survey immediately, traveling to California on a ship by way of the Isthmus of Panama. Brewer was the field head for the first four years of the survey. At the end of this period, he received an appointment as Chair of Agriculture in the Sheffield Scientific School at Yale, a post he remained at until his retirement.

Brewer specifically traveled to Los Angeles to buy mules and fully equip the expedition, as he was told that Los Angeles was a center for the mule trade. In his published account, *Up and Down California, The Journal of William H. Brewer*, edited by Francis P. Farquhar, he relates journeying to Los Angeles to organize their first field trip:

> *We have nine fine mules, saddles, harness, spurs and all. A four mule team drew our wagon, in which two rode; the remaining 5 were mounted on similar brave animals, some of them scarcely half broken, just half wild from the ranches with these queer Mexican saddles, still queerer Mexican bridles, and most queer of all Mexican spurs.*

The spade-bits and Mexican spurs that he mentioned can have their origin traced back to the Moors in Morocco. Brewer also hired a packer, Pete, and a camp cook, Mike, for the party.

In June of 1863, Brewer, Josiah Whitney, Charles Hoffman, a topographer, and a packer, John, planned to cross the Sierra via Yosemite Valley by the Coulterville Trail and return by the Sonora Trail. Brewer wrote:

> *Besides our riding horses, we have 2 pack mules which carry provisions and such blankets as we cannot carry behind our saddles. Of course, our personal baggage*

is cut down to the very lowest figure—only what little we can carry in our saddle-bags. So, too, our cooking arrangements must be primitive—4 knives and forks, 4 tin cups, a coffee pot, a tin pail to cook beans in, a pan to wash dishes in and a frying pan in which we fry meat and bake bread—no tent, no shelter, fewer blankets than we used to have in our wagon, compass, 2 barometers, and other instruments.

Pack mules with a professional packer in charge transported the scientific instruments and camp gear, while the men rode saddle horses and mules.

Most of the fieldwork in the Sierra was done between 1863 and 1870. Brewer was the field chief from 1860 to '64, Charles Hoffman was the topographer, and James Gardner and Clarence King were geologists. Richard "Dick" Cotter was hired as the packer in 1862, but he was called the "Man of all Work." Cotter was strong and agile, and climbed many of the peaks. He was the man Clarence King most trusted to climb with him. In 1864, the Whitney Survey explored the Kings River high country and discovered there were many peaks at 13,000 feet elevation and over. They did not expect to learn there were also a number of peaks over 14,000 feet. Clarence King and Dick Cotter climbed and named Mt. Tyndell, at 14,023 feet, and viewed Mt. Williamson, at 14,384 feet, and Mt. Whitney, at 14,505 feet.

The Survey produced a vast amount of valuable information about the state and particularly the Sierra Nevada Mountain Range before it ended in 1873. The outstanding scientists of the Geological Survey kept careful journals and sketches of their travels. Brewer collected plant specimens, discovering new species. Their accounts of their experiences are recorded in books they later published. Their maps were also published and were the first accurate maps of the Sierra, and in the process, they pioneered new trails. These men of the Survey, as the surveyors and mappers of the mountains, were also early explorers and mountaineers.

UNITED STATES GEOGRAPHICAL SURVEY AND THE WHEELER SURVEY EXPEDITION

The newly organized United States Geographical Survey was formed in 1871, and worked out of Fort Independence in the Owens Valley, mapping, collecting specimens, and surveying the terrain. The direction from Washington was to conduct a survey of a portion of the United States lying west of the 100th meridian. It was referred to as the Wheeler Survey Expedition after its supervisor, Lieutenant (later Captain) George M. Wheeler.

George M. Wheeler graduated from West Point with a commission of Lieutenant in the Army in 1866. He was appointed to the staff of the Command General of the Department of California of the U.S. Army. In 1869, he made his first exploration at the age of twenty-seven. Two divisions or parties were organized. The first party was organized under Captain George M. Wheeler, and the second under Lt. D. A. Lyle.

These survey expeditions were considerably larger than the Whitney Survey. In addition to the scientists, each party included one guide, one chief packer, one cargadore and five or six packers. The cargadore was responsible for making up the pack loads while the packers loaded them on the mules and tied the hitches. Only the warm months were spent in field travels, and the mules were kept at Fort Independence on pasture during the winter months.

While most of their work was east of the Sierra Nevada, fieldwork in the Mt.

Whitney, Lake Tahoe, and Yosemite areas was completed between 1875 and 1879. The map of Yosemite Park became the standard map of Yosemite for many years after. The Wheeler Geographical Survey ended with the creation of the new Geological Survey in 1879.

FIRST CLIMBS OF MT. WHITNEY

Mt. Whitney, the tallest peak in the United States, had not yet been climbed in 1872. This region of the Sierra has some half-dozen peaks over 14,000 feet elevation, and about 500 over 12,000 feet.

Clarence King had made two attempts to climb Mt. Whitney but was unsuccessful. He and Richard "Dick" Cotter climbed Mt. Tyndall in 1864, identifying it as Mt. Whitney. When King and Cotter reached the summit of Mt. Tyndall, they observed a higher peak beyond them and realized they were not standing on Mt. Whitney. King tried to find Mt. Whitney again later in the summer and was unsuccessful. On his next trip in 1871, he hired Newt Crabtree as his guide, naming Crabtree Meadows for him. This time, he climbed Mt. Langley with French climber, Paul Pinson, mistakenly believing that he was on Mt. Whitney. For two years, King believed that he had climbed Mt. Whitney, writing about the climb in his book, *Mountains of California.*

In his book, *History of the Sierra Nevada*, noted California historian Francis P. Farquhar chronicles the colorful climbing history of Mt. Langley and Mt. Whitney. In July of 1872, two separate tourist groups from the nearby towns of Lone Pine and Independence had packed into the Kern River at Soda Creek. These two parties included Sheriff Cyrus Mulkey, Sheriff of Inyo County, Mrs. Mulkey, and their daughter, Mattie. Two others were Watson Andrew Goodyear, a civil engineer with the California Geological Survey, and Mortimer W. Belshaw, a mining engineer, who was an owner of the Union Mine in Cerro Gordo. They had packed in to escape the heat of the Owens Valley, and "indulge in fishing and other sports." In addition to fishing, they explored the surrounding mountains, riding sure-footed mules. Mulkey Creek was named for Sheriff Mulkey.

While there on July 27th, they rode their mules to the summit of Mt. Langley, at 14,042 feet elevation, and Belshaw and Goodyear took measurements. They found the coin on which Clarence King had scratched the date, his name, and that of Paul Pinson, who had made the climb with him. They also found King's record of his climb, believing he was on top of Mt. Whitney. The men were familiar with Mt. Langley and knew that this peak was not Mt. Whitney. They could also see another higher peak several miles away.

The California Academy of Sciences, chaired by Professor Josiah Whitney, held their meeting on August 4, 1873, and W. A. Goodyear read a paper reporting on the discovery concerning Mt. Langley and Mt. Whitney. Goodyear described in detail his trip and proceeded to prove that the other peak, five or six miles away and considerably higher, was the one named by William Brewer in 1864 as Mt. Whitney. Clarence King was stunned when he learned of this news.

In the summer of 1873, the group were again camping on the Kern River, and Sheriff Mulkey, along with his wife and daughter, were again part of the party. Three of the men, who called themselves the fishermen—Albert H.

Johnson, John J. Lucas, and Charles "Charley" D. Begole—rode first to the top of Mt. Langley, where they could see a taller peak and determined that they would climb it. They rode their horses to Ramshorn Springs, where they camped for the night. The next morning they proceeded on foot up the southwestern side of the great mountain. At noon on August 18, 1873, they stood on the summit of the great elusive mountain, built a monument, and christened the mountain in honor of themselves, "Fishermen's Peak." The summit of this massive mountain, after examining its sheer east and north faces, is surprising, as the top is flat and is several acres in size, before sloping to the west.

A short time later in August, another vacationing group of fishermen from the mining community of Cerro Gordo packed into a campsite on the Kern River. Two of the Cerro Gordo miners' party, William Crapo and Abe Leyda, climbed the soaring peak. The local newspapers published reports of these two climbs, and of the rivalry between the two parties to prove who climbed Mt. Whitney first. A third party of Cerro Gordo miners then packed in, and on September 6th, 1873, four of them climbed the soaring and elusive mountain.

When this disconcerting news reached Clarence King, now residing in the East, he immediately hurried across the country to Visalia by train, hired a professional pack outfit and two guides, and rode across the Hockett Trail to the Kern River. On September 19, 1873, King and packer Frank Knowles became the fourth party to climb the real Mt. Whitney, correcting his initial mistakes. He discovered the names of the previous climbers who had preceded him in climbing the highest mountain in the contiguous United States, as they had signed their names and placed them in a rock cairn on top of the peak. On this climb, King reported that he discovered a Native American arrowhead on the summit and "other indications that the peak had been visited by natives prior to the first ascent by whites." The previous parties believed King was being a bit of a spoilsport by this statement, as they had not observed arrowheads or other signs of people while on the summit.

John Muir's party of three was the next group to attempt the climb of Mt. Whitney. After failing the first time, the party retreated to Independence to rest and regroup. Muir, after resting, left his riding mule, pack animals, and companions behind in Independence, and climbed the mountain in an amazing hike, alone and on foot. He hiked up the North Fork of Lone Pine Creek, reaching the summit on October 21, 1873, with a first ascent of the now termed Mountaineer's Route. He made some sketches while on the summit and returned to Independence by the same route. Two years later, in 1875, Muir guided two companions, Charles Washburn of Wawona and George B. Bayley, manufacturer and expert climber, to the top by a slightly different route from the east side. The previous climbs had been made from the west side of the mountain.

James Hutchings, John Muir's former employer from Yosemite Valley, organized an expedition to climb Mt. Whitney in 1875. After these first climbs, numerous people climbed Mt. Whitney, many packing into the west side of the peak and base camping on the Kern. Other prospective climbers began their trips in Lone Pine or Independence, and rode up to Onion Valley, and then over Kearsarge Pass. Most of these parties rode to within two miles of the top and scrambled up the last two steep and rocky miles to the summit plateau.

In 1878, an expedition of men and women from Porterville packed into the Kern River. At Soda Springs, in Kern Canyon, they found a "jolly crowd of over thirty people from Inyo County already camped there." The Porterville party included Miss Anna Mills, lame since childhood, but who was determined to climb Mt. Whitney. She reinjured her back when her horse jumped a creek but refused to give up her dream. The party rode their horses as far as possible and climbed the remainder of the distance on foot. In spite of her injury and disabilities, Anna Mills reached the summit of Mt. Whitney, along with three other women in the party. Mills published her account of the trip in 1902, called *A Trip to Mt. Whitney in 1878.*

A Lone Pine party of eight, including three women, reached Mt. Whitney's summit in 1881. A very narrow foot trail had been built that year from Lone Pine. In 1883, another party from Bakersfield included two women who reached the top. Nearby Charlotte Lake was named for Mrs. Charles Houle of Independence, who used to camp at the lake during the 1880s. One has to remember that these women rode and climbed in cumbersome clothing, and some even rode their horses on sidesaddles. This was no easy feat!

UNITED STATES GEOLOGICAL SERVICE

The United States Geological Survey was formed in 1879, with Clarence King as its first chief. King was formerly of the California State Geological Survey, also called the Whitney Survey, and the fourth party to climb Mt. Whitney. The new agency absorbed the former United States Geographical Survey and the Wheeler Survey.

However, intensive geological surveys of the Sierra Nevada Range were not done until 1894 and '95. At the time, the only maps of the Sierra that were available to the public were the Whitney Survey and Wheeler Survey map sheets. Between 1890 and 1910, the U.S. Geological Survey made considerable progress in mapping the Sierra Nevada—not an easy task. The Yosemite Quadrangle was completed in 1893-1894, the Mt. Lyell Quadrangle was completed in 1898-1899, and the Mt. Goddard Quadrangle was published in 1912.

FRESNO FLATS TRAIL

The Fresno Flats or Mammoth Pass Trail was formerly a trans-Sierra Native American path, annually used by westside Miwoks who traveled eastward for a trade rendezvous with the Long Valley and Owens Valley Paiutes in Long Valley. They also enjoyed the pleasures of the Casa Diablo Hot Springs and Hot Creek while trading, and built wickiups adjacent to the hot springs.

This trail became an important thoroughfare for men driving their herds of cattle and sheep into the high mountains for summer grazing. Sheep and cattle ranchers packed in their camp supplies on pack horses and mules. It was the sheep men and cattlemen who were responsible for much of the trail system of the Sierra Nevada. Most of these trails just happened while moving livestock to and from summer ranges in the higher mountains using the easiest and most direct routes. A suspension bridge was constructed across the North Fork of the San Joaquin River and was called Sheep Crossing for the many flocks that crossed the river on the bridge.

The first mining claim on Red Mountain, adjacent to the Mammoth Lakes, was filed in June of 1877. A rush to the area followed, more claims were established, and several mining towns sprang up. In 1878, John S. French, a mining promoter with interests in the Mammoth area, built a toll trail across the Sierra, following old, established Native American trails to the new gold strikes in the eastern Sierra. The trail was variously called the Mammoth Pass Trail, Fresno Flats Trail, or the French Trail, and began at Fresno Flats (the town of Oakhurst) forty-six miles from Fresno. It passed through Jackass Meadow, Clover Meadow, Soldier Meadow, and 77 Corral, and crossed the North Fork of the San Joaquin River. From there, the trail traveled up the Granite Stairway to King Creek and Summit Meadows, down to the Middle Fork of the San Joaquin River through Red's Meadow, and over Mammoth Pass to Pine City and Mammoth City.

French offered a twice-weekly pack train service from Fresno Flats to the new Mammoth gold mines for fifteen dollars. Passengers were permitted up to twenty pounds of luggage. The Pine City Feed and Livery Stable, just below Lake Mary, also advertised regular pack train trips to Fresno Flats. The Fresno Flats Saddle Trains departed from the Monumental Hotel on Central Mammoth Avenue in Mammoth City on Tuesday and Friday, leaving at five a.m. for the fifty-four-mile journey. Travel and transportation of supplies and machinery for the new boomtowns depended on the surefooted pack strings of mules and horses and their skilled packers prior to construction of wagon roads. The Mammoth Pass Trail was never improved to a wagon road although it was proposed and vigorously promoted.

FURTHER EXPLORERS

In the 1860s, many accounts of trips into the Sierra were published in newspapers and magazines from communities on both the east and west sides. Reports of the incomparable beauties of this mountain fastness reached valley cities, and summer expeditions to these mountains began. These accounts generated much interest by local citizens, and even the remotest parts of the mountains were visited.

The early explorers were young, vigorous, and physically strong. Daring travelers explored unmapped country, visiting the sparkling lakes, streams, and glorious canyons. They enjoyed fishing, climbed rugged peaks, and hiked new trails. Surveying, exploring, and vacationing expeditions set out from communities near the base of the vast range. Wagon roads were lacking, and trails were narrow and precipitous. Pack train freighting and transportation were essential to access the mountains.

Fort Independence, in the Owens Valley, became a staging area for many exploration trips into the Sierra. In July of 1872, nationally known artist Albert Bierstadt joined Louis Agassiz, a paleontologist, and Clarence King of the Whitney Geological Survey. They met a U.S. Army contingent at Fort Babbitt in Visalia, and traveled with the large army pack train, crossing the Sierra via Walker Pass and the Hockett Trail to Fort Independence. Bierstadt and King remained at Fort Independence through that fall and made many exploratory pack trips into the Sierra, Bierstadt sketching and painting, and King climbing peaks.

They packed over Kearsarge Pass to Kings Canyon, where Bierstadt made sketches and studies. These studies were used for a large oil painting of Kings Canyon. The completed studio oil painting sold for $25,000 and hung in a great castle in Europe. When snow drove them out of the mountains, they packed out by way of the San Joaquin River, and thence to San Francisco. Bierstadt returned again in 1873, along with his wife, for a stay at Fort Independence.

Among the early scientists who explored the Sierra Nevada was Israel C. Russell, a geologist and geographer with the U.S. Geological Survey, who spent 1881-1884 studying the Mono Basin surrounding Mono Lake. He wrote of his first journey to Mono Lake in 1881 in the annual USGS report, *Quaternary History of Mono Valley, California,* "Explorers in the far west have found that the most practicable method of carrying forward their work is to travel on mule back, the desert character of much of the country and the consequent scarcity of grass and water making the use of horses less satisfactory."

Theodore S. Solomons, an early and influential member of the Sierra Club, conceived the idea for a trail along the backbone of the High Sierra, keeping as near to the main crest as possible. From 1892 to 1897, Solomons made extended pack trips of exploration, principally in the upper branches of the San Joaquin River. His trips were extremely hazardous, especially to his horses and mules, and he survived one trip only by the fortunate presence of a sheepherder camp in the area. His writings and detailed maps added greatly to the overall knowledge of the High Sierra.

Bolton Coit Brown began spending summer vacations in the higher reaches of the Sierra, mapping and sketching, in 1895. Brown was a Professor of Fine Arts at Stanford University, and his maps and drawings were especially accurate and descriptive. In 1896, his wife, Lucy, accompanied him and, three years later, he returned with Lucy, as well as their two-year-old daughter, Eleanor. They spent two months exploring and climbing peaks, joined the Joseph LeConte party, and climbed several peaks together. In 1898, LeConte, a professor at the University of California, Berkeley, joined the search for a north-south Sierra Crest trail route, keeping careful notes and maps of their travels. The Sierra Club had published LeConte's first map in 1893.

The author Stuart Edward White and his wife, Elizabeth "Billy," spent their honeymoon packing in the Sierra in 1904. With their ranger friend, Wes, they pioneered a difficult, previously untraveled route from the Roaring River Fork of the Kings River over a rugged divide at 11,400 feet elevation to the Middle Fork of the Kaweah River. They decided that it should be named Elizabeth Pass, honoring Billy as the first woman to cross the pass. White wrote about their pack trip adventures in *The Mountains* and *The Pass.* He also offered advice to novice packers on what to learn before attempting to pack into the backcountry, with detailed information on equipment and gear, as well as how to choose the right type of horse for a pack trip.

Many early trips during this period were large parties of friends and families from urban regions of the state. Packers, livestock, equipment, guides, and cooks were hired to service the trips. Wealthy families and businessmen were used to hiring and dealing with "servants," and San Francisco area visitors often hired Chinese cooks such as they had at home. Unfortunately, not many of these trips recorded the names of these service packers and cooks, or the names of businesses that provided services, animals, and gear for these trips.

LOCAL FAMILIES ENJOY RECREATIONAL TRIPS

Owens Valley families journeyed to far distant areas of the Sierra during summer vacations by horse and pack animals. Most people had saddle horses, draft horses, and buggies or wagons. Everyone rode and used extra horses to pack their camp and provisions. The many local livery stables and ranches also provided stock and equipment.

Writer Mary Austin and her husband Stephen, a newspaper publisher and editor from Independence, often packed in and camped at the lakes near Kearsarge Pass in the 1890s. She related that June and July began the camping season in the eastern Sierra, and wrote eloquently of this area and the guides and their pack mules. Her books, *The Land Of Little Rain* and *The Flock*, describe her deep love of the eastern Sierra. In *The Flock,* she wrote about Peter "Little Pete" Giraud, an Inyo County sheepherder. Little Pete Meadow below Muir Pass on the John Muir Trail is named for him. *The Land of Little Rain*, set in the Owens Valley, has become a classic and her most popular book.

In 1893, nineteen-year-old Jim Sherwin, along with his brother and a friend, determined to attend the Midwinter Fair in San Francisco. From Bishop, they packed across the Sierra via Rock Creek and Mono Pass with three horses and one pack mule. Upon reaching Fresno, they boarded their livestock, caught a train to San Francisco to enjoy the fair, and returned by the same route. Sherwin wrote a wonderful story of this trip, published in the Inyo Register newspaper.

The Wash Brierly family packed from Bishop to Yosemite during the 1880s. They took one pack mule. The two children rode double on one horse while the small family dog rode double with Mrs. Brierly on another horse. That same summer, the Watterson family of Benton took a pack trip to Yosemite, traveling all the way from Benton with their own stock, making the lengthy journey to the Sierra.

SIERRA CLUB OUTING TRIPS

The Sierra Club was organized with John Muir as its first president in 1892. A goal of the newly formed Club was "to explore, enjoy and render accessible the mountain regions of the Pacific Coast; to publish authentic information concerning them; to enlist the support and cooperation of the people and the government in preserving the forests and other natural features of the Sierra Nevada." Another objective was to make the scenic attractions more widely-known so that the public would support preserving and protecting these wild lands. Steps were taken to encourage the building of roads and trails by which the public could reach the scenic attractions of the mountains. Most of these early members were affluent persons and families from the San Francisco Bay Area, and many of the 182 charter members were scientists.

Under the direction of William Colby in 1901, the Club introduced its First Annual Outing Trip with a pack trip to Yosemite Valley and Tuolumne Meadows, in order to personally acquaint members with scenic mountain wonders in California. These trips were later called the Sierra Club High Trips. Colby was an attorney from San Francisco, and had joined the Sierra Club shortly after finishing law school. He became secretary of the organization, a post he held for many years. He also assumed the position of

Outings Director.

The first trip had ninety-six participants (a third of whom were women), who spent a month camping, riding, hiking, and climbing peaks. The first participants were primarily professors, scientists, college students, lawyers, and businessmen, along with their families, from the Bay Area, who had the time and could afford a month-long vacation in the Sierra.

The horseback riders and hikers first enjoyed a base camp in Yosemite Valley at the foot of Glacier Point. They hiked and rode horses or mules to all the points of interest. After a week, the group, by way of the Yosemite Falls Trail, climbed up to Porcupine Flat and traveled along the Tioga Road (then a rough dirt toll road) to Tuolumne Meadows. A base camp called Camp Muir was established at Tuolumne Meadows, and the commissary was hauled to the meadows by freight wagons. The packing, animals, and wagons were contracted out to professional commercial packers. Colby hired a separate cook crew of Chinese cooks and chefs, reflecting the life and times of San Francisco, to handle the food preparation and cleanup. The chief cook was Charlie Tuck, and he cooked on many future Outings as well. A Buzzacott wood range was hauled by wagon. This stove was especially designed for the Klondike trail, and was much too heavy for pack stock to carry, as it had a cast iron stove top. Bread and pies were baked in camp daily, requiring large ovens. It is hard to imagine that sometimes as many as a hundred loaves of bread a day were pulled out of those ovens.

An active social program was planned for the participants, but the trip was not to be just another pleasant vacation in the mountains. Prior to the trip, the guests were given reading assignments so that they would be prepared for this adventure. The two most important texts were *The Mountains of California* (1894) by John Muir and *A Journal of Ramblings Through the High Sierra of California* (1875) by Joseph LeConte. Colby insisted that the leaders were to guide the members to appreciate, be inspired by, and understand the beauty of the mountains so that they could become defenders and advocates of these special places. There were lectures by John Muir in the evening around a blazing campfire, as well as lectures by William Dudley, C. Hart Merriam, and Theodore Hittell, college professors and members of the Sierra Club.

John Muir was accompanied by his two daughters, Wanda and Helen. Both the girls were skilled horsewomen and rode their horses wearing divided skirts. They enjoyed hiking, riding, and camping, accompanying their father on many excursions. Muir was quite proud of his daughters' hiking and riding prowess.

Joseph LeConte and his daughter, Sallie, were Sierra Club campers, along with William Keith, the Yosemite artist, and his wife, Mary. LeConte, a professor at the University of California, Berkeley, was an avid explorer of the Sierra Nevada and an influential member of the Sierra Club. LeConte took ill suddenly on July 5th and died the following day of a heart attack in Yosemite Valley. This was a stunning upset to this fledgling trip, but his family insisted that the planned Outing continue, as that was what he would have wanted. His son, Joseph LeConte, Jr. was on his honeymoon in another part of the Sierra so didn't learn of the sad event until later.

At the Tuolumne Meadows base camp, campers climbed many peaks and participated in planned hikes throughout the basin. Mt. Dana was climbed by forty-nine hikers, and Mt. Lyell by twenty. Women, in spite of fashionable but bulky clothing, climbed and hiked alongside the men. A number of college girls were on this trip and were often referred to as Berkeley or Stanford girls. These girls climbed Mt. Dana, impressing the gentlemen hikers.

In 1902, the Second Annual Outing explored Kings Canyon. Ione "Poley" Napoleon Kanawyer operated a store, camp, and pack station at Millwood in Hume Meadow on the way to Cedar Grove. William Colby, Outing Manager, persuaded Poley to purchase more pack stock, enough to pack in the Sierra Club, and contracted him to service the trip. This was the first trip using just pack mules and no wagons. There were approximately 200 hundred Sierra Clubbers and a large support staff with 25,000 pounds of supplies on this historic trip.

On this trip, an army stove was packed into the Kings River, but it was still too heavy for the pack stock. After using these cumbersome stoves, Colby designed and had specially constructed a stove resembling the Klondike stove but made out of sheet iron. Colby designed the stove to be carried on a mule, but it still necessitated a large mule to carry it. Each stove weighed over 200 pounds. A special string of large mules packed in the stoves, and aparejo packsaddles were used. After the first few years, a sheet of heavy aluminum was placed on the top of the stove, and when moving, the stovepipe was telescoped inside the oven. Three or four of these wood-burning stoves were packed in on the Outings, and the Club used them for many years. The ovens were used to bake bread and pies. In later years, crackers were substituted for bread in the trail lunches, but the packers still insisted on having "regular" sandwiches prepared for their lunches.

Again, rides, hikes, and climbs were planned for the participants. Fifty participants climbed Mt. Brewer, and John Muir led a group to the summit of Mt. Whitney. Lectures were given around the campfires, and the singing of campfire songs was popular. After this trip, anyone desiring to ride would make arrangements with the stock contractor. The Sierra Club encouraged walkers.

In 1903, Broder and Hopping Company, stock contractors from Three Rivers, arranged and supplied the necessary horses, mules, and services for the five week Third Annual Sierra Club High Trip with 143 guests. One must remember that in order to partake in these Sierra mountain pack trips, Club members had many prior days of travel just to reach the start of the actual trip. This travel included trains, stagecoaches driven by four or six-up hitches of horses or mules, and finally saddle horses to ride to the base camp. The guests on the 1903 Outing took trains to Visalia, stage coaches to Three Rivers and Mineral King Valley, and hiked or rode horseback from there into camp at Coyote Creek and the Kern River.

William Colby and the Broder and Hopping Packing Co. contacted the U.S. Cavalry, from the Presidio Headquarters in San Francisco, concerning the plans for this large trip. There were many complaints from exploring and tourist parties over the lack of feed in the meadows for the horses and mules because of banned sheep flocks entering this remote country early in the summer from the east.

Captain Charles Young of the 9th Cavalry, superintendent of Sequoia National Park, was stationed at the Presidio. He sent an advance detachment of fifteen soldiers under the command of Lieutenant Howard with orders to keep the flocks of sheep out and clear trails. He detailed these cavalry soldiers to construct a trail from Guitar Lake (where the trail had ended) to the summit of Mt. Whitney. The cavalry was successful in completing their orders prior to July 10th.

The trip began at Mineral King Valley in June, and snow still blocked the trail over Farewell Gap, making crossing the passes difficult. Despite challenges, the Sierra Clubbers made it to the base camp along with all the supplies carried by the pack mules. There were perhaps eighty-five head of pack and riding animals that grazed on the lush grass of the backcountry that had been saved from the sheep, which John Muir had described as white locusts.

Climbing peaks had become an important activity on these trips. On this trip, the Club guided a large number of participants to the summit of Mt. Whitney on the newly completed trail. The surrounding areas were always well-explored, and fishing was also a popular activity, with Clubbers enjoying the addition of fresh trout to the menu. The trip returned to civilization by way of Kaweah Gap to Giant Forest, making a circle.

In 1904, the Outing Trip packed to Hetch Hetchy Valley in Yosemite. Hetch Hetchy was a beautiful valley that was parallel to Yosemite Valley and boasted similar beauties. In 1892, when the Sierra Club was organized, San Francisco had already proposed a dam at Hetch Hetchy Valley to provide water storage for the City, with the Club opposing it at that time. The 1907 trip again camped at Hetch Hetchy Valley. However, Sierra Club members were mostly from San Francisco, and, after the 1906 San Francisco fire, many now favored a dam in the valley. The fire had demonstrated that San Francisco needed another source of water. John Muir was adamantly opposed to the dam and was distressed by the Club's defection. He considered leaving the Sierra Club. A long battle ensued. In 1914, the Club camped again for the last time in the doomed Hetch Hetchy Valley prior to the dam construction. The Raker Bill was signed that year by President Woodrow Wilson, and sadly John Muir died on Dec. 24, 1914 without being able to save Hetch Hetchy.

The early Outings rotated between Yosemite National Park, the Kings River/ Canyon region, and the Mineral King/Kern River Area for many years. Later, the upper regions of the San Joaquin River were added to the rotation. The early Outings were for four weeks, and then later were divided into two two-week sessions. High Trips were to travel for two weeks at a time throughout the Sierra Nevada, with a different camp almost every night.

The Club contracted arrangements for the necessary pack and saddle stock, along with professional packers, each year. There were only a few Sierra pack stations with enough mules and equipment to cater to the needs of the Sierra Club. Eventually, the Robinson Pack Trains under Charlie and Allie Robinson contracted all the Sierra Club trips. For a number of early years, the Club arranged that the packer crew ate their meals and set up their camp away from the Club participants. Presumably, the commissary and camp staff also had the same arrangement. This arrangement was reflective of the urban San Francisco social community. Many packers on these early Sierra Club Outings learned how these large trips successfully functioned, loved the wilderness country, and remained with the packing industry for the rest of their lives.

The Club members, the large commissary and camp crew, one hundred head or more of pack mules, riding horses, and fifteen to twenty professional packers made for a very large group of up to two hundred and fifty people. However, one leader remarked, "the crowd somehow became a community." Bandanas were a necessary item for every participant, and their required tin cups were known as Sierra Club cups.

The Sierra Club informational literature sent to prospective guests, as quoted in *History of the Sierra Nevada* by Francis P. Farquhar, contained some helpful advice concerning proper attire for women participants. "For the women riding horseback, divided skirts are recommended. It would be unsafe to ride otherwise than astride on portions of the trip." Women who rode astride usually camouflaged their method of riding with billowing layers of skirts. They also wore elaborate hats. "Skirts can be short, not be halfway from knee to ankle, and under them can be worn shorter, dark colored bloomers." Women who walked were expected to hike up to twenty miles a day. A proud John Muir once observed that his daughters could easily hike twenty-five to thirty miles a day on these trips.

In 1911, a further change in women's clothing was announced—the bloomers worn under their skirts could be the same color as the skirt. In 1914, again there was modification in proper dress for women. "Bloomers or knickerbockers should be worn under the skirt as the latter are essential for the more difficult mountain climbs where skirts are dangerous for wear." In 1923, the literature suggested that, "Women usually wear knickerbockers or riding trousers" for the entire trip. In 1925, the Club clarified that women's "pants" were called hiking or riding breeches. After that year, women were not advised on what clothing to wear, and grateful women soon adopted practical blue jeans as the standard mountain attire. It was assumed that men could always wear whatever they wished on the trips.

An outfitted party, with a packer and mules, arrive at a camp near a High Sierra lake. Circa 1914. (Laws Museum)

The Sierra Club on the second High Trip to the Kings Canyon in 1902.
(Laws Museum)

On this Sierra Club Trip in 1919, the pack mules are loose herded,
crossing Murphy Creek near Tenaya Lake in Yosemite. (Laws Museum)

CHAPTER FIVE

THE ROLE OF GOVERNMENT AGENCIES

THE U.S. CAVALRY

Congress established Sequoia National Park, the second national park in the United States, on September 25, 1890. One week later, a bill was signed expanding the new park, as well as designating Yosemite as the third national park and General Grant Park as the fourth. All three of these parks are in the Sierra Nevada of Central California.

Yosemite Park Preserve encompassed 932,600 acres. Yosemite Valley itself, along with the Mariposa Grove, was still a California State Park, although surrounded by the new national park. It wasn't until 1905 that a bill was passed joining the Valley to Yosemite National Park.

The government assigned U.S. Cavalry troops to protect these newly created parks. The Cavalry patrolled the parks primarily to keep the sheep herds in check. Troop K of the 4th U.S. Cavalry from Georgia, a black troop, patrolled Sequoia and General Grant Parks. Their Captain, Joseph H. Dorst, was the first Acting Superintendent of these parks in 1891 and 1892. Captain Dorst was also in charge of troops stationed in Mineral King, just outside of Sequoia Park. In 1903, the Acting Superintendent for Sequoia National Park was Captain Charles Young, who was the third black cadet to graduate from West Point Academy. The 9th U.S. Cavalry was then patrolling the park.

While on patrol, the Cavalry troops cleared and improved many of the cattle and sheep trails that had developed through use, along with constructing some new, improved trails. Some of the trails were further developed and improved into wagon and stage roads. Army Pass was originally a sheepherder route and was rebuilt as a horse trail by the Cavalry in 1892. Tools, supplies, and the camp outfits were packed on Army mules.

In 1903, Captain Young, having listened to requests to build a trail from Crabtree Meadow to the top of Mt. Whitney, directed his troops to construct the trail before the Sierra Club arrived with their Outing Trip. The Cavalry kept sheep flocks from entering and grazing off the meadows needed for exploring and tourist parties. When Broder and Hopping's pack strings arrived with all the supplies and the camp for the Sierra Club, good grass for grazing was there.

When that trail was completed, Captain Young sent the trail building crew to Lone Pine, on the east side of Mt. Whitney, to build a trail to the top of the mountain from Lone Pine. There was a rough trail there already, but it was not in good shape and could no longer safely accommodate horses and mules. The troop worked on that trail until the snow prevented further construction, around the first of October. They had planned to complete the trail before leaving, but were just short of the top when winter storms prevented them from continuing. Captain Young met with the citizens of Lone Pine and urged them to complete the trail the following spring. The following year in 1904, the town of Lone Pine completed that last section to the peak.

In Yosemite, the Army headquarters were established in Wawona, at Camp A. E. Wood, named after Captain Abram Epperson Wood of the 4th U.S. Cavalry, who administered Yosemite National Park beginning in 1891. The State of California still administered Yosemite Valley. The U.S. Cavalry patrolled the park and constructed a large horse barn and corrals to handle their many pack and saddle animals. Usually, 150 Cavalry troopers from the Presidio in San Francisco were detailed to the park from May through October. A large number of pack mules and wagons pulled by mule teams accompanied the Cavalry.

The grazing of stock was banned in the park, but trespass by sheep and cattle was a major problem and intensified each year. The cattle owners who accompanied their cattle to summer pasture became cooperative with the Cavalry. One rancher, Timothy Carlon, was commended by the Army for keeping his cattle out and assisting the Army any way he could. But the sheep owners (wool growers) were not out on the range with their herds, and held a different viewpoint. Over 90,000 head of sheep were in close proximity to the park borders, and herders slipped the herds across to graze whenever they found an opportunity. The sheepherders, not the owners, were mostly Basque (artzainas) or Mexican (boregeros), and frequently spoke little English. A lesser number of sheepherders were French, Portuguese, and Scotch. According to Army records, the sheepherders had divided up the park area among themselves. Certain canyons and mountains "belonged" to certain men, and they drove out or killed any sheepherders who attempted to trespass on their range. The grass and forage was devoured by the sheep, leaving little grazing for the Army horses and mules, as well as pack trips organized for recreation by the public.

When Lieutenant Harry C. Benson arrived at the park in 1896, his job was to arrest illegal poachers, drive out the herds, construct and improve trails in order to clear the region of sheep herds, plant fish, and generally improve the third national park. He devised a method for clearing out the sheep flocks while, at the same time, developing the trail system. During the day, the troops worked on the trails. After dinner, Benson would go out alone and on foot to scour the nearby countryside for tracks. The sheepherders were supplied at least once a month by a pack string supplied by the herd owner. They also had burros and goats that stayed with the flock. Benson tracked these hoof prints to the camps and blazed the trees with an H. The next day, a detail of troopers would then ride to the camp, take charge of the herd, and scatter them outside of the park. Benson, with troops, would arrest the sheepherders and take them to the headquarters at Camp Wood on the other side of Yosemite, where they were released outside of the park. The sheepherders were also thought responsible for the growing number of wildfires that the troops had to fight to control and put out. The improved trail system allowed the Army to thus gain control over the trespass by sheep flocks.

Above Yosemite Valley, there were no trout in the upper lakes and streams in the park. The California Fish Commission had constructed a fish hatchery at Wawona. Transplanting the fish was difficult, and the percentage of young fish that survived the journey was too small. Benson devised a system to transport the fish, personally supervising each expedition. Milk cans were lashed to pack saddles on the mule strings. An elaborate lid of metal gauze and hoses was designed by Benson because the water in the cans had to be replaced often in order to keep the young fish alive. The packer with the string would stop at creek crossings and quickly perform this task before continuing on to the destination. This led to successful transplants.

The 24th Mounted Infantry, Company H, and the 9th Cavalry, black army regiments, were assigned to protect Yosemite in 1899. These "Buffalo Soldiers" patrolled for trespass by livestock, both sheep and cattle. The soldiers constructed and established the trail system throughout the park. Many trails followed old Native American trails, and sheep and cattle routes. They worked on various construction projects throughout the park and planted fish in the backcountry lakes and streams.

First Lieutenant N. F. McClure of the 5th U.S. Cavalry was stationed at Wawona in 1894. He described an expedition to "scout for sheepmen, who were reported to be unusually thick in the vicinity of Tuolumne Meadows." The expedition included twelve mounted soldiers and five mules loaded with their camp and provisions. They found sheep herds near Mt. Conness and arrested four herders, taking them along with their pack train back to Wawona.

In 1905, now Captain Harry C. Benson was appointed Superintendent of Yosemite National Park through 1908. In 1906, California receded the state park lands (Yosemite Valley and the Mariposa Grove) back to the federal government as part of the national park. John Muir had been appalled at the deterioration of the valley since he had lived there, and the Sierra Club had lobbied the federal government to take back the Valley. The State of California had financial shortages and did not want to spend State funds in the Valley. Locals living there objected to the transfer, as the administration from the State had been minor, and they regarded the Valley as theirs. Hay was cut in the meadows, domestic chickens still roamed the meadows, and settlers grazed their animals there.

The Army moved their headquarters from Wawona to Fort Yosemite in Yosemite Valley, where Yosemite Lodge now stands. A large barn was constructed in 1908 near Leidig Meadow in the Valley. The Army administered the park through 1914. They hired civilian packers and utilized their enlisted men to move supplies and equipment around the park. Gabriel Sovulewski, an immigrant from Poland, served as a corporal in the Cavalry in Yosemite. After leaving the Army, he became the earliest civilian packer in the Valley, hired in 1899. He remained in Yosemite for the rest of his life, working for the Park Service before retiring in 1936.

U.S. FOREST SERVICE

In 1891, Congress passed the Forest Reserve Act that allowed the president of the United States to create forest reserves. President Benjamin Harrison established the Sierra Forest Reserve, consisting of four million acres, in 1893. This forest block was later enlarged and divided into eight national forests.

The Forest Service Organic Administration Act, passed in 1897, formed the

National Forest System. President Grover Cleveland established thirteen new forest reserves. The Stanislaus National Forest was among those created in 1897.

Gifford Pinchot, a professional forester, was appointed Chief Forester in the Department of Agriculture, and a corps of young forest rangers was hired by the General Land Office to manage the reserves. Pinchot trained his young men in proper techniques to keep the forests healthy and sustainable. Some of the work done by these first rangers was building trails and ranger cabins, making maps, harvesting timber, packing and shoeing horses and mules, and fighting forest fires. Theodore Roosevelt became President in 1901 and shared Pinchot's vision of the forest reserves. In 1905, the Forestry Division took over the management of all the public forests, and Pinchot renamed the department the U.S. Forest Service.

In 1907, the Inyo National Forest was established by proclamation of President Theodore Roosevelt, setting aside 221,324 acres. Much of the land was along the floor of the Owens Valley and the Owens River, and was withdrawn for the purpose of protecting these lands from homesteading. Like San Francisco, Los Angeles was in need of another source of water. This Owens Valley land was desired by the Los Angeles Department of Water and Power in order to build their planned aqueduct system. It was reported back to President Roosevelt that there were serious doubts about the value of these Owens River lands for a national forest, because of interest in water resources. In 1911, President Taft rescinded the public land withdrawal along the Owens River and restored 275,000 acres to public entry, asserting that the land was inappropriate national forest land.

President Roosevelt issued another executive order that reorganized the Sierra National Forest in 1908, and transferred 1,521,107 acres of its east side to the Inyo National Forest. This part of the Sierra National Forest had been administered by a head ranger from 1904 to 1908 and was known as Sierra East. President Roosevelt also signed an executive order establishing the Mono National Forest.

After the U.S. Forest Service was formed in 1905, the new federal agency eventually began issuing resort permits for pack stations, along with lodges, recreation residences, and camps in the national forests. Grazing permits were also written for recreational pack and saddle stock grazing on national forest land. From 1916 on, the Forest Service was very interested in establishing and managing recreation activities in the Inyo National Forest, as well as other forests. A major part of the recreation work of the Forest Service has been constructing and maintaining access trails throughout the forests.

NATIONAL PARK SERVICE

Stephen Mather, a native Californian, worked for the Pacific Coast Borax Company and then helped found the Thorkildsen-Mather Borax Company. By 1914, he was a millionaire and could retire to pursue his interests in the scenic areas of the country that needed protection and management. He had joined the Sierra Club in 1904 and became acquainted with John Muir. At the urging of the Secretary of the Interior, Mather was appointed Assistant Secretary of the Interior in 1914. His assistant, Horace Albright, was the son of a miner raised in Bishop, California, growing up very familiar with the Sierra. He attended the University of California, Berkeley, becoming an attorney.

Mather organized the Mather Mountain Party of 1915, aided by his young assistant, Albright. Mather had hosted an earlier camping trip in July of 1912 that had included his wife and five-year-old daughter. Both pack trips were ten-day journeys from Visalia to Giant Forest, using the Hockett Trail to cross the crest of the mountains to Lone Pine in the Owens Valley.

The 1915 Mather Mountain Party trip consisted of thirty men, eleven of them commercial packers with one chief packer, and fifty head of horses and mules. Two Chinese cooks were also employed. Both of these men were experienced backcountry cooks, having worked on previous expeditions for the U.S. Geological Survey. The other men, guests and hosts, represented California and its concerns. Mather hoped at the end of the two week trip, they would come together to map out the future of the national parks.

This was a most strenuous trip over high elevation passes and narrow trails. Many of the guests rode mules, including Mather, who rode a white mule. The party explored, fished, and discussed the importance of a National Park System for America. Mather's enthusiasm and boundless energy proved successful.

The National Park Service was organized in 1916, and Mather was appointed the first Director of the newly created agency in 1917. Horace Albright continued as his assistant, being named Deputy Chief. These two men, Mather and Albright, became the first and second Chiefs of the National Park Service.

During Mather's extended absences because of debilitating illness, Albright, who shared his vision of the National Park System, put the early plans for the organization of the Park Service into place. When Mather resigned in 1928, after suffering a stroke, Albright was named to the top position and remained Chief until 1933.

A civilian administration took over Yosemite Park management from the Army. The newly formed National Park Service leased horses and mules from local stock suppliers and ranchers as it commenced accumulating stock for the government's packing operations. By 1924, the park had acquired forty-six head of stock and leased another ninety-four from a local rancher. The U.S. Army had already built the necessary stock facilities during its tenure. Government stock was used for road and trail work, planting fish, hauling garbage, and distributing firewood.

Stephen Mather, as Chief, had formed a concessionaire system as a method of providing needed guest services to the visiting public. There were a number of private innkeepers and livery stables operating in Yosemite Park prior to this decision. He foresaw merging these smaller entities into one concessionaire.

The first concessionaire contract went to D. J. "Joe" Desmond of San Francisco, who had a small business in Yosemite. Desmond formed a company called the Desmond Park Co. and purchased the livery stable business of Coffman and Kenney Yosemite Stables. He established tourist camps at Tenaya Lake, Tuolumne Meadows, and Merced Lake in 1916, but the company went bankrupt in 1918. After reorganization, it became the Yosemite National Park Co. The David Curry family, who had established Camp Curry in 1899, formed the Yosemite Park and Curry Co. by merging with the Yosemite Park Co. They became the concessionaire for the park, supplying visitor services for many years. The company operated four pack stations and stables in the park and was the largest pack station operator in the Sierra. They reopened the tourist camps now called High Sierra Camps and built others.

Yosemite National Park and Sequoia National Park already had a fairly good trail system created by the U.S. Army during their management of the parks. However, the remainder of the Sierra Nevada lay in national forest land, with mostly sheep, cattle, mining, and Native American trails. The Forest Service had constructed a few trails, and local communities and counties had built or funded the construction of trails in their regions.

CALIFORNIA FISH AND GAME

In the early years of exploration and settlement, people supplemented their diet and lived off the ample stocks of fish and game. But as the areas were settled and more people flocked in, the necessity of maintaining the populations of both fish and game became the responsibility of the State. The Game Act of 1852 was passed by the California State Legislature, covering some birds, deer, elk, and antelope. Later that year, action was taken to protect the salmon runs.

In 1870, the legislature organized a Board of Fish Commissions, and in 1871, they enacted the state's first fish and game laws, including appointing game wardens. The next year, the first laws to protect specific species were enacted. The name of the department was changed in 1909 to the Fish and Game Commission, and in 1927 to the Department of Fish and Game. The name was not changed again until 2013, when it became the Department of Fish and Wildlife.

The California Department of Fish and Game began officially stocking fish in Sierra lakes and streams in 1909. In 1916, the historic Mount Whitney Fish Hatchery was constructed. Beginning in 1917, the first rainbow trout (*Oncorhynchus mykiss)* eggs were collected from Rae Lakes and packed out in milk cans over Baxter Pass, at 12,300 feet, to Oak Creek, just north of Independence, by mule strings. A spawning station was built there in 1917, and this source was used until the end of the 1927 season, when the station was closed due to difficult access. The first golden trout (*Oncorhynchus aguabonita*) eggs were collected at Cottonwood Lakes in 1918, and were reared at the Mt. Whitney Fish Hatchery.

Crews from the hatchery journeyed on horseback with mule strings to the lakes and stripped and collected eggs from the females, loading them on pack mules for the long trip back down to the valley. In two months, fingerlings were ready for planting. Fish roe are still packed out by mule strings today. Golden trout fingerlings were planted above the falls on McGee Creek up McGee Canyon on the eastside in September of 1919. Golden trout readily hybridize with rainbow trout, producing what is termed a rainbow-golden cross.

Additional hatcheries were built to meet the demand for fish stocking along the length of the Sierra. The Hot Creek Fish Hatchery was constructed in the 1920s, and by the 1940s, Black Rock and Fish Springs Hatcheries were also operating.

The Department of Fish and Wildlife has planted other species of trout in Sierra waters and most have proved successful. Loch Leven and German brown trout were originally two subspecies but have been crossed, both in the wild and in hatcheries, and are now considered one species, termed brown trout *(Salmo trutta)*. They are prized by fishermen and seem to prefer lower elevation waters. Frequently, they grow to a large size and are long-lived. The hardy eastern brook trout *(Salvelinus fontinalis)* is prolific and well adapted to mountain streams and lakes, and so is probably more widespread and abundant than any other species in the Sierra. Lake trout *(Salvelinus namaycush)* were introduced in some larger lakes, where they became large and fed on smaller fish. Most of these fish have naturalized and are no longer planted.

Commercial packers and their mule strings were contracted to transport the small fish to wilderness lakes and streams as demand increased. Special fish cans were packed on sawbuck saddles, and the movement of the animals kept the water in the can circulating to provide necessary oxygen. For lakes beyond stock trails, Fish and Game personnel and packers would carry the cans on their backs the remainder of the way to the lakes. Golden trout were always stocked in the highest lakes, requiring much effort to get them there. These early fish planters named many of the lakes and streams. Lee and Cecil Lakes in the Fish Creek drainage were named for packers Lee Summers and Cecil Thorington, who planted the lakes for the Fish and Game Department.

In 1952, Phil Pister and Cliff Brunk, of the Department of Fish and Game, and packer Russ Johnson packed golden fingerlings up Baldwin Canyon by mules as far as they could go. Then they scrambled upward through shifting talus, carrying the fish cans on their backs, to where the fingerlings were released in the high-elevation Baldwin Lake in McGee Canyon.

Also in 1952, a record size golden trout weighing in at nine pounds fourteen ounces was caught in Lake Virginia on the John Muir Trail. My husband, Lou Roeser, was a packer for Mammoth Lakes Pack Outfit at the time. He packed the fish out and reported that the man who caught it had wrapped it in his sleeping bag and that the large fish stuck out on either side of the bedroll. Golden trout on average are not over ten inches long.

Beginning in 1947, fish hatcheries collected eggs from spawning fish in the mountains, packed the roe carefully back to the hatchery, then incubated and grew them to fingerling size (3 inches), in order to be airdropped from planes into high lakes. In 1954, the Department of Fish and Game reported that they had stocked 540 Sierra backcountry lakes. For the lower elevation lakes accessible by vehicles, the department raised and planted catchable-size trout. Mistakes were sometimes made, however, and rainbow fingerlings were mistakenly air dropped in Virginia Lake, home of the record golden trout, so now many of the fish caught there are rainbow-golden crosses.

The Department of Fish and Game also regulated game hunting. As California was settled, more and more people depended on game for their meat. Deer and antelope herds were depleted and even vanished in some areas. Hunting licenses were issued, and deer, antelope, and elk hunting seasons were established. Gradually the herds returned, and hunting became a sport rather than subsistence. Hunting was banned in the national parks, so that put more pressure on the national forests where hunting was permitted. Urban hunters relied on commercial pack stations to outfit and guide them to hunting locations in the Sierra.

The Inyo National Forest packers and mules supported major trail work on the Mt. Whitney Trail in 2013. (Lee and Jen Roeser Collection)

Inyo National Forest packers Lee Roeser and Michael Morse on the 2013 Mt. Whitney Trail Project. (Lee and Jen Roeser Collection)

CHAPTER SIX

SPORT FISHING IN THE SIERRA

Fishing has long been a major visitor attraction in all the waters of the Sierra. Early explorers and settlers reported lakes and rivers swarming with fish. William Brewer and Clarence King wrote that the Kern River was teeming with trout in 1864.

The main crest of the Sierra divides the water drainage and fish fauna. To the east are those rivers of the Lahontan Basin—the Truckee, Carson, and Walker Rivers—as well as some lesser streams, the few Mono Basin streams, and the Owens River drainage. All other rivers drain to the west, mostly into the San Joaquin and Sacramento River systems. In the Mammoth Lakes basin, during an earlier geologic time, the waters had drained westward into the Middle Fork of the San Joaquin River. Volcanic action occurred, closing that drainage, and the glacial melt water cut through volcanic rock to allow Mammoth Creek to flow east into the Owens River drainage.

The glaciers that had formed during the Little Ice Age period were much more extensive than today's remnants throughout the central and southern Sierra.

INDIGENOUS FISH SPECIES OF THE SIERRA

In the Sierra Nevada, two species of trout are native, the Lahontan cutthroat *(Oncorhynchus clarkii henshawi)* of the eastside and the rainbow of the westside. There are subspecies of these trout found throughout the range. Originally, the rainbow trout *(Oncorhynchus mykiss)* were the trout of all cool water streams and lakes west of the main Sierra crest. Rainbow trout are very adaptable and are now found in most suitable waters of the Sierra.

The Lahontan cutthroat trout, also called the black spotted trout, is a subspecies of cutthroat trout, a wide-ranging species that includes at least fourteen recognized forms in the western United States. Lahontan cutthroat trout were originally and still are found in the Truckee, Carson, and Walker River drainages. The Lahontan cutthroat reached maximum size in Lake Tahoe and formerly provided an important food source for the Washoe tribe. In 1882, a thirty-one-and-a-half-pound cutthroat trout was speared in the West Walker River. Before dams, it was common to find this species in the Bridgeport Valley and lakes connected to the East and West Walker River system. Heavy commercial fishing after 1860 drastically curtailed cutthroat populations in the largest lakes.

The Lahontan cutthroat was once very abundant in eastern Sierra waters, but has been largely replaced by more adaptable and aggressive brown *(Salmo trutta)*, rainbow, and eastern brook trout *(Salvelinus fontinalis)*. The cutthroat interbreeds readily with the rainbow trout. Fish in different drainages often vary somewhat in color and shape. The cutthroat seems to thrive best in waters where it does not need to compete with other species. Lahontan cutthroat trout have been planted in some westside creeks, namely Cow Creek and the West Fork of Portuguese Creek. They are also raised in fish hatcheries.

The golden trout *(Oncorhynchus aguabonita)* is a subspecies of the rainbow trout and is believed to have evolved from rainbow trout of the Kern River. The subspecies of trout occupying the Kern River drainage were the Kern River rainbow trout *(Onchorhynchus mykiss gilberti)*. Natural barriers such as lava flows occurred, isolating fish populations on some of the upper tributaries, and gradually those populations evolved into the golden trout. Golden trout are particularly adapted to the high, cold lakes above 9,000 feet in elevation. These flashy trout are distinguished with a spotted olive top and tail, golden sides, a pink stripe over oval spots running down the middle, and a red belly.

Henry W. Henshaw was a young natural history field collector with the Wheeler Survey from 1872-1879. In 1875, he served with the U.S. Geological Survey and reported seeing the beautiful golden trout in the South Fork of the Kern River.

Sherman and Augustus Stevens were sons of Sherman Stevens, who owned a sawmill at the head of Cottonwood Canyon. The Stevens Sawmill provided lumber for the busy mines at Cerro Gordo. The brothers caught thirteen of the golden beauties with hook and line in a little stream in Mulkey Meadow, where the Hockett Trail enters the meadow. They transported the fish in coffee pots over the Hockett Trail and planted them in Cottonwood Creek, about a mile above the sawmill. The trout then worked their way up stream toward the lakes until they met an obstacle they could not penetrate. These fish became well established and, in 1891, one hundred fish were moved beyond the impassable waterfalls and planted in the Cottonwood Lakes, where they have served as brood stock ever since.

In 1893, Dr. David Starr Jordan, president of Stanford University, named the new fish *Salmo mykiss agua-bonita*. That classification was later changed to *Oncorhynchus aguabonita*. These colorful fish inhabited various branches of the Kern River including Volcano Creek (now called Golden Trout Creek). There are color variations in several of the streams. During the summer of 1904, the National Commissioner of Fisheries investigated the fish in the Kern River and Mt. Whitney region. Three scientists and an artist explored the area. Dr. Barton W. Evermann, chief of the Division of Scientific Inquiry, U.S. Bureau of Fisheries, wrote a lengthy report describing the fish and claimed two new species. However, both populations of golden trout were later determined to be the same species. The golden trout has not only survived in its natural habitat, but has been transplanted to many other streams and lakes and is raised in hatcheries. Golden trout have also been exported to other states.

The Paiute cutthroat trout *(Oncorhynchus clarkii seleniris)*, a subspecies of the Lahontan cutthroat, was discovered and identified in Silver King Creek in the upper East Fork of the Carson River drainage in the early 1930s. These Paiute cutthroat trout were an isolated population in Fish Valley, and may have evolved similarly to the golden trout in the southern Sierra. Early sheepherders transplanted these fish throughout the area.

In 1968 and 1972, the California Department of Fish and Game planted Paiute trout in Sharktooth Creek and Stairway Creek in the Central Sierra. These creeks are located in the drainage of Fish Creek, a tributary of the Middle Fork of the San Joaquin River. They were also introduced to Desert Creek in the Sweetwater Mountain Range, a spur range of the Sierra. In 1946, in the White Mountain Range of eastern California, the North Fork of Cottonwood Creek was planted with the Paiute cutthroat, and that area has remained closed to fishing since that time to protect the fishery.

During the late Pleistocene Epoch, at the end of the last ice age, large, glacial meltwater lakes covered much of the Great Basin and Mojave Desert. As the climate of the region became much warmer and more arid during the altithermal period 4,000 to 9,000 years ago, the large Pleistocene lakes dried up, leaving the remnant habitats that are present today. When the lakes and rivers dried and receded, the larger fish probably became extinct first. Since cutthroat trout are present in the Lahontan Basin, it is possible to assume that the Owens River system might have contained trout in prehistoric times. Many glaciations and volcanism probably played an important role in the early distribution of fish fauna.

Some scientists believe there may have been connections between the Lahontan System and the Colorado River System, allowing an exchange of fish species. The fish of the connected Death Valley/Colorado River System, of which the Owens Valley is a part, were probably much more diverse and abundant during the Pleistocene than they are today. It is reasonable to assume that there may have been larger species of fish as well as the ancestors of the small modern forms. Remnants of Lahontan System lakes such as Pyramid Lake and Walker Lake contain indigenous trout as well as other desert fish.

Paiute and Shoshone tribes caught and dried native fish for sustenance. Four species of desert fish were found in the lower elevation waters, including the Sierra. In the Owens River drainage, several species that require abundant cool water have persisted. Two species that survived are the tui chub *(Siphateles bicolor)* and the mountain sucker *(Catostomus platyrhynchus)*. Smaller fish, the Owens pupfish *(Cyprinodon radiosus)* and speckled dace *(Rhinichthys osculus)*, survive in small isolated springs and marshes. All but the pupfish are found in the Upper Owens River region, at an elevation of 6,500 feet. Pupfish are native (endemic) to California. They belong to a group termed the killifish and are apparently the most adaptable of the native fishes. Owens pupfish historically inhabited the Owens Valley from Fish Slough in Mono County to Lone Pine in Inyo County, dwelling in springs, pools, sloughs, and ditches. In 1964, Phil Pister, a biologist for the Fish and Game Department, rediscovered the pupfish in Fish Slough north of Bishop, and the fish were listed as endangered in 1967.

EARLY FISH PLANTING

When pioneer settlement began in the 1850s, the Owens River drainage on the east side of the range did not contain trout species in the waters. Settlers, miners, packers, and summer visitors soon planted barren lakes and streams. They gathered native cutthroat, golden, and rainbow trout from lower streams teeming with fish. Fish were transported in coffee pots, water barrels, and coal oil cans hung over the wooden forks of pack saddles. As the trout quickly adapted to their new habitats, the Sierra became known for superb trout fishing.

In 1867, a mining company diverted water from Virginia Creek, in the East Walker River headwaters, across the divide to a Mono Basin drainage. Virginia Creek contained cutthroat trout. Shortly after, LeeVining Creek and Rush Creek were planted with the same cutthroat trout. After a lawsuit settlement, Virginia Creek was reestablished in its original channel on the north side of Conway Summit, draining into the Walker River drainage. The Walker River drainages supported cutthroat trout, and the fish were distributed to other drainages by settlers. The trout were sometimes carried in water barrels hung on freight wagons.

1873 was a busy year of fish planting by settlers. Charles Wonacott, an Owens Valley rancher, planted the lakes at the head of the Upper Owens River with rainbow stock from what the pioneer settlers called the "South Fork of the San Joaquin River." This river is actually Fish Creek, a tributary to the Middle Fork of the San Joaquin. During the 1870s, settlers planted rainbow trout fry, obtained from the Kern River and the South Fork of the Kings River on the westside, in the Upper Owens River and streams in Long Valley.

In 1872, J. W. McMurry, a resident of Big Pine, brought two dozen rainbow trout from the Kings River and planted them in reservoirs on his property at Fish Springs. Thomas Bell, also from Big Pine, raised rainbow trout from a stock of ten trout brought from the Kern River in 1873. He built several reservoirs to raise the trout. A. B. Kitchen of Big Pine planted Big Pine Creek with trout from the South Fork of the Kings River. This was a fifty-eight-mile mule pack train trip over Kearsarge Pass, with the fish transported in kitchen coal oil cans. Eighty fish survived out of the 200 brought to Big Pine. Kitchen also planted about sixty small rainbow trout in Little Pine Creek, now called Independence Creek. Additional trout were brought from the Kings River and planted in Baker, Birch, Tinemaha, Red Mountain, Oak, Independence, Shepherd, Bairs, and George's Creeks. William Harrell and the Russell Brothers, Owens Valley residents, stocked Bishop Creek with Walker Lake cutthroat trout brought from Carson City by H. Parker. In 1874, Andrew Thomson planted Walker River cutthroat in lakes of the Upper Owens River Valley. These trout, from near the headwaters of Walker Lake and Mill Creek, were transported in coal oil cans.

In 1876, thirteen golden trout from Mulkey Creek, near Monache Meadows, were transported in a coffee pot to Cottonwood Creek. In 1877 and 1878, Rock, Hilton, Convict, McGee, Laurel, and Sherwin Creeks, as well as the Mammoth Lakes, were all stocked with trout from Bishop Creek. Lake Mary, in the Mammoth Lakes basin, was planted in 1877 and 1878 with fish from the Middle Fork of the San Joaquin River. In 1879, Colonel Sherman Stevens of Lone Pine planted Cottonwood Creek with golden trout taken from Mulkey Creek. E. H. Edwards planted Lone Pine Creek with trout from Oak Creek.

In 1878, the newspaper of the early mining town Mammoth City reported that the Paiute tribe was catching large rainbow trout in the Middle Fork of the San Joaquin River and Fish Creek, hauling them to town to sell to the miners. The rivers and streams west of the crest had always contained native rainbow trout, whereas the Owens River system did not. There was little commercial fishing carried on by the settlers, however.

Franklin Buck reported in a local newspaper on a fishing trip to the South Fork of the San Joaquin (Fish Creek) on July 23, 1880. He and his party packed in about twelve miles, possibly near Island Crossing. He reported that there were deer, quail, a creek teeming with native rainbow trout, and rattlesnakes.

During summer months, residents living adjacent to the Sierra, on both the east and west sides, spent time in the mountains as the inland valley heat became extreme and valley insects became annoying. Local citizens moved to the mountains for weeks at a time and fished to supplement their diet.

In 1884, Albert Wonacott stocked local lakes in the Upper Owens River Basin with trout from the San Joaquin River. In 1891, one hundred golden trout were planted in the Cottonwood Lakes. More fish were planted throughout the area in 1897-1898, and again in 1903.

It was reported in the 1908 *Inyo Register* newspaper, "that the large trout in Convict Lake are Walker River variety and weigh up to 30 pounds. The other lakes contain mostly the San Joaquin variety (rainbows), and in the rivers are the Walker River (cutthroat) variety."

Prior to World War II, the Rainbow Club, an early sportsmen's club in Bishop, planted fish throughout the eastern Sierra. Other communities organized sportsmen's groups to support fish planting in their areas.

The Calif. Dept. of Fish and Game has designed fish cans to transport the trout fry by mule back. (Russ and Anne Johnson)

Fish Creek in Cascade Valley teems with rainbow trout.
Packer Dan Price enjoys fly fishing.

As a mule is added to the string, the packer keeps them circling to generate
oxygen in the cans. (Russ and Anne Johnson)

CHAPTER SEVEN

RECREATIONAL PACK TRIPS FOR SUMMER PLEASURES

EARLY RANCHERS

In the not-so-distant past, ranchers trailed their herds of cattle and sheep to the mountains for summer grazing. Sheepherders and cattlemen had developed passable livestock trails before the turn of the century. Cattle ranchers packed in to their summer line camps, small cabins outfitted for the season, along with their herds. They also often packed their families into the mountains for the summer to escape the intense heat and insects of the inland valleys. Families set up tent camps near lakes and creeks on their livestock grazing leases. Eventually, many ranchers who drove their herds and flocks to the Sierra for the summer began to pack their friends into the backcountry.

Tom Rickey, Alney McGee, and Charlie Summers, eastern Sierra cattle ranchers, trailed their cattle into the Fish Creek basin, a tributary to the Middle Fork of the San Joaquin River, deep in the heart of the Sierra fastness. These ranchers developed cattle and sheep trails for summer grazing. Sheep were pastured in upper Fish Creek and Mono Creek, trailing in from the west side of the Sierra

Gene Tully was a Forest Service ranger who patrolled Fish Creek basin for six weeks during the summer, monitoring the sheep flocks for several years after 1908. He often base-camped with his pack string at Tully's Hole Meadow, which bears his name. An old log sheep corral can still be detected at Upper Fish Creek, several miles above Tully's Hole on the McGee Pass Trail.

Drought is a reoccurring weather pattern in California. The severe droughts of 1876 and 1877 in the Central Valley forced livestock owners to move many herds to mountain grazing lands. In 1880, the sheep population in California was 4,152,349, the largest in the United States. As the sheep bands left the higher grazing lands and returned to the lower valleys for the winter, some sheepherders set fires behind them to improve future grazing and clear the trails and driveways, the open sections of land where stock was driven. Local valley newspapers reported that large fires could be seen, and mountain summits were blanketed in smoke. Since there was no fire suppression at that time, fires often burned until the winter snows arrived and eventually put them out. While the fires might have opened up the country somewhat, the unintended consequences did much resource damage that took years to recover from.

During the 1880s and early 1890s, the Sierra experienced wet and stormy weather cycles. Summer storms were more frequent and powerful. The high country contained large snowdrifts and snowfields that lasted all summer.

Frank Dusy was a Central Valley sheep man who drove his flocks to the Sierra in the summer, especially to the North and Middle Forks of the Kings River. He discovered Tehipite Valley in 1869 and explored north to Palisade Basin in 1877. Dusy, along with Winchell Lilbourne, a Fresno farmer, spent five months exploring in the Sierra in 1879. Dusy lugged a large, heavy camera, packing it carefully on a mule, and took the first photograph of Tehipite Valley. These trips opened a new business venture for Dusy when he offered guide and pack mule services to the public. The timberline lakes basin near Bishop Pass, the Dusy Lakes Basin, is named after Frank Dusy.

Winchell Lilbourne, who also made numerous trips to the Sierra over many years, wrote a book, *The History of Fresno County and the San Joaquin Valley*. In 1881, James William, Albert Wright, F. H. Wales, and W. B. Wallace took a pack trip to the Kern River and Mt. Whitney. Wright drew a map of the area that was later published in Lilbourne's book.

Tom Williams, a rancher in the Mammoth Meadows, drove his cattle from Mammoth Meadows over the Mammoth Pass Trail to his Forest Service grazing permit on abundant meadows in Deer Creek. A sheep camp was located on a lower bench below Deer Creek, where a livestock trail dropped abruptly into Lower Fish Creek. That trail became thickly overgrown with dense brush when the sheep no longer grazed the area.

The Blassingame Ranch family of the Central Valley trailed their cattle to Jackson Meadow in the Silver Divide country starting roughly around the turn of the century. Other westside ranchers grazed mountain meadows and the grassy side hills during the short summer months.

Jeff Davis, a Woodlake cattle rancher, purchased the Mineral King Butcher Store in 1904 to market beef to summer visitors in the Mineral King Valley. His family soon expanded their activities to begin a tourist packing business. Commercial packing in the early 1900s was sporadic, but Jeff Davis and his five sons gradually increased their packing services as high country touring became popular with urban visitors.

Gus Cashbaugh of Bishop held a Forest Service grazing permit in Pioneer Basin and Mono Creek in 1910. He drove his cattle over 12,000-foot Mono Pass to reach these verdant meadows, and built a log cabin line camp at First Recess.

EARLY ADVERTISING

Communities near established trailheads advertised their scenic attractions and outfitting services to potential tourists. Livery stables in nearby towns advertised the availability of camping outfits, pack trains, and professional packers. Every town had at least one livery stable and most towns had several. The stables provided stabling for travelers, blacksmith services, and horses and pack mules for hire, as well as buggies and teams. They also bought and sold livestock. They outfitted pack trips and supplied knowledgeable guides.

Railroads also advertised the beauties of the High Sierra. Tourists traveled by trains to nearby towns, then boarded stages, and finally, rode horses to their ultimate destination. It required some time to arrive at the departure site to begin a High Sierra vacation. Tourists from cities and towns discovered the wonders of the High Sierra, and the recreational outfitting industry became well known in the region.

Owens Valley newspapers carried the following advertisements:

Mt. Whitney Hotel and Anton's Resort, J. C. Anton, Lone Pine, "Anton's Resorts – 16 miles from Lone Pine on Cottonwood Creek on the Hockett Trail. We outfit parties at Lone Pine for Sierra trips. Saddle and pack horses for hire."

E. H. Edwards mercantile, Lone Pine, since 1874, "Outfitting Store for camping expeditions to Mt. Whitney, Cottonwood Lakes etc."

BUILDING THE MT. WHITNEY TRAIL

By 1903, Lone Pine citizens realized they needed a direct pack train trail to the summit of Mt. Whitney to accommodate visitors wishing to climb the tallest mountain. The U.S. Cavalry troops under Captain Charles Young worked on the trail in the early fall and almost reached the summit. Snow storms forced them to cease their trail work for the season. At the urging of Captain Young, the citizens of Lone Pine raised money to complete the remaining trail work needed to accommodate saddle and pack stock.

The following spring, in 1904, contractor George F. Marsh and trail workers were packed up the switchback trail to a base camp by Carmen Olivas and his Olivas Pack Trains. The men constructed a pack trail from where the soldiers had stopped the previous fall, up Lone Pine Creek to the summit. They completed it on July 17. On July 22, three pack trains loaded with firewood and led by packers climbed up the trail to the summit. They built a huge celebration fire that night and set off fireworks on the summit that could plainly be seen in Lone Pine. The builders enthusiastically reported that the pack trains had no difficulty in climbing the mountain, saying, "The trail is in good shape and parties are going over it every day."

The Smithsonian Institution was interested in obtaining weather observations from the summit of Mt. Whitney and requested a cabin be built on top for prolonged stays. Marsh was again the contractor, and construction of the cabin began on July 28, 1909. Olivas Pack Trains packed all the materials, tools, equipment, and builders for a stone cabin to the top of the mountain. Rock was readily available on the mountaintop. The stone cabin was completed by the end of August when the scientific team arrived. Stone corrals were also constructed next to the cabin to corral the mules and horses needed for riding and the transport of supplies for the scientists.

LOS ANGELES DEPARTMENT OF WATER AND POWER CREATES CHANGE

Circumstances were changing significantly on the east side of the range in regards to water. In 1905, the Los Angeles Department of Water and Power planned an extensive aqueduct system to transport Owens Valley water to the growing city. In order to secure the water rights for their vast plans, the department commenced purchasing Owens Valley farms and ranches. As ranches and farms went out of production, the economy of the agriculturally-based Owens Valley communities was devastated. The little towns greatly suffered from the demise of the agricultural economy.

To offset this change in the economy created by removing irrigated farmland from production, local community groups and the Los Angeles Department of Water and Power promoted tourism. With the reduction in agriculture, the towns needed to provide a new economic base, and encouraged development of tourism and recreation. The large presence of the City of Los Angeles, with its extensive water system, had made this region well-known to Southern California residents, and tourists soon discovered the pleasures of camping and summering in the eastern Sierra.

In 1908, both Inyo and Mono Counties published advertising booklets promoting the counties' attributes, along with camping, fishing, and hunting opportunities. The backcountry scenery, with its lakes and streams, was highly praised. Each of the towns in the Owens Valley wrote glowingly of the scenic backcountry wonders that could be reached by beginning an expedition from their town. Lodges, camps, and pack stations sprang up near many of the lakes, streams, and passes into the backcountry.

Many horses and mules were no longer needed for work on valley ranches and farms, along with an increasingly idle workforce. So, men, animals, and winter pasture were available for the burgeoning tourist packing and outfitting industry. Cowboys, ranchers, blacksmiths, and farmers organized pack stations to meet this tourist demand, and outfits sprang up at every trailhead. Livery stables in towns expanded their operations to include outfitting mountain pack trips. In addition to the required animals and guides, complete camping equipment and cooks could be provided.

In the 1912 *Inyo Register Magazine,* local outfitters advertised:

The Nevada Stables, Louis Bodle, Bishop, "Tourists and Campers' Outfits."

Pioneer Livery Stable, F. E. Herrick, Bishop, "All kinds of outfits for tourists' mountain trips."

Ben R. Ransome a guide out of Big Pine, in Guide of the Sierras, advertised: "Outings in the Sierras for 10 days, 15 days, 30 days and plus tourist trips, Headwaters of the San Joaquin for 30 days, Yosemite Valley for over 30 days."

EMERGENCE OF PACK STATIONS

In the 1870s, Cerro Gordo, near Owens Lake, was an active mining area, along with other mines in the southern Owens Valley region. Nearby Saline Valley provided vast acres of salt, and salt works soon sprang up. Packers, with mule strings loaded with salt, packed it to the numerous cattle and sheep herds on the Kern Plateau and Monache Meadows, to supplement their diets. These areas depended on packers with mule trains to bring supplies.

Frank Olivas, who was a vaquero and arrierro, had arrived in the Owens Valley by pack train from Mexico. His family engaged in the commercial packing business in Lone Pine. Olivas also cut wood that he hauled to the Cerro Gordo mining town, packing ore on the return trips. The town of Lone Pine had a constant need for wood for heating and cooking, and ice for refrigeration. By 1890, his son, Carmen Olivas was running the packing business and, in 1901, Carmen advertised as Olivas Pack Trains, with corrals at Olancha and Sage Flat on Loco Creek. He used his traditional methods of packing.

The Tourists' Saddle and Pack Livery in Lone Pine was one of the early commercial pack outfits in the Owens Valley. Charles W. Robinson was a teamster, raised mules and horses, and, starting in 1872, packed commercially.

In 1901, he established a tourist-packing outfit under C. W. Robinson & Son, Prop. Charlie and his son, Allie, produced an advertising brochure declaring that they would meet parties at all points of interest in the national forest, and that no charges would be levied until leaving "your point." Moving to Independence, they established their business in town, with corrals where their trips commenced. Allie Robinson continued the packing enterprises when Charlie retired, and contracted the large Sierra Club trips until World War II. Outfitting these trips required a large number of mules.

John Broder of Sequoia Ranch and his partner, Ralph Hopping, both owned ranches along the Lower Kaweah River. They opened Camp Sierra on the North Fork of the Kaweah River and also established a stage line into Sequoia National Park, using the Old Colony Road to the road's end. Guests took the stage and then rode horseback four miles to Round Meadow, near Giant Forest, for their vacation stay at Camp Sierra. Broder operated the stage line, and Hopping and his wife operated Camp Sierra. They then established a packing service operating out of Three Rivers, with eighty-five head of stock, corrals, ten tents, and a cook house. From there they conducted pack trips across the mountains, where their clients could camp below Mt. Whitney and climb the great mountain. In 1903, they were contacted by the Sierra Club and contracted to pack in the Club on their third Outing Trip to the Kern River. While there, over a hundred of the Clubbers climbed Mt. Whitney. They camped at Camp Olney, part of old Camp Lewis on the Hockett Trail near Coyote Creek. Camp Lewis had been homesteaded in 1876 and was later acquired by John Lewis of Lone Pine.

Peter Napoleon "Poley" Kanawyer was a miner who prospected in the Kings Canyon in the 1880s, where he had a copper mining claim. He homesteaded property and established a camp. By 1898, it had evolved into Camp Kanawyer and Pack Station, where he served tourists. His wife cooked for these groups. William Colby of the Sierra Club persuaded the Kanawyers to invest in more mules and horses in order to accommodate the Club's trip. They catered the 1902 Sierra Club Outing Trip to Kings Canyon for a two week base camp. This was the first outing trip totally packed in by mules and horses.

Charlie Summers and his brother, John, ranchers from the Owens Valley, purchased the large Cyrus Rawson cattle ranch in the Upper Long Valley in 1908. Charlie's headquarters was on Laurel Creek south of Mammoth Lakes, and as local ranchers, he and John packed family and friends into backcountry cattle camps during the summer. This service evolved into the commercial packing business at Mammoth Camp as the tourism business grew.

Mammoth Camp, located in the Mammoth Meadows on Mammoth Creek, was growing into a summer visitor destination. People had camped along the Mammoth Creek since the 1890s, and some had erected log cabins.

Charles F. Wildasinn purchased 160 acres in 1891 for back taxes and continued purchases through 1901. Prior to 1905, he built a sawmill and then a small two story hotel that he called El Casa Sierra in the meadow. An old hotel register shows a good summer business at the hotel. Wildasinn also constructed a general store to supply the campers and a large barn across the road.

By 1915, Charlie Summers and his son, Lloyd, operated a commercial pack trip business, loosely called Mammoth Camp Pack Outfit, out of the barn and corrals across the road from the hotel. They packed customers into the Mammoth Lakes Basin, over Duck Pass to the Fish Creek Basin, and to the Middle Fork of the San Joaquin River. In 1917, Summers purchased Wildasinn's hotel, resort, and property, and built a new, larger hotel named the Mammoth Camp Hotel. In 1919, the old wagon road, winding up to the abandoned mines and mining towns of Mammoth City and Pine City by Lake Mary, was improved by the new Forest Service to accommodate automobiles. Charlie Summers then built a corral at Lake Mary, and pack trips began there. Horses and mules were trailed up to Lake Mary from Mammoth Camp's grassy meadows. On the south side of the lake, Lloyd Summers had fenced in a small meadow and constructed a corral as a base for the pack trips.

JOHN MUIR TRAIL

At an evening campfire in 1914, Meyer Lissner suggested to the Sierra Club that the State of California should appropriate money to establish a good trail system in the Sierra Nevada. The current trail system was mostly unmarked and poor, and even had no accessible trails in some of the most spectacular regions. Lissner promoted a Sierra Club program to seek appropriations for trail development. A committee was formed, with William Colby chosen to write the trail bill. John Muir had recently died, and their proposal included the name "John Muir Trail" to memorialize him. John Muir's name for the Sierra Nevada was "The Range of Light," and his love of this superb mountain range was honored by this proposed John Muir Trail.

State Engineer Wilbur McClure selected the final route of the John Muir Trail, and the State of California allocated funds of $10,000 to begin the construction. The route was chosen to stay as close as possible to the high main crest of the remarkable chain. Actual trail construction began in 1915 under the direction of Roy Boothe, a Forest Service ranger. Boothe was later Supervisor of the Inyo National Forest from 1926 to 1945. The trail was built and supervised from the east side of the range, because the distance was shorter than from the west side. The Sequoia and Sierra National Forests also did much construction work, and commercial pack stations provided packing services for the trail work. Pack animals, saddle horses, and draft teams were essential in trail and bridge construction. In addition to the necessary tools and supplies, a camp with all of its provisions had to be maintained for the trail crew.

By 1927, most of the trail had been completed. Side trails that accessed the John Muir Trail were improved and relocated in some areas. In 1930, the Sequoia National Forest and National Park began construction of Forester Pass. Before completion of this pass, the Muir Trail went east over Junction and Shepherd Passes. Forester Pass, a most spectacular pass and engineering marvel, provided a direct crossing of the high, precipitous Kings-Kern Divide. It is the highest pass on the John Muir Trail, at 13,153 feet elevation. The last section slated for construction, called the "Golden Staircase" for its many steep switchbacks, started on a cliff below Palisade Lakes and then traversed across granite rock to complete Mather Pass (12,100 feet). This last segment was completed in 1938. Muir Pass, at 11,955 feet, to the north of the Golden Staircase, was also finished in 1938. Volunteer Sierra Club members later

56

constructed a small round rock hut with a fireplace on top of the pass, calling it the Muir Hut.

The John Muir Trail traverses the range lengthwise from Happy Isles in Yosemite Valley to the top of Mt. Whitney for 211 spectacular miles, staying as close as possible to the higher regions of the range. Including the access trail from the top of Mt. Whitney to the Whitney Portal trailhead, the actual trail mileage is 222 miles. The length of the trail is not bisected by any trans-Sierra highway.

THE PACIFIC CREST TRAIL

In 1932, Clinton C. Clarke of Pasadena, California, visualized a trail running from Mexico to Canada through California, Oregon, and Washington along the crest of the mountains, including the Sierra Nevada Range and the Cascade Range. His original proposal included linking the John Muir Trail with the Tahoe-Yosemite Trail through the Sierra and two other trails in California. Many miles of the route were already on completed trails.

Clarke was founder of the Pasadena Playhouse and Chairman of the Mountain League of Los Angeles. He organized a conference called the Pacific Coast Trail System Conference that included the Boy Scouts and the YMCA. The goal was to plan the route of the trail and push for the support of the Federal Government. The YMCA explored 2,000 miles of the proposed trail from 1935 to 1938. Their routes were very close to the current route of the trail. Much work on the trail was accomplished by the CCC prior to World War II, when work was halted for the duration of the War. In the Sierra, pack stations along the route packed in trail crews and supplies for maintenance on established trails, as well as new construction on linking trails. The trails were all designed for horse and mule travel as well as hiking. Pack stations provided support, with resupplies to travelers and crews along the way.

In 1968, the PCT, as it was termed, was put on the National Trails System, and in 1993, it was called complete, although work still continues on some portions. It is 2,653 miles long, with the majority of the trail in national forests, national parks, and protected wilderness areas. The highest elevation along the PCT, at 13,153 feet, is Forester Pass on the Kings-Kern Divide in the Sierra, which is also on the John Muir Trail.

FIRST AUTOMOBILE ROADS IN THE EASTERN SIERRA

Eastern Sierra tourism had been slowed by the lack of all-weather roads. As early as 1878, a rough wagon road led from Bishop to the mining towns of Mill, Mammoth, and Pine Cities, as well as Mineral Park. By 1912, an improved wagon road had been constructed to Mammoth Lakes. The Inyo Good Roads Club, an Owens Valley association, was formed in 1910. They urged the State of California to build a state highway on the eastside and, by 1916, the Sherwin Grade between Bishop and Mammoth Lakes was completed. Mammoth Lakes and the eastern Sierra became a staging area for trips into the backcountry. Later, in 1931, a paved road called El Camino Sierra was completed from Los Angeles to Bridgeport.

These improved roads encouraged more automobile traffic and tourists to visit the many beautiful areas of the Sierra. As automobiles became more common, tourists drove their own vehicles to the mountains to camp, stay in the lodges, and pack into backcountry campsites.

Beginning in 1915, Forest Service trail crews constructed the JMT from Yosemite to Mt. Whitney. (Russ and Anne Johnson)

In a steep, rocky draw, a trail is built up like a ramp. (Russ and Anne Johnson)

CHAPTER EIGHT

BACKCOUNTRY TRAVEL INCREASES AFTER WORLD WAR I

At the close of World War I, recreational use of the Sierra Nevada increased rapidly. The region was often referred to as the High Sierra. This tourism spurt was made possible by the availability of automobiles and better roads. As automobiles became more common, new roads were constructed and wagon roads were improved to accommodate this new mode of transportation.

PACK STATIONS SPREAD THROUGHOUT THE REGION

The number of pack stations grew during the 1920s and early 1930s, with at least one station at each suitable location. The stations were located adjacent to trailheads that led to lakes and streams, preferably at or near the end of the accessible road. Some popular road-end destinations had two or three pack stations, and most were busy. After 1935, there were no new stations, and outfits began to merge where there was more than one.

Sierra pack stations were issued resort permits in the 1920s from the U.S. Forest Service and developed permanent facilities at their sites. The owners were also issued grazing permits to graze in the backcountry on overnight, extended, or traveling trips. Many pack stations had adjoining or nearby pastures for their stock. Since little hay was available in the early years, and hauling it to the high mountain locations was difficult, pack stations were issued grazing permits in nearby meadows and grasslands on national forest land. The pack station owners built drift fences to manage and control grazing. The horses and mules were turned out at night to graze, and rounded up the next morning to be saddled for work.

Most stations were small family businesses, with the entire family assisting in the operation of the business. Wives and daughters cooked for their family, crew, and customers, as well as handling the reservations and bookkeeping. Children also helped and learned to saddle their own horse as soon as they were big enough. Some stations, like Rainbow Pack Outfit on the South Fork of Bishop Creek, above the town of Bishop, even kept a milk cow. There were no telephones or electrical services in these early days. Running water was a pipeline to the nearest creek, spring, or lake.

The term "packer" is widely used in the Sierra, but there are two quite separate classifications. The pack station operator is the owner whose business is the commercial tourist packing business. The other type of packer is the person who is employed by a pack station as a packer, wrangler, or guide.

A majority of the early professional packers were cowboys and teamsters, born and raised around stock, who also enjoyed spending summers in the mountains. They were experienced with horses and mules, could shoe, and had excellent packing skills. Many packers worked for the same outfit each summer, and some eventually bought or began their own outfit. During the Great Depression, work was scarce, and pack stations were able to hire exceptionally skilled packers for the summer season.

Career packers sometimes brought their families to the mountains, where they resided in tent cabins. Many such children raised around pack outfits eventually worked for the outfit when they were old enough, and some eventually became owners of their own pack stations.

Packers, wranglers, and guides often worked on ranches during the winter and packed in the Sierra during the summer. A few packers worked on dude ranches in the Southwest during the winter and became quite talented at entertaining the guests with stories, music, and cowboy poetry.

As new roads were pushed farther into the mountains, some pack stations had to relocate to new sites at the end of a new road. The rough dirt roads were usually one-way with few pullouts, and often were steep and winding. Some pack stations had to move several times following the construction of new roads penetrating farther into the Sierra wilderness.

Don Cecil began his station at Eshom Creek west of Cedar Grove in 1923. In 1925, he moved the station to Big Meadow west of Hume Lake. His eldest son, Ernest, ran the station, which included a store, at Big Meadow in 1935. Then, in 1936, the road was cut through seven more miles to Horse Corral Meadow, south of Cedar Grove, so by 1939, Ernest Cecil had moved the station again to Horse Corral. The buildings had to be removed and then reassembled at Horse Corral. In 1940, a road was completed to Cedar Grove, and the Cecils built a second station at Cedar Grove.

At trailhead sites where there was more than one outfit, one owner would gradually buy out the others until there was only one in each canyon or drainage. Pack stations in less used areas sold out to a nearby operator in a more popular location or, if the station was financially unviable, went out of business. Some outfits were small, with only a few head of stock, and they either increased the size of their operations, sold, or went out of business. Some pack stations developed cabins, tent camps, a cafe, and a store to provide for summer guests.

PACK TRIPS

Packers improved on and added to the original Native American, mining, livestock, and army trails. If necessary, they constructed new trails to better access desired camping locations near favorite fishing spots. This trail system grew gradually, providing access to most lakes and streams.

In the Sierra, fishing was a vital interest and motivation for many clients, and formed the major part of many stations' businesses. Deer hunting was an important fall activity for areas outside of the national parks, which no longer permitted hunting. Sierra pack stations did not establish permanent hunting camps like the big game hunting outfitters did in the Rocky Mountains. Hunters used the same campsites used by fishing parties earlier in the season, and many hunting parties fished as well.

Since it took time to reach the start of a Sierra pack trip in these earlier years, trips tended to stay for a long time. Trips were often ten days to two weeks, and were sometimes traveling or all inclusive trips, where the packer and stock, and possibly a cook, stayed with the party, moving camp as desired. However, most trips were spot trips where the party was dropped off at a campsite, with the packer and stock returning to pack them out, and the average size of parties was small—up to six customers. The only really large trips were the Sierra Club Outings, and they were handled most often by Allie Robinson's pack outfit. The majority of the pack stations did not have enough mules to handle these huge trips.

Some families of affluence took up camping and enjoyed deluxe pack trips of some length throughout the Sierra that lasted up to a month. Outfitters supplied the usual basic camp gear such as tents, chairs, tables, stoves, and sleeping cots. They sometimes supplemented the camp with rugs, tablecloths, and even china and glassware so guests could still enjoy the niceties of civilization while camping in the wilderness. A few outfits, mostly on the west side of the range like Mineral King Pack Station, catered to this type of client.

Eleanor Roosevelt, First Lady of the United States, with her secretary, Lorena Hickok, vacationed in Yosemite National Park from July 21-24 of 1934. She was packed into the Young Lakes from Tuolumne Meadows with four Yosemite park rangers. The Young Lakes are located in the northeastern section of the park at 10,000 feet elevation at the foot of Mt. Conness. The chief ranger, Forest Townley, was the guide and in charge of the trip. Rangers Otto Brown, Billy Nelson, and John Bingaman set up camp and looked after the food and sleeping gear, with Brown doing the cooking. It is reported that Nelson provided Mrs. Roosevelt with a hot water bottle each night to warm her feet.

Mrs. Roosevelt was an excellent horsewoman and rode her horse almost every day when she was home in Washington, D.C. As this was also a fish planting mission, the rangers were planting fish in the upper lakes, and Mrs. Roosevelt assisted in planting rainbow trout. The uppermost, unnamed lake was named Roosevelt Lake in honor of the First Lady.

The Mammoth Camp Pack Outfit was owned and operated by Charlie Summers and his son Lloyd. They also owned the Mammoth Camp Hotel and a nearby cattle ranch. Horses and mules were pastured and corralled in Mammoth Meadows, and packers trailed them up the Mammoth Road, either the evening before or on the morning of a trip, to Lake Mary to begin trips into the backcountry. The road climbed 1,000 feet in elevation to the Lake Mary corrals at the small meadow on the south side of the lake. Other fenced meadows were located below Heart Lake and Emerald Lake.

Clark Keely, whose family stayed at the Mammoth Hotel in Mammoth Camp, described pack trips out of Mammoth Camp Pack Outfit in 1920 and 1921. Dave Jackson, an Owens Valley Paiute, was their packer and a long time packer for the outfit. Jackson Meadow and Jackson Lake (now called Grassy Lake) were named for him. In 1920, Keeley packed in over the old Duck Pass trail from Emerald Lake, Skelton Lake, and the two Woods Lakes, and over the top of the crest to the east of the current Duck Pass.

In the 1921 summer, the Keely family packed in from the Mammoth Hotel and corrals over Mammoth Pass to the San Joaquin River. They camped at Soda Springs near Devils Postpile for ten days, and reported that there were very few campers at the river then.

The City of Los Angeles Department of Recreation and Parks acquired land and built Camp High Sierra in 1924. Automobile travel from Los Angeles to

Mammoth Lakes was a two or three-day trip over a rough road. Guests from Los Angeles stayed at the camp at least a week, enjoying fishing, horseback riding, and hiking. Some guests based there before and after their pack trips into the nearby backcountry.

In 1938, a new paved road was completed to the Lakes Basin that bypassed Mammoth Camp. Access to the Mammoth Lakes Basin was easier now, and the village businesses in the meadow moved their facilities several miles north in the forest, to the newly completed Mammoth Lakes and Lake Mary Road.

MINERAL KING PACKING COMPANY AND IKE LIVERMORE

In Mineral King Valley, Phil Davis became the lead packer in the Davis family packing business. He was the largest and most successful packer in the area. Phil Buckman became Davis's assistant in 1927 and his business partner in 1929.

In 1929, a very tall young man had just graduated from high school at the Thacher School in Ojai, California. His name was Norman "Ike" Livermore, and he was to become a very positive force in the Sierra packing industry. Growing up on his family's ranch in Northern California, he had developed a love of horseback riding, hunting, and fishing. Ike went to work that summer for Davis, learning the packing business. His jobs included assisting with cooking and doing whatever chores needed doing, as well as shoeing the horses and mules.

After a long dispute with the Forest Service, Davis lost his packing permit at the end of the 1929 season, but he and his brothers continued their packing services from another nearby location. In 1930, Phil Buckman obtained the Mineral King Pack Station permit from the Forest Service. Ike Livermore, now attending Stanford University, packed for Buckman in the 1930 season. He took his first long traveling pack trip that summer, beginning at Mineral King Packing Company corrals.

Mineral King Packing Company had arranged a trip that would begin at Yosemite. Ike and another packer deadheaded the stock—or led them without loaded packs—from Three Rivers all the way to Yosemite by trail. Reaching Yosemite, they rendezvoused with the party of four persons. They packed all the camp supplies, equipment, and personal gear on the mules, and mounted the guests on horses to begin the pack trip from Yosemite, traveling the entire length of the John Muir Trail to Mt. Whitney. They then trailed the party from Mt. Whitney to Mineral King Pack Station.

By 1933, Phil's cousin, Ray Buckman, who had packed for the old Broder and Hopping outfit, joined the pack station, now financed by Ike Livermore. It had become a large operation with a store and dining room in addition to the pack station. Livermore became a partner in 1937 and continued a long association with the Mineral King Packing Company.

Roland and Bart Ross owned the Ross Brothers Pack Station, also in Mineral King Valley. By 1934, they had sixty head of stock and a store. There seemed to be enough business for both operations, as Mineral King was a popular trailhead area, with many directions that trips could take from there. A third pack station was located about six miles below the valley at Silver City, an old mining area. In 1940, Ray Buckman bought out the Ross Brothers and combined their businesses into one pack station in the valley.

IKE LIVERMORE SURVEY AND CREATION OF
THE HIGH SIERRA PACKERS' ASSOCIATION

At the end of the summer packing season in September of 1934, Livermore rode his motorcycle up and down both sides of the great mountain range, surveying and studying the various pack stations. His field of study was the region he called the, "High Sierra wilderness area, that stretch of country between Tioga and Walker Passes which is yet unspoiled by roads," as quoted from his survey thesis.

At that time, there were seventy-one pack stations located on the east and west sides of the range. The estimated number of people who took stock pack trips the summer of 1934 was 32,000. Packers estimated that between thirty to a hundred and fifty mule loads of fish were planted annually for the California Department of Fish and Game.

As he surveyed pack stations, some findings by Livermore indicated that the Tehama packsaddle was the most popular and was used extensively. Most packers believed Porter and Hamley dude saddles were the best all-around saddles. Most packers liked and used simple curb bits and bridles with chin straps, but Allie Robinson preferred a split ear headstall. For pack tarps, a five by six foot pack cover was considered the right size, although Navy hammocks obtained from Army and Navy stores also made good pack covers. Furniture pads (quilts) used by moving companies were sometimes used as packsaddle pads. The diamond hitch was used almost exclusively to secure loads. Only Earl Pascoe and Warren Halliday preferred the box hitch. Packers thought 150 pounds packed on a mule was the right weight over mountain trails, but in reality they believed many mules were sometimes packed with loads of up to 200 pounds.

Livermore returned to Stanford University that fall with his research notes and used his study to write his Master's thesis, earning an MBA. He printed the results of his thesis, titled *The Tourist Packing Business of the High Sierra Region*. We are honored to have a copy of this report. As a result of his study, he urged the packers to form an association to benefit their members.

Livermore organized a group of packers from the westside to gather in Porterville in May of 1935. At this first meeting, the group in attendance formed an association called the High Sierra Packers' Association, with Ike Livermore as the secretary-treasurer and Art Griswald, the packer from Camp Wishon, as temporary president. The packers agreed to follow this meeting with a second meeting including the eastside packers.

The initial members of the new association were: Rae Crabtree, Coolidge Meadows; Earl McKee, Giant Forest; Craig Thorn, Silver City; Roland Ross, Mineral King; Phil Buckman, Mineral King; Phil Davis, Three Rivers; Art Griswald, Camp Wishon; Walter Greig, Quaking Aspen Meadows; Ed Snider, Pine Flat; H. M. Culkins, Durrwood on the Kern; Earl Pascoe, Camp Pasco; and H. P. Thelan, Kennedy Meadows.

The Eastside Packers' Association had previously been organized in 1928, with mostly Owens Valley packers, and a bylaw booklet had been printed. The association had only been functioning minimally, so Ike Livermore helped reorganize them in 1935, under the name Eastern High Sierra Packers' Association. The two associations would be loosely joined together but met separately because of geographical distances and the fact that they were divided by an over-14,000-foot-tall mountain range.

TOURIST SADDLE AND PACK LIVERY

In 1913, the Tourist Saddle and Pack Livery, owned by Charlie Robinson and his son, Allie W. Robinson, began outfitting the very large Sierra Club trips from their headquarters in Independence in the Owens Valley. The outfit was now called Robinson Pack Trains. The Robinson headquarters on Main Street in Independence were close to High Sierra Pack Train, owned by Archie Dean, another early Owens Valley packer. The Robinson Ranch, where the stock was pastured, was a city lease (Los Angeles Department of Water and Power) on Mazourka Canyon Road.

By 1931, Robinson Pack Trains, now owned by Allie and Doris Robinson, was the largest pack station in the Sierra. It was larger and did more packing at that time than the Curry Company Stables in Yosemite National Park. Allie Robinson packed the Sierra Club High Trips for many years. The Sierra Club trips were huge events of two hundred people plus staff, requiring sometimes three hundred head of pack and riding horses, with as many as fifty packers.

By the 1930s, Sierra Club trips were so popular that they had become unwieldy. So, to alleviate this problem, the Club created three separate excursions each summer. The High Trip was the traditional, stock-supported trip, lasting four to six weeks. People could join the party for portions or the entire trip. The Burro Trips were small hiking trips with burros furnished by pack stations, which packed the camp gear and provisions. The burro trips appealed to families with children. Knapsack trips were small backpack trips supported by prior food caches deposited at campsites by commercial pack stations. These trips focused on athletic adults desiring a strenuous off-trail/cross-country hike.

The Robinsons (Charlie and his son, Allie) owned exceptionally good mules, raising some of them. Some of the pack strings were matched by color, including the packer's horse—all black, all gray, all sorrel, etc. Because of the need for large numbers of mules, many were still broncs. Allie loaded those mules with 250 pounds and stated that he wouldn't give five cents for a mule if he couldn't pack that much weight on it. One string of large mules was called the stove string, since they carried the heavy stoves and ovens. Allie had one hundred stock bells, and on trips, he belled all of the animals without hobbling them. Other packers preferred just belling one mare or gelding that the mules would stay with, possibly hobbling that animal or others.

Allie hired mostly Owens Valley cowboys as packers, and there wasn't much turnover from year to year. The packers had good gear and were proud of looking sharp with fine animals. On large trips, a "nighthawk" (night watchman) was hired to watch the stock at night.

At the pack station in Independence, before the start of a large Sierra Club trip, a rope corral was set up. In the early morning, the stock was herded inside, with the packers circling the corral. Many of the mules were broncs, ready to kick or strike. Allie and Charlie would enter the corral on foot with a manilla catch rope about thirty-five or forty feet in length. They would rope each mule using a backhand hoolihan throw. The mule was led toward the middle of the corral, and Allie would yell a packer's name. When his name was called, the packer, with a halter and lead rope, would go to the mule, halter it, and lead it to the hitching rail. The packer would then tie the mule to the hitching rack, roach or clip off its mane, and fit it with a packsaddle.

Allie knew every horse and mule in the Owens Valley and, according to his contemporaries, was an excellent roper. He could throw a hoolihan loop unerringly either on horseback or on foot.

On the 1932 Sierra Club Trip, the Club camped on the stream below Hitchcock Lakes beneath Mt. Whitney. Gerry Mack, a packer on that trip, wrote a delightful account of the whole adventure in his recollections that he wrote for his family at their urging after he had retired (courtesy of Carl and Arlene Pearce):

The enthusiasm was high the next morning, not only among the members but also some of the packers were interested, for Allie told us this was a day off and anyone could ride to the top of our highest mountain peak! Anyone who wished to make the trip! There was a catch in the bargain though because the saddle horses would all be left behind and anyone going must ride a mule from their string! Some of the boys had never been on Whitney, and now a bit of wild mule riding occurred, as by the same token, some of these hybrids had never felt a man on their back! The fellows picked the animals that seemed the most gentle; sometimes they were right and introduced the mules to their first riding saddle. A very few, if any, had ever been that close to one and did not take kindly to the experience.
I certainly expected to witness some falls, but a mule is a funny critter. They don't care to be hurt and will watch for their own safety far better than will a horse. Besides, the men were all good hands and they knew how to handle wild livestock. No injuries were reported to pedestrians or mule jockeys as approximately 240 people made the round trip that day.

Fifty packers mounted on these bronc mules rode to the summit of Whitney safely. On the return trip, the mules ran all the way back to the camp, with all the packers managing to remain aboard. Among the top hand crew—the most experienced packers—on this trip, in addition to Gerry Mack, were his brother Lauren Mack, Wendell and Harold Gill along with their brother-in-law Relles Carrasco, Pete Garner, and Orville Houghton. The skilled Gill brothers handled the aparejo packs.

In 1937, Ike Livermore packed for Robinson Pack Trains on a Sierra Club High Trip that used 300 head of stock. Since the headquarters were located in Independence, preparations were organized there. Pete Buckley, Allie's top packer, spent several weeks shoeing the stock before the trip began. On the trip that year, there were thirteen strings of mules and thirteen packers. The packers then drove the stock from Independence to Agnew Meadows where the trip was to begin, a distance of over a hundred miles. In the heart of the summer heat, Livermore reported casually that it was very hot driving the stock through the Owens Valley.

The following year, Livermore became a broker between the Robinsons and the Sierra Club, managing the stock and selecting the campsites. In 1940, Livermore led the first Sierra Club High Horse Outing Trip, which was a horseback riding trip lasting two weeks in length. The new trip began in the Owens Valley at Division Creek northwest of Independence and ended at Carroll Creek southwest of Lone Pine, including a ride to the crest of Mt. Whiney in the itinerary. Packers for this trip were Pete Buckley, Roy Alvin, Austin Amick, Pete Garner, Russ Hatfield, Steve Fost, and Tommy Scott.

Buckley packed a large gray mule string with the kitchen and heavy ovens. There were seventy head of stock, twelve crew members, and twenty-nine guests.

PLANES FLY TOURISTS INTO BACKCOUNTRY CAMPS

After the end of World War I, interest developed in flying airplanes into backcountry hunting and fishing areas in the Sierra. Monache, Tunnel, and Templeton Meadows on the Kern Plateau offered flat grassy landings and take-off fields. Henry "Leaky" Olivas developed Tunnel Pack Station/Tunnel Air Camp. Chrysler and Cook, a large pack outfit operating out of Lone Pine, then took over, operating out of the Lone Pine Airfield. Bruce Morgan acquired the station from owner Ted Cook, and operated it until World War II. After World War II, Bob White, an exceptional pilot, ran the camp and air service.

Fly-in service was also offered from the Airlift Pack Station headquartered at the JG Motel in Olancha. Guests flew out of the Grant Airpark, close to the motel, to Monache Meadows or the South Fork of the Kern River, a twenty-minute flight. Mr. and Mrs. John Herbert managed Monache Lodge in the backcountry, and Harold Burdick provided horses and guided trips to the many lakes and streams. Also located in Olancha, the Airborne Pack Station, owned by Ed Roman and operating out of the Union 76 Station, flew in guests to Monache, Tunnel, or Templeton Meadows.

BACKCOUNTRY CAMPS

Golden Trout Camp on Cottonwood Creek, about three miles below Cottonwood Lakes, at 10,000 feet elevation, was another backcountry lodge and camp that was accessed by airplanes as well as pack trains. The camp boasted tent cabins with wood stoves and wonderful home cooked meals in the lodge dining room. Cottonwood Pack Station and Mt. Whitney Pack Trains packed luggage and provisions into the camp on pack mules while guests rode in on horseback. Day hikes or horseback rides to fishing spots were undertaken from the base camp.

In Big Pine Canyon below Palisade Glacier, Glacier Lodge became a popular vacation area beginning in the early 1900s. The Camp at Upper Palisade Lake was a backcountry lodging facility. A few tents were maintained on the cliff above Fourth Lake, at 11,000 feet elevation. During the 1930s, the Upper Lodge was built, replacing the tents. All construction materials were packed in on pack station mules. Bob Logan's Big Pine Pack Outfit packed guests in first to the tents and later to the Upper Lodge.

Hilton Lakes Camp boasted a log cabin lodge, dining room, and tent cabins on the shore of Davis Lake. There are ten lakes nearby in that gorgeous basin. Guests rode two and a half hours into the camp from the pack station corrals on Hilton Creek. After the passage of the Wilderness Act of 1964 and the inclusion of this area in the John Muir Wilderness Area, the Forest Service required that these permanent facilities be removed.

HOLLYWOOD MOVIE INDUSTRY DISCOVERS
THE EASTERN SIERRA

Lone Pine became a center for the blossoming Western movie industry beginning in the early 1920s. This was partly because of the large numbers of ranch and pack station mules and horses available, as well as packers who functioned as cowboys, wranglers, stuntmen, and extras. The region was in close proximity to Los Angeles, where the movie industry was located, and the eastern Sierra provided many scenic looks for filmmakers. In the Great Depression years, the film business was an important boost to the economy in the Owens Valley and surrounding areas.

Henry and Pete Olivas were fourth generation Lone Pine vaqueros, whose father, Carmen, and grandfather before him, had been vaqueros and professional packers. Henry "Leaky" Olivas operated a fifty-head pack outfit at Lone Pine with a corral at Sage Flat and rented his stock to the film companies. The Olivas brothers became very active in the new film business. Henry possessed the first Screen Wranglers card in the Owens Valley, while his brother Pete was issued the first Screen Actors card.

The town of Lone Pine honors this early industry with the annual Lone Pine Film Festival in October of each year. In the spring of 2006, the Beverly and Jim Rogers Museum of Lone Pine Film History opened to the public.

Republic Films used the Mammoth Lakes area for many of their films, often headquartering at Twin Lakes and Tamarack Lodge. Tamarack Lodge was built in the early 1920s by Mary Foy, the daughter of actor Eddie Foy, and the resort, on the shore of Twin Lakes, was enjoyed by people involved in the Hollywood film industry.

William Boyd was selected to play the cowboy hero Hopalong Cassidy, despite the fact that he was not a cowboy or a rider. Hopalong Cassidy was the titular character of a western movie and television series that began in 1935 and ran through 1955. Boyd was sent by the film company to the Mammoth Lakes Pack Outfit and the tutelage of young Lee Summers, son of the owner. Lee taught him to ride and rope, and Boyd spent much time riding in the Mammoth Lakes backcountry for many years. Lee Summers was hired as a film extra and stunt double in many early Western films. Many early movie companies stayed at the Summers' Mammoth Camp Hotel until it burned in 1927. The 1934 film *The Trail Beyond* with John Wayne was filmed in Mammoth Lakes.

TRAIL BUILDING

The Civilian Conservation Corps or CCC was formed during the Great Depression to provide employment. These crews, under the direction of the Forest Service, built and improved many trails in the Sierra. The skilled trail-building crews were important in the final construction of portions of the John Muir Trail. Pack stations packed in their camps, tools, and provisions and assisted in the construction work. A CCC camp was located at Big McGee Lake in the 1930s, where the men worked on McGee Pass and Hopkins Pass.

The Park Service and the Forest Service were also very active in building new trails and bridges over treacherous streams and rivers. The High Sierra Trail, built for recreational purposes, was begun in 1928 and completed in 1932. Beginning on the westside at Crescent Meadow in Sequoia National Park, the trail crossed over the crest of the Sierra to end at Whitney Portal on the eastside, a length of forty-nine spectacular miles.

Forester Pass, on the John Muir Trail, was constructed beginning in 1930 to provide a direct trail across the Kings-Kern Divide. The notch in the ridge had been discovered as part of a wildlife trail the previous summer, and it was determined possible to build a stock trail through it. It is the highest pass on that trail at 13,153 feet elevation. The long dogleg trail around to Junction and Shepherd Passes could now be bypassed. Sequoia National Park and Sequoia National Forest joined forces to complete the construction. The Park Service worked on one side of Forester Pass, and the national forest trail crews worked on the other.

Sadly, during a blasting incident with a resulting rockslide, four trail crew workers were seriously injured. One young man died, and the others had to be transported by litter out of the mountains. There were no helicopters to rescue the injured men in those days. Boys from Bishop High School hiked in and carried litters out on foot, with four boys per litter, one on each corner. Dudley Boothe, who later owned Rainbow Pack Outfit, was one of the stretcher bearers and recalled carrying out one injured young man over Shepherd Pass.

PRIMITIVE AREA DESIGNATIONS
In the years from 1928 to 1930, the Forest Service considered boundaries for a new primitive area designation, the first protected designation within national forest land. Wilderness proponents and the Sierra Club recognized the public interest at the time in at least one trans-Sierra road route south of Tioga Pass Road, and pushed for primitive area designations. The Mammoth Pass region was agreed upon by the Forest Service and selected for a future trans-Sierra road, partly because of existing mining access roads.

On April 21, 1931, the Secretary of Agriculture established the High Sierra Primitive Area in recognition of its outstanding wilderness characteristics. The nominated area encompassed 761,750 acres in the Sierra and Inyo National Forests, and five years later it was increased to 826,561 acres. On the same date, the Chief of the Forest Service also established the Mt. Dana-Minarets Primitive Area. This primitive area enclosed about 82,372 acres. A corridor between the two primitive areas was intentionally left out for a future trans-Sierra road if and when needed.

FIRST GUIDE BOOK
Starr's Guide to the John Muir Trail, first published in 1934 by the Sierra Club, had become the standard guidebook for travel on Sierra trails. Sadly, the author, "Pete" Starr, died in a solo mountain climbing fall from Starr Minaret in the Ritter Range in 1933 before his book was completed. His father, Walter Starr, completed, edited, and published the book that came out a year later. This indispensable guidebook contains maps and details of travel, mileage, campsites, etc., which were extremely helpful to both packers and hikers. Many a packer, when first traveling in unfamiliar territory, stashed a copy of the book in his saddlebags and checked out the next day's travel itinerary when the clients weren't around. He certainly needed to appear knowledgeable to his customers.

RAINBOW DAYS
Held in 1937, Rainbow Days in Bishop, was a "rodeo" of packing skills. The residents of the Owens Valley were more familiar with packing events than traditional rodeo events. Wilfred Partridge, a packer at Glacier Pack Train, won a number of those early contests. The program included a ladies'

packing event, with three Bishop packers winning first, second, and third. This concept was later revived in 1970 with the organization of the Mule Days Celebration event in Bishop. Wilfred Partridge was the arena announcer for the early shows. This celebration, highlighting mule and packing events, is now held every Memorial Day weekend and is annually attended by more than 30,000 people.

Packer Allie Robinson, on a 1918 Sierra Club High Trip, is second from the left wearing 'wooly' chaps. (Laws Museum)

A packer returning from a spot trip with the pack and saddle animals, 'loose herding' the stock.

Packer Bud Hall is repacking on the trail, using blinders to cover the mule's eyes to keep it calm. (Bud Hall Collection)

At the lodge at Fourth Lake in Big Pine Canyon, a boat is being christened. Circa early 30s. (Kenneth Partridge Collection)

Through the Smithsonian Museum in 1908, a stone hut was constructed at the top of Mt. Whitney. (Ed Turner)

Murray Hall waits with his mule string until the preceding string reaches the top of Forester Pass. (Bud Hall Collection)

Russ Johnson leads his party from Upper Fish Creek towards McGee
Pass with Red Slate Mtn. looming.   (Russ and Anne Johnson)

Pack strings from Hallidays' Rainbow Pack Outfit in the late 1920s on their way to
the Bishop Pass trail. (Photo by Burton Frasher-Laws Museum)

CHAPTER NINE

WORLD WAR II
AND ITS AFFECTS
ON TOURISM

With the advent of World War II, pack station operators throughout the Sierra were compelled to drastically downsize their operations for the duration of the war. Some pack stations closed temporarily, and others went out of business. Younger cowboys, packers, and pack station owners were inducted into the various armed services. Their urban clients had to deal with gas and tire rationing, making it difficult to reach distant vacation locations. The Army also requisitioned some horses and mules. The pack stations at the southern and western areas of the Sierra saw more vacationers than the more northern and eastern regions, as they were located closer to the population centers. Food rationing impacted pack stations with a restaurant component, and even leather boots were in short supply.

Fred Wass, at Fish Camp on the southwestern border of Yosemite National Park, reported that business was good for him during the war. Gas was rationed so his customers were only able to obtain enough gas to drive to the pack station. He would pack them in for a week and when they packed out, they were eligible for another tank of gas on which to drive home.

On March 4, 1940, Kings Canyon National Park was created by Congress and included the tiny General Grant National Park. This area covers 462,901 acres. It is north of and contiguous to Sequoia National Park. John Muir visited the region in 1873 and declared that it was a rival to Yosemite National Park. Kings River Canyon is a steep walled valley, 8,000 feet deep from ridges to the river, deeper than the Grand Canyon.

Hunting was banned in the national parks, and many former good hunting areas were now located in the new park. This impacted pack stations that could no longer provide pack trips for hunters to these backcountry areas. Deer hunting had been an important segment of the short Sierra vacation season. Some pack stations were able to lease their animals to packers located outside of the parks in the national forests for hunting season. Packers were sometimes able to find packing jobs to finish out the season at stations out of the parks.

THE GENERALS' PACK TRIP

In the summer of 1944, during World War II, General H. H. "Hap" Arnold, Chief of the U.S. Air Force, contacted Roy Boothe, Supervisor of the Inyo National Forest, requesting that he arrange a fishing and traveling pack trip through the central Sierra Nevada. Boothe had accompanied General Arnold on previous trips during the past ten years and knew the general's preferences and how much he enjoyed these backcountry excursions. Boothe organized all the special arrangements, including the itinerary, food, and details for the trip.

This "rest and relaxation trip" would begin in Mammoth Lakes at the Mammoth Lakes Pack Outfit, owned by Lloyd Summers. Early in August, a test trip was taken by a Forest Service radioman and an Army communications man to ascertain that radio contact could be made throughout the trip. The names of the men going on the trip were to be kept a military secret. Boothe learned only the day before the plane arrived in Bishop that General George C. Marshall, Chief of Staff, was also to be a member of the party.

After the Japanese attack on Pearl Harbor, the U.S. airfields along the coast were no longer considered safe from attack. In anticipation of needing to move the Air Force into the interior of California away from the Pacific Coast, the Army had searched out possible airfields to enlarge and possibly establish bases at. The landing strip in Bishop had been reconfigured in 1942 to 7,500 feet long in order to accommodate larger planes. On August 23, 1944, the party of Generals Arnold and Marshall flew into Bishop on a DC4 plane from Washington, D.C. and landed at the Bishop Army Air Field (as it was then known) at 6 a.m. They had already eaten breakfast on the plane and were immediately driven to Mammoth Lakes in two cars. The general public were not aware of this planned trip.

Besides the two generals, the party included Roy Boothe, Colonel Peterson, General Arnold's aide, Lieutenant Waldron, Del Fausett, Bevier Show, Joe Elliott, Supervisor of Lassen National Forest, and Mr. Cronemiller from the Regional Forest Service Office. Joe Elliott had also been on previous pack trips with General Arnold. Mr. Cronemiller "Croney" would be the backcountry chef.

Because of the War, the packers were older men not in the service. Dave Jackson, Don Douglas, and George Brown, along with another unnamed man, packed on this trip. Don Douglas's winter job was Dean of Boys at Whittier High School in Whittier, California. George Brown owned Pine Creek Pack Outfit, and Dave Jackson was a long time packer at Mammoth Lakes Pack Outfit.

After the party was mounted on their horses, with their stirrups adjusted and fishing gear tied onto the saddles, the party proceeded up the trail. As they headed up the Duck Pass Trail from Lake Mary, they were escorted overhead by two circling planes, an L-5 and a larger plane, possibly a B17, that were to be part of the trip. The L-5 was piloted by a female flyer, a WASP, and her job was to drop the daily mail packet to the party.

The group rode horseback over Duck Pass, traveling on the John Muir Trail, and reached Purple Lake, the first night's camp, that afternoon. The packers with the mule strings followed the riders, and, along with the Forest Service rangers, set up the camp. The generals put together their fly fishing rods and soon caught enough trout for breakfast.

The second night's camp was at Tully's Hole, an exquisite meadow on the John Muir Trail with Fish Creek meandering through it. As the name implies, excellent trout fishing for golden/rainbow crosses is to be had.

Mail, war communications, and supplies were airdropped to the generals daily, and they were in daily radio contact with the planes. On the third morning of the trip, on August the 25th, the L-5 plane, which had an open air cockpit, circled low over the meadow. The pilot physically reached out and dropped several bundles, but the most important, a twenty-five-pound mailbag, was whipped out of her hand about a half a mile too soon. After an intense two-hour search by the entire party, the important missing bag was fortunately located on a nearby rocky, timbered mountainside.

The third night found the expedition camped in Quail Meadow on Mono Creek, along the John Muir Trail, where the group laid over for a day in a very comfortable camp. The elevation was lower and the temperatures were warmer. They fished in the creek, and some of the party rode upstream toward the canyons called the Recesses for additional fishing waters.

The next camp move was to the Hilgard Branch on the North Fork of Bear Creek, with the party continuing up the creek to about one and a half miles below Lake Italy. Lake Italy is a large, deep lake at 11,154 feet elevation in a spectacular glacial cirque. Five peaks well over 13,000 feet surround the lake: Mt. Hilgard at 13,361; Mt. Gabb at 13,711; Mt. Abbot at 13,715; Mt. Dade at 13,635; and Bear Creek Spire at 13,713. The campsite on the Hilgard Branch was their highest campsite, at about 10,700 feet in elevation.

Lake Italy provided ample small golden trout fishing from shore, but fishing for the larger fish was slow. An aide radioed a request from camp for an inflatable rubber raft. A raft was obtained, probably in Bishop, and was airdropped to their campsite with a yellow silk parachute. The next morning, the generals launched the raft and paddled out into the lake, catching fish, but still not any of the legendary, elusive golden trout. Two of the packers had ridden over to a nearby lake, where they caught some very large rainbows for the generals to take home with them.

On the last day, packer George Brown led the party out over Italy Pass at 12,359 feet elevation. The trail was a sheep route marked by small stacks of rocks, rarely-used, rough, and rocky, to Granite Park and then to Pine Lake, where the better trail was accessed. General Marshall commented on that section of trail from Lake Italy, saying, "Hell was probably paved with such trails." The distance to the trailhead at Pine Creek was thirteen or fourteen tough miles, with a steep descent of about 5,000 feet in elevation.

At the Pine Creek trailhead, cars were waiting, and the party drove to Bishop for an informal banquet at the Golden State Restaurant on Main Street. The group highly praised the delicious meals prepared by Croney in the backcountry. The two generals generously invited Forest Service Supervisors Boothe and Elliott to accompany them back to Washington, D.C. that night on their huge airplane. The two rangers accepted and enjoyed a grand trip to America's capital.

This had been a rugged and strenuous pack trip at a high elevation for this party, particularly since they were from sea level, but these men were tough. General Arnold had suffered two heart attacks in 1943, one as recent as May. Following the trip, he flew almost immediately to London to proceed with the war.

An interesting sidelight to this event is the following recount. From 1943 until 1946, at Manzanar, a former orchard-growing region in the Owens Valley, an internment camp was built to house thousands of Japanese-Americans from Southern California. After the attack on Pearl Harbor, the government was afraid that some Japanese-American citizens might be serving Japan as spies.

President Roosevelt ordered that these citizens be placed in internment camps in the interiors of California, Oregon, and Washington.

According to a number of accounts, some of the young boys sneaked out of the camp during the hot valley summers, and hiked up into the nearby High Sierra mountains to fish. Apparently, some of the guards liked these teenage boys and provided them with fishing gear and maps, and looked the other way when the boys slipped out under the fence.

After the camp was discontinued and the detainees released, many former internees packed into the High Sierra to camp and fish during their vacations. In the 1970s, a group of Japanese dentists from Southern California packed in most every summer to fish and relax. While enjoying coffee in the dining room of the Mammoth Lakes Pack Outfit, after their return from their pack trip to Virginia Lake on the John Muir Trail, one of the men related this story. While living in Manzanar in 1944 at age sixteen, he related how the guards gave him and his friends fishing equipment and how he had spent that summer hiking around the Sierras, living off the trout he caught. Having heard about the fishing in Lake Italy, he had hiked there and happened to arrive when the generals' pack trip was there. He spotted the party, and witnessed the planes circling in the air. Quickly ducking out of sight, he was terrified and thought they must be searching for him and would believe he was a Japanese spy. He immediately ended his fishing expedition and slipped away, hurrying under the cover of darkness back to Manzanar and safely crawling under the fence. He was relieved that no one was searching for him. Everyone in the dining room at the pack station, so many years later, chuckled with him over his predicament. He had become enamored by the Sierra when he was sixteen and treasured every summer pack trip afterwards.

LOGGING, MINING, AND ROADS

Immediately after the War, among the issues that were of major concern to members of the Eastern and Western High Sierra Packers' Associations were the possibilities of more new road construction and mining roads, obtaining winter pasture and feed, and the possibility of helicopter packing into the backcountry. In 1953, the Eastern High Sierra Packers' Association wrote a resolution opposing any new trans-Sierra roads. In 1964, they reiterated this stance.

On the west side of the mountains, logging was pushing further into the roadless areas, with logging roads remaining after an area was logged. Jeeps were now available to the public and could be driven on the new logging roads, making areas more accessible to hunting.

Mining roads continued to be built or extended into backcountry areas of the Sierra. Miners were avidly prospecting for tungsten, and new claims were established that necessitated access roads. The pack station owners were concerned that the Sierra backcountry was being slowly whittled away. Often, the mine failed shortly after inception, but the road was left, providing access to army jeeps, pick-up trucks, and various four-wheel drive vehicles into the High Sierra Primitive Area.

The Scheelore Mine was discovered in 1940 near Baldwin Lake in McGee Canyon on the east side of the range, at an elevation of 11,000 to 11,600 feet. Mining for tungsten commenced there in 1942, and a road was cut in up

Baldwin Canyon. In 1944, the Public Roads Administration built the McGee Creek Road as a mining access road to the Scheelore Mine. It was a ten-mile-long road accessed by trucks. Since it was in the High Sierra Primitive Area, a locked gate about a mile above McGee Creek Pack Station was placed at the primitive area line. A mill and mine buildings were built, and ore was trucked out to the Pine Creek Mill of Union Carbide Mine. Tactite was mined for tungsten, and ore was hauled out until 1955.

The California Department of Fish and Game had planted golden trout in Baldwin Lake adjacent to the mine. They used the road to drive up by pick-up truck to monitor the fish population in the lake. By 1955, the mine was no longer in use, but the gated road remained. Gradually, over time, the road has disappeared, with nature reclaiming it. By 2004, the road was barely discernible.

NEW OWNERS AFTER THE WAR

When the war ended in 1945, the request for pack trips quickly resumed. Clients had missed their favorite lakes and streams and were anxious to once again camp in the spectacular High Sierra backcountry. However, there were no longer the seventy-one plus pack stations as there had been in 1934 when Ike Livermore conducted his survey. By 1946, the number of stations had decreased to twenty-eight. Many pack stations increased their number of saddle and pack animals in order to accommodate the demand from the general public. Various types of trips were offered to their customers. Hour, two hour, half-day, and all-day horseback rides became popular with visitors staying in nearby lodges, cabins, and campgrounds.

Before 1945, Murray Hall had worked as a packer for the Forest Service in the Los Padres National Forest, had been head packer for Sequoia National Park, and had leased the Silver City Pack Station in Mineral King. The Forest Service offered him a pack permit at Kennedy Meadows. Murray and his wife, Lothelle, next purchased the Onion Valley Pack Station from long time packers, Harold and Wendell Gill, and leased a ranch in the Owens Valley. They built facilities at both locations and moved their cattle to the Black Rock Ranch, north of Independence. In the winter, they took over the Death Valley Stables horse operation at Furnace Creek Ranch that Bruce Morgan, of Mt. Whitney Pack Trains, and his family had operated for some years. The Halls drove their herd of horses between Big Pine and Death Valley in the fall and back again in the spring.

Ike Livermore, an owner of Mineral King Pack Station, had served in the Navy as a Second Lieutenant during World War II and participated in the Allied landings at Sicily, Okinawa, Iwo Jima, and Palau. After his discharge in 1945, he recognized the need for an outfit with many mules that could handle the Sierra Club and other large group trips. In 1946, he purchased Chrysler and Cook's Mt. Whitney Pack Station at Carroll Creek and Barney Sears' Monache Meadows Pack Station, as well as equipment and stock from Sage Flat to form his new pack station. Ted Cook recommended Bruce Morgan to him, and Morgan became a minor working partner and manager. Morgan managed packing operations until 1950, when he became general manager for the pack station.

The new merged pack station became Mt. Whitney Pack Trains, with three locations: Carroll Creek, Sage Flat, and Whitney Portal. Livermore assembled over 130 head of stock, including some Nevada bronc mules, and began operations as the largest pack outfit in the Sierra. Mt. Whitney Pack Trains contracted for Sierra Club Trips, with Ike Livermore as the packing contractor, from 1946 to 1968.

At the Mammoth Lakes Pack Outfit, Lloyd and his wife, Sybil, kept the pack station open during the war with help of their younger son and some of their older packers. The Summers' two older sons were in the armed services, Lee in Alaska and Verne in the South Pacific. Two horses that the Summers bought that year were named Alaska and Fiji after the boys. Sadly, on Aug. 25, 1945, when Lloyd was leading a horse out of the corral, he suffered a fatal heart attack and died by the corral gate. Lee Summers returned from Alaska, and, the following season, took over and operated the pack station until 1960, when it was sold to my family.

During the War, Russ Johnson worked in the defense industries in San Diego as a tool and die designer. Russ and his wife, Anne, took summer pack trips into the Sierra at Mammoth Lakes and Rock Creek. Due to gas rationing, they rode the Greyhound Bus to Bishop and Mammoth Lakes for their annual pack trip.

A group of partners who worked for United Airlines in Southern California, led by Herb London, purchased the Rock Creek Pack Station in 1947. Russ and Anne Johnson went to work for Rock Creek Pack Station, realizing their dream of spending their entire summer packing in the mountains. They conducted the all-expense trips from 1948 through 1950, with Russ packing and Anne cooking. Then, in the winter, they worked at Stovepipe Wells resort for the Park Service permittee in Death Valley Monument, and also did mine packing.

Then in 1951, the Johnsons purchased McGee Creek Pack Station and began repairing, enlarging, and improving the base facilities, as well as adding to the stock numbers. Russ and Anne became active in the Packers' Association and revamped the yearly advertising brochure. Russ edited and printed the association pamphlet of bylaws.

Lou and I, newly married, worked for the Johnsons at McGee Creek in 1953 and '54. Russ and Anne were wonderful mentors, and we learned many skills from packing to business. Bob Tanner worked with them in 1952, and again after he was discharged from the Navy. He later bought Red's Meadow and Agnew Meadows Pack Stations. We took all-expense traveling trips, Lou as a packer, and myself as a cook. It was from Anne Johnson that I learned how to cook gourmet meals for groups on traveling pack trips and how to bake in a reflector oven. These learning experiences were invaluable to us when we later became pack station owners.

Pack stations began to employ more college students as wranglers, guides, and packers. As most pack stations were many slow, twisting miles from towns, they provided lodging and meals for their employees. Students had their summers free and enjoyed working with the stock and staff, mingling with the guests, and treasuring a summer in the mountains. More and more young women were employed. In earlier years, women were hired mostly as cooks and secretaries although pack station wives and daughters always had to function in all capacities. Women were hired as guides when horseback rides became popular, as well as backcountry cooks and packers. It was hard physical work with long hours for a very compressed season, but it was exhilarating and exciting for young people to work outdoors in such a glorious setting.

New and better vehicles were on the assembly lines in Detroit, along with availability of good tires and plentiful gasoline. Passenger airlines were thriving, and now Easterners flew across the country to experience the fabled Sierra backcountry. With better-paved roads, vacation trips occurred more often and for a shorter length of stay. Most trips were for a week, and traveling trips were shortened to accommodate the shorter time frame. In the 1950s, the Yosemite National Park Service rebuilt the Tioga Pass Road through Yosemite into a wider, two-lane paved road. More visitors from the San Francisco and Central Valley areas now accessed the eastern side of the Sierra Nevada Range.

Winter Sports Shows, held in the metropolitan areas of Los Angeles and San Francisco, were very important venues for spreading the word about the revitalized packing industry and vacation opportunities in the Sierra Nevada. The Sports Shows were a popular winter activity. Pack station owners assisted in the show booths, answering questions, passing out brochures, and explaining pack trips to potential customers. The shows lasted for about ten days. The packers provided a gentle horse and mule to be kept on display in the auditorium during the show times, and conducted packing demonstrations for the public. The Los Angeles booth was a combined cooperative effort by the City of Los Angeles, the Eastern High Sierra Packers' Association, and the eastern Sierra chambers of commerce. The State of California Tourism Department as well as the Automobile Club also promoted pack trips into the Sierra.

The neophyte ski industry burgeoned in the 1940s and '50s, introducing many more visitors to the High Sierra. In Mammoth Lakes, Hans Georg built a rope tow and small lodge on the road to the Lakes Basin. Dave McCoy built a rope tow in 1955 on the north side of Mammoth Mountain, and quickly developed that mountain to become one of the largest ski areas in the Sierra. With the expansion of new ski lifts, more lodges, resort complexes, and condominiums were constructed near the lifts. Roads were improved and paved to the new resorts. Skiers soon discovered that the winter lodges and condominiums also provided lodging access for summer recreation. The nearby backcountry lured adventurous visitors to ride horseback and experience a pack trip, where they could explore, camp, and fish.

LARGE GROUP TRAVELING TRIPS

During the War, the Sierra Club suspended its large traveling and base camp trips. Allie Robinson, who had contracted with the Sierra Club to supply the necessary packing services, began downsizing his operations. He lacked the desire to continue packing the huge trips, so he no longer had the need for the large number of stock, particularly mules. He sold an interest in his Onion Valley location to Harold and Wendell Gill, who had worked as packers for him for many years. By 1952, Robinson was owner of the Leavitt Meadows Pack Station near Sonora Pass. This outfit catered to fishermen and hunters, and serviced the nearby U.S. Marine Corps Cold Weather Training Base, established during the Korean War.

The California Alpine Club organized large pack trips into the Sierra. It contracted with pack stations up and down the Sierra to furnish pack and saddle stock, packers, provisions, and the camp set-up. Other large riding and hiking clubs also contracted for pack trips throughout the Sierra. The Sierra Club resumed its large annual pack trips, using the services of Mt. Whitney Pack Trains, owned by Ike Livermore.

In 1946, Hall's Pack Trains at Kennedy Meadows agreed to assist Harold Gill at Onion Valley with packing in the Southern California Alpine Club. This large pack trip would be for thirty days with 170 people. The trip would begin at Onion Valley above Independence, pack over Kearsarge Pass, and end at Carroll Creek near Lone Pine. Murray Hall, his son Bud Hall, and Brock Cole, their packer, drove their horses and mules to Onion Valley from their pack station at Kennedy Meadows through the Owens Valley summer heat.

When the tired men and stock reached Onion Valley to join with Gill's pack station stock and crew, they found about 250 head of stock tied everywhere in the small valley. It seemed that Mt. Whitney Pack Trains, and others assisting them from Lone Pine, were packing in the Sierra Club on the following day over Kearsarge Pass. The next morning, when the two large trips packed out, there were over 300 head of horses and mules on the Kearsarge Pass Trail, plus numerous hikers and riders. It seemed as though the trail was full from Onion Valley to Bullfrog Lake with stock and people, according to Bud Hall. He further commented that it rained for twenty-eight of those thirty days spent in the backcountry. The Gills later sold the Onion Valley outfit (formerly Allie Robinson's) to Murray and Lothelle Hall.

David Brower had been a member of the Sierra Club since 1933, and had been on the Board of Directors since 1941. During World War II, he served in the United States Mountain Troops in Italy. After the War, he became manager of the Sierra Club High Trips in 1947, working with Ike Livermore to organize the highly successful trips, and continued in this capacity for many years.

Brower wrote this account in the *Sierra Club Bulletin* about the packing crew on the 1947 trip that began at Agnew Meadows:

The pack stock had already been trucked in from Lone Pine and was now happily dispersed in the meadows, except for those being shod or otherwise worked over in the corral improvised with rope in a small, out of the way opening in the lodgepole forest. There were some seventy five head in all, watched over by Ike Livermore and his contingent, as pleasant a group as ever gave a string of mules a bad time or a good time depending upon the need of the moment. Pete Garner, whose ancestors were in this country when the Mayflower arrived, was second in command to Ike, and a veteran packer who handled with equal ease and serenity the heaviest loads—the stoves—and the mules that carried them. Bud Steele, another veteran, was one of the men—if you would believe him— who helped the devil pack in and set up the Devils Postpile. If he didn't look old enough for that role, at least he was talented enough. Tommy Jefferson, a full-blooded Mono, had a tireless smile that let you know you were welcome to the land of his fathers. During the day, he charmed one of the strings of mules that carried commissary impedimenta; and in the

80

evenings, we knew from last year, he could charm both a guitar and those who listened to his repertoire of songs. Among the others who handled a horse and a string of five mules per man were old time packers from the Owens Valley and college students who wanted to learn something about livestock in its least prosaic environment. Ed Thistlethwaite, Owens Valley artist with a broad accent that was anything but indigenous, was our nighthawk. It was to be his job, when the camp should be heavy with sleep on a moving day—and that is earlier than would sound reasonable in print—to get up and watch the dawn in the high and relatively inaccessible pasture lands to which the stock had been pushed, then to round them up and bring them down to work. A lad from Yale watched over the saddle horses, a few of which had been brought along for persons who either already knew they weren't in condition for a hard day on the trail or who would find out before the day ended. Ike Livermore thought that his wife, who came along to take care of the man who was taking care of the packing operation, should have some title; and so Dina Livermore was the Assistant Saddle Horse Boy.

Joseph Wampler was a crew member on Sierra Club High Trips from 1946 to 1949 and conceived the idea of organizing his own John Muir Trail Trips. He began his commercial Wampler Trail Trips in 1950, with trips organized for either hikers or riders. The 200-mile-long segment was organized into a series of weekly segments so guests could join or leave the trip at these intervals. From June to early September for eight or nine weeks, he guided twelve to twenty-five people during a period, traveling up and down the Sierra. Wampler contracted with commercial packers to handle the livestock portion of the trips. Glenn Burns and later Sam Lewis Jr. supplied the necessary stock for many years.

Glenn Burns, a native of the San Joaquin Valley, began packing in 1920, and soon opened his own outfit at Huntington Lake. He packed guests throughout the Sierra from 1926 to 1954, with up to 140 head of horses and mules. He always had an excellent reputation for having the best stock in the mountains and satisfied customers. After selling his pack station to Floyd Fike in 1951, he continued to take a few custom trips—only ones that he wanted to. Burns kept about thirty head of stock and operated from his San Joaquin Valley ranch. He had some of this stock for twenty years, and they all stayed together. While grazing in the backcountry, he said he kept them happy with a little barley each morning. Burns stated, "I'd rather lead a string of mules up a switchback trail and over the divide to the next camp than eat. That is unless it's eating deep-fried trout around a campfire. This high country life sort of gets in your blood."

WAR SURPLUS CAMPING GEAR AND NEW PRODUCTS

During World War II, The United States Marine Corps and Army developed camping and backpack equipment for their infantry. At the conclusion of the war, this equipment found its way into Army/Navy surplus stores. Pre-war equipment had been heavy and bulky, while the new camping equipment was lighter in weight, utilizing nylon, plastics, and aluminum. The pack stations purchased this new equipment to outfit their trips, and campers eagerly purchased these products for their personal use on spot pack trips, where they would be packed into the mountains to camp on their own. More campers were now better outfitted with tents, sleeping bags, air mattresses, cook kits, stoves, and other camping equipment at a reasonable cost.

Dehydrated meals, developed for the Armed Services, were now available as backcountry fare. Companies such as Dri-Lite and Bernards manufactured food packets for campers and sportsmen. Packers seldom used the new dried meal packets on their catered, all-expense trips, as customers still preferred traditional camp foods, including fresh meat, vegetables, and fruits.

Backpacks were still heavy, awkward, and one-size-fits-all. The Trapper Nelson pack frame weighed four and a half pounds, and the Army rucksack weighed in at six pounds. Lightweight aluminum external pack frames with nylon bags were developed by sporting goods manufacturers. These new packs came in several sizes and were comfortable on the back. The manufacturers made many improvements and continued developing lighter weight camping equipment. This new lightweight pack and camping equipment gradually led to the increase in backpacking occurring in the late 1960s and the early 1970s.

During and after World War II, aerial photography added to map-making skills and corrected former inaccuracies. For several weeks in 1953, my husband, Lou, packed two U.S. Geological Survey geologists through the Fish Creek Basin, doing new survey work on the Mt. Morrison Quadrangle. New Quadrangle maps surveyed and printed by the U.S. Geological Survey were highly accurate and made journeying into the mountains safer and easier for the general public.

By 1953, the U.S. Army had become mechanized and began dispersing their no-longer-needed good pack mules and horses. On December 15, 1956, at Fort Carson in Colorado, the U.S. Army deactivated the last two operational mule units, the 35th Quartermaster Pack Company and Battery A of the 4th Field Artillery Pack Battalion. Yosemite National Park was able to acquire thirty mules with the army brand on their necks and Kings Canyon National Park obtained twenty of these mules. Some commercial pack stations also purchased surplus Army mules and horses that proudly wore the U.S. brand.

HORSE DRIVES

Winter pasture for pack and saddle stock was often some distance away from the summer headquarters. The pastureland needed to be out of heavy snow zones, with plenty of feed for the horses and mules. There were few stock trucks and horse trailers were small. The stock was driven to and from the winter pasture, sometimes a long distance away.

The Mammoth Pack Outfit made some especially noteworthy long drives. For several years in the early 1940s, packers drove their stock to Yerington, Nevada, near the old town of Wabuska, to the ranch of Howard Rogers. This was a distance of over 150 miles. In the spring, on the return drive, the packers let the horses and mules trail themselves the last few miles to the pack station located below Lake Mary. At Glass Creek, the animals were left on their own while the packers hastened to the pack station by truck to open the corral gates and set up corral posts, hopefully before the returning herd arrived. A few wise bell mares with mules in attendance always seemed to know where home was and led the herd in. In 1946, the pack station drove their stock to Fish Lake Valley on the east side of the high White Mountains over Westgard Pass. Again, this was a distance of over 150 miles, with a rugged, dry trip over the pass.

In 1951, Lee Summers, owner of the outfit, drove the horses and mules to Coarsegold, California, to the ranch of his father-in-law, Don Douglas. Before reaching the lush green grass of the western foothills near Oakhurst, the stock traveled across the historic Mammoth Pass Trail to Fresno Flats. The herd gingerly crossed the old swinging suspension bridge at Sheep Crossing across the North Fork of the San Joaquin River. Originally, this bridge, built in the 1920s by the Forest Service, had no rails and crossing on it could be quite hazardous. It had been used in the past by the many sheep flocks moving to the Sierra for summer grazing.

The winter of 1951-52 was one of the heaviest snow years on record. The snow was late in melting, and it was over the Fourth of July that the horse herd was driven back over the Sierras to the pack station on the east side of Mammoth Pass. When the horse drive reached Sheep Crossing, the packers were stunned to observe that the old swinging bridge had been washed out in high spring floodwaters. The packers would have to attempt to swim the herd across the raging San Joaquin River. Lee Summers found a spot where he could jump his saddle horse into the torrent, while the other packers pushed the herd into the current behind him. The wild waters washed them downstream to a sandbar, where they miraculously climbed safely out of the river on the other side. All the animals survived the turbulent, chilling waters.

As the fatigued herd approached the pack station above Mammoth Lakes, at 9,000 feet elevation, they traveled over the deep snow packs of the record winter. On sun-warmed patches, they broke through the hard pack. The tired herd and even wearier packers finally arrived at the pack station after a very difficult crossing minus a few head. These stragglers eventually made their way to Red's Meadow Resort a few days later. My husband, Lou, on his first packing job at the outfit, then trailed them from Red's Meadow up over Mammoth Pass to the pack station at Lake Mary. Later, he was proud to have the three ex-army mules in his string.

The following fall marked the first time the Mammoth Pack Outfit stock was hauled to pasture in the Owens Valley near Fort Independence in large commercial stock trucks and trailers. The horse and mule herd must have been amazed at this new change. The availability of a new trucking company with large cattle trucks made this possible. Three pack stations had negotiated with the Los Angeles Department of Water and Power for winter pasture north of Independence in the Owens Valley. The three outfits, Rock Creek Pack Station, owned by Herb London, Red's Meadow Pack Station, owned by Arch Mahan, and Mammoth Pack Outfit, leased the 5,000-acre "Pool Field." In the early years, other pack stations were also accommodated in the field. This winter pasture lease is still in use by those three pack stations. Most outfits began trucking their stock to winter locations in the late 1950s and continued doing so for twenty years. In the '70s, some outfits started offering horse drives to guests as a practical and profitable activity. These drives have continued to be very popular, and have been a way for pack stations to expand and embrace changing clientele and times.

TRAIL WORK

By 1947, the Mt. Whitney Trail was overdue for serious maintenance and reconstruction. Henry Thorne was the acting forest engineer in charge of construction for the Forest Service at that time. The trail project to rebuild the section of the trail from Consultation Lake to Whitney Pass included the infamous ninety-six switchbacks. It was necessary to reroute part of the trail up a sheer granite wall in order to avoid deep snowdrifts that often buried parts of the trail most of the summer.

The Forest Service contracted with the Mt. Whitney Pack Trains at Whitney Portal to haul all equipment and supplies for the project and the camp on the backs of mules to the 12,000-foot elevation trail camp. Thorne reminisced in the 1986 Mule Days Program that, "If it hadn't been for mules, the whole job couldn't have been done at all." Relles Carrasco was foreman of the hardy twelve-man trail crew, with Lizzie, his wife, cooking for the men. Mrs. Carrasco was famous for her backcountry meals.

A heavy Schramm air compressor that weighed 10,000 pounds had to be taken apart and then reassembled up at the work site, along with 1,500 feet of pipe to transport air to the compressor. The compressor was used to power the rock drills. The heaviest piece was the crankshaft that weighed 344 pounds and had to be carried in one piece on one mule. Presumably, that mule had to be a large, sturdy, draft-type animal.

Packing the heavy equipment, dynamite, supplies, and firewood required four strings of five mules each up the trail almost every day. Regular sawbuck packsaddles could not be used to pack the heavy machinery and equipment, so aparejo saddles were put into service. At that time there were still a number of qualified packers who had the experience and technical skill to pack these heavy loads on aparejo saddles—not an easy task. One string of mules carried the camp supplies and necessities up the trail almost daily. Since the camp was well above the tree line, wood to supply the cooking fires as well as heating fires for the cool nights had to be packed up to the camp.

The often-hazardous trail project took two summers to complete. In working on the steep cliffs, the men had to be secured with ropes. The project was safely completed in September of 1948. On September 8, the first pack trip, the Wilderness Riders of America, packed in by Mt. Whitney Pack Trains, used the new section of trail to the top of Mt. Whitney. The party, including pack station packers and cooks, Forest Service personnel, and club participants, numbered thirty-five all together, with at least seventy head of horses and mules. Of the many hikers who climb the famous trail daily today, few are aware of the enormous difficulty in constructing and maintaining it. Even fewer know of the essential part played by the humble mule.

After a backcountry pack trip in 1959, Supreme Court Justice William O. Douglas suggested to Russ Johnson at McGee Creek Pack Station that a collaborative trail project, possibly with the Sierra Club, could be a solution to the backlog on trail maintenance. Justice Douglas had crossed McGee Pass at the end of a traveling trip. He thought the Sierra Club or a similar organization might be willing to participate in trail projects with the stock assistance of pack stations and the technical trail building management of the Forest Service.

Three years later, the first maintenance trail project with the Sierra Club,

McGee Creek Pack Station, and the Inyo National Forest was successfully completed on the McGee Pass Trail. Twenty-two strong young people from colleges across the United States did the physical labor at a high elevation. McGee Pass is 11,900 feet. The Forest Service directed the work and supplied the necessary trail tools, and McGee Creek Pack Station supplied the camp and provisions by mule string.

The High Sierra Packers' Association participated in Sport Shows
in L. A. and S. F. (Blake Jones)

Eastern High Sierra Packers' Association members pose at a
1949 Sports Show in L. A. (Blake Jones)

Supreme Court Justice William O. Douglas, 2nd from L at McGee Creek
Pack Station, 1959 trip. (Russ and Anne Johnson)

Ike Livermore, on horse Kitty, is crossing Cottonwood Pass, in the
Southern Sierra, 1936. (Livermore Family Collection)

At this old hunting camp, someone with carpentry skills has fashioned a comfortable table with benches.

Biscuits baked in a Dutch oven are always welcomed at dinner or breakfast.

At this innovative branding chute, Lou Roeser brands while packer
Red Altum mans the squeeze.

These horses display fresh brands, while Lou Roeser and
Red Altum check the Independence pasture.

CHAPTER TEN

THE WILDERNESS ACT OF 1964 AND CHANGES IN BACKCOUNTRY USE

The wilderness experience is considered so valuable in the national philosophy of the United States that we have set aside vast areas of land in wilderness designation and continue to withdraw further lands. Many eminent historians credited the frontier wilderness experience with development of traditional American character values, including self-reliance, strong work ethic, independence, optimism, confidence, humor, and honesty.

PRIMITIVE AREA DESIGNATION

In 1929, the Forest Service adopted regulations designating the establishment of primitive areas. The Hoover Primitive Area near Sonora Pass was the first to be created in 1931.

On August 20, 1963, the Mt. Dana-Minarets Primitive Area boundary was adjusted and the area reclassified as the Minaret Wilderness by the Secretary of Agriculture. The Forest Service stated that the Minaret Wilderness, south of Yosemite, contained some of the most scenic high country in the Sierra Nevada.

WILDERNESS ACT OF 1964

In 1964, after some years of heated debate and revised legislation, Congress passed the Wilderness Act. The High Sierra Packers' Association, who did not wish to see the spectacular High Sierra region further bisected by roads, actively supported this Act. Sierra pack station owners and their customers lobbied for passage of this bill, recognizing what a treasure the Sierra backcountry was and how important it was to keep this long stretch of high mountains free of further roads. The act ended most threats of more trans-Sierra roads and creation or expansion of local roads invading the Sierra heartland.

The Wilderness Act of 1964 declares that a purpose of the act is enjoyment by the public, and clearly articulates that wilderness shall be untrammeled. Webster's Dictionary defines "untrammeled" as "Something that is unconfined, unrestrained, or unshackled." It does not mean "untrampled," as sometimes misstated. Congress determined that wilderness land, under the act, is intended for humans, as well as flora and fauna, and human use was not to be regulated out of a wilderness area.

Congress intended, supporters believed, and the act so states, that current activities and uses of the land would continue under the new 1964 Wilderness Act designation. Historic uses and activities that were present when an

89

area was designated a Forest Service Wilderness Area would continue, but permanent facilities would not be permitted. This designation does not cover National Park Service wilderness lands; however, national parks do have a wilderness component. Yosemite National Park has permanent camps and bathrooms in their wilderness areas.

The John Muir Wilderness Area, in the Sierra and Inyo National Forests, was formally established on September 3, 1964. This huge wilderness encompasses over a half million acres within four California counties and extends one hundred miles along the crest of the Sierra. The Minaret Wilderness was incorporated into the National Wilderness Preservation System at this same time and contains 109,559 acres across the Sierra and Inyo National Forests.

This act created large expanses of national forest land that were designated to remain primitive in character, with no motorized vehicle access. This designation also meant no wheeled vehicles such as bicycles and no motors, including on boats. There were several permitted boat rental concessions on larger lakes that had to remove their boat motors. A motorized exception is helicopter use, authorized only for emergencies such as rescues and fire suppression, along with occasional chainsaws and other equipment used by trail crews.

Permanent lodges and camps were eventually ordered to be removed from the wilderness areas. There were formerly a number of backcountry camps and lodges in areas that are now a part of a wilderness designation. The Hilton Lakes Lodge at Davis Lake and the Upper Lodge in Big Pine Canyon were among those that were ultimately torn down and removed.

The popular High Sierra Camps in the Yosemite National Park backcountry were not included in the ordered removal of permanent camps and lodges, as they are located within the national park lands. So popular are these five unique backcountry camps that every summer, the public must participate in a drawing to obtain reservations. Tent cabins, with comfortable beds and bedding, delicious meals, and hot showers are furnished, and visitors can either ride mules or hike to the camp locations. Since sleeping accommodations and meals are provided, backpackers only need to carry their clothes, camera, fishing gear, and personal items, making for a much lighter load.

In 1964, at the time of the act's passage, backpacker use in the John Muir Wilderness Area was eighty percent of total backcountry use, whereas in 1944, backpacker use was only twenty percent of total use. In 1944, stock supported visitors comprised eighty percent of total use. Lighter-weight camp gear, as well as lighter backpacks, dried food, and nylon tents, had encouraged a surge in backpacking.

NEW ROAD CONSTRUCTION

In the late 1960s, the Disney Corporation launched an ambitious proposal to create a ski resort complex in Mineral King Valley. The Forest Service favored the application as a plan to provide additional recreation opportunities for the public. Ski clubs, local chambers of commerce, and local businesses added their support for the plan. Ray Buckman sold his Mineral King resort to the Disney Corporation, believing in their winter resort concept, while his partner, Phil Buckman opposed the plan.

Construction of a new all-weather road to access the valley from Sequoia National Park or Three Rivers was a major stumbling block. The one-lane, seasonal, unpaved road that currently accesses Mineral King was not adequate for a first class ski resort. The original Mineral King Road was constructed in 1879 from Three Rivers to the Mineral King Valley. It was twenty-five miles of steep, narrow, twisting turns. The 698 curves in the road were most unnerving to many potential visitors. In the proposal, the existing road was to be improved, but it became apparent that the steep terrain, even with major improvements, would still not be suitable for a major access road. The Mineral King Road still remains a mostly one-lane unpaved road.

The Sierra Club vigorously opposed the road and the ski resort development plan. Ike Livermore was appointed by Governor Ronald Reagan to be his Director of Natural Resources for the State of California. Being intimately familiar with the access into Mineral King Valley and its natural resources, Livermore opposed the plan. Livermore had owned the Mineral King Packing Company for many years.

Mineral King Valley was originally in the Sequoia National Forest. Since the creation of Sequoia National Park, Mineral King had been persistently looked at as a future addition to the park. Because of the mining activities in the region, it had originally been excluded. The Park Service quietly opposed the ski resort plan, still hoping to add Mineral King to Sequoia National Park. After the proposal for the controversial Disney winter resort was withdrawn, Mineral King Valley was quietly added to the boundaries of Sequoia National Park in 1978.

The Horseshoe Meadows Road construction began around 1969 to access a proposed new ski area/winter sports complex called Trail Peak in the Lone Pine area. In 1972, the Forest Service cancelled the permit to build the facility, but made plans for campgrounds and trails in the area. Cottonwood Pack Station, previously located at the mouth of Cottonwood Canyon, moved up to the end of the road. It was now a shorter distance to access the backcountry lakes and streams of this region. The road is steep but well-constructed and offers spectacular views of the Owens Valley. Shortly after climbing out of the valley, the road crosses Carroll Creek and passes by the old Carroll Creek headquarters of the Mt. Whitney Pack Trains. This old homestead is now a private residence.

MAMMOTH PASS/MINARET SUMMIT ROAD PROPOSAL

In 1965, the specter of construction of a trans-Sierra highway over the Mammoth Pass/ Fresno Flats corridor again surfaced, with intense pressure from Central Valley towns to add it to the State of California Highway System. Prior to 1928, six trans-Sierra roads had been proposed. In 1930, the primitive area boundaries had left a corridor between what later became the John Muir Wilderness and the Minaret Wilderness boundaries for the purpose of a road, referred to as the Minaret Summit Road. The Mammoth Pass/Minaret Summit route was selected because of some existing mining roads already in the area. A 32.8-mile gap between Minaret Summit and Squaw Dome existed. Members of the High Sierra Packers' Association, as well as business owners in Mammoth Lakes at the eastern terminus of the proposed road, had continuously lobbied against the construction of this road.

A bill to construct the road was proposed in the U.S. Congress in 1940, but the proposal died in committee. Proponents of the road from the San Joaquin Valley became active in pushing for the road again in the late 1950s. Fresno, Madera, and Merced Counties were actively lobbying for a road, claiming economic necessity for access to "rich markets to the East." Supporters proposed that a year-round highway be added to the State Highway System.

In 1957, the Bureau of Public Roads, along with the Forest Service, completed a feasibility study and reached a conclusion that the road could be constructed. Hearings were conducted in 1961, and in 1962, Forest Highway 100 became official. This was a joint action of the Bureau of Public Roads, the U.S. Forest Service, and the California Division of Highways.

The proposed year-round highway would bisect the roadless section of the High Sierra from Tioga Pass to Walker Pass, as well as the John Muir Trail. It would be very expensive to build. Several bridges would have to be constructed over deep canyons. The snow removal costs would be sizable, as snow level records confirmed that snow depths along the road corridor were some of the deepest in the state. There would be no services for a long distance. The highway would then connect Califa and Benton, not exactly large metropolises.

The California State Highway engineer, after studying the report, recommended in 1966 that the Mammoth Pass or Minaret Summit Road not be added to the State Highway System and not be included in extension of the Interstate Highway System. These conclusions stated that construction costs would be high and the use low. By this time, the John Muir and Minaret Wilderness Areas bordered either side of the road corridor.

A small group of residents and businesspeople in Mammoth Lakes and some Sierra Club members organized to defeat the road proposal. In Mammoth Lakes, local business owners formed a group called the Mono County Resources Committee to fight against the highway. Packers, including my husband and myself, along with Bob Tanner, were involved. The committee met with local residents and businesses, garnering the support of a large number of eastern Sierra people to object to the road construction. The Mono County Board of Supervisors also refused to support the proposal. The Eastern and Western High Sierra Packers' Associations lobbied against the bill.

However, the legions of San Joaquin Valley supporters hugely outnumbered the eastside residents. Petitions were signed and were presented at a hearing in Fresno. By 1965, the proponents were well on their way to having the road included in the State Highway System.

A hearing on the proposed Bill AB 290 before the Assembly Transportations and Commerce Committee was scheduled for April 18, 1967 at the State Capitol in Sacramento. Despite the fact that the Highway Commission had already recommended against including this highway months before, the Madera and Fresno County proponents continued to press for the road.

A small contingent from the Mono County Resources Committee agreed to attend the Sacramento hearing. My husband represented the Packers' Association, Doug Kittredge represented the Mammoth Lakes Chamber of Commerce, and Chip Van Nattan represented the Mono County Resources Committee. The group embarked for the hearing in Van Nattan's 1957 Ford station wagon. A late snowstorm hit them when they reached the Carson

Valley in Nevada, so they elected to drive over Donner Pass, as other passes across the Sierra were closed. Their vehicle did not have four wheel drive (not many passenger cars were so equipped at that time), but they installed chains on the wheels and plowed through the snow drifts. On Donner Pass, the Highway Department had just closed the highway to traffic, but the group pleaded successfully, and they were reluctantly permitted to proceed. The soft blowing snow kept drifting up over the hood of the vehicle, and they had to continually stop and brush the snow off the headlights and the hood. After what seemed an eternity, the weary travelers reached the home of Lou and Dorothy Fitzhugh, my brother-in-law and sister and our pack station partners, in Sacramento. The tired group rolled their sleeping bags out on the living room floor for the night.

In the morning, accompanied by Lou and Dorothy, the small group went to the State Capitol to meet with the Highway Committee members before the Assembly hearing commenced in the afternoon. They divided up and talked to all the members of the committee, explaining the facts of the road proposal and urging them to vote no on the bill. These members were surprisingly uninformed about the actual terrain of the proposed highway and were interested in hearing details from the group. The committee members were also impressed with the story of the Mono County group driving over Donner Pass in a snowstorm just the day before. Even a major trucking route can be closed by snow to traffic in April. The hearing began at 1:30 p.m. When the bill came to a vote, it was defeated eleven to one. The proponent of the bill from Fresno was furious and vowed to continue the fight on the federal level. One of the Assembly committee members voting to defeat the bill was Pete Wilson, who later became Governor of California.

After the Sacramento hearings, the State declined to build the road. However, the Forest Service had Forest Highway 100 on their road system and continued with plans to construct the road. The new plan was to construct a two-lane, seasonal road. The opposition now had to rally to defeat the federal proposal.

Ike Livermore was Governor Reagan's Secretary of Resources for eight years from 1967 to 1974. He opposed the proposed Forest Highway 100 and stated, "Completion of this road, in my opinion, would be the greatest tragedy since Hetch Hetchy Dam in Yosemite was built." Livermore brought the road situation to the attention of Governor Reagan. Members of the Sierra Club also opposed the road and urged the protection of the John Muir Trail by closing the road corridor permanently. Behind the scenes, the opponents continued their pressure on the Reagan administration to take action. In 1971, stakes had been driven into the ground on Minaret Summit where the new road would be located. The Forest Service had obtained necessary funding, and road construction was ready to begin.

Several days before June 28, 1972, my husband was informed that an event concerning the road was planned. Bob Tanner telephoned him and asked him to transport a truckload of saddle horses to Red's Meadow Resort on the morning of June 28. A press conference was to be held by Governor Reagan at a site along the road corridor. Tanner did not have enough horses for the expected party of about one hundred people that was expected to ride to Summit Meadow on the old Mammoth Pass Trail. There would be a number of press people, the Governor's staff, Secret Service personnel, local officials, and a small number of packers. Some people would be packed into King Creek, about an hour and a half ride from Red's Meadow, on the day before and would meet the rest of the group riding in on the 28th.

My husband and my son, Lee, hauled Mammoth Lakes Pack Outfit horses down the precipitous Agnew Meadows Road (part of the old Minaret Summit Road) to Red's Meadow from Mammoth Lakes early that morning of the 28th. They joined the large group of people waiting for Governor Reagan to arrive. He flew in from Sacramento in the morning and was then driven to Red's Meadow Resort where the party was assembled. Reagan was attired in western riding clothes and ready for the mountain ride. He was led to a group of horses tied to a hitching rail and allowed to choose which horse he would like to ride. He was apparently quite happy with his choice, and according to the packers, he had picked the best one.

It was about a three-hour ride to the site of the press conference. Once on the narrow trail, there was some jockeying around, as the Secret Service men were not positioned quite where they wanted to be, and all the cameramen wanted a good view of Reagan. Lee and several other wranglers had to retrieve horses occasionally, as cameramen, spotting a good photo, would leap off their horse to get the shot, and the horse would keep walking up the trail.

At Summit Meadow, a news release was arranged. A large map of the area of interest was displayed on panels. The horses were tied to trees around the perimeter of the meadow, and the group gathered around Governor Reagan. After explaining the history of the road project to the assembled group, Reagan reached into a pocket in his Levis and pulled out a rumpled telegram, stating, "Well, folks, I have good news for you." He then read the telegram from President Richard Nixon, stating that he had ordered a halt to Forest Service plans to construct the controversial highway and funding was being withdrawn. Reagan further proposed that the existing corridor be closed forever by adding the corridor route to one of the two adjoining wilderness areas.

Following this announcement, the group ate lunch and visited with the Governor before riding back to Red's Meadow. Lee, a newly-turned seventeen-year-old packer at the time, was impressed that when he shook hands with the Governor, Reagan looked him straight in the eye and gave him his full attention. It was a long ride for many of the novice riders, but Governor Reagan, an accomplished horseman, relished the trip.

GOVERNOR REAGAN AND IKE LIVERMORE'S PACK TRIP

In 1973, Ike Livermore arranged for Governor Reagan, his wife, Nancy, and family to go on a High Sierra pack trip in July into the wilderness area of Yosemite National Park. Ike and his wife, Dina, were also participants on the four-day pack trip. The accomplishment that Ike Livermore stated that he was most proud of was that he was a key influence in persuading Governor Reagan and President Nixon to "deep six" the proposed road. He was happy to share his love of wilderness with Governor Reagan.

Bob Barnett, manager of Yosemite Park and Curry Company Stables, provided the stock, camp equipment, and supplies. Ike's son, Sam, who packed for the Curry Company for four years, was a packer on the trip.

Johnny Jones, a long time westside pack station owner and Most Honored Packer at Mule Days in 1985, was a guide and packer. The traveling trip began at Mugler Meadow east of Bass Lake and traveled over Chiquito Pass to Moraine Meadows and the South Fork of the Merced River. Ike had "collected" passes in the Sierra of over 10,000 feet elevation during his many pack trips and had boasted that he had been over all fifty Sierra passes except one. That one, Fernandez Pass, he crossed on an easy side trip during this trip. On the way out to Yosemite Valley, the party stopped at Illilouette Falls and then traveled down to Nevada Falls and on to the stables on the Valley floor.

In 1974, Mule Days in Bishop honored Governor Ronald Reagan as Grand Marshall of the parade. Riding Jeannie, a handsome, stocking-legged mule, he was enthusiastically cheered by spectators as he rode along Main Street to the Tri-County Fairgrounds. In 2007, Ike Livermore was honored as Most Honored Packer posthumously.

NEW WILDERNESS AREAS

The Ansel Adams Wilderness Area, formed in 1982 from the Minaret Wilderness, included in its redrawn boundaries this remaining primitive area designation corridor where the proposed state highway was routed to go, thus permanently ending any further road proposals in this area. In 1984, Congress passed the California Wilderness Act. This act established the Golden Trout Wilderness Area in the southern Sierra and the Ansel Adams Wilderness Area, formerly called the Minaret Wilderness Area, including the corridor. The Southern Sierra Wilderness Area was established by the California Desert Lands Protection Act.

PACK TRIP PARTY SIZE AFFECTS THE SIERRA CLUB HIGH TRIP

Recreational use of pack and saddle stock increased steadily after World War I and peaked in the 1930s. Use declined in the 1940s during World War II and increased again in the early 1950s after the war ended. Backpacking increased in the late 1960s, peaking in the early 1970s. The peak year for wilderness use in the Minaret Wilderness Area was 1968. Overall wilderness use has continued to decline since then. Although August was still the most popular month with the general public for Sierra vacations, school schedules with year-round school or earlier beginnings in August changed many family vacation options to July.

Beginning in 1946, the Sierra Club limited the number of guests allowed on their Annual High Trip to 125 persons. This number did not include the large staff these trips required. As the years passed, with an increase in smaller backpack trips in the Sierra, there were more complaints from the small groups, even other Sierra Clubbers, who were concerned about the impacts from such a large group. The Sierra Club approached the Packers' Associations concerning support for the large participant numbers on their high trips. They maintained that having one large, organized group in their control, with one kitchen, eating, and sleeping area, was less damaging to the forest than many small pack trips. However, it became a social issue with non-Sierra Club campers who objected to camping near such a large group on their wilderness vacation. Environmental organizations lobbied for trip size reductions.

The Forest Service and the Park Service began limiting group trip size throughout the region with their permit process. The final Sierra Club High Trip was conducted in 1972. Special dispensation was given to allow this last trip. The trip had fifty paying participants plus the commissary, packing, and leadership crews, and lasted two weeks. The trip began at the King's River and looped through the high country, crossing Pinchot and Cartridge Passes, and ended the loop tour at Cedar Grove. The Mount Whitney Pack Trains was deeply affected by this decision, as they had been providing the packing services to the Sierra Club since 1946. That year, owner Ike Livermore decided to turn his interest in Mt. Whitney Pack Trains over to a partnership of Tommy Jefferson, Herb London, and Bob Tanner. The former pack station headquarters at Carroll Creek was not included in the sale, as it was on private property of the Morgan and Jefferson families.

GROWTH OF BACKPACKING

The outfitted public, served by commercial pack stations, had not increased substantially in number of customers over the previous twenty years, and in 1978, only represented five to ten percent of the total backcountry use according to some Forest Service surveys. Backpacking use had increased explosively, mostly due to the availability of new lightweight backpacking and camping equipment, dried meal packages, and more importantly, good maps and guidebooks to the trails. Previous to this surge, ninety percent of the use was on horseback.

In 1978, the Sierra and Inyo National Forests wrote wilderness management plans for the John Muir and Minaret Wilderness Areas. At the time of writing of the John Muir Wilderness Plan, there were nineteen commercial pack stations located near the trailheads they served. They had special use resort permits to operate in the John Muir Wilderness Area. There were thirteen who operated on the east side of the Sierra and six from trailheads on the west. These pack stations had remained the same for quite a few years. There were four pack stations operating in the Minaret Wilderness Area in 1978.

BACKCOUNTRY GRAZING

According to the fossil record, large numbers of horses and camels grazed the Great Basin region during the Pleistocene era. The largest mammals, such as mammoths, bison, and oxen, were not as abundant. Several varieties of horse bones have been located at various sites. Undoubtedly, the region's ecosystem evolved around large grazing animals. Horses and mules today graze on the rich grasses and forbs, leaving behind manure that enriches the nitrogen-poor mountain soils. Many garden experts recommend that horse manure is the best fertilizer to use for healthy plan growth. Just as manure benefits cultivated gardens, it performs the same magic in the wilderness. Grasses and many other plants have evolved to be eaten, and horses and mules perform the task of a power lawn mower. The indentations of hoofprints from livestock and deer plant seeds of grass and forbs, providing a bed for the seeds to germinate.

The commercial pack industry has been accused of overgrazing meadows with recreational stock. However, the incidental number of recreational stock grazing occasionally in the backcountry meadows during a short season is very small compared to the past heavy grazing of sheep and cattle herds in meadows all summer and fall. That heavy grazing in the previous century did not permanently destroy the meadows and surrounding countryside. The 20th century droughts that lowered the water tables have been overlooked. As the meadows became drier, lodgepole pine invaded them. A prolonged drought occurred in 1915 to 1934, followed by a long interval of high precipitation from 1937 to 1986, when the meadows again became lush. It is oversimplification to blame drier meadows on overgrazing by incidental recreation with pack and saddle stock.

The John Muir Wilderness Plan of 1974 states:

> *Grazing is a legitimate use of the Wilderness. Due to the unique geologic character of the Sierra Nevada, little early season grazing damage occurs from recreation stock. In early summer many of the higher basins are protected by deep snow in the passes to the east and by long canyons with heavy run off to the west. Rarely are the passes freed from snow until after the first of July. By this time most of the meadows are firm and little or no damage results from stock.*

The Forest Service and National Park Service commenced a policy of closing more mountain meadows to grazing or severely limiting the use of them. These closures have affected traveling trips, as it is difficult and impractical to pack bulky feed for the stock. Having to pack hay or pellets means more pack animals on the trail for each trip.

Quotas were imposed on some trails as a means of limiting public visitations. The Forest Service began issuing wilderness permits and instituted a wilderness ranger system to patrol and monitor the wilderness. Quotas on trails and use allocations called service days were assigned to commercial pack stations. The Forest Service assigned wilderness permit books to each pack station and collected them during the season. The pack trip party had to keep their copy with them during their wilderness stay to display to a backcountry ranger checking permits.

PACKING SAND AND CEMENT TO REPAIR
A BACKCOUNTRY DAM

The Southern California Edison Company is the owner of power dams on the Rush Creek series of lakes, Alger, Gem, and Waugh Lakes. In 1977, the company made plans to repair the uppermost dam, located at Waugh Lake in the Minaret Wilderness Area. The elevation of Waugh Lake is about 9,500 feet. The repairs required 500 tons of cement at the dam site. Because of provisions of the Wilderness Act, the Forest Service would not allow a permit for the material to be packed into the site by helicopter. The hauling of sand and cement had to be accomplished in time for the project to be completed before winter's cold weather prevented concrete work from continuing. Packers with strings of sturdy pack mules could be used to provide that service.

A contract was signed between Southern California Edison Company and three commercial pack stations: Frontier Pack Station, Red's Meadow Pack Station, and Rock Creek Pack Station. The three contracting pack stations, plus Leavitt Meadows Pack Station, Mammoth Lakes Pack Outfit, and McGee

Creek Pack Station, agreed to haul the sand and cement to the storage site located at the dam. The contract had to be completed in ninety days. Each of the six pack stations contributed packers, pack mules, and horses.

The two stations closest to the dam site were the designated loading areas—Frontier Pack Station at Silver Lake, elevation 7,225 feet, and Agnew Meadows Pack Station, a second location of Red's Meadow Pack Station, elevation 8,300 feet. Sand and sacks of cement were trucked to these two stations. The cement was already sacked but the sand was in bulk piles and had to be sacked at the staging centers. A ground crew at each loading site filled and weighed the sacks of sand by hand. Special pack bags were constructed that would accommodate the sacks of sand and concrete. Mules packed an average of 200 pounds each. The cement, in ninety-six pound sacks, was loaded two sacks to a mule.

Up to ten strings of five to eight mules each were loaded at each departure site early every morning. Some days, as many as fifteen strings made the round trip. From Silver Lake, using the steep and hazardous Angels Flight Trail, it required a seven-hour round trip, not including packing and unloading time. From Agnew Meadows, it was an eight-hour trip via the John Muir Trail, plus time to pack and unpack.

The other pack stations kept their stock at the departure corrals. Packers commuted back and forth from the departure locations to their individual pack stations. They carried their slickers with them daily, as it was a rainy summer. Many young packers learned packing skills that summer. The days began early and ended late. Pack station cooks prepared early breakfasts, packed lunches, and stayed late in the kitchens to provide dinners for tired returning packers. All of this activity had to be worked around the normal busy summer season with scheduled general public pack trips. Owners dealt with complicated logistics.

At the Waugh Lake dam storage site, over one hundred mule loads were unloaded each day. Altogether, over 4,000 loads of sand and cement were hauled over steep, rocky trails by sure-footed mules to the unloading site. Over a hundred mules and pack horses were used, and they had to be re-shod every four weeks because of the granite rocks. There were some wrecks along the trail but with no serious injuries, and all of the mules and horses, as well as their packers, were still working at the end of the project period.

Even though it was a wet summer with many thunderstorms and rainy days, the contract was completed in seventy-four days. The dam was repaired that fall. When packers get together to relate packing tales, this mighty effort by men and mules and horses is still reminisced about over coffee.

MULES AND MARINES

In 1952, during the Korean War, the U.S. Marine Corps established the Mountain Warfare Training Center at Pickel Meadows on Sonora Pass. The purpose of the base was to provide survival training during the Korean War. The base is not far from the Leavitt Meadows Pack Station and has access to many acres of backcountry in the Sonora Pass region.

Realizing the mobility gained by using pack animals, as had been done in World War II, the Marine Base acquired their first pack mules in 1985. Packing skills were added to the many skills being taught at the center, and some potential packers were sent to packing schools offered at several commercial pack stations. Mark Romander was the first instructor and used both sawbuck and decker saddle packing systems. He also designed some special panniers for carrying heavier weapons. In 2009, the base had around forty head of mules, and had added burros to their stable to accommodate war situations in the Middle East. Many of their riding horses are mustangs obtained from the Bureau of Land Management in Carson City, Nevada. Their color guard consists of all mustang geldings. During the heavy winters on Sonora Pass, the base sends their stock to winter pasture grazing on a Naval base near Hawthorne, Nevada, and more recently, to the Antelope Valley of northern Mono County. Tony Parkhurst has managed the mule operation and training at the base for many years now. Following the Marine Band in the 2010 Rose Parade, Colonel Norman Cooling, Commander of the Mountain Warfare Training Center, led a loaded sorrel pack mule string, followed by Tony Parkhurst with his string. This base is the only center in the Marine Corps that offers this kind of training.

Ike Livermore taking notes on a 1967 Calif. Dept. of Fish and Game pack trip. (Livermore Family Collection)

Gov. Ronald Reagan, Ike Livermore, and their families, on a pack trip
to YNP in 1973. (Livermore Family Collection)

Reagan describing the Trans-Sierra Minaret Road before reading a
telegram from Pres. Nixon halting the road. (Russ and Anne Johnson)

Gov. Reagan enjoying lunch before the 100 riders ride back down the trail with cameras clicking. (Russ and Anne Johnson)

Bob Tanner with Governor Reagan saddling up to ride to Summit Meadows for the 1972 press conference. (Russ and Anne Johnson)

At Frontier Pack Station corrals, 1977, sand and cement were stockpiled for packing to Waugh Lake dam site. (Russ and Anne Johnson)

Agnew Meadows was busy with pack strings carrying boxes designed to transport sand to the dam site. (Russ and Anne Johnson)

CHAPTER ELEVEN

SIERRA PACKING PRACTICES

Traditional packsaddles still jingle in rhythm to the clink of iron mule shoes on rocky granite trails leading into the craggy mountains. Self-reliant packers carefully tend their dependable animals, carrying loads of supplies over narrow trails pioneered by Native Americans and travelers countless years ago. The packing industry in the Sierra had its beginning in the Gold Rush, and the mule packers with their strings of saddle and pack animals look much the same today as they did in those long past days. Even the attire worn by mule packers of today looks as if it has stepped out of an old, faded photograph.

My son, Lee Roeser, who grew up working at our pack station, and who now owns McGee Creek Pack Station with his wife Jennifer, along with packing for the Forest Service, has this to say about Sierra packing history, "The Sierra Nevada Mountain Range has had the largest scale mule packing operation in this country for the past 100 years. This history of packing experience has helped the Sierra packer develop packing methods second to none."

TYPES OF PACK TRIPS

By the 1920s, the types of tourist trips offered by commercial pack stations were fairly well standardized and established throughout the Sierra. In the early days of tourist packing, almost everyone rode horseback, and very few people hiked or backpacked.

Campsites are mostly located near scenic and popular lakes and streams. They are chosen for a flat area to place tents and fire circles, and, if stock is staying overnight, near suitable grazing and watering for the animals. Regulations require camping 100 to 200 hundred feet away from streams and lakes.

The four basic types of trips still offered today are: all-inclusive trips, extended trips, spot trips, and dunnage trips. These trips are customized per individual clients' requests. Each individual party chooses the type of trip, the dates, and the destination for their vacation. Within the arrangement and organization of the pack station, trips are programmed into a workable schedule as much as possible to meet the requests of the customer. The earlier in the year that the client contacts the station, the more feasible it is to meet their vacation time frame. Today, because of tight Forest Service quotas on trails and destinations, grazing and fire restrictions, and obtaining a Wilderness Permit from the Forest Service, it is much more difficult to arrange and accommodate each customer's desires.

Before telephone service, customers wrote letters to the pack station making their reservations. When pack stations acquired telephone service, reservations could be made much more quickly and efficiently. Fax machines and more recently the Internet have made reservations easier. Today, most stations have a web page supplying information and some have online booking options.

In the past, some pack stations rented burros to hikers, who would pack and lead the animals on their trip itinerary. The Sierra Club offered burro trips, contracting with various pack stations that had them. In the distant past, some stations allowed experienced horsemen to rent saddle and pack animals and pack themselves into the backcountry, but this practice ended shortly after World War II. Very few stations handle burros today, and seldom allow any riding or pack animals on the trail without a pack station wrangler or packer leading them. Liability insurance policies and good animal husbandry now dictate many practices.

As customers began assembling their own camp gear, the basic spot trip became the most popular type of trip. Customers ride horseback or hike while mules carry their provisions. On a prearranged date, the packer and stock return to pack the party back out to civilization. Depending on how many miles into the wilderness a destination is, the trip may be termed a one or two-day trip. On a one-day trip, the packer and stock are able to reach the campsite and then return to the station on that same day. Two-day trips require the packer and stock to remain overnight with the party before returning to the station the following day. When in the backcountry, the party feeds their packer while he or she is with them. On the pack out, the packer travels to the camp the day prior to the party's out date.

On an extended trip, the packer and stock remain with the party for the duration of the trip, enabling the party to ride each day or travel to new campsites. The customers supply the camp and prepare the meals. Both extended and all-inclusive trips can be riding or hiking trips. Guests can also choose to have a base camp and take day horseback trips to other nearby lakes or streams.

On all-inclusive trips, the pack station makes all the preparations and often plans the itinerary. The station plans the camp, menu, and provision, and provides packers, cooks, and livestock. The trip can be a traveling trip or a base camp trip with input from the customers. Clients only need to bring personal items and equipment such as sleeping bags, tents, fishing gear, and cameras. The packer, mules, and saddle horses remain with the party for the duration of the trip. All-inclusive trips were very common, with the pack station supplying the camp and provisions, and most importantly, a cook. Many people did not have the necessary camping gear and relied on the pack station to outfit their trip. These trips are still very popular, as many urban customers have neither the camp equipment nor the wilderness knowledge to feel relaxed and comfortable camping on their own. Vacationers love the luxury of a carefree trip without having to cook.

Some pack outfits offer open group all-inclusive trips for customers who do not have a group of their own. The trips are often organized around themes such as fly-fishing, photography, painting, or natural studies of the mountains, and are very popular with singles and couples that wish to join a larger trip. Patrons are supplied with everything except their sleeping bags and personal gear. These trips are pre-scheduled by the station and advertised in advance.

Dunnage trips are arranged for hikers who wish to have their gear packed in while they hike to their destination and have become increasingly popular. Some dunnage trips are one-way, but many hikers arrange to have the packer return for their gear on a predetermined date. As hikers age, many find it difficult to hike and carry a heavy backpack. Since most Sierra visitors live near sea level and Sierra trailheads begin at seven to nine thousand feet in elevation and proceed upward to as high as twelve thousand feet on some passes, adjusting to the altitude change can be a challenge. Packers also pack in food resupplies for backpacking parties hiking the Pacific Crest Trail and the John Muir Trail.

There were no limitations on the size of trips in the early days, other than what the individual pack station could provide. Most trips were not large. The Sierra Club trips were the largest and an exception to the average. There were a few other groups, such as the Wampler Trips, Riders of the Wilderness, and the California Alpine Club, who conducted large trips and contracted with a pack station to supply the packing and riding services. The Forest Service now regulates party size and has imposed quotas on trails and destinations.

On earlier trips with older styles of heavy camping equipment, the packer reserved one pack mule per person. Today, with lighter camp gear available, trips can entail fewer pack animals to transport customer gear. However, because of grazing restrictions in many areas, hay and cubed or pelleted horse feed must be packed in for the stock, entailing more pack animals.

In the '70s, many youth groups packed into a base camp. These groups, such as the Boy Scouts and YMCA, as well as church groups, consisted of twenty-five to thirty-five or more members and often stayed a week. In Mammoth Lakes, the YMCA had an established summer camp in the '60s and sent in pack trips with the Mammoth Lakes Pack Outfit all summer. The pack station established their camp away from the popular backpacker camps, allowing for as much privacy as possible.

RECREATIONAL GRAZING IN THE BACKCOUNTRY

In the Sierra, professional packers turn their stock loose for grazing at night, rounding them up early in the morning. Some packers will give the animals a little grain before turning them loose. "Homing pigeons," animals that want to head home, are a problem. They are kept tied up close to camp and watched closely for a little grazing in the evenings and again in the morning. One animal deciding to go home can lead the whole herd with them. The packer bells his horse if the mules have bonded with it or selects the most popular animal. A popular bell mare, who geldings and mules will stick close to, is used when available. The bell mare or gelding, wearing the identifying bell and sometimes hobbled, will hopefully keep the rest of the stock with them during the night. Packers call the sound of the bell "mountain music." In some strategic narrow areas, there are drift fences or gates across the trail that help keep stock from returning home to the pack station when they are turned out to graze. The packer arises hoping to hear the comforting sound of the bell. Either on foot or riding the wrangle horse, who is left tied on a high-line rope overnight, the packer follows the sound and the tracks to locate the herd—hoping they are all together. He catches the belled animal, often leading it back to camp with the rest of the group following. Back in camp, the animals are given grain to encourage them to remain close.

If animals must be tied up for the night, a high-line rope is strung high between two trees on a hardened site where they can be safely tied. Stock is not tied up within camp or within a hundred feet of lakes and streams, except to load or unload. Where grazing is not permitted, stock must be fed commercial hay cubes. In recent years, there are more Forest Service restrictions on grazing and meadow closures that have greatly reduced the availability for commercial stock grazing. So the need to pack in feed is much more prevalent than in earlier times. With the advent of electric fences, some packers are exploring their use in the backcountry.

The pack and saddle animals on a pack trip that are turned loose to graze and move around for the night have minimal impact on the resource that has evolved to withstand large animal grazing. Grazing by horses and mules is not confined to open lush meadows. Stock will spend a considerable amount of time in forested areas, as well as dry slopes and benches, where they are protected from mosquitoes and wind, preferring this to wet areas. Forest forbs, grasses, and sedges provide abundant nutrition for stock, and dry slopes supply bunchgrass. Just as lawn mowers improve city lawns, grazing can improve meadows and rangeland. If pack and saddle stock is to be picketed, it is for only short periods for safety of the animals and protection of the grazing resource. Hobbles are preferred over picketing; however some animals become quite adept at traveling with their hobbles.

Loose herding of horses and mules on trails is only permitted now for safety reasons when going over very dangerous trails or in an emergency. Loose stock could pose a threat to hikers or other stock groups on the trail. When loose herding, the packer prefers to lead on the trail, with the loose stock stringing out behind him, and a second packer following behind if one is available. In previous times, when animals were returning back empty in the dark to the pack station, the packer would turn them loose and get ahead of them, and they would follow behind him. Sometimes it worked out better with the packer riding behind to keep the stock from dropping off in grassy meadows for a snack.

PACK GEAR AND HITCHES

Basic pack gear and equipment have not changed very much in design. The old standby, the wooden sawbuck saddletree, has been and is still the standard packsaddle used in the Sierra. According to Lee Roeser:

> The predominant type of pack saddle used in the Sierra is a double rigged Tehama style sawbuck—a functional and reasonably easy to use outfit that can be adapted to carry a variety of loads. The sawbuck pack tree most commonly used on mules and horses is the Tehama, which has larger bars to distribute the load over a broader area.
>
> The most important factor to consider in using these trees is their proper fit to the back of the pack animal. A good tree is wide enough to set properly on a mule's back without pinching or putting pressure on its withers or spine. The bars of the tree should be fairly flat and allow a sufficient amount of front to back rock, creating a maximum and uniform bearing surface on the animal. Because all backs are not the same, most pack outfits stock a variety of trees to enable them to properly outfit their entire string.

The sawbuck packsaddle has cross forks on the front and back made of oak that are riveted to carved, well-shaped wooden sidebars constructed of pine or sometimes cottonwood. The bars are of softer wood that can be rasped on the bottom to better fit a particular animal. The saddle is double rigged with leather straps, rings, snaps, and buckles that can be adjusted to fit a particular animal. To this is added double cinches, a breast collar, and britching (a harness around the rump of the animal to keep the saddle and load from moving forward), with proper quarter straps to hold the tree in place.

Lee further explains:

> *This outfit provides maximum stability, reducing the amount of rock in the load that can sore an animal. Proper padding is crucial when packing a mule. It should be large enough to keep the saddle and load from touching the mule's back, and thick enough to protect the mule. The padding material should resist slippage. Most packers use large canvas covered pads with quilts or blankets underneath them.*

With this packsaddle, the packer uses pack boxes constructed of wood. In the past, packers sometimes covered their wooden pack boxes with rawhide or haired cowhide, shrinking the hide to fit. Since World War II, adjustable leather straps called ears have been attached to fit over the sawbuck saddle. Canvas bags with heavy leather ends, or all-leather bags with looped straps called kayaks or panniers, are also hung over the packsaddle. An overstrap is a long strap sometimes attached to a set of pack bags. Manty loads are also used occasionally in the Sierra. This involves loads that are wrapped and tied securely in a tarp package, called a manty, and then slung in various ways.

Slings constructed of heavy canvas and leather, with wooden or aluminum bars on the top, are commonly used in the Sierra. Leather ears hang the sling on the forks of the packsaddle. Two long leather straps on the outside of the canvas encircle the load, making it snug. Slings are very useful for packing a variety of items such as duffle bags, boxes, stoves, and large tents. When hay is packed, it is mantied in canvas and slung. Cubes and pellets are usually packed in pack bags, but sometimes a whole sack may be mantied and slung. Side loads need to be evenly balanced so they ride without slipping or turning on steep trails. After the side loads are in place, duffle, tents, poles, etc., are loaded on top (called a top load). Good packers pride their ability to pack and balance a load that rides correctly on the mule to the destination without rubbing the mule or having to be adjusted. No experienced packer wants to repack on a steep or narrow trail, or be seen traveling down the trail with a load riding lopsided.

Most commercial packers use a platform or hanging scale at the pack station to weigh loads. Experienced packers learn to judge weights by lifting each box, bag, and slung load. For tourist packing, 150 pounds per animal is the average weight each mule carries.

A canvas tarp is thrown over the entire load. A lash cinch attached to a long rope ties it all down with either a diamond hitch or a box hitch. The single diamond hitch and the box hitch are the most commonly tied hitches in the Sierra. Mt. Whitney packers appropriately called their diamond hitch the "Mt. Whitney Diamond." Packers on the Kaweah River used another version. The

Mammoth Lakes Pack Outfit diamond hitch is the reverse of the Mt. Whitney pattern. Hitches are thrown and tied off from the onside, or the left side of the animal.

Occasionally, Decker saddles are used for heavy or unusual loads. The decker saddle, designed by the Decker Brothers in Idaho, came into use around 1910. Decker packsaddles, although quite popular in the Rocky Mountains, have never become widely used by Sierra packers. Sierra packers occasionally use this saddle for difficult loads that work best slung.

Heavy aparejo saddles have virtually disappeared from use in the Sierra today, and there are very few packers who can correctly use them. The heavy weight of the saddle and the technical method needed to correctly pack them make them impractical for most recreational packing. Aparejo saddles are used primarily for packing very heavy and difficult loads and are still unsurpassed. The wide and heavy pads protect the backs of the mules. The Salmon River saddle is a cross between an aparejo and a sawbuck, and is an excellent saddle for steep and rough country.

SELECTING SADDLE HORSES, PACK MULES, AND RIDING SADDLES

Each pack outfit has developed certain criteria to select saddle horses and mules for use in the mountains. Much depends on how the animal is to be used and in what kind of mountainous terrain the pack station operates. In the eastern Sierra, most stations are located at elevations of around 8,000 to 9,000 feet, and the trails are steep and rocky. Typically, the westside enjoys lower elevations, with gentler terrain and thick dense forests until reaching the high mountainous crest of the Sierra.

Generally, riding horses and mules must be sound, with sturdy leg bones, good feet, and good backs. Being a "good keeper" means that the animal can maintain its weight during hard use. Pack outfits look for animals that are best suited for these circumstances. When the owner is searching for appropriate saddle stock, they keep these criteria in mind, but most of all, they look for an animal with a good disposition. In the early years of packing, many people rode horses and could handle them well, but today, most of the people who ride at pack stations are novices. There is a great range in ages of riders as well as riding experience, so all the saddle horses and mules have to be gentle-natured. Pack stations use both horses and mules. The Sierra has a rich history of saddle mule use—particularly on all-day rides and pack trips. Yosemite National Park uses surefooted saddle mules for all their backcountry trips and on the High Sierra Camp circuit, and saddle horses for their short day rides.

When purchasing new horses, age and size are also taken into consideration. Horses with more size are more practical because a bigger horse can also carry a smaller person, but a smaller horse may not be capable of carrying a larger person. The general visitor population tends to be taller and heavier today than they were seventy-five years ago. All colors, types, and breeds of horses are found at Sierra pack stations. A few owners breed some of their animals and raise the colts. Part draft horse animals are bred or acquired to accommodate larger persons. In recent years, some outfits have adopted mustangs for their horse remuda. Quarter Horses are the most common breed selected for pack stations, although most are not registered. It is prudent to look for fairly young horses so they can be used for ten to fifteen or more years. Most stations purchase horses when they are four or five years of age and ready to go to work. Some stations prefer only geldings, but most outfits have both mares and geldings in their dude string.

New, young horses are sometimes packed until they understand rocky mountain trails and stream crossings and are ready to be ridden. The packer's riding horse is ideally strong and quiet-natured, and permits the packer to safely lead a string of packed mules. When a packer is returning from a trip empty, he will also have the saddle animals that were ridden by clients added to his string.

Saddles and bridles must be fitted to each animal, and this set will generally stay with that horse or mule the rest of the season. Guests are matched to a horse or mule according to their equestrian capabilities, age, and physical size. Saddles come in various sizes to match the diverse sizes of people. It is important that saddles are carefully fitted to particular horses and mules and will not make their backs sore. Very large people may not always be safely accommodated at a pack station, depending on the availability of strong, larger horses and saddles, length of ride, and terrain.

Selecting pack animals is very important to the pack station owner. In the Sierra, mules are used almost exclusively as pack animals. Good strong legs and feet, as well as a straight back, are desirable. Packers look for mules that have gentle-natured dispositions and are easy to shoe. Some outfits have or have used stocks—chutes where the animal can be safely secured—for shoeing and doctoring more difficult animals. Behavior and attitude are as important as physical structure in a mule. Animals with a calm disposition, who are easy to catch and pack, are very important to the packer on the trail and in the backcountry. The packer also has guests to be concerned about and care for safely.

Pack animals are corralled together at the pack station since the animals will function together as a herd. Often the packers' lead horses are corralled with the mules, encouraging bonding. In the backcountry, when the stock is turned loose to graze, animals that are used to being together usually stay together.

THE BUSINESS END OF PACK STATIONS

Pack stations are expensive operations. Sierra pack stations have a short operating season and high overhead. The summer season is brief, and stations are open seven days a week with early mornings and late evenings. Horses and mules have to be cared for all year, supported by income generated over approximately a three to, at best, four-month season. Winter pasture and feed are costly. Seasonal buildings and facilities, barns, and corrals must be maintained. Horses, mules, and equipment are costly to purchase. Liability and workman's compensation insurance, as well as other types of insurance, must be purchased for the entire year. Leases to the Forest Service must be paid as well.

A pack station owner has many concerns. Owners not only manage and operate the business part of the outfit, but also pack and guide trips. The owner or manager must schedule where each horse and guide operating in the riding string, as well as every packer and mule in the pack string, travels each day.

His or her worries include: planning around the weather; opening strategy for when snow melts in the spring; scheduling and reservations for trips; keeping saddles, gear, and pack equipment in good repair; advertising; transportation for hauling stock; purchasing hay and and grain; procuring veterinarians; obtaining winter pasture and feed; and hiring employees. They also must maintain good relations with their customers, the Forest Service, and the Park Service, as well as the neighboring communities and the public at large. Pack station stock and personnel may also need to assist in fighting backcountry forest fires, rescues, and trail work.

Employees have to be selected, hired, trained, paid, housed, and fed. The qualities looked for when hiring are: excellent horsemanship, a friendly personality with the public, honesty, and a willingness to learn new skills and follow the procedures set up at that particular pack station. At most stations, it is very desirable that packers know how to shoe the stock. Iron shoes only last, at best, six weeks on the rocky granite trails of the Sierra. In the backcountry, a packer has to be able to shoe any stock under his care when they lose a shoe. Because of the large volume of shoeing necessary, many stations hire the services of an outside horseshoer to keep their stock shod.

Veterinarian bills can be very expensive, especially when dealing with a large herd of horses and mules. In order to reduce this expense, the pack station staff worm, give shots and vaccinations, and care for minor injuries themselves. A veterinarian is consulted when the problem is more serious. This means having to haul the animal to the veterinary hospital, often fifty or more miles away. College students with an animal science or veterinary major are a plus on the summer crew.

Some pack stations operate rental cabins, restaurants, stores, campgrounds, and associated activities to provide necessary services to the public, and to make the most of their location and the short summer season. Other outfits offer short rides, special trail rides, and horse drives outside the wilderness areas, where more clients can be accommodated. By the end of the season, owners have worked seven days a week with very long hours to maximize their income potential. Pack station wives often consider it a day off driving to a distant town to resupply. Shopping is done for varied hardware supplies and food for the crew to last a week or more, and errands are run for family and employees, which includes going to the local boot repair shop.

In order to get through another season, most owners have another job during the winter months to supplement their family's yearly income. They work at various diverse occupations that will allow them the necessary four summer months off each year.

WINTER OCCUPATION IN DEATH VALLEY

The resorts at Death Valley National Park have provided winter activities for a number of eastside pack stations over the years. The resorts close in April for the hot summer months, and that allows pack station owners to return to the mountains for their summer season. When winter snows force the closure of the high elevation pack stations, Death Valley is just opening for the busy winter season. Before stock trucks and trailers were available to haul the stock, eastside packers drove their saddle stock back and forth to Death Valley. This was not an easy task!

Charlie Summers, of Agnew Meadows, and Glenn McNinch ran the stables at Furnace Creek Ranch in Death Valley, providing winter work for their horses. Other packers at Furnace Creek and Stovepipe Wells over the years were: Bruce Morgan of Mt. Whitney Pack Trains, Herb London of Rock Creek Pack Station, Murray Hall of Hall's Pack Trains, Gene and Lona Burkhart of Sequoia Kings Pack Trains, Slim Nivens of Pine Creek Pack Station, and Mark and Robin Berry of Rainbow Pack Outfit and Sequoia Kings Pack Trains. Mark and Robin Berry and their family have continued operating the Furnace Creek Ranch Stables even after they sold Rainbow Pack Outfit. Currently, the Berrys' daughter, Samantha and her husband, Luis Moya, manage the stables during the winter season.

Herb and Marge London, along with two partners, purchased Rock Creek Pack Station in 1947. That following winter, the Londons were running the stables at Stovepipe Wells. Herb played the guitar and sang to guests at the evening campfires, where Stan Jones, the park ranger who wrote the immensely popular song, "Ghost Riders in the Sky," sometimes joined him.

Russ and Anne Johnson went to work for Rock Creek Pack Station the following summer in 1948. During the winter of 1948 and 1949, the Johnsons ran the stables at Stovepipe Wells, where Russ also did a great amount of mine packing. He packed in mining equipment and packed out ore for the Gold Hill Dredging Company, often packing mules with aparejo saddles. The miners lived at the site, so Russ also packed in groceries and supplies for them.

In 1950, the mine was continuing operations later in the spring, after the temperatures in the valley soared to from 110 to 120 degrees, so Russ had to carry out the packing operation at night by the light of a Coleman lantern. The major hazard on the trail was the sidewinder snakes curled up in the path. When moving the stock from Immigrant Springs, out of Stovepipe Wells, again in the dark, Russ loaded one bunch of stock in the stock trailer and hauled them to Independence. Anne strung up the remainder and led them over Towne Pass and across hot Panamint Valley to the Panamint Springs Resort. Russ then trailered them the remaining distance to Independence.

A strong work ethic and a passion for the mountain way of life are necessary for this strenuous and demanding lifestyle.

TRAILS, TRAIL MAINTENANCE, AND CAMPSITE CLEANUP

Pack station owners, along with their employees, have accomplished much trail maintenance over the years in their areas. They have rocked trails, cut fallen timber along with low hanging branches and brush, repaired washouts and slides, shoveled snow off trails in the spring, diverted water from heavy cloudbursts off trails, cleaned water bars (logs or lines of rocks built in across the trail to channel water off), and have generally kept the trails open and passable. Trails must be maintained to their constructed standard, or they can be lost to erosion in a very short time. Heavy spring runoff and summer cloudbursts and thunderstorms make water erosion on the trails a constant maintenance concern. Maintenance must be performed on a regular and timely basis to prevent this damage, as soil for trail treads in this rocky region is valuable and easily lost. In the higher basins and on the passes, trail bed material often must be hauled in from some distance on pack mules.

The Forest Service trail crews perform maintenance and reconstruction, but their crews are limited, and in order to open the trails in the spring, the local packers also work to open the trails in their area. In the spring, the snowpack lingers in shady areas of the trails and high passes. Snow has to be shoveled off sections of the trails to make them passable for hikers, as well as riders and pack strings. In earlier days, the deepest hard-packed icy drifts were sometimes dynamited and left to melt for a few days before the crews went back up to shovel the drifts. On some trails, packers sprinkled sand across the route to assist the melting process. After several days, the sun would heat the sand and help melt the path. The packers would then shovel a route through the snow. In heavy snow years, after the shoveling process was completed, there were often cut banks three or four or more feet high on the sides of the trails.

Avalanches provide a special challenge, as downed trees can block a trail completely. Forest Service administrators interpret the Wilderness Act to mean that chainsaw use is not permitted in the wilderness except under unusual circumstances. Trail work is to be done using the "least minimal tool," using Forest Service terminology. Cutting large downed trees with hand saws and two-man crosscut saws is slow and laborious.

The life of a trail depends to a great extent on its location and the quality of the original trail construction. Water bars must be properly installed to drain water off the trails. Damage to trail switchbacks is another constant maintenance problem, and is most often caused by hikers shortcutting the trail, especially when hiking downhill. Pack animals rarely cause this problem since the animals being led have to stay on the trail bed.

Another problem is the placement of rock or log steps in the trail. As the trail washes and erodes, and is not maintained to construction standards, the steps become exceedingly tall. Hikers and backpackers then skirt these high steps, causing parallel trails on either side. Pack mules will always seek the safest route on a trail, and will bypass what they see as a dangerous obstacle that could possibly endanger them. Seeing these alternate trails, they may try to use one and get themselves and the string in trouble, causing a wreck.

Mostly, the local packers handled wilderness camp cleanup in the past. Packers cleaned up camps used by their customers and packed out cans, plastic, tin foil, and other litter left by other visitors. Years ago, to encourage hikers to clean up their camps, Arch Mahan at Red's Meadow Resort hung gunny sacks on trees in popular camping areas. When his packers were in the area, they packed out whatever trash was collected. He advocated this successful cleanup method to the Packers' Association. Other packers had similar methods of keeping the campsites clean. No packer wants to lead their party into a beautiful campsite only to find it dirty from previous campers. When a packer was coming out empty after dropping off his party, he packed out bagged trash on his mules.

After the wilderness ranger system was put in place, the initial rangers cleaned up backpacker camps and carried the trash to the main trail, where packers would pick it up on their way out with an empty mule string. This practice continues today. Forest Service packers also pack out litter when they are packing trail crews in and out of areas.

Today, wilderness campsites are very clean and litter-free. Both the pack stations and the Forest Service have had successful educational programs to alert visitors to wilderness areas on proper conduct and camp cleanup. Each packer must make certain that his party has tidied up their campsite and bagged any litter to be packed before he packs them out. "Leave your camp cleaner than when you arrived here!" is the passed-down wilderness etiquette. The Forest Service motto on the wilderness signs is, "Take only photographs, leave only footprints!"

Pictured is the Mammoth Lakes Pack Outfit mule corral.

These MLPO saddle sheds have racks for each saddle and bridle with the horse's name signed above.

Packers Red Altum and Carl James are shoveling the snowy chute to open the JMT.

Dudley Boothe rides through a shoveled route on the top of Bishop Pass.
(Boothe Family Collection)

The Owens Valley Trucking Co. in Bishop hauled stock to pack stations, to/from winter pastures.

Huge stacks of hay are required at pack stations to feed the hard-working stock.

**Louie Fitzhugh is feeding grain to the horses and mules
at MLPO before they are saddled.**

**Lee Roeser at the old mule pack saddle rack at MLPO,
with name signs for each muleshoe hook.**

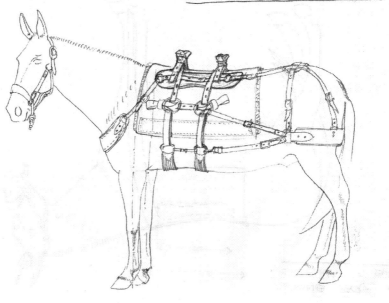

THE "SAWBUCK" PACK SADDLE.

SAWBUCK
RD '97

Drawing of the sawbuck pack saddle on a mule, along with the harness rigging.
(Rene Duykaerts)

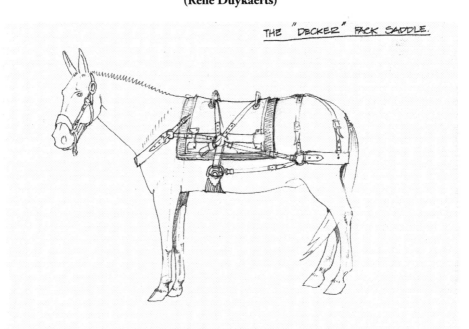

THE "DECKER" PACK SADDLE.

. DECKER .

Packer Rene's drawing of a mule with a decker pack saddle and rigging.
(Rene Duykaerts)

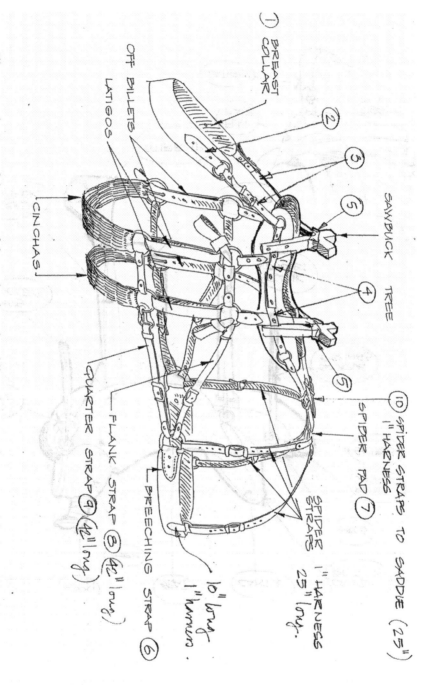

Illustration by Rene of the parts of the sawbuck pack saddle and rigging that was used for his packing classes at Thacher High School in Ojai. (Rene Duykaerts)

CHAPTER TWELVE

PACK STATIONS PROVIDE VARIED RECREATION OPPORTUNITIES

Hal Roth, in his 1965 book, *Pathway to the Sky*, observes these thoughts about the packing industry in the Sierra:

> *The packing business as practiced in the Sierra Nevada is unique. The Appalachians in the eastern United States have nothing comparable nor do the Alps in Europe (travelers from abroad are always amazed at pack stations). Packers and pack stations are an important part of the mountain scene in California and a way that someone not suited to hiking can ride a horse, meet a different breed of Americans and find a sure trail to the wilds.*

The 1965 *Sierra Club Wilderness Outings* brochure, edited by Genny Schumacher Smith, aptly described their famous High Trips:

> *The traditional Sierra High Trip is a roving pack trip with stock carrying all the loads and trip members hiking to a series of camps usually located near timberline. The High Trip pattern was developed over sixty years ago, when the young Sierra Club offered an Annual Outing each summer that more people could travel the largely trail-less Sierra Nevada. You stay in the same camp from perhaps one to three days. A commissary crew sets up camp, cooks the meals and packs and cleans up on moving days, although everyone expects to help occasionally. Your personal duffel is limited to thirty pounds.*
> *High Trips are limited to 100 people. If this number sounds large to you, remember that the mountains are big. On moving days people choose their own pace and their own companions; on layover days they scatter in all directions. About the only time you realize you are with a hundred others is when you see them at breakfast and dinner.*
> *On moving days, after breakfast, you start on the trail. There is no need to hurry or reach the next camp until dinnertime. You need carry only your lunch and extra clothing. The pack train may pass you on the trail and your duffel bag may be in camp when you arrive. You hike from 5 to 15 miles. Camps are usually above 9,000 feet; passes may be 11,000 or 12,000. Layover days, when we remain at the same camp, are yours to enjoy as you please.*

VARIOUS TYPES OF PACK TRIPS AND TRAIL TRIPS

Pack trips by organized groups such as the Boy Scouts, YMCA, Sierra Club, church groups, and various college and university classes increased markedly after WWII. These groups required services provided by the commercial pack stations and averaged twenty-five to thirty participants. Commercial group trips such as the Sierra Club, Wampler Trail Trips, Outward Bound, and various mountaineering groups had also been steadily increasing.

Pack stations, catering to the public and their customers' requests, launched a variety of pack trips and trail rides. University and college sponsored classes evolved, with classes in veterinary care in the backcountry, horsemanship and trail riding, natural history studies of the Sierra, watercolor painting, and photography. Along with these, fly-fishing, campfire and Dutch oven cooking, and packing school trips were offered for the interested public. Several pack stations conducted cattle drives, horses drives, and mustang viewing trips. 1985 was the peak year for traveling college and university trips through the Sierra. Rock Creek Pack Station made these educational trips the core of their operation for a number of years.

In 1972, a group size limitation of twenty-five people per group, including pack station personnel, was initiated in the Minaret and John Muir Wilderness Areas, thus ending the large Sierra Club High Trips as well as other group trips. In around 1991, the Forest Service instituted a further maximum group size limitation, lowering the number of people on a trip to fifteen persons and twenty-five head of stock. Limited or no grazing has also increased the need to pack feed in on trips, necessitating more mules. The group size of fifteen, including pack station crew, makes it very difficult for most youth groups, church groups, and college educational classes to conduct pack trips for their members and students. Youth groups need enough participants to pay for the transportation costs of getting there, and enough adult counselors to supervise the youth. Colleges need to have a certain number of enrollees in order to pay for the instructor and college overhead and make the trip viable. College educational trips are all-inclusive trips, with meals and the camp provided. These trips include a cook and helper, as well as necessary packers, all part of the magic number of fifteen. This doesn't allow for very many paying guests. After the group size was lowered to fifteen, including instructors and pack station crew, this type of trip was inevitably less available. Ironically, as more visitors are urban residents, there is an increased demand for open group and customized all-inclusive pack trips. With smaller group size, increased expense per person, and increased overhead for the pack station, the trips have become less profitable and less economically feasible to operate.

Individual pack stations have various specialties, such as wagon rides, hayrides, sleigh rides, and always-popular dinner and breakfast rides. Clients can choose experiences and activities that appeal to them. Mammoth Lakes Pack Outfit and Red's Meadow Resort offer various trail rides for three or four days outside of the wilderness, such as the Bodie Ghost Town trips. The horses and riders are transported by truck and trailer to the location of departure and then picked up at the final destination four days later. A cook trailer and camp meet the riders at a prearranged location each night. This type of trip is very versatile because of its mobility.

Several outfits organize mustang viewing trail rides in Adobe Valley and the Pizona Mountains, northeast of Bishop, in the spring. Rock Creek Pack Station and Frontier Pack Station have wild horse experts on the mustang viewing trips and offer college credits. European tourists particularly enjoy the mustang rides and horse drives. In coordination with local ranchers, cattle drives have been conducted by some pack stations.

Some outfits have been able to use their stock in other activities during the winter, such as movie and film work, horseback riding, stables, wagon and hayrides, trail rides, and other western activities. Furnace Creek Ranch in Death Valley has been a Sierra packer-operated winter stable business since the 1930s and perhaps even earlier. Into the 1950s, a certain amount of mine packing occurred in the Death Valley area, offering winter work for pack strings. Today, outfits try to maximize the shoulder seasons (spring and fall) with trail rides, mustang sighting rides, and horse and cattle drives. McGee Creek Pack Station offers trail rides in the Alabama Hills to view western film locations during the winter months. Many outfits use their pack mules not only to pack, but to drive and ride as well.

HORSE DRIVES

Pack outfits began trucking their horses and mules to winter pasture locations in the late 1950s and continued doing so for twenty years. Cattle trucks were used where available. Some stations began to invest in stock trucks, but these could seldom haul more than ten head. Horse trailers were still small, usually for only two horses. On the eastside, the pack stations relied on a trucking company located in Bishop to haul their stock. With a large stock truck and trailer, a large number of stock could be hauled with each load. However, in the early 1970s, this trucking company, who had been hauling pack station stock for years, went out of business. It was difficult and expensive to locate cattle trucks that were not double deck rigs. Horses and mules are too tall to fit into double deck livestock trucks designed for shorter cattle and sheep.

Interest in the Old West was high, and riding and pioneer heritage adventures were popular with the public. The great cattle and sheep drives no longer trailed up and down the old livestock trails between valley pastures and mountain meadows. The eastern Sierra is particularly suited for horse drives, with the wide-open spaces and good camping areas. By 1968, Rock Creek Pack Station had begun conducting three-day spring and fall horse drives from Independence to the pack station near Rock Creek Lake with guests.

For some years, my husband, Lou, had been interested in organizing horse drives to and from the winter pasture in Independence in the Owens Valley, and believed that, with paying customers, it would be financially feasible. In 1976, our outfit, Mammoth Lakes Pack Outfit, and Red's Meadow Pack Station conducted a joint trial fall drive from Mammoth Lakes to Independence, with crew and a few participating guests. It was a strenuous hundred-mile three-day drive with a 4,000-foot drop in elevation. Dr. Don Blackman, who participated in and survived that first horse drive, is still participating on every drive with the Mammoth Lakes Pack Outfit.

Having found that a horse drive with customers was feasible, both stations planned separate drives for the next year. Other outfits followed suit, constructing their own versions of a horse drive. Many of the outfits tried cattle drives as well, but since that meant working around the local ranchers' schedules, most of them were discontinued. Besides, horse drives are much more exciting for the riders. The horses know where they are headed and are anxious to get there, so it is more of a holding operation than a slow, driving or pushing operation such as a cattle drive.

The following year in 1977, we at Mammoth Lakes Pack Outfit commenced annual spring and fall hundred-mile horse drives between the pack station in Mammoth Lakes and winter pasture near Independence. The first drives were along the old cattle trail called the Rickey Trail that was very grueling on the horses, mules, guests, and crew. The next year, we extended the drive to a four-day trip, with shorter riding miles each day. Then, Lou pioneered the Dry Trail, as it was called in pioneer days, when it was an old cattle and sheep trail on the north side of Long Valley that avoided fences, gates, and all but two major road crossings. The drive was eventually expanded to five days, making the ride less arduous for the guests and the livestock. The crew also welcomed that change.

Guests and crew camp out together along the trail, with ranch-style barbecues and campfire entertainment in the evenings. This is a very exciting experience for guests because they are able to participate in an actual working trail drive. The Mammoth Lakes Pack Outfit drive became more and more popular, with up to sixty-five guests participating. This required a large support staff of a kitchen crew, a camp crew, and a wrangler crew. Hay had to be hauled to each camp. A water truck accompanied the drive, as the Dry Trail lived up to its name. Accompanying the drive was a "pop" wagon that was, on some drives, pulled by a four-up hitch of mules, carrying water, lemonade, and iced tea to keep riders hydrated on the long, warm, and dusty trail. A truck and horse trailer for tired or lame stock followed the drive and picked up tired riders who could "hitchhike" to camp in the truck. The lunch wagon met the drive at prearranged lunch stops with a scrumptious "spread," and riders welcomed the chance to stretch tired muscles.

In August of 1991, the movie, *City Slickers*, a humorous tale of a cattle drive, hit movie theaters throughout the country. Telephone calls poured in to pack stations that offered horse and cattle drives in the fall. The Mammoth Lakes Pack Outfit five-day drive was already booked, so after a consultation with all of our family and crew, it was a consensus that two additional drives could be done. Both of the additional horse drives quickly booked up, and the pack outfit conducted three fall drives. This must have confused the horses and mules, who expected a long winter vacation when they arrived at the pasture in Independence. They were kept in the corrals and not turned loose to graze on the 5,000 acre "pool field."

The kitchen and camp crew, headed by my daughter, Kerry, and her fiancé, Mike Elam, quickly reprovisioned and reorganized the camp for the second drive. This drive was for four days and traveled north back up the Owens Valley to Laws Railroad Museum, where the herd was again corralled, and where the camp crew provisioned the camp for the third group of fifty guests. The third drive turned around and went back down the valley to winter pasture. This time, the tired horses were turned out for their well-deserved winter rest. The even more tired crew headed for hot showers. Kerry and Mike had to reschedule their wedding plans for a week later in order to accommodate this additional activity.

When the stock reached the end of the drive, their shoes were pulled, they were wormed, and new animals were branded with our ML brand, before being turned out in the 5,000-acre Owens Valley pasture, shared with Rock Creek

Pack Station and Red's Meadow Pack Station. The packer crew and cooks camped in the pasture for a few days, finishing up these fall chores. Fences needed to be checked and repaired, as herds of tule elk summer in the pasture and are notoriously hard on fences. Sometimes, the wooden working corrals at the pasture need some attention. In the spring, the stock was rounded up and shod for the spring drive back to the mountains.

McGee Creek Pack Station, owned by my son and daughter-in-law, Lee and Jennifer Roeser, also participated in these biannual horse drives. McGee Creek Pack Station stock was hauled across the valley to nearby Eight Mile Ranch, Lee and Jennifer's ranch headquarters, for winter pasture.

The present owner of the Mammoth Lakes Pack Outfit, John Summers, continues these annual drives. When his grandfather and father, Lloyd and Lee Summers, owned the outfit, the crew managed the semiannual horse drives, with no guests. Spring and fall horse drives are a glimpse into the past and allows urban dwellers to participate and be a working part of historical activities once common in the Sierra.

These new types of trips helped to offset the decline in hunting season. With the creation of Kings Canyon and Sequoia National Parks, hunting was banned in a large area of the Sierra. Deer numbers on the east side of the range declined drastically due to a number of factors, including increased numbers of protected mountain lions who prey on the deer and bighorn sheep. The California Department of Fish and Game responded with less available deer tags. Without a large hunting season, many stations will close earlier in September. Horse drives fill in the hole for some eastside outfits.

MULE DAYS CELEBRATION IN BISHOP
The first Mule Days at the Fairgrounds in Bishop occurred in 1970, organized to honor the mule and its role in the packing industry of the Sierra Nevada, and to showcase traditional packing skills. The goal of the Mule Days Celebration was to create an activity that would show the versatility and value of the mule. The Owens Valley did not have a Memorial Day Celebration, and that was a time slot the Bishop Chamber of Commerce and Hotel Association were seeking to fill. A group of people representing the Packers' Association and the Town of Bishop, along with a Forest Service representative, met at the home of Wilfred Partridge, long time pack station operator and rancher, to plan that first competitive event, not imagining that it would still be taking place in 2019. The group meeting regularly that winter included Wilfred Partridge; Leo Porterfield of the U.S. Forest Service; Roland Christianson, Head of the Bishop Chamber of Commerce; Herb London of Rock Creek Pack Station; Art Schober of Schober Pack Train; Dudley Boothe of Rainbow Pack Outfit; Bob Tanner of Red's Meadow Pack Station; packer Orville Houghton; and others. Mule Days celebrated its 50th Anniversary in 2019.

The town of Bishop participated enthusiastically. Packers ran the events and contests and came with their mules from all across the Sierra to partake in a fun day of a parade and contests at the fairgrounds. The first show in 1970 was a one-day affair on the Saturday of Memorial Day weekend, with mostly local competition. 1971 was also a one-day contest, and the judge was former pack station owner, Johnny Jones.

Slim Tatum, former owner of Frontier Pack Train, was the first Grand Marshall of the parade in 1970, and Ike Livermore, owner of Mineral King and Mt. Whitney Pack Trains, was Grand Marshall in 1971. In 1973, the tradition of Most Honored Packer was established, with pack station owners Arch Mahan honored in 1973 and Art Schober in 1974.

The parade is advertised as the largest non-motorized parade in the country and boasts having had two California governors as Grand Marshalls. Governor Ronald Reagan was Grand Marshall in 1974, riding a mule, and Governor George Deukmejian was Grand Marshall in 1986, riding on the Sam Smizer parade wagon, pulled by an eight-up hitch of mules.

In 1981, Bob Tanner and his son, Bobby, put together a twenty-mule team of Red's Meadow Pack Station red mules to pull the ninety-nine-year-old Borax wagons from Death Valley. Henry Olivas, former pack station owner, helped put the teams together, as he was experienced in how to train the mules and repair and rig the equipment. Olivas had worked with Bruce Morgan and Russ Spainhower, of the Spainhower Ranch in Lone Pine, to train, organize, and drive the 1949 Centennial Twenty Mule Team trek from Lone Pine to Death Valley, to commemorate and celebrate its first 100 years of operation. Olivas also helped Bobby Tanner learn to drive the mules and walked beside them during the many weeks of training for the parade and area events. Since then, Tanner's Twenty Mule Team continues to perform at various parades around the West, including the Rose Parade in Pasadena.

Bob and his wife, Jean Tanner, rode in the Rose Parade with an appaloosa horse-riding group for many years. The group had a large entry in the Rose Parade, with pack strings, young riders, and government officials, and one year, they included Gail Norton, Secretary of the Interior. For several years, Tanner was associated with the Los Angeles Department of Recreation and Parks with a program providing backcountry pack trip experiences to urban, underprivileged teens.

Mule Days has grown by leaps and bounds since its beginnings, and people attend and compete in the competitions from all over the country. The Bishop show is a unique event at the right time of the year, and the public loves it. The event is now a six-day celebration with an attendance of over 30,000 people. Mule Days has encouraged the breeding and showing of mules, as well as education about traditional packing skills. The concept has even spread to many other towns across the West. Pack station owners serve as officers, board members, and committee chairman, along with community members. In 2007, our son, Lee, was the president of the event. Previously, Bobby Tanner and Craig London, both also second-generation packers, had served as president. Lou and I were honored to be selected as Most Honored Packers in 1982, and to serve as Grand Marshals in 2012. In 2018, I was surprised to be selected Favorite Backcountry Cook, which our daughter, Kerry, had been chosen for in 2011. Bob Tanner, Mule Days' ramrod for many years said, "It's been fascinating to watch the event grow and transform itself from a day of fun for mule skinners into a nationally known event. It worked out to be a community event, and a good old country fair where everyone can participate."

Through this colorful event, many more people are introduced to the magic of backcountry pack trips in the Sierra each year and have a greater understanding of the distinctive mule packing industry. Mule Days has certainly encouraged the packing industry over the years.

Experienced packers and wranglers at the reservation office at MLPO.

The saddle shed at McGee Creek Pack Station is well-planned and efficient.

Kerry Roeser and Kiera Elam saddle up the day ride horses
at the beginning of a busy day at McGee Creek Pack Station.

Trail guide Johanna, at MLPO, gives instructions to the horseback riders.

Kerry Roeser gives her instructional talk to trail riders at McGee Creek Pack Station.

Wrangler, Kiera Elam, on a trail ride in McGee Canyon.

Leslie Roeser leads a scenic ride through meadows,
with Mammoth Mountain behind.

Following a wrangler, saddle horses trail back to the
saddling area from their day corral.

Butch Willmon is analyzing, making up loads, and packing gear on the mule, Grey.

After World War II, aluminum pack boxes were used in
addition to wooden pack boxes.

Canvas and leather pack bags were used extensively with
wooden sawbuck pack saddles.

Lee Roeser is placing a top load on the pack mule.

Rene Duykaerts leads a pack string out of the yard at MLPO.

Jennifer Roeser looks back at her string on a difficult section of trail.
(Lee and Jen Roeser Collection)

This campsite on a bluff overlooking Grassy Lake offers
stunning views and great fishing.

The UC Riverside Extension pack trip on natural studies
earned students college credits.

Riders on the fall 100 Mile MLPO Horse Drive lead the stock to the next camp at Crowley Lake.

The remuda is led by packer Lou Roeser through a crossing at Layton Creek, fall Horse Drive.

**Dave Stamey (well known cowboy music artist) plays cowboy
music on MLPO horse drives.**

**Chef Jay Elam prepares barbecued steaks and chicken for
dinner at an Owens R. campsite.**

Wranglers on the horse drive, Matt Engelhart and
Gene Cooper, are waiting for the herd.

Lou and Marye Roeser were Grand Marshals in the Mule Days Parade
in Bishop in 2012.

Gov. Reagan was Grand Marshal in the Mule Days Parade
in 1974, riding Jeanie. (Russ and Anne Johnson)

The herd at Casa Diablo Grade are contained by the riders forming a strong front line.

CHAPTER THIRTEEN

THE SIERRA PACKING INDUSTRY TODAY

Riding clubs, "Old West" groups, Back Country Horsemen chapters, and heritage and historic societies have sprung up around the country. Interest in pioneer life and traditions has grown exponentially. As California has become more urbanized and populated, many Americans are looking for active, adventurous vacations that reflect this interest in a historic culture. There has always been a deep interest in summer camping traditions in the Sierra.

A Sierra pack trip is a journey back in time where life assumes a slower pace, with time for fishing, photography, sketching, and discovering what lies just around the next bend in the trail. There is time for camaraderie around a campfire with good conversation and fellowship. A wilderness camping adventure can be the experience of a lifetime, drawing campers into the spirit of the past, following the hoof prints and footprints of those who traveled these trails before. John Muir wrote of seeing "a new heaven and a new earth every day."

For many years, pack stations have met this historic interest and love of the incomparable Sierra backcountry by providing memorable vacations for the American public. The urban population relies on commercial pack stations in order to access the public lands of the Sierra backcountry. The stations provide them with horse and mule transportation, knowledgeable guides and packers, and competent backcountry cooks. The vacationing public that pack stations serve depend on these guides to instruct them in low impact camping techniques, the lore of the mountains, and an understanding of natural systems and resources. The outfitted general public that uses pack station services can be a strong advocate for wilderness values and access.

Commercial packers, like their Forest Service and Park Service partners, deem themselves "stewards of the land," serving visitors, providing enjoyable access, and conserving the natural resources of the wilderness areas. The various government agencies, including the Forest Service, have depended upon commercial packers to pack in camps, supplies, equipment, and people for their wilderness administrative activities.

Pack stations in the Sierra are still mostly small family outfits. Many owners are second and third generation packers. On the eastside, Dennis Winchester, Murt Stewart, Mike Morgan, Brian Berner, Craig London, Lee Roeser, Jennifer Ketcham Roeser, John Summers, Bobby Tanner, and Dave and Kent Dohnel have carried on historic family traditions. John Summers is a fourth generation packer following his great-grandfather, Charlie Summers, grandfather, Lloyd, and father, Lee, in the packing business. On the westside, Owen Topping, Jay Barnes, Larry Knapp, John Cunningham, Tim and Lee Loverin,

Hilary and Luke Painter, and Richard Ross operate second and third generation family businesses.

The Back Country Horsemen of America was organized by private stock-owners that enjoy packing into the national forests and parks as well as other public lands, and who work to protect the continuance of their access rights. Their goals declared in their mission statement are to:

1. Perpetuate the common sense use and enjoyment of horses and mules in America's backcountry and wilderness areas.
2. To work to insure that public lands remain open to recreational stock use.
3. To assist the various government, state and private agencies in their main tenance and management of said resource.
4. To educate, encourage and solicit active participation in the use of the backcountry resource by stock users and the general public commensu rate with our heritage.
5. To foster and encourage the formation of new state organizations and BCHA.

The Back Country Horsemen organization engages in many trail mainte-nance projects every summer in partnership with the Forest Service and local packers in order to keep trails open and passable. Back Country Horsemen volunteers contributed 650,000 service hours, valued at 12.3 million dollars, in a six-year period. The organization also educates their members as well as the general public in gentle use camping techniques to minimize any adverse impacts on natural resources.

Horses and mule strings still have the right-of-way on the trails and most backpackers cheerfully step off the trail on the downside. Hikers often com-ment to the packer that, next year, they'll have the mules carry their packs as they labor up a steep trail. Pack station owners are very aware that a large percentage of their customers are ex-backpackers who still like to hike without heavy packs on their backs, love the backcountry, and wish to continue camp-ing in the wilderness.

A newer type of use in the Sierra is the increase in backpacking on the Pacific Crest Trail, which travels from Mexico to Canada, border to border. PCT usage began with mostly horseback travelers, but primarily consists of back-packers today. While the trail crosses public lands, there are many different agencies managing the lands. The trail crosses national forests, national parks, state parks, Bureau of Land Management land, wilderness areas, and wildlife reserves in three states—California, Oregon, and Washington.

Some special interest and environmental organizations proposed elimina-tion of the historic packing industry from the High Sierra landscape. Certain organizations attempted to advance their agendas, not through legislation, but through the court system, by filing continuous lawsuits and appeals. These organizations contended that pack stations' commercial use was in violation of the Wilderness Act, and that their activities caused irreparable resource dam-age in wilderness areas. They asserted that horse and mule transportation was not appropriate for wilderness as they sought to ban this recreational use.

The 1964 Wilderness Act states that lands admitted into the National Wil-derness Preservation System will continue the existing activities and conditions as permitted when accepted into the system. In order to be accepted into the Wilderness System, lands must meet established criteria for wilderness. Established wilderness areas are, by law, open for all the American public to access and enjoy. Commercial pack stations were permitted and operating many years prior to the passage of the 1964 Wilderness Act.

This statement issued to the public from the Inyo National Forest briefly stated the recent events that had occurred:

> *In April 2000, a lawsuit filed against the Inyo and Sierra National Forests (by Wilderness Watch and High Sierra Hikers Association) alleged violations of the National Forest Management Act, National Environmental Policy Act (NEPA), and the Wilderness Act. The judge overseeing the lawsuit issued a ruling on the litigation and found in favor of the plaintiffs, although only on the NEPA claim. The Court determined that in authorizing the Special Use Permits for the pack stations, the Forest Service failed to adequately document environmental impacts as required by the NEPA. A Court Order was issued that required the Forest Service to complete the site specific NEPA process for these permits no later than 2006.*

In 2001, the new Wilderness Management Plans for the John Muir and Ansel Adams Wilderness Areas were completed and issued by the Sierra and Inyo National Forests. These plans reflect the demands by the San Francisco court ruling for the plaintiffs against the Forest Service. Severe regulations and restrictions against the public using commercial stock-supported services was the unfortunate result. The High Sierra Packers' Association then filed a lawsuit against the Forest Service over elements of the other lawsuit, and the new 2001 Wilderness Plan that had been adjusted to appease environmental organizations threatening to appeal.

The nineteen permitted pack stations in the two wilderness areas, with specified conditions and restrictions, were court ordered to conduct twenty percent less business (handle less customer pack trips and day rides) in those wildernesses, until the NEPA analysis was completed. This meant there were twenty percent less opportunities for the general public to use these services to access the wilderness areas.

From Forest Service reports at the time stated:

> *In 2001, the Northern California U.S. District Court issued a Court Order that required the Forest Service to evaluate the cumulative impacts of commercial pack stock operations in the AA/JM Wildernesses by December 2005. The Court also ordered that the site-specific impacts of each special use permit issued the commercial pack station be analyzed in a subsequent NEPA analysis to be completed by December 2006.*

During the course of this lawsuit, the Federal Court ordered the Forest Service to do a Cumulative Effects Analysis EIS (Environmental Impact Study), June, 2004, on commercial packing. In the introduction to the DEIS (Draft EIS), the Forest Service explained the details of the court order:

> *A Court Order was issued that required the Forest Service to complete a two-step process for issuing commercial pack stock special use permits. First, a cumulative impact analysis of pack stock operations in the AA/JM Wildernesses was to be completed no later than December 2005. Secondly, by December 2006, the Forest Service was to complete a site-specific analysis for each permittee. The*

last requirement is fulfilled through this document. The court allowed all nineteen pack station operations on the Inyo and Sierra National Forests to continue to be authorized, with specified conditions and restrictions imposed by the court. The pack stations have been operating under this restriction since 2002. It should be noted that, due to this court injunction, the 2001 and 2005 wilderness directions have not been fully implemented as designed.

The Forest Service interpreted the court-ordered two-step NEPA process in a way that the two documents ordered were not meant to revisit the same topics covered by the 2001 Wilderness Plan.

Pack station permits had been held in limbo, since most expired in 1999 through 2006, with the Forest Service issuing one-year temporary permits to them. This was a difficult, unpleasant business climate and a ruinous economic situation for pack station owners. The Forest Service completed the 2005 *Trails and Commercial Pack Stock Management in the Ansel Adams and John Muir Wildernesses* Draft EIS in December of that year. The ninety-day public opportunity to comment on the draft, where people could express their concerns, contribute input, and propose changes, ended in May of 2006.

In January of 2007, the Forest Service issued the *Final Environmental Impact Statement for Commercial Pack Station and Pack Stock Outfitter/ Guide Permit Issuance* by both the Sierra National Forest and the Inyo National Forest. A Record of Decision on the FEIS documents by both Forest Supervisors stated that they intended to reissue twenty year Resort Special Use Permits to the nineteen commercial pack stations operating in these areas who had applied for a reissue of their permit. In the Record of Decision, Supervisor Edward Cole of the Sierra National Forest wrote, "Every packer receiving an SUP [Special Use Permit] is serving a demonstrated need and granting the permits will not degrade wilderness character."

Jennifer Roeser, representing the High Sierra Packers' Association, Eastern Unit, and the National Forest Recreation Association, testified before the Congressional House Sub-Committee on National Parks, Recreation, and Public Lands on September 30, 2003, on the *Right-to-Ride Livestock on Federal Lands Act of 2003.* She testified:

> *Our link to the past is important as it provides us with an understanding of the processes that shaped our American history and culture. Many users of pack and saddle stock seek to find and experience the historic activities of an earlier time. To be able to view and live as our early explorers did provides many users the opportunity to connect with history outside of a museum setting. Our link to the past is our ability to carry out this tradition and culture of the early-day pioneers and to work to insure that these traditional skills are not lost to future generations. As we begin our journey into the twenty-first century, free and unrestricted wilderness travel is fast becoming an anachronism. Incremental restrictions and regulations threaten the very essence of a wilderness experience, and the ability to continue historic patterns and types of travel in remote, unroaded backcountry is eroding year by year.*

Jennifer Roeser continued:

> *Perhaps Aldo Leopold, a wilderness advocate and U.S. Forest Service Ranger in New Mexico in the early 1900s best expressed the concept of packing history as being an important value of wilderness when he wrote, 'The time is almost upon us when a pack train must wind its way up a graveled highway and turn its bell*

mare into the pasture of a summer hotel. When that day comes, the diamond hitch will be merely a rope; Kit Carson and Jim Bridger will be only names in a history lesson... If, once in a while man has a chance to throw the diamond hitch and travel back in time, he is just that much more civilized than he would have been without that opportunity...'

In the 2005 *Back Country Horsemen of America Newsletter*, Steve Didler, Public Lands Officer, wrote the (BCHA Position Statement on a Wilderness Purity Concept.) Included in the statement is the following clarification of the current situation:

The efforts of the managing agencies to place a higher emphasis on restoring pristine conditions are the result of a misguided preservation/purity bias that has been prevalent since before the Wilderness Act was passed. The purity doctrine was addressed by Congress during the 1970s in two important pieces of legislation. The first was a statute adding numerous areas of forest in the eastern states to the wilderness system. The second was the Endangered American Wilderness Act of 1978. The House Report of the Endangered American Wilderness Bill (Report 95-540, July 28, 1977) specifically directed the managing agencies to abandon the purity approach. Congress clearly expected that wilderness would accommodate a wide spectrum of Americans who desired wilderness-type recreation experiences of a nature that were established at the time the law was passed. The intent of Congress (emphasized throughout the Congressional Record) was to preserve existing conditions while providing for existing and future use. Nowhere does the Wilderness Act or Congressional Record require restoring wilderness to a condition more pristine than that which existed prior to designation, and nowhere does it define 'special' categories of users that will be favored through implementation of the law.

Didler further wrote:

As a result of a perceived need to provide 'stock free' opportunities, zones are being created to accommodate a 'wilder-elite' who prefers not to see horses and mules (or signs of their presence). In doing so, customary and historical users are being excluded from areas commonly and historically frequented by pack and saddle stock users.

In the January 2007 Record of Decision, Supervisor Edward Cole of the Sierra National Forest clarifies the following concerning wilderness character and pureness:

If we were to analyze the effects of any action (including those not within the scope of this analysis) in wilderness as compared to 'pure' wilderness, then any action would be a violation of agency regulations because every action that would allow for any kind of human impact (including any kind of visitor use) would have an adverse impact to wilderness character and would violate the Forest Service's non-degradation policy. Furthermore, this comparison would not align with the intent of Congress, which clearly intended to allow for the 'use and enjoyment' (the Wilderness Act, Public Law 94-577) of wilderness areas, which inherently means that some human impacts are acceptable, so long as the level of the impacts are below a certain threshold and wilderness character is not being degraded below current conditions.

For the vast and remarkable Sierra Nevada wilderness areas to continue to exist in this changing California, there must be a broad, diverse user base. It needs to include those who will be advocates and champions for the whole historic and cultural wilderness experience. If our young people are not experiencing hands-on wilderness trips by participation in youth group, family, or organizational pack trips, they will be less likely to become future responsible wilderness proponents.

Adeline Smith of the Muir Trail Ranch wrote these words for their advertising:

> We have offered the ranch for public use because we believe that America's wild lands should be experienced by people so they don't lose touch with the things that inspired generations of our ancestors. An outdoor program on the Discovery Channel or the manicured lawn and neatly trimmed trees of an urban park aren't a good substitute for the real thing—the wild land in its natural state that surrounds us.

Enjoyment should never be regulated out of a wilderness experience. Wilderness is more than an aesthetic, scenic place to view, and limiting it to that role degrades wilderness experiences. Wilderness is not a museum or a Disney theme park, where people are merely allowed to pass through and look, but not to touch, leave the trail, camp, or interact with the environment.

David Brower prophetically wrote these words of advice in 1947 in the *Sierra Club Bulletin*:

> The argument that John Muir presented remains essentially valid. If we want mountain wilderness—the spacious scenic wilderness that means something—we must make it known to the men who, in knowing it, will protect it. Those who like best the most Spartan of wilderness trips—cross-country backpacking—must make haste slowly in any attempts to impose such trips upon others, or there may be too few men in the wilderness to protect it.

Brower continues:

> To hold the wilderness, however, we need defenders of all ages who have at some time in their lives traveled the wilderness trails. We need so many of them that we must, as the pressure for all types of mountain-recreation grows, get as many of these defenders out on those trails as we can with the least possible damage per man per visit.

These words are incredibly true today and should be considered conscientiously by all advocates of the wilderness experience.

Let us embrace prudent use by all the public desiring to visit our spectacular Sierra Nevada Mountains. We need enough conservation to protect our abundant natural resources, while encouraging the public visitors to experience wild spaces in a user-friendly way. A reasonable amount of human and stock impact does not permanently damage the natural environment. Vacationing people and packers with pack and saddle stock have long been part of the natural environment in the Sierra. Between the extremes of natural resource exploitation and resource preservation, there is a vast middle zone of sustainable wilderness to be enjoyed by all the American public.

Packers, horses, and mules continue to traverse the switchback trails of the Sierra. They provide services, accessibility, and memories for a lifetime to vacationers in order to enhance their experiences of the American wilderness.

INYO NATIONAL FOREST PACK STOCK PROGRAM
R5 REGIONAL PACK STOCK CENTER OF EXCELLENCE

The Inyo National Forest Service packing program has stock and packing facilities in Bishop at the Mann Ranch, in Mammoth Lakes at the Tack Room on Sherwin Creek Road, and at other stock facilities throughout the Inyo Forest. A new packing facility was built near the old Tack Room in 2008. In the distant past, when their programs were smaller, the Forest Service contracted with commercial pack stations for packing services, but now, the agency uses their own packing operation in managing the wilderness lands. They pack in trail crews, fire crews, wilderness rangers, biologists, administrators, and others into the various federal wilderness areas. The Forest Service still depends on commercial pack station services when their packing team is gone on fire assignments.

Michael Morse is the Forest Pack Stock Program Manager and Region 5 South Zone Pack Stock Co-Director. He has packed for the Inyo Forest since 1974, when he was first hired in a trail crew/packer position. Lee Roeser, my son, has packed for the Inyo Forest since 2002, utilizing his extensive knowledge of commercial packing, stock, and gear. He works as the Regional Master Packer for the R5 Regional Pack Stock Center of Excellence, overseeing the packing operations in the Inyo National Forest. Michael and Lee implement packing and fire training programs to standardize packer procedures and methods for Forest Service personnel and other government agencies. They also give public presentations for Back Country Horsemen groups, Mule Days visitors, and other educational venues. They have created a trainee program to mentor and prepare selected packers to transition into lead pack stock positions with the Forest and Park Services.

Michael and Lee are an integral part of R5 Regional Pack Stock Center of Excellence, created in 2013 to coordinate logistics and assist with stock-supported backcountry fire and trail crews, packing in necessary supplies, equipment, and materials. During the normal operating season, their packing program is available 24/7 for emergencies as needed within the wilderness areas, such as fire, natural disasters, and damaged bridges. Their exemplary program and their commitment to training, mentoring, and teaching at a high level of professionalism is passing along traditional, historic packing skills in the Sierra.

Lee Roeser with his Forest Service pack string in Big Whitney Meadow. (Lee and Jen Roeser)

Michael Morse and Lee Roeser of the Inyo National Forest during a packing seminar.

Inyo National Forest packer Lee Roeser giving an educational packing demonstration.

Inyo National Forest mules packing heavy bridge planks to repair a backcountry bridge. (Lee and Jen Roeser Collection)

Inyo National Forest mule dragging logs for construction projects. (Lee and Jen Roeser Collection)

145

Jen Roeser rests her string on McGee Pass, with Fish Creek Basin to the south.
(Lee and Jen Roeser Collection)

Lee and his saddle mule on the F. S. Mt. Whitney Trail Project 2013.
(Lee and Jen Roeser Collection)

Lee and Jen Roeser are knowledgeable leaders in the packing industry in Calif. (Sandy Powell Photography)

Bear cans and boxes are now required on trips to keep bears out of customers' food.

Lee and Jen Roeser's Twenty Mule String of matched black mules, opens each arena show for the National Anthem at Mule Days over Memorial Day. (Lee and Jen Roeser Collection)

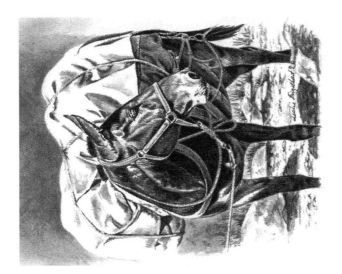

Pack Mule John

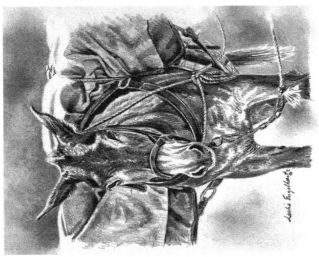

Sorrel Mule Alice

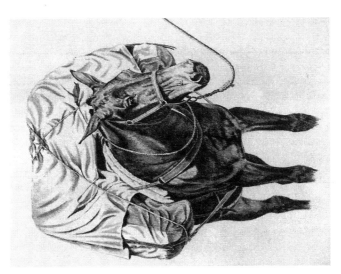

Loaded Sally

Leslie Roeser Engelhart is a skilled western pencil artist, her drawings accurate to the last detail.

THE ACTUAL DIAMOND IS COMPLETED.

DIAMOND
~ MLPO ~
HITCH
(RJD)

Rene 's sketch of the complete sequence of a MLPO packer tying the
diamond hitch on a packed mule. (Rene Duykaerts)

"The Long Drive"

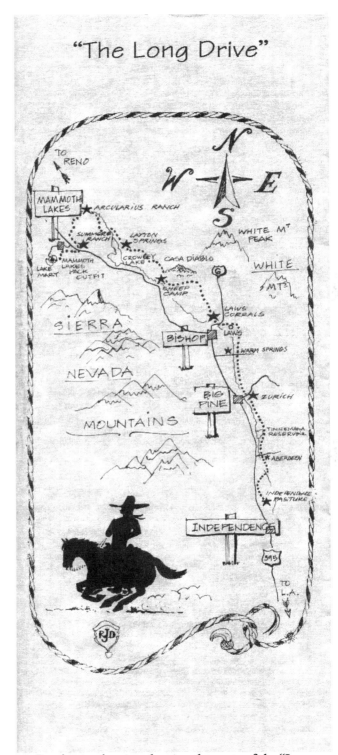

Rene's map drawing showing the route of the "Long Trail," detailing MLPO Horse Drives.   (Rene Duykaerts)

151

MLPO family and crew pictured at the end of a Horse Drive. Rear L-R: Lou Roeser, Kerry Roeser, Mike Elam, Maryl Roeser, Jen Roeser, Rene Duykaerts, Lee Roeser. Front L-R: Marye Roeser, Scott Lee. (William Shepley Photography)

Jen Roeser with pack string on Laurel Pass Trail overlooking Genevieve Lake. (Sandy Powell Photography)

Lee Roeser with pack string in McGee Canyon. (Sandy Powell Photography)

**Mule string led by packer Bobby Tanner in front of Rainbow Falls in the 1970s.
(Russ and Anne Johnson)**

Kerry Roeser leads a string above Duck Lake heading for the Silver Divide.

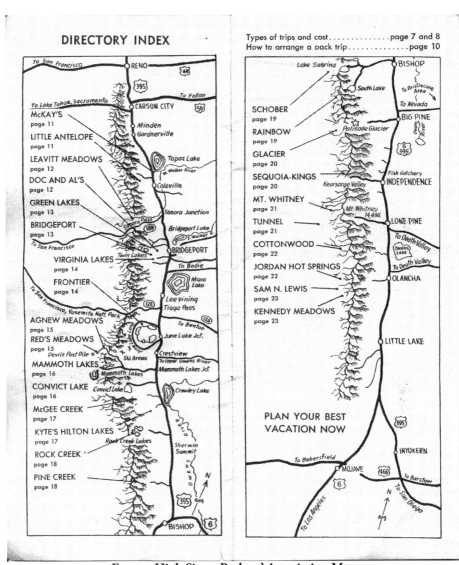

DIRECTORY INDEX

Types of trips and cost.............page 7 and 8
How to arrange a pack trip.............page 10

PLAN YOUR BEST
VACATION NOW

Eastern High Sierra Packers' Association Map.

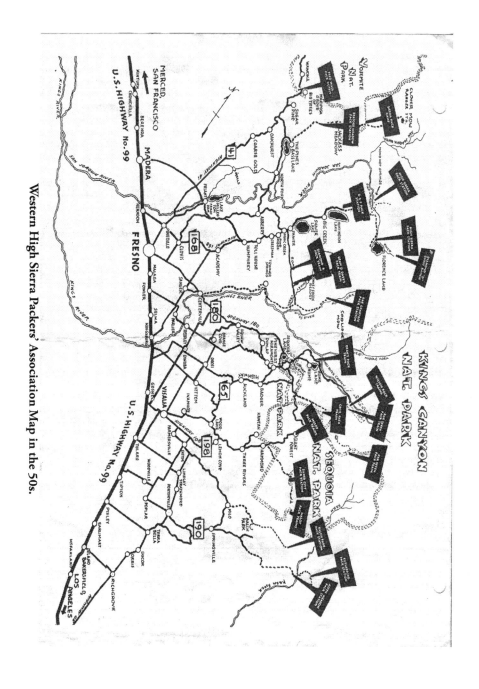

Western High Sierra Packers' Association Map in the 50s.

The Roeser family in front of office at MLPO in 1987.
Pictured from L-R: Lou, Kerry, Leslie, Maryl, Marye & Lee Roeser.

Mike Elam leads his string of mules to the packing dock.

Packer Scott Lee is shoeing by the corrals at MLPO.

Trail ride at McGee Creek Pack Station.

Maryl Roeser helps packer Ed Leos tie a diamond hitch to secure the pack load.

**Lee Roeser, wearing chinks, is ready to mount his horse
and lead his pack string up the trail.**

Scott Lee heads out of the MLPO yard leading his string.

MLPO packers, '65. L-R: Barney Chapman, Lou Roeser,
Red Altum, Butch Willmon.

MLPO crew, '76. R L-R: Gene, Steve, Al, Rob, Dan, Lee, Lou.
F L-R : Hank, Patti, Kerry, Leslie.

MLPO packers "take five," '70s. L-R: Rob Willis, Lee Roeser,
Brad Harlan, Gene Cooper.

Stock trucks were used to haul horses and mules at each station.

Kerry Roeser tops Duck Pass with her string.
At camp, she trades spurs for an apron.

Matt Durham leads his party up and over Duck Pass.

Rene Duykaerts looking back at his string and packer behind him on Duck Pass.

Lou Roeser will throw a pack tarp over the load before tying on a diamond hitch.

Lou Roeser leads his party on the John Muir Trail.

Leslie Roeser packs a party out of an upper lake in the Mammoth Lakes Basin.

Packer Wilfred Partridge assists cook Kerry Roeser, with a fire, on a UC Riverside trip.

167

A "nice mess," of rainbow trout, alongside a wicker creel. (Russ and Anne Johnson)

Matt and Leslie Engelhart welcome hot coffee on a chilly backcountry morning.

Packer/cook Larry Maurice, well known cowboy poet, preparing
his signature chicken cordon bleu.

Dan Farris' party looks forward to his famous pancakes, along with cowboy coffee.

169

A delicious peach cobbler, prepared in a dutch oven, is ready to enjoy.

Marye Roeser prepares breakfast on a collapsible
sheepherder stove that folds up.

Custom cook boxes assist camp cook Kerry Roeser, creating storage and a work space.

In camp, pans are placed at the cooking fire circle, which is topped with a steel grate.

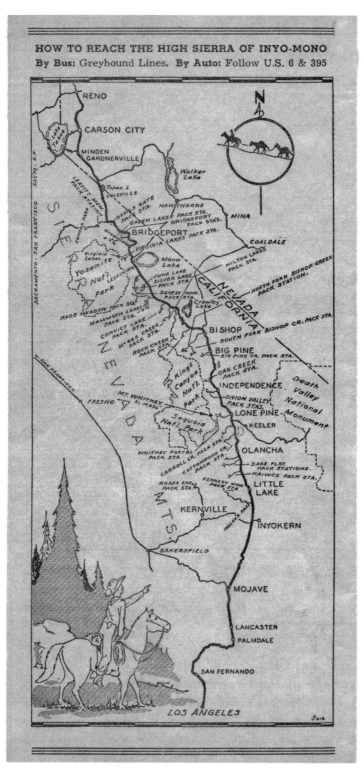

A 1950s map of Eastern High Sierra pack stations was drawn for a brochure.

APPENDIX

EASTERN HIGH SIERRA PACK STATIONS

SOUTHERN SIERRA AND THE KERN PLATEAU

The Kern Plateau is a high-elevation tableland located at the southern tip of the Sierra Nevada Mountains, and comprises more than 950 square miles of country. The country is rolling hills and ridges covered with forests, interspersed with vast sprawling meadows, with the South Fork of the Kern River and Little Kern River running through. It was not glaciated like the mountains just to the north.

The Inyo and Sequoia National Forests cover the Plateau, intermixed with some private property. The Golden Trout Wilderness, the Southern Sierra Wilderness, and the Domeland Wilderness Areas are located on parts of the vast plateau.

Beginning with the advent of the California Gold Rush in 1849, the huge population surge of miners and new towns demanded more meat. Sheep were brought in from New Mexico and Mexico, wintering in the Central Valley and summering in the mountains. From about 1860 until 1893, when sheep grazing was banned, innumerable sheep herds summered in the many meadows. By 1898, most of the sheep were gone from the plateau, and cattle herds began replacing the sheep flocks. By 1915, cattle ranchers with Forest Service grazing permits had built permanent cow camps in many of the meadows. Some cattle grazing still continues in this backcountry, and ranch cowboys stay at the cow camps.

Dee Gill was an early packer who packed salt to the many herds on the Kern Plateau from the Saline Valley salt fields near Death Valley. This was a three-week trip, crossing two mountain ranges with very heavy loads packed on the mules.

The Kern Plateau is the home of the California State Fish, the Golden Trout. These colorful trout evolved in the creeks on the plateau, such as Volcano Creek and the South Fork of the Kern. Early sheepherders and ranchers helped spread these golden beauties throughout the area.

After World War I, in the 1920s and '30s, airplanes flew into landing strips built in the meadows. Hunters and fishermen packed into backcountry camps, campsites, and lodges. Movie companies discovered the area, and early films were shot on the Kern Plateau.

U.S. Highway 395 travels the length of the eastern Sierra in California. As the southern Sierra region was the closest to population centers in Southern California, pack stations were established in this region first. Many mountain fishing and hunting pack trips originated in this area. The Kern River and Kern Plateau were early popular and accessible destinations.

LITTLE LAKE AND COSO JUNCTION

Little Lake Pack Station was located at the Little Lake Hotel by Little Lake, north of Mojave. It was owned by Charles Whittock until 1915, when

Bill and Elvira Bramlette purchased the property. Bill Bramlette, who had arrived at Little Lake in 1910, was a race car driver and a founder of the AAA Auto Club. Bramlette built many new structures to provide for the growing tourist trade, and eventually purchased 1,200 surrounding acres to form the Little Lake Ranch.

In the early 1900s, James Cowan homesteaded a site ten miles north of Little Lake on the Midland Trail. In 1923, he operated a pack station with about seventeen head of stock. Highway 395 was realigned north from Little Lake in 1929, and this changed the course of the Midland Trail. Cowan moved west to what is now called Dunmovin and called his station **Cowan Station**. Sam Lewis packed for Cowan when Lewis first arrived in the area, and later purchased the packing operation, merging it with his outfit. In 1936, Charles and Hilda King purchased Cowan Station. Charlie renamed it Dunmovin, as he asserted he was "done moving." They operated the gas station and store, but no longer packed parties into Kennedy Meadows.

Sam Lewis intended to look for a job on the construction site of the Los Angeles Aqueduct. In 1914, riding a horse and leading a packhorse with all of his possessions, he headed north from Los Angeles to Little Lake. Here he remained, breaking horses for Bill Bramlette at the Little Lake Ranch, as well as working at Little Lake Pack Station. In 1916, Lewis homesteaded a place at Portuguese Bench, a grassy bench up against the Sierra, about two miles west of Highway 395 and eight miles north of Little Lake. Lewis called the place High Lonesome Ranch. He then left to serve in the Navy during World War I until 1918, when he returned. He married Olive Truax from Inyokern and built a home on his ranch property.

When Lewis returned to the area, he commenced purchasing horses for the pack station he planned to establish. He considered Bill Bramlette his mentor, and said he was the one who helped him break into the packing business. After he bought out Bramlette's small Little Lake Pack Station, he purchased Cowan's outfit. These purchases gave him Forest Service permits for additional backcountry areas and Haiwee Canyon. Haiwee Canyon is north of Little Lake, fifteen miles north of Portuguese Bench and High Lonesome Ranch, and is at 8,200 feet in elevation.

At the end of the road, at the mouth of Haiwee Canyon, he built his new pack station on the desert flat looking toward the Haiwee Reservoir, calling it the **Sam Lewis Pack Train**. From the summit of Haiwee Pass, it is only about a mile and a half to the South Fork of the Kern River, and then up to Dutch John Flat and Deer Mountain. Lewis packed into Haiwee Canyon, Deer Mountain, Dutch John Flat, Fish Creek, Olancha Pass, and the headwaters of the South Fork of the Kern River. His pack trains traveled from Kennedy Meadows to Mt. Whitney, throughout the Monache Meadows and Kern Plateau, from Mt. Whitney to Domeland, and from Summit Meadows to the main Kern River.

Lewis built large log cabin camps at several locations, cutting the logs himself and hauling them to the campsites with a team of horses. By 1928, he had built four of these cabins at Troy Meadow (ten miles from Kennedy Meadows), Dutch Flat, Deer Mountain, and Casa Vieja. He constructed these backcountry cabins for his packers and customers. His wife, Olive, often accompanied them and cooked for the parties, assisted by their six children, who were great helpers early on. There were many hunting trips in the fall.

The Nine Mile Canyon Road to Kennedy Meadows and Blackrock was improved in 1933. By 1934, Sam ran forty head of stock. He packed only horses, and was one of the few Sierra packers not to pack mules. His pack stock was not strung together; the packed horses were loose herded to the camps on the Kern Plateau. Apparently, the animals knew the way and the routine, as they trailed themselves to the corral at the designated camp, accompanied by their packer. During the winter, Lewis pastured his stock to the west of his homestead on Portuguese Bench, near the mountains.

In 1946, his son, Sam Lewis Jr., joined him in the business, and in 1959, Sam retired and his son took over the business. Sam Lewis Jr. continued the packing operations, and in 1964, he was president of the Eastern High Sierra Packers' Association. Sam Lewis Pack Train packed the fully-catered Joseph Wampler traveling trips up and down the John Muir Trail for six weeks during the summers for some years. Joseph Wampler personally led these trips, and his customers could join along the way for a week, two weeks, or more.

After he was released from the U.S. Army Signal Corps at the end of World War II, Joe Wampler renewed his love of the Sierra. He went on the Sierra Club High Trips as a wood cutter from 1946 through 1949. This led him to organizing his own trips. His headquarters were in Berkeley, California. In 1950, he began his schedule of John Muir Trail Trips, with groups from twelve to twenty-five at a time. Besides himself, he had a cook, second cook, and one or two college students as camp helpers. During the remainder of the year, he led wilderness trips in Arizona and Mexico. In 1960, he wrote and published a book on the Sierra titled *High Sierra Mountain Wonderland.*

By 1965, Sam Lewis Jr. had ceased his packing business. The Forest Service permit lease for Haiwee Canyon and the pack station facilities became available again in 1967. John Slaughter from Altadena, California, quickly snapped it up. He had been coming to the area since 1950 and loved it. He renamed the pack station the **Sierra Lady Pack Station**. He conducted pack trips over Haiwee Pass to Dutch Flat, and utilized three of the old Sam Lewis log cabins. In the fall of 1972, the main cabin at the pack station burned. At the same time, the Forest Service closed the lease, as the area of the Haiwee Pass and the cabins (part of the lease) were located in the new Golden Trout Wilderness Area. The Forest Service also burned down the backcountry cabins.

The **Thelan Pack Station** at Coso Junction was on the old Midland Trail, about two miles north of Little Lake. Horace Percy Thelan and his wife, Mabel, homesteaded the property in 1922. They operated a store, post office, and gas station there. They also owned a pack station with twenty head of horses and mules that packed into Kennedy Meadows. In 1934, Thelan was a charter member of the Westside High Sierra Packers' Association.

In 1921, brothers Chester and Kenneth Wortley began operating a pack station called **Wortley Brothers** at Sand Canyon, just above the Mojave Desert and off of Highway 395. They packed parties into the South Fork of the Kern River. A year later, a heavy cloudburst and flash flood wiped out their facilities. The brothers then moved their headquarters to Nine Mile Canyon. At that time, the road ended at the Los Angeles Aqueduct, so they had to construct a road from that crossing to their new headquarters three miles up the canyon.

They quickly earned a highly respected reputation as good packers and were soon packing in many prominent people from Southern California. In 1925, the brothers moved again, this time to the Bloomfield Ranch in the Kern River Valley, near the South Fork of the Kern River. Chester died in 1932, but Ken continued on, and later operated a pack station at Beach Meadow, northwest of Troy Meadow and Blackrock, in 1962.

TROY MEADOW AND KENNEDY MEADOWS

Jerome and Kirk Troy ran sheep in the meadows beginning in 1871, thus giving their name to Troy Meadow. Cattle ranchers from the west and south settled Kennedy Meadows in the 1880s, grazing the meadows during the summer season. Small homesteads were filed by ranchers. The meadows have also been called Cannell Meadows.

The Nine Mile Canyon road to Kennedy Meadows from Highway 395, up Nine Mile Canyon, was constructed in 1929 and improved in 1933. It is a twenty-seven-mile drive to the South Fork of the Kern River and Kennedy Meadows from the junction of Highway 395. The Pacific Crest Trail travels through this area. This road also accesses nearby Troy Meadow, where pack stations were located. Troy Meadow is located west of Kennedy Meadows, with Fish Creek running through it. Ranchers have continued to own private land in the meadow. The road continues on to the Blackrock Ranger Station and Blackrock Trailhead. Many summer homes have been built in the area today.

At the turn of the century, this was a very busy region. Besides the cattle herds grazing during the summer, there were many recreationists from both sides of the Sierra accessing the area by the Jordan Trail. Monache Meadows and the Kern River were popular destinations. The summer season opened here earlier than many other areas because of the relatively lower elevation.

The Sherman Pass Road from the North Fork of the Kern River is now paved and intersects the Kennedy Meadows Road near Black Rock. Thus, one can drive from the North Fork of the Kern River, above Kernville, to the Sherman Pass Road, to the Kennedy Meadows Road and Nine Mile Canyon, and then to Highway 395 near Olancha.

In 1945, the Forest Service offered a new pack station permit to Murray and Lothelle Hall to establish a pack station in Kennedy Meadows/Troy Meadow. Previously, Murray Hall had packed in the Los Padres Forest, packed for the Forest Service, and was head packer for Sequoia and Kings Canyon National Parks for three years during World War II. He then leased and operated the Silver City Pack Station, below Mineral King, from Craig Thorne for two years.

After accepting the Forest Service permit, the Hall family, which included their two sons, Bud and Dave, moved to the China Lake Naval Station, where they operated a riding stable and leased a cattle ranch in Jawbone Canyon.

The Halls called their pack station **Kennedy Meadows Pack Trains** or Pack Station. Their headquarters were built on private property, upstream on Fish Creek from Troy Meadow. The location was about ten miles from Kennedy Meadows. They built a kitchen, dining room, office house, bunkhouse, saddle shed, corrals, and other facilities, as there were previously none there. Murray's older son, Bud, was actively involved with his dad in the operation of the pack station. Dave, the younger son, packed in the summers and went to school in the winter. Murray Hall also purchased a pack station in Onion Valley from Harold Gill in 1946.

In 1958, the Halls sold the Kennedy Meadows Pack Trains, along with the pack station at Onion Valley, to Irwin Burkhart and his nephew, Gene Burkhart. Twenty-three head of stock were included with the pack station sale. After their first season, the Burkharts split their partnership, and Irwin and his wife, Alice, took the Troy Meadow location, and Gene and his wife, Lona, chose the Onion Valley station.

Irwin and Alice Burkhart, along with their son, Bob, later purchased Jordan Hot Springs. The staff and livestock were moved between the two locations as business demanded. For trips into Jordan Hot Springs Resort, the stock was trucked to Blackrock Trailhead, then trailed two miles to Casa Vieja Meadow, and then turned west for three more miles down Nine Mile Creek to the resort.

Irwin Burkhart also owned and operated the historic Onyx Store on the Isabella/Walker Pass Road (Highway 178). Their horses and mules were pastured on the nearby ranch of their son, Bob, who was associated with them in the business in later years. The ranch was just east of Onyx village.

Their season began with a fifty-mile horse drive from the winter range east of Onyx on the Walker Pass Road. From Walker Pass, they traveled cross-country to the Troy Meadow headquarters. In the fall, after deer season was over and snow began to fly, the horses and mules were again driven back to winter pasture. In 1981, they operated with fifty to seventy head of horses and mules. They packed into the Kern Plateau for hunting and fishing trips and the Kern River. Irwin and Alice Burkhart operated Kennedy Meadows Pack Trains, which included Jordan Hot Springs, for twenty-four years.

Former packer Bob Quinn and his wife, Tiese, purchased the pack station from the Burkharts in 1982. The Quinns began proceedings to have the old buildings of Jordan Hot Springs accepted into the Historic Buildings designation. In 1985, Jim and Julie Porter acquired the pack station. The resort permit for Jordan Hot Springs expired in 1990 and was not renewed by the Forest Service, as it was now located within the newly designated Golden Trout Wilderness Area.

In 1992, Don and Phyllis Bedell, owners of Mineral King Pack Station, took over the Kennedy Meadows permit from the Porters. The Bedells' location was just off the Blackrock Road and did not have any facilities, so Don moved in a camp trailer and put up a corral. He had to haul water to the site. The Forest Service requested that the pack station site be established about one mile below the Blackrock Ranger Station on Forest Service land. The road ended a short distance beyond Blackrock at the trailhead. After 1997, the Bedells dropped the permit due to difficulties in building a new facility.

Stanley Carver, owner of a ranch in Troy Meadow on private property, then operated for one year, in 2000, on his private land, and called his station **Troy Meadow Outfitters**. He offered hunting and fishing trips as before and guided day trail rides. The huge Sequoia Forest Fire burned the whole area in 2001, and Carver did not reopen.

Into the early '60s, Sam N. Lewis Pack Train operated at **Troy Meadow Pack Station,** where Sam Lewis Sr. had built a log cabin camp in the late '20s, and at Haiwee Canyon during hunting season.

JORDAN HOT SPRINGS

Jordan Hot Springs Lodge and Pack Station was located on Nine Mile Creek at 6,680 feet elevation, a four-hour ride from Troy Meadow. The trail follows the Kern River to the turn-off to Nine Mile Creek, which contains a fine golden trout fishery. The area was also called Jordan Junction.

Buildings were constructed there as early 1875, and a log lodge was built in 1890. After 1893, the vast sheep herds were banned on the Kern Plateau and were gradually replaced by cattle. The cattle ranchers built cow camps on their Forest Service grazing permits and brought their families in for the summer grazing season. The cabins and corrals were constructed of logs cut near the site and dragged to the cabin area. The time from about 1900 to 1950 is considered the Cow Camp Era.

In 1915, people packed into the historic resort area, particularly from the west side of the Sierra, with families staying most of the summer. It was a busy local gathering place. Dances were held on a wooden platform, and the hot springs were very popular. By 1916, there was a telephone line into Jordan Hot Springs which ran from the Tunnel Meadow Forest Service Station through Casa Vieja, Jordan, Monache Meadows, and on to other Forest Service stations. A store was located there, and local ranchers could buy needed groceries. Early packers on the eastside, including Henry Olivas from Olivas Pack Train and Ollie Dearborn from Carroll Creek Pack Station, packed in store supplies, as well as guests and their gear. The store permittee accepted outgoing mail from area ranchers and visitors, and was required to take mail out at least once a week to Inyokern. Mail was almost the only method of communication. The telephone line in 1916 was unreliable and only went to the Forest Service Station.

Hal L.Womack had the Forest Service permit at Jordan Hot Springs in 1920, and built some early resort buildings. Walter Dow, who owned the Dow Hotel in Lone Pine, bought the permit and resort in 1925. Dow installed a Pelton wheel, as well as a sawmill powered by a Model B Ford motor that sawed the needed timber on location. He constructed the dining room, kitchen buildings, and tent platforms with lumber milled in Monache Meadows. There were four sleeping cabins, a dining room and kitchen, three bath houses for the mineral baths, two tent cabins, a cook's cabin, and a saddle shed with corral, in addition to the main lodge. The kitchen contained two wood stoves. One was a household sized stove, and the other was a huge stove salvaged from an old steam ship that burned fireplace-sized logs. Irwin Burkhart claimed that he was told it took twenty mules to pack the monster stove into the resort. The lodge, kitchen, and dining room were powered by a generator that was run by the small Pelton wheel. This provided power only for lights. Servel refrigerators ran on propane.

There were fourteen hot springs located on Nine Mile Creek, and just below the resort, three cement bathing tubs were developed. One tub was a curiosity. It was a hollowed out log that was just coated with cement. The hot springs permit was held by the resort.

In the 1920s and '30s, the resort was very popular with ranch families from the San Joaquin Valley and the Owens Valley. Families packed into the resort to escape heat of the valleys. Families would stay for long periods of time, and the men would come to the resort as soon as the haying and harvesting were finished. A cement dance floor was constructed, and remnants of that floor can still be seen.

The pack station operated with thirty head of stock. From this area, trips were conducted into Tunnel Meadow, Lloyd Meadows, Grasshopper Flat, Little Whitney Meadows, and the Upper Kern River. Trips via Casa Vieja accessed Monache Meadows, Templeton Meadows, and the South Fork of the Kern River. At Casa Vieja, the Forest Service had a ranger camp that was a hub for various trails.

From the eastside, Jordan Pack Station, gateway to the lodge, was located twenty-two miles northwest of Little Lake. After turning west, it was another six miles over a steep, narrow, gravel road to where guests met the packer and stock.

By 1935, Walter Gregg had bought the resort. Airstrips had been built in Templeton, Tunnel, and Monache Meadows. Airplanes flew into Monache Meadows from Owens Valley airfields and were met there with saddle and pack animals by appointment. Visitors then rode saddle horses, and their duffle was packed by mules down to the Jordan Hot Springs resort. The pack station also met guests at Sage Flat and packed them into the lodge.

In 1941, Clarence R. Purnell of Palm Springs, along with his brother, Elmo, and Tom Madar, purchased the resort and pack station, calling it **Purnell Bros. Pack Station** and **Jordan Hot Springs Dude Ranch and Pack Station**. Purnell pastured his stock in the winter near Independence in the Owens Valley, and operated the resort for twenty-three years. They restored the sawmill and Pelton wheel, and operated a mill for a while.

In 1964, Dr. Reginald Stocking, a veterinarian, purchased the resort from Purnell, calling it **Jordan Hot Springs Pack Station**, but had Purnell operate it for two more years. Stocking utilized the resort only for his private use as a retreat for family and friends. The number of stock used was less now—only fifteen head. It was then sold to Bob Burkhart, the son of Irwin, in 1972, and the Burkharts merged it with Kennedy Meadows Pack Trains. Bob and his wife operated it until 1981. The Quinns, who had purchased Kennedy Meadows Pack Station in 1982, were the next owners. They started the paperwork for establishing it as a Historic Landmark. The Porters then took over until 1990, when the permit expired.

Congress designated the Golden Trout Wilderness Area on Feb. 24, 1978, and Jordan Hot Springs was located within the new wilderness boundaries. This would eventually affect the operation of a resort there, as permanent structures and resorts are not permitted in designated wilderness areas. In 1990, when the permit expired, the Forest Service did not renew it. In 1992, it was registered as a Historic Landmark, and the remaining buildings are protected. The Inyo National Forest plans to maintain the buildings of the resort in a state of arrested decay.

FLY-IN MEADOWS

After World War I, with the advent of airplanes, airfields were located in a few of the larger meadows of the southern Sierra, where camp resorts were built. Airplanes flew in tourists from the Lone Pine airfield and other nearby flying fields. Flying time from Olancha or Lone Pine to Monache Meadows, located near the South Fork of the Kern River at 8,000 feet elevation, was about twenty minutes. Monache had two landing strips, while Templeton Meadows only had one. Some of these flying services were: Coso Air Pack Station, Airlift Pack Station, Symons' Flying Service, Airborn Pack Station, Sierra Airways, and Bob White's Flying Service.

An early sheepman, Ben Templeton, grazed his flocks in what came to be called Templeton Meadows from the 1860s through the 1880s. The meadows lie at 8,600 feet elevation. Hollywood discovered the eastern Sierra as a location for Western films in the 1920s. The Virginian was filmed in Templeton Meadows in 1923. Packers with their mule pack strings traveled up and down the trail daily, supplying the movie crews. The film crew built log cabins for the movie sets in what is now called Movie Stringer Meadow, and a number of these cabins are still there. The landing strip was created or improved for the use of movie crews flying in and out. Many of the cast stayed at the Dow Hotel in Lone Pine and were flown in and out.

Tunnel Meadow is a large, high meadow at 9,100 feet elevation, and derives its name from an early water scheme. During the 1880s, a severe drought gripped the Kern River Valley, and local farmers and ranchers needed more water to irrigate their fields. They devised a plan to divert Golden Trout Creek into the South Fork of the Kern River, where they needed additional water. In 1883, men from the South Fork tunneled through a low ridge separating the two streams. However, the tunnel collapsed, either on its own or with help from irate Tulare County farmers, who also coveted the water. By 1900, further efforts to divert the creek were discontinued.

Henry " Leaky" Olivas developed the **Tunnel Meadow Pack Camp and Station** in the 1920s in Tunnel Meadow. The Olivas family pack outfit dated back to the 1870s and was located in Lone Pine. The high meadow is fifteen miles southwest of Lone Pine and twenty-two miles northwest of Olancha. The airfield in the meadow was created in 1931. A Dr. Shook paid Leonard Shellenbarger, a local resident, forty dollars to form the runway so that he could fly in to fish. Shellenbarger's father, Everett, was a forest ranger there. Shellenbarger arranged to have a Fresno scraper packed in by Chrysler and Cook's Mt. Whitney Pack Trains on mules to the high meadow. A mule then pulled and dragged the scraper to create the landing field, which was 1,800 feet long.

That same summer, Colonel Hap Arnold and a friend flew in from March Air Force Base, where he was stationed, on a fishing trip. When they attempted to fly out, they had difficulty gaining altitude, and the plane crash landed in the meadow, with both men walking away. Colonel Arnold apparently was not injured and went on to have many further adventures in the Sierra. He became chief of the Air Force during World War II.

Ted Cook of Chrysler and Cook Pack Trains purchased the camp and airfield from Henry Olivas. It was named **Tunnel Pack Station/Tunnel Air Camp.** In 1936, Bruce Morgan purchased the camp from Ted Cook. Bruce and Grace Morgan and their family of five children lived at and operated the resort through 1941, when it closed due to World War II.

After the war, in 1946, Morgan sold the camp to Bob White, a pilot who owned Bob White's Flying Service at the airport in Lone Pine. White called it **Tunnel Air Camp and Pack Station** or **Tunnel Pack Station.** Accommodations were tent cabins on wooden platforms (furnished with cots and a wood stove) that encircled the compound. An office tent cabin was in the center. Two large tents held the kitchen and dining rooms, where home-cooked meals were served. Leppy Diaz managed the camp in the 1950s, followed by John "Bud" O'Keefe.

Late model Cessna aircraft were used by the flying service. White operated Cessna 170 and 206 planes. He kept a tractor at the airfield to move planes around and take gear and provisions to the camp. A mountain phone line ran out to the Lone Pine Airport.

Guide services and saddle and pack animals were available at the camp. Guests rode with a guide to nearby lakes, including the Rocky Basin Lakes, and streams to fish for golden trout, or just to enjoy visiting the beautiful surrounding country. Within easy walking or riding distance from the camp, the South Fork of the Kern River and Golden Trout Creek could be accessed. Duane Rossi, a cowboy from Big Pine, was a packer at the camp for several summers. Pack trains at Cottonwood, Onion Valley, Carroll Creek, and Mt. Whitney also packed in guests to the camp. Clint Hershey, of Walker in Mono County, packed for Bob White from 1957 through 1960, after his grandfather, Leo Rogers, sold Cottonwood Pack Station.

In 1979, after Bob White passed away, John Langenheim purchased his flying service, changing the name to Eastern Sierra Flying Service. He operated until 1988, when the backcountry camps were all closed. When the new Golden Trout Wilderness Area was established in 1978, including Tunnel Meadow, the camp and airfield had to be phased out. In 1978, the Forest Service banned private aircraft from flying into the airstrip. 1981 marked the fiftieth year of airplane operation on the Tunnel Meadows Airstrip.

Next, Murton A. Stewart and his wife, Jean, of Glacier Pack Train, purchased the **Tunnel Meadows Pack Station**. In 1982, the Forest Service closed the airstrip and the camp to all use, but determined that the pack station could still operate with the packing permit out of Sage Flat. In 1988 both the airfield and camp were closed.

Prior to the 1970s, several guide services provided anglers the opportunity to quickly access the Sierra backcountry for a fly-in fishing trip. (Stephanie Rekas)

181

OLANCHA, SAGE FLAT, COTTONWOOD CANYON, AND HORSESHOE MEADOWS

OLANCHA AND SAGE FLAT

Olancha is situated along the southwestern edge of the now dry Owens Lake. Until the 1940s, Owens Lake was an inland sea, a remnant of vast Pleistocene lakes filled by melting glaciers. Owens Lake had been gradually drying and shrinking. In the 1860s, the lake covered about a hundred square miles and was thirty feet deep. It was the center of a thriving silver mining region, and the large Cerro Gordo mine. A tramway hauled salt from Saline Valley. Two paddlewheel steamers plied the lake waters, hauling supplies from Cartago on the southwest shore to Keeler on the north. Ore from the Cerro Gordo Mine and salt were hauled on the return trip.

John Jordan blazed a trans-Sierra Trail across the mountains from Visalia to Olancha in 1861. Unfortunately, he drowned in the Kern River before completing his trail project, and G. W. Warner completed the trail over Olancha Pass. A bridge was built over the Kern River. In 1862, John Hockett constructed a more northern branch of the trail that exited the mountains over Cottonwood Pass and continued on to Lone Pine.

Sage Flat is located at the end of the Loco Ranch Road near Loco Creek, west of Highway 395. Several pack stations had corrals and facilities there. The trail up to Olancha Pass is a tough, dry trail, with little water available now, but in the past there was an old rock water trough about two thirds of the way up. The creek there is often dry. The summit of the pass is a broad sagebrush saddle, through which the trail swings down into Summit Meadows. The elevation of the trailhead on the west slope of the Owens Valley is 5,750 feet, and the pass tops off at 9,200 feet. From there, the trail heads into Tunnel Meadow.

At Summit Meadow, a trail branches off to Olivas Camp, built in 1938, and the main trail continues on to Monache Meadows. The Olivas cabin is situated along the stock driveway. Henry and Ethel Olivas and their family often fed the cowboys who were driving cattle herds to Monache Meadows.

Olivas Pack Train, started by the Olivas family, with headquarters in Lone Pine, operated out of Olancha and Sage Flat on Lobo Creek. They used Olancha Pass to pack into Monache Meadows, Tunnel Meadow, and the South Fork of the Kern River. Olivas had his corrals on one side of the mostly dry Lobo Creek bed. Barney Sears' **Monache Pack Train** had a small facility located on the other side, operating in the 1930s and '40s.

Fred Burkhardt was an early packer in the Lone Pine area and was associated with a number of partners in various early packing operations. He was born in Aurora, Nevada, but moved to Lone Pine as a child. Fred Burkhardt and Fred Cook, younger brother of Ted Cook, who later owned Chrysler and Cook Pack Station, were packing in the Sage Flat area in the 1920s. Burkhardt also packed with the Gill brothers, Harold and Wendell, local packers and pack station owners. His younger brother, Oscar, frequently packed with him. In 1923, Dick Burns and Burkhardt were operating in the Olancha area.

Fred Burkhardt and Frances Gragg operated **The Oaks Pack Train**, about five miles west of Olancha. Besides the pack station, they constructed several guest cabins. By 1934, Dick Burns was running it with forty head of horses and mules. Ralph Bauer purchased the station in 1947. From the Bauers' resort, a trail joined the Olancha Pass Trail at Sage Flat. The little ranch is now operated as a wild burro refuge.

Dan N. Cook ran a small outfit in 1923. Cook, along with Frank Chrysler, operated a packing operation in the Sage Flat area in 1934 with twenty-eight head of stock. It only operated briefly, and Chrysler bought a larger station in Lone Pine.

COTTONWOOD CANYON

Cottonwood Canyon is ten miles north of Olancha and five miles west of Highway 395. The old Cottonwood station was located on the floor of the canyon. The pack trail wound up a steep, narrow canyon past the Stevens Timber Company sawmill, then passed through Golden Trout Camp, and a right fork traveled up to the Cottonwood Lakes and over Army Pass. At a left fork beyond the camp, the trail crossed Horseshoe Meadows and then traveled over Cottonwood Pass.

The California Department of Fish and Wildlife still harvests golden trout eggs from mature fish in several of the Cottonwood Lakes. The eggs are then raised to planting size at Black Rock Fish Hatchery, north of Independence. There are twenty-eight lakes in the region containing golden trout.

Army Pass lies above the lakes and accesses Rock Creek and Miter Basins. Mt. Langley, at 14,042 feet elevation, is the southernmost peak in the Whitney group of 14,000+ foot peaks.

The Cerro Gordo Mine in the Inyo Mountains, north of Owens Lake, required huge amounts of wood, and the more accessible nearby pinion and juniper-covered hills were soon denuded of trees. In 1873, Colonel Sherman Stevens, early Inyo County pioneer, built a small sawmill about eight miles up Cottonwood Canyon. In 1873, the Stevens Sawmill had constructed a flume, with water from Cottonwood Creek turned into it. From the mill above, lumber was floated in the flume down the canyon to the Owens Valley. From there, mule trains packed the lumber to the Cottonwood Landing wharf on Owens Lake, where it was boated across Owens Lake to Swansea.

Barney Sears' Pack Trains began as one of the original pack stations in the southern Sierra in 1920. Sears was a long-time muleskinner and teamster who raised exceptionally good mules. His first mule-packing job was at the age of twenty-one, when he packed gold ore on burros near Silverton, Colorado. Two packers loaded eighty-five burros twice a day. Sears was a big man, at six foot, three inches, and 225 pounds. He worked on construction and hauling jobs with mules and teams all over the West.

In 1908, he worked on the railroad grade from Mojave to Olancha. He liked the area, and with his fishing rod and a pack mule, he packed up into the Monache country. With his mother, sister, and brother, he homesteaded a claim, planting a ten-acre orchard three miles south of Olancha. Barney continued building railroads, levees, ditches, and pipelines, and leveling land in Southern California.

Sears bought 1,000 head of mohair goats and shipped them to Olancha. He ran them on the range from Little Lake to Death Valley, but learned they weren't very profitable. He figured he knew more about mules than goats, so in 1920, he put together a small pack outfit, moved into Cottonwood Canyon, and began "wrangling dudes," or guiding paying customers. In the fall, he moved part of his outfit down to Olancha and packed up the trail to Monache and Tunnel Meadows for deer hunting. In 1923, Sears had his headquarters in Cottonwood Canyon on Cottonwood Creek, called **Barney Sears Cottonwood Pack Station,** as well as a corral at Sage Flat by Loco Creek.

During the winters, Sears worked for the highway department building roads. In 1935, he decided to shorten the trip from Cottonwood Canyon to Sage Flat by building a road from the old ranger station on Loco Creek three and a half miles to Sage Flat. He built the road with six mules, a light grader, and a Fresno (a mule-drawn grader and plow) with only one other man besides himself.

Sears packed out of Sage Flat over Olancha Pass up to Monache Meadows, where deer were plentiful, for deer hunting trips. He had corrals and a storage building at Sage Flat that he called Monache Pack Train. In 1936, Sears ran fifty head of pack and saddle stock.

The Cottonwood Pack Station serviced the Golden Trout Camp, operated then by Barney Sears' brother, on Cottonwood Creek. The camp was eight and a half miles, or a four-hour ride, from the pack station at the foot of the canyon.

By 1946, Sears ran about a hundred head of horses, mules, and burros. He branded his animals with his LZ7 brand on their left sides. (John Lacey, an Olancha cattleman, now has the brand, but his cattle are branded on the right side.) In 1946, Sears sold Monache Pack Station at Sage Flat, along with stock and gear, to Ike Livermore, who merged it with Chrysler and Cook's Mt. Whitney Pack Trains to form Mt. Whitney Pack Trains. Sears continued to operate the **Cottonwood Pack Station**, and at the end of the 1946 season, he sold it to Leo Hastings Rogers and his wife, Merta, from Bakersfield, who had worked for Sears for some time. Sears was eighty-two years of age and attributed his long and healthy life to "wrangling dudes in the invigorating air of the High Sierras."

The Leo Rogers family settled in Cartago near Owens Lake and Olancha, and, during the winters, worked at various available jobs in the area. Their grandson, Clint Hershey of Walker-Coleville, remembers growing up around the pack station and packing his first solo pack string up to Horseshoe Meadows when he was twelve years of age. Pack station children learned to work at a young age, and the young ones looked forward to each new responsibility. Rogers operated with forty-five head of stock after ten years of operation. His brand was the Quarter Circle 7, which he branded on the left shoulder of his animals, and the iron is still treasured by Clint Hershey. At the end of the packing season in 1956, Rogers sold the pack station to Bob Vinnedge.

Clair William "Bob" Vinnedge, his son, Ken, and his family owned the Hansen Dam Stables in the San Fernando Valley of Los Angeles for many years. Bob's daughter, Vonda "Tiny," was married to Bob Moore, and together, they operated the Cottonwood Pack Station from 1960 until 1970. They increased the number of stock to sixty head. Bob Moore was the vice president of the Eastern Sierra Packers' Association in 1967.

In 1970, Dennis Winchester, grandson of Bob Vinnedge and nephew of Vonda and Bob Moore, took over the station. Winchester had worked for his grandfather beginning in 1958. He wintered his stock at his ranch in Independence. He also worked as a movie wrangler on film shoots and regaled his fellow wranglers with the humorous stories that he was noted for. Winchester was vice president of the Packers' Association in 1979. He owned and operated the station until 2018, when he sold to Craig London at Rock Creek Pack Station.

HORSESHOE MEADOWS

Beautiful Horseshoe Meadows is two miles long, and nearby Cottonwood Creek is famous for golden trout. The South Fork of the Kern River is the indigenous home of the golden trout, the state fish of California. Foxtail pines, some 3,000 years old, adorn the ridges surrounding Horseshoe Meadows. The foxtail pine is a close relation of the bristlecone pine found in the White and Inyo Mountains east of the Owens Valley.

In the 1960s, an optimistic plan was underway to build a downhill ski resort, called Trail Peak, in Horseshoe Meadows, which was a catalyst to build an access road to the site. The Horseshoe Meadows Road rises sharply from southwest of Lone Pine, at 4,399 feet elevation, passes the old Carroll Creek location of the Mt. Whitney Pack Trains, and climbs to nearly 10,000 feet at the road's end. The view of the Owens Valley is superb from the road. In 1968, the dirt road was completed from the valley floor to the summit. Cottonwood Pack Station, located in Cottonwood Canyon, had to move their facilities to the top of the grade, about six miles up.

However, the Forest Service canceled the developers' plans for the big ski resort for various reasons. Instead, the Forest Service constructed a new campground near the end of the road. In 1984, the road was paved and completed to its present form. The pack station was then moved to its present location, and permanent facilities were built. The station is now the highest pack station in the eastern Sierra, located at 10,500 feet elevation.

Mt. Whitney Pack Trains also packed out of Horseshoe Meadows from Carroll Creek until the Forest Service determined, after the road was paved in 1984, that Cottonwood Pack Station would be the primary local packer in the Horseshoe Meadows area. Mt. Whitney Pack Trains, operated by Rock Creek Pack Station and Red's Meadow Pack Station, are allowed a certain number of trips from Horseshoe Meadows and other southern Sierra trailheads; however, they no longer have a headquarters facility in the area, and haul their stock and equipment from their pack stations to permitted trailheads. Craig London of Rock Creek Pack Station purchased the Cottonwood Pack Station from Winchester in 2018, and operates with a complete variety of trips. Rock Creek and Red's Meadow still own the Mt. Whitney Pack Trains permit to operate trips in the southern Sierra.

Golden Trout Camp is another privately owned, commercial backcountry resort camp. It is on the North Fork of Cottonwood Creek, at 10,000 feet elevation, near Horseshoe Meadows, and is situated below Mt. Langley to the north. Construction of the Golden Trout Camp began in 1923, and the camp was in operation by 1925. Cottonwood Pack Station and Mt. Whitney Pack Trains packed guests and supplies into the resort. It was a ten-mile, or four-hour, horseback ride from Carroll Creek with Mt. Whitney Pack Trains. Guided horseback trips were provided by Cottonwood Pack Station. Boats were available on the Cottonwood Lakes for golden trout fishing, with fifteen lakes in the basin for a variety of fishing experiences.

The dining room was a log cabin with a small store that even had a telephone in later years. Another cabin offered hot and cold shower baths. The dozen ten cabins had good wooden floors and wood stoves. Housekeeping services were provided in some cabins, which included a small kitchen. Three additional log cabins were built in the 1950s. Mr. and Mrs. C. E Towler operated the camp in 1933. John "Bud" O'Keefe purchased it from the Towlers in 1949, and he and his wife operated it until the Thacher School purchased it in 1972.

In 1972, Ike Livermore, who owned Mt. Whitney Pack Trains, arranged for the Golden Trout Camp to be purchased by the Thacher School of Ojai, where he had attended high school. The Thacher School is a private boarding high school and includes teaching horsemanship and packing skills in its curriculum.

The Golden Trout Wilderness Area in Inyo and Tulare counties on the Kern Plateau was designated on February 24, 1978. The Forest Service wrote the Wilderness Management Plan in 1982.

The camp is now located just within the Golden Trout Wilderness Area, but is still permitted to operate by the Forest Service. Now, the Thacher School operates the camp as the Golden Trout Wilderness School, and offers wilderness education programs for Thacher high school students and alumni during the summer. With construction of the Horseshoe Meadows Road, it is now only a two-and-a-half-mile hike into camp.

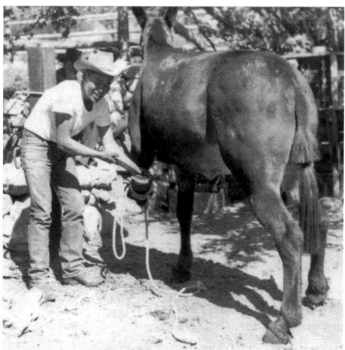

A young packer, Tommy Jefferson, shoes a mule at
Mt. Whitney Pack Trains, '50s. (Lee and Jen Roeser Collection)

LONE PINE AND MT. WHITNEY

Over 10,000 visitors climb popular Mt. Whitney, elevation 14,505 feet, each year. Mt. Whitney is the highest mountain peak in the continental United States, and is part of a massive granite wall that stretches fifteen miles from Mt. Tyndall in the north, at 14,024 feet, to Mt. Langley in the south, at 14,042 feet. There are twelve peaks in this portion of the Sierra range that are over 14,000 feet in elevation. Mt. Williamson, a prominent peak on the Owens Valley line, is 14,384 feet. Whitney Portal, at the beginning of the trail, is 8,367 feet, and, from there, it is an eleven-mile trip to the summit, with an elevation gain of 6,000 feet. The trail, although steep, was constructed as a stock trail and is reasonably wide and gradual. The mountain summit is several acres in size and almost flat. A rock shelter building, constructed shortly after the turn of the century, is still there.

Frank Olivas, his son, Carmen Olivas, and brother, Joe, were vaqueros or arrieros, and had arrived in Alta California by pack train from the northern part of Sonora, Mexico, where the Apache had chased them out. Frank rode a horse, and the boys rode burros. They went to Los Angeles first, but soon after, traveled on to the Owens Valley, settling in Lone Pine.

In the late 1870s, Frank Olivas was engaged in commercial packing as a freight packer to the mines in the area and Saline Valley. Much of their early packing was mine packing, including packing for the mines around Cerro Gordo, and transporting commercial goods. They also cut and hauled wood to the mines and hauled salt from Saline Valley by mule trains to the herds of sheep and cattle in Monache Meadows and the Kern Plateau area. Compressed snow was also packed from Lone Pine Canyon to Lone Pine for refrigeration.

Carmen was born in about 1869, and helped his dad as a youngster. There have been four generations of Olivas vaqueros, using Mexican mule packing methods and providing packing services to the southern Sierra. Carmen married Petra Diaz, who was from a prominent Lone Pine family, and they raised a large family. All of the children grew up riding, roping, and packing. Around 1912, Carmen homesteaded their headquarters ranch, located on Olivas Ranch Road in the Alabama Hills. The Olivas Ranch Road, where the house still stands, is west of Lone Pine.

By 1890, Carmen Olivas was running the commercial packing services. In 1901, he called it **Olivas Pack Train**. Olivas packed up Lone Pine Creek Canyon and, when the Mt. Whitney Trail from Lone Pine to Mt. Whitney was completed in 1904, Olivas Pack Train packed all the supplies for the project. From 1905 to 1907, they packed dirt and materials to build the Yosemite Valley Railroad.

Carmen's two sons, Henry "Leaky" and Peter J. "Pete," joined the packing business and advertised their pack station in 1923 as **One Bar One Pack Train.** The two sons packed for their father and cowboyed for other ranchers in the Owens Valley.

In the 1920s, Hollywood filmmakers discovered Lone Pine, the Alabama Hills, and the Owens Valley. Russell Spainhower, local rancher, supplied livestock and wranglers for early Western films. The Olivas Ranch was located in the Alabama Hills, where much of the early filming took place. Henry "Leaky" Olivas and his brother Pete began working for Spainhower and the movie producers, supplying livestock and wranglers. Henry owned about fifty head of stock with his pack outfit and was issued the first wranglers card in the Owens Valley. Pete was issued the first screen actor's card. In later years, Henry's wife, Ethel, and their daughter, Charlotte, sometimes catered meals for the film companies.

Both Henry and Pete packed for Allie Robinson and Ike Livermore on early Sierra Club trips. In 1934, Fred Burkhardt, a well known packer in the area, was a partner with Henry Olivas in the packing operation in Lone Pine for a while. Olivas leased a pasture south of the Alabama Gates and pastured his stock there. He also leased stock to other pack stations when they had large pack trips and needed extra stock.

In 1946, Henry Olivas married Ethel Dearborn Ruiz, daughter of Ollie Dearborn, previous owner of Carroll Creek Pack Station. Ethel's children, Margaret and Joe Ruiz, were also raised at the Olivas pack staton, learning the packing trade. Henry and Ethel's daughter, Charlotte, was born in 1948.

The 1949 Death Valley Centennial Twenty Mule Team was organized, and the original Borax wagons were borrowed to use. Bruce Morgan of Mt. Whitney Pack Trains supplied the mules. Henry Olivas organized the gear and harness, and trained the mules. He drove the wagons on the eight day trip from Lone Pine to Death Valley. Ethel Olivas and their ten-month-old baby, Charlotte, accompanied the trip as well. Henry's brother, Pete, was the brakeman.

In 1952, Henry's stepson, Joe Ruiz, was associated with him in the packing business. Henry was active in the packing business until about 1954, when he retired, sold his stock and equipment, and went out of business.

The Olivas family kept their cabin lease in Monache Meadows, spending summers there. In 1977, a reunion ranch rodeo was held in Monache Meadows, and Henry was an official and one of the sponsors. Ethel was the surprise Rodeo Queen of the event.

The property of **Carroll Creek Pack Station** was homesteaded in the early 1860s, and was located along the old Hockett Trail that crossed the Sierra to the west side of the range. In around 1879, Alfred W. Carroll purchased forty acres on the creek that is now called Carroll Creek after him. He was a founder of the Sierra Club and operated a pack station from the property.

Oren "Ollie" F. Dearborn operated the pack station beginning in 1912. As a young packer, he had packed supplies to construct the rock shelter on the summit of Mt. Whitney in 1908. Dearborn's daughter, Ethel, married Henry Olivas from the Olivas packing family. The Carroll Creek private property is now located off the Horseshoe Meadows Road, constructed in the 1960s.

From 1921 to 1934, James F. "Frank" Chrysler and Daniel N. Cook (not related to Ted and Fred Cook) packed out of Lone Pine Creek. They packed tourists to Cottonwood Lakes twenty-one miles away. Frank Chrysler was a cowboy, packer, and teamster who worked for many Owens Valley ranches and was considered to be a top hand. As a young man, he had driven twenty mule teams in Death Valley. He had also worked for the Saline Valley Salt Works, packing salt to the Kern Plateau for the livestock herds grazing there. From that experience, he went into mine packing and then tourist packing.

From 1923 to 1925, Chrysler, along with Vinton A. Hoegee, had a permit to pack out of Carroll Creek into the Cottonwood Lakes area. Hoegee, from Sierra Madre, owned a resort in Big Santa Anita Canyon in the San Gabriel Mountains called Hoegee's Camp and Stables. He was partners with Frank Chrysler for several years before selling his interest to Ted Cook.

Edgar H. "Ted" Cook grew up in Aberdeen in the Big Pine area. He served in the Army in World War I, and after the war, in the 1920s, he packed with Fred Burkhardt in the Lone Pine area. In the spring of 1935, Ted Cook and his wife, Margaret, purchased Mt. Whitney Pack Trains from Hoegee, with Frank Chrysler remaining as a partner with Cook. The partners called their business **Chrysler and Cook Mt. Whitney Pack Trains**. They established headquarters at Carroll Creek on the old homestead, ten miles southwest of Lone Pine. Cook was the businessman of the pair, and Chrysler was the stockman. The barn, corrals, tack room, and office were west of the house and along the creek. These facilities burned before 1946.

Another corral, called **Hunter's Flat Pack Station**, was fourteen miles west of Lone Pine at the end of the new automobile road. William L. Hunter was an early rancher in the valley, and made the first ascent of Mt. Williamson with C. Mulholland in 1884.

The CCC completed the new auto road, now called the Whitney Portal Road, in 1936. Mt. Whitney Pack Trains built a store and corrals there.

In 1938, the Mt. Whitney Trail was rebuilt, with Chrysler and Cook packing the supplies and equipment to the trail crew. There are a hundred switchbacks up to Trail Crest Pass at 13,780 feet. Pack trips could now pack up that trail to the summit of Mt. Whitney. The rock shelter on top was used as an emergency shelter, but was not a regular campsite. Riding and hiking stock are no longer permitted on the Mt. Whitney Trail because of the heavy hiker use.

During the construction of the John Muir Trail, the great barrier of the Kings-Kern Divide was considered too rough for pack stock and would have to be detoured. Forester Pass was one of the last passes completed on the John Muir Trail route, and is the highest, at 13,153 feet elevation. After that trail completion, Junction Pass, at 13,000 feet, was bypassed and abandoned.

Chrysler and Cook Mt. Whitney Pack Trains ran a hundred head of stock, making them one of the largest stations in the eastern Sierra. The animals were branded with a JF on the neck. This was Chrysler's brand, standing for James Franklin. In addition to their many pack trips into the nearby backcountry, they packed guests into Tunnel Meadow Camp and Airfield. Mt. Whitney Pack Trains had three locations—Carroll Creek, Whitney Portal, and Hunter's Flat. The outfit was associated with the Golden Trout Camp, and packed guests into that camp. In addition, they rented stock to the movie companies frequently filming in the area. Ted Cook had a screen actor's guild card and acted as an extra in early Western movies filmed in the area.

One suggested trip for private customers started from the Carroll Creek headquarters and went to the Cottonwood Lakes, Army Pass, Rock Creek, and Crabtree Meadows. Their other trail started from the mouth of Lone Pine Canyon, followed the course of Lone Pine Creek, and then ascended up to the summit of Mt. Whitney, where the two trails joined. On the Mt. Whitney Trail, packers loose herded their mules from Trail Camp westward up and over Trail Crest Pass, at 13,800 feet.

Beginning in 1938, Ike Livermore brokered Chrysler and Cook Mt. Whitney Pack Trains' pack stock for large Sierra Club trips. Mt. Whitney Pack Trains packed many large Sierra Club trips, supplying stock and packers. Norman "Ike" Livermore was a partner in Mineral King Pack Station, had organized the High Sierra Packers' Association, and was the organization's secretary for many years. During World War II, Livermore was a Second Lieutenant in the Navy.

In 1945, after completing his Navy service, he recognized the need for an outfit with many pack mules to handle the large Sierra Club trips. Allie Robinson had packed these trips for many years out of Independence, but he sold his Robinson Pack Trains during the War. In 1946, Livermore purchased the Chrysler and Cook Mt. Whitney Pack Trains from Frank Chrysler and Ted Cook. He also purchased the Monache Meadows Pack Station at Sage Flat, along with equipment and mules, from Barney Sears. The merged pack stations became known as **Mt. Whitney Pack Trains**. Livermore leased some stock from Ray Buckman at Mineral King Pack Station on the westside, which he previously had owned with Buckman, and more stock from Wendell Gill at Rock Creek Pack Station. He also purchased twenty bronc mules in Fallon, Nevada. By assembling over 130 horses and mules, he began his operation as the largest outfit in the Sierra. This number of stock was necessary to handle the large trips. Their packers used a one-man diamond hitch on their pack mules, termed a "Mt. Whitney Diamond Hitch," and each packer led five mules. Livermore was the pack contractor for the Sierra Club pack trips from 1946 to 1972.

The Mt. Whitney Pack Trains had three locations: Carroll Creek, Sage Flat, and Whitney Portal. Stock was pastured at the Elder and Moffat Ranches in the Alabama Hills, where the outfit had corrals and pens. Ike constructed an office/tack room on the Whitney Portal Road, just west of Lone Pine. The lumber for it was cut on the Livermore family ranch on the north coast and hauled to Lone Pine.

Bruce Morgan was made a working partner on a recommendation from Ted Cook, and then managed the packing operations. Morgan had operated the Tunnel Meadows Camp for a number of years before World War II. In 1950, Morgan became the general manager of the outfit. Bruce, his wife, Grace, and his family of five children lived at the Carroll Creek station. The Morgan and Livermore children grew up at the pack station, learning to pack at an early age.

Tommy Jefferson of the Mono tribe began packing for Mt. Whitney in 1946 as a young teenager and became a lauded packer. He married Barbara Morgan, Bruce's daughter, and later managed the outfit. He became an owner of Mt. Whitney Pack Trains and remained in that position until 1974, when he sold his interest to London and Tanner. He was a favorite on pack trips, playing his guitar and singing.

The Outpost Camp (also called Ibex Camp) was located at Bighorn Peak, at 10,365 feet, just below Mirror Lake, and many visitors camped there. Mt. Whitney Pack Trains operated the guest camp, where beds and meals were available for travelers to Mt. Whitney. People still rode horses to the summit of Mt. Whitney. After the 1964 Wilderness Bill became law, the camp had to be removed, as it was located in the John Muir Wilderness Area. The next camp, Trail Camp, was three miles further up the trail at 12,000 feet, and was above timberline. Mountain bighorn sheep were sometimes seen in the vicinity of these camps, but no longer. There are a hundred switchbacks from Trail Camp to Trail Crest Pass, at 13,800 feet.

In the winter, the Morgan family operated the riding stables at Furnace Creek Ranch in Death Valley. They drove the Mt. Whitney horses to Death Valley from Lone Pine each fall. At Furnace Creek, they put on barbecues and square dances. Grace Morgan was an excellent square dance instructor. In 1949, Russ Spainhower, Bruce Morgan, and Henry Olivas hitched up a Twenty Mule Team for the Death Valley Centennial Celebration. They drove the mule team from Lone Pine to Death Valley. Morgan and Olivas were credited as being the last Pacific Coast Borax Twenty Mule Team muleskinners until Bobby Tanner, of Red's Meadow Pack Station, drove the Borax wagons again in 1981.

Bruce Morgan later managed the Dow Hotel in Lone Pine, helping to coordinate and accommodate the film companies filming in the area. Walter Dow had constructed the Dow Hotel in 1923 to accommodate the new movie industry that made Lone Pine its center, and later added the motel section, the Dow Villas. Dow next opened the Winnedumah Hotel in Independence in 1925.

Morgan divided his interest in the pack station between himself, his eldest son, Charles C. "Charlie" Morgan, and son-in-law, Tommy Jefferson. Charlie Morgan and Tommy Jefferson alternately managed the outfit. Charlie's son, Mike Morgan, is still in the packing business, owning Bishop Pack Outfitters at North Lake out of Bishop.

In 1972, Tommy Jefferson, Bob Tanner of Red's Meadow Pack Station, and Herb London of Rock Creek Pack Station formed a partnership to acquire Ike Livermore's interest in the permit. Two years later, London and Tanner bought out Jefferson's interest.

In 1973, at the end of the season, the Forest Service closed the Mt. Whitney Trail to use by pack and saddle stock because of the heavy use by hikers. Ironically, the trail was constructed for stock use in 1904, and used by horses and mules continuously from 1904 to 1972. Now, over 10,000 hikers trudge the trail to Mt. Whitney each year, and only occasional Forest Service administrative stock are permitted on the "old pack trail."

The pack station facilities were no longer needed at Whitney Portal, so Mt Whitney Pack Trains moved out of Whitney Portal, removing their corrals and packing sheds. The store and café are still there, serving the many hikers going up the trail.

Since the Mt. Whitney Trail was closed to horseback riding and pack stock parties, the Forest Service permitted Mt. Whitney Pack Trains the use of other southern Sierra passes and trails. Their permit allows them to pack both north and south of Horseshoe Meadows and Whitney Portal. Passes that they can use include Haiwee Pass, Olancha Pass out of Sage Flat, Shepherd Pass, Sawmill Pass, and Taboose Pass. Rock Creek Pack Station and Red's Meadow Pack Station still use the packing permit for trips in the southern Sierra. Both pack stations continue to share the Mt. Whitney pack station permit. Another Forest Service permittee operates the store and café at Whitney Portal under a separate permit. Jen and Lee Roeser of McGee Creek Pack Station are also allotted permits for mule-supported hiking trips to climb Mt. Whitney.

Other early packers in the Lone Pine Area who operated packing services at various times were Elvis Bonner and Agner, who packed in the 1920s. Edward C. Overhulser and Raymond W. Spear also did packing in that period. Wally Wilson operated from 1928 to 1941, and also ran cattle in the 1940s and 1950s.

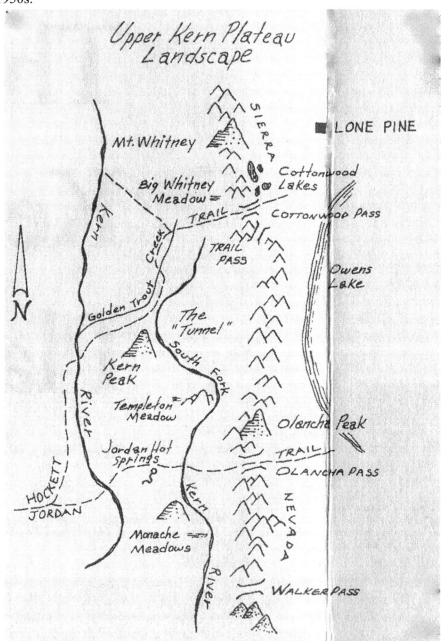

Hand-drawn map of the Kern Plateau.

INDEPENDENCE

MANZANAR

Manzanar was a ranching and farming community south of Independence on Highway 395. Claude Morton Kreider was a fireman with the Long Beach Fire Department and arranged with the department to have his summers off. He loved the High Sierra out of the Owens Valley and, in 1918, was hired out as a packer with an Owens Valley pack outfit. He then purchased an apple orchard in George Chaffey's Irrigation Colony. This area at Manzanar had been subdivided into small farms, of which many were orchards, in 1922. It became the headquarters of his business, **Krieder's High Sierra Pack Tours**. He personally conducted tours starting in Independence. In 1923, Kreider advertised in his brochure that he was a Sierra Club member, and that the trips were three to fourteen-day tours, with a ten-person limit. The trips, arranged with other stations, were all-expense, with everything needed for the trip provided, and the tourists needed only bring their personal items. In 1924, he sold his fruit ranch to the City of Los Angeles when they began buying up the ranches in Manzanar.

He continued conducting his High Sierra trips and wrote about them for various outdoor magazines. Needing a new bamboo fly rod, he learned how to build them himself and built over 500 during his lifetime. They were much in demand by ardent fly fishermen. In 1951, he wrote a book called T*he Bamboo Rod and How to Build It.*

INDEPENDENCE AND ONION VALLEY

The Sierra Nevada reaches its greatest height north and west of Lone Pine, all the way to Big Pine. There are dozens of peaks over 13,000 feet in elevation. Mt. Williamson, south of the Onion Valley Road, is the second highest mountain in the Sierra at 14,379 feet in elevation, dominating the skyline. Onion Valley is a glaciated hanging valley, located fifteen miles west of Independence, and five miles above the Owens Valley floor. The new Onion Valley Road was completed in 1962.

Kearsarge Pass is a popular entrance into Sequoia and Kings Canyon National Parks from the eastside. Kearsarge Pass, out of Onion Valley, is the shortest and only relatively easy pass accessed from the Owens Valley, and was originally a Native American trail. The pass lies at 11,823 feet elevation, and is five strenuous miles from Onion Valley at 9,200 feet. Pack trips over the pass reach the Kearsarge Lakes, Charlotte Lake, Bullfrog Lake, Rae Lakes, Bubbs Creek, and the Kings River, all in Sequoia and Kings Canyon National Parks. Other passes in the area are as high as most Sierra peaks. The other trails begin low on the dry sagebrush slopes of the Owens Valley at around 4,600 feet, and steeply climb 6,000 feet to the summits.

The early gold mining camp of Kearsarge City, located in Onion Valley, was founded in 1864 and later destroyed by an avalanche in 1867. At the time, it was the largest town in Inyo County and was seriously considered as the site for the county seat.

Three pack stations operated out of Onion Valley at one time and all were busy. The headquarters and corrals for **High Sierra Pack Train** were located on Highway 395 in Independence, near the facilities of Allie Robinson. The pack station also maintained corrals at Onion Valley (sometimes called Kearsarge Valley) and Sawmill Pass trailhead. This pass is opposite 8-Mile Ranch, north of Independence. From the corral at the end of Division Creek Road, they also packed over Sawmill Pass to Woods Lake and Woods Creek. From the corrals on Symmes Creek, pack trips went over Shepherd Pass to Wallace Lake, Milestone Basin, and Upper Kern Canyon. Pack trips went over Kearsarge, Sawmill, Taboose, Baxter, and Shepherd Passes. The 1953 brochure advertised, "We will meet you anywhere in the Sierra and have your car waiting for you at any given point on coming out for a reasonable charge."

Archie Cornelius Dean began his packing business, called High Sierra Pack Train, when he was a young man in 1912, and built his business up to seventy head of stock. He always advertised "grain-fed horses and pack mules." Dean had packed materials to build the rock shelter on the summit of Mt. Whitney with Garth Goodly in 1908.

Archie Dean married Mary Fitzpatrick, a capable horsewoman from a ranch in the San Joaquin Valley. In later years, Mary, her son, John, and three daughters did most of the packing while Archie remained at headquarters. Mary's daughter, Tansy, and her husband, John K. Smith, both packed for Archie Dean, and, along with their son, John Hylas Smith, were associated with the pack station until it was sold in 1958. Mary and the girls were reported to be as expert at packing as the men.

Lona Tankersly Burkhart worked for the Dean family in 1951. Her father was a cattle rancher in the Mojave Desert near Barstow. She and her future husband, Gene Burkhart, would later own the Sequoia Kings Pack Trains out of Onion Valley, merging the existing outfits, Hall's Pack Trains, High Sierra Pack Train, and Parker Pack Train, together.

Ed Thistlewhaite, a tall, dignified English artist and long time packer, first worked for the Parker family at their pack station, Parker Pack Station, out of Oak Creek and Onion Valley. He then packed for the Deans for many years at High Sierra Pack Train, then at Convict Lake Pack Station, and then for the Burkharts at Sequoia Kings Pack Trains until he died. He packed on several of the large Sierra Club trips for Mt. Whitney Pack Trains. Many of his pencil and pen and ink drawings, along with paintings, can still be seen in the Owens Valley, as he often paid his bills with his artwork.

In 1954, Dean sold his packing business to Dudley and Ardyce Carter, along with seventy head of stock and thirty burros. Dudley Carter had formerly worked for Dean. Carter called the station **Dud Carter's High Sierra Pack Train**. In 1958, the Carters sold the station to Bill and Ginny Muckle, along with fifty-eight head of stock.

In 1963, Gene and Lona Burkhart purchased High Sierra Pack Train from the Muckles and combined it with Hall's and Parker's outfits, which they had previously purchased in 1958, to make one pack station in the valley. They named their business **Sequoia Kings High Sierra Pack Trains**. When they purchased High Sierra Pack Train, they acquired the headquarters in Independence and moved their headquarters there from the Parker Ranch, northwest of Independence. They also acquired the 8-Mile Ranch lease north of Independence. There was a pack station at 8-Mile for a time, and they had a permit to pack out of Onion Valley as well.

194

The Tourists' Saddle and Pack Livery was established by Charles W. Robinson in 1901, and was located in Independence and Lone Pine. He had been packing commercially since 1872, and was also a teamster, owning many horses and mules. Charley's father, A. W. Robinson, had stocked many of the lakes and streams in the area with trout. Charley's son, Allie William Robinson, grew up packing and joined Charley in their business. In the 1920s, they called their business **Robinson Pack Trains and Auto Camp**.

The Robinson headquarters in Independence were located almost next door to Archie Dean's headquarters for the High Sierra Pack Train on Highway 395. Before the Onion Valley Road was improved, corrals were at the bottom of the grade off the lower Onion Valley Road. After the road was extended, they built corrals in Onion Valley. The Robinson ranch, where they pastured their livestock, was on the Mazourka Canyon Road.

The Robinsons packed out of Onion Valley and Sawmill Canyon, as well as Symmes Creek, and Oak, Davis, and Taboose Creeks. Pack trips went to Rae Lakes, Bubbs Creek, and the Kings River. They also used the Hockett Trail and Cottonwood Pass Trail from Lone Pine, and maintained four corrals at various trailheads. In 1928, Allie W. Robinson, Charlie's son, took over operation of the pack outfit. In 1934, the pack station was owned and operated by Allie and his wife, Doris. With 170 head of stock, it was the largest station in the Sierra, larger even than the Curry Company Yosemite Stables in Yosemite National Park.

The Robinsons began packing Sierra Club trips before 1918. They had the quantity of mules needed to handle these large trips. As many as fifty packers and two hundred and fifty head of mules and horses were on these trips. Beginning in 1938, Ike Livermore became a broker between the Robinsons and the Sierra Club, managing the stock on their trips and selecting the campsites. That year, the Sierra Club High Trip left from Agnew Meadows near Mammoth Lakes.

At the Independence headquarters, the packers had previously spent weeks shoeing the stock before the drive and the pack trip. Equipment also needed readying and packing for the long trip. Not having large stock trucks at that time, the packers drove the stock from the headquarters in Independence to Agnew Meadows during the heat of the Owens Valley summer. There were probably seventy-five head of mules plus riding horses on the over-100-mile horse drive.

After the start of World War II, Allie Robinson began down-sizing his operations. He lacked the desire to continue packing the huge Sierra Club High Trips, so he no longer needed the large numbers of stock, particularly mules. He had a packing operation at June Lake for a time, and then purchased Leavitt Meadows Pack Station on the West Walker River. In 1944, He sold an interest in the Onion Valley outfit to Harold and Wendell Gill, who had packed for him. The facilities consisted of a hog wire corral, a tent cabin, and thirty-five head of stock.

In 1947, Harold Gill sold the Onion Valley outfit to Murray Hall and his partner, Fred Moore. Fred Moore had packed for Chrysler and Cook for many years and was an uncle of Harold Gill. Murray Hall owned Kennedy Meadows Pack Trains in 1946. The Halls changed the name of the old Robinson outfit to **Hall's Pack Trains** at Onion Valley. They also acquired a ranch lease at Black Rock Springs north of Independence, where they pastured pack station stock and ran 300 head of cattle.

After Bruce Morgan of Mt. Whitney Pack Trains ceased operating the Furnace Creek Stables in Death Valley during the winter, the Hall family took over that operation for several years. They drove the pack station stock to Furnace Creek in the fall and back to the Owens Valley in the spring. The first night's camp on the long, dry, and dusty horse drive was near Dirty Sox Hot Spring, and the second night was spent at Panamint, an area in the Panamint Mountains on the road to Death Valley. On the third day, they drove the stock to Stovepipe Wells in Death Valley. Finally, on the fourth day, they reached the Furnace Creek Ranch further south.

The three pack stations operating at Onion Valley then were Hall's Pack Trains, Parker Pack Train, and High Sierra Pack Train. In 1949, the Halls bought out their partner, Fred Moore. Murray Hall built the first permanent facilities in Onion Valley, including a house for the family to live in. In 1952, he ran about fifty head of stock at the pack station.

Bud Hall, Murray's son, was active in the business and the Eastern High Sierra Packers' Association until they sold their stations. Bud was secretary of the organization when he was just eighteen. Both of the Hall's sons, Bud and Dave, learned to ride as soon as they learned to walk and were packing at an early age. Murray's wife, Lothelle, kept all the many facets of their sprawling ranching and packing businesses together.

In 1958, Irwin and Alice Burkhart and Eugene "Gene" and Lona Burkhart purchased Hall's Pack Trains at Onion Valley and Kennedy Meadows Pack Trains from Murray and Lothelle Hall. Irwin was Gene Burkhart's uncle. The Burkharts renamed the pack station **Sequoia Kings High Sierra Pack Trains**. The two couples lived at Onion Valley the first summer, but after that year, Irwin and Alice Burkhart took over the Kennedy Meadows station, and Gene and Lona kept Onion Valley and ran cattle at Black Rock. Lona and their son, Randy, did much of the packing, and Lona was known as a first-rate packer.

In 1963, Gene and Lona merged the two other pack stations that had been operating out of Onion Valley, High Sierra Pack Train and Parker Pack Train. Now there was just one outfit in Onion Valley that used Kearsarge Pass, and at peak times, they utilized about a hundred head of stock. The station also furnished burros to hiking parties, and used corrals at Symmes Creek, Sawmill Pass, Taboose Pass, Sawmill Canyon, and Shepherd Pass trailheads.

For three winters, beginning in 1959, the Burkharts ran the Furnace Creek Stables in Death Valley in partnership with Slim Nivens of Pine Creek Saddle and Pack Train. The Burkharts obtained a permit from the Park Service to capture wild burros, and after breaking and gentling them, they were placed in their burro pack string. Slim Nivens also had Death Valley burros for rent at his Pine Creek Pack Station.

The Burkharts were also able to purchase some good reject mules from the Fred Harvey Company, which conducted the mule rides into the Grand Canyon. At the Grand Canyon, mules were trained to turn sideways on the trail when they stopped, but the Bright Angel Trail is wide. On narrow Sierra trails, the mules would attempt to follow their training, but soon learned that this stance was not possible.

Gene Burkhart ramrodded the Packers' Association Sports Show booth in

Southern California each winter. The association sent a mule and a horse to the exhibit, and the packers presented packing demonstrations for the general public. These shows did much to promote and familiarize the Southern California visitors with the eastern Sierra. Fishing, hunting, lodging, camping, and packing in the beautiful Sierra backcountry received much publicity in the Los Angeles area.

In 1971, the Burkharts sold **Sequoia Kings Pack Trains** to Gary Kulper. The Burkharts took it back in 1975, and resold it to Larry and Marie Wolfe. The Wolfes were in the ranching business in Fallon, Nevada. Fat Jones and his brother were movie outfitters from Hollywood. When they retired, some of their movie wagons were for sale at an auction in Fallon, and Wolfe purchased the collection. He sold the collection to my husband, Lou, who used the various wagons in many Marlboro film commercials, as well as other film shoots throughout the eastern Sierra. One of the chuck wagons was used in the John Wayne movie, The Cowboys, and that wagon is now parked on loan at the entrance to the Lone Pine Western Film Museum.

The Kings Canyon National Park Service cancelled Wolfe's National Park use permit because of poor performance. Wolfe then backed out of his sales agreement with Burkhart. Burkhart resold the station in 1977 to Jim and Donna Howell, who were also the owners of Rainbow Pack Outfit on Bishop Creek. Howell obtained the necessary Park and Forest Service permits and was a member of the Packers' Association.

After dispersing their properties, Lona Burkhart moved to Oregon, raised cattle and horses, wrote several books of prose and poetry about the West, and was selected Most Honored Packer at Mule Days. Gene Burkhart ran the Pines Café in Independence for some years before retiring to the Colorado River.

In 1981, Dale, Mark, and Joanne Berry purchased the Sequoia Kings Pack Trains from the Howells, along with their purchase of Rainbow Pack Outfit. In 1993, the Berrys sold the Sequoia Kings Pack Trains permit separately to Brian and Danica Berner, who owned Pine Creek Pack Station. The Berners were active in the Packers' Association, with Brian serving as president and Danica as secretary. The Berners continue operation of the station at Onion Valley today.

Parker's Camp and Pack Train was located on the South Fork of Oak Creek, north of Independence. George V. Parker homesteaded 160 acres on Oak Creek. The Parkers remained there from 1912 to 1958. With a partner, Albert M. Blunt, Parker ran a pack outfit called **Parker and Blunt Pack Train** from about 1925 to 1929. They had a corral in Onion Valley and used Kearsarge Pass and other desert passes to access the backcountry. Later, George and Vida Parker operated the pack station until 1954.

There were seven cabins and a dining room at the resort, besides the corrals and packing sheds. An apple orchard provided fruit for pies and jam. Vida was very capable and active in the running of the pack outfit. In about 1955, Daniel "Danny" G. Harris, their grandson, assumed management of their resort. They ran about forty head of stock in 1954, and packed in from Onion Valley over Kearsarge Pass.

In 1958, Lewis "Bud" and Jeanne Corwin purchased the resort and packing operation in Onion Valley, **Parker Pack Train**. In 1963, Gene and Lona

Burkhart operated the ranch and pack station operations, and pooled them with their Sequoia Kings Pack Trains. They lived at the ranch, and Lona ran the dining room at the resort for several years. Later, the ranch resort was sold to the Bright family, who operated it as a cattle ranch, and the resort no longer functioned. In the 2007 Inyo Complex Fire, much of the old ranch was burned, and in the 2008 summer flood, the remaining buildings washed away.

Circle Dot Pack Train operated at 8-Mile Ranch in Independence in the 1920s and 1930s. In the early 1900s, the 8-Mile Ranch was one of the largest ranches in the area, along with the Black Rock and Taboose Ranches, all of which were considered beautiful ranches. The packing operation was owned and operated by C. H. "Buck" Hyers, Stoddard, and L. H. Pitts. They had a Los Angeles Department of Water and Power city lease on the ranch and about sixty head of stock. Their pack trips used Sawmill Canyon, along with Kearsarge and Taboose Pass Trailheads, to access the Kern and Kings River country. The station operated until about 1941, during World War II, when they closed and went out of business.

Gene and Lona Burkhart acquired the City of Los Angeles ranch lease, and Lona's father lived in the small house. Gene planted forty acres of alfalfa. Russ Johnson purchased the ranch lease for 8-Mile Ranch from the Burkharts and attached it to his McGee Creek Pack Station permit. Russ also acquired the old Circle Dot branding iron and branded McGee Creek stock with it. When Dave McRoberts purchased McGee Creek Pack Station in 1968, he assumed the ranch lease and lived there with his family during the winter.

The Ketcham family, John, Suzy, and their daughter, Jennifer, acquired the ranch in 1978, with their purchase of McGee Creek Pack Station, and John Ketcham put in many more acres of alfalfa. After Lee and Jennifer Ketcham Roeser were married, they purchased the ranch and McGee Creek Pack Station from John Ketcham, and have added more facilities to the beautiful ranch oasis. Lee Roeser built his saddle shop at the ranch. The 2007 firestorm, the Inyo Complex, burned through the ranch, but miraculously missed the house and saddle shop. Miles of fencing were burned in that very hot fire and had to be replaced, and trees replanted.

Three Corner Round Pack Outfit, Inc. was established in 1919 in New Hampshire. The camp was organized as a backcountry leadership camp for teenage boys and is a non-profit organization, with headquarters in Ohio. The camping program provides wilderness experiences and leadership training to boys. Although most trips are in the Sierra Nevada, the foundation has provided trips all over the world. In 1940, the Cleveland Museum of Natural History took over the ownership of the outfit, but by 1950, they no longer had any affiliation.

In 1947, the camp was required to have commercial Forest Service and Park Service permits for their activities. The campers and their leaders travel throughout the Sierra backcountry during summers for six weeks, varying their itinerary each summer.

The leaders operate a base camp at the end of the road along Pinyon Creek near Independence. The boys spend two weeks there, learning packing skills and how to care for the burros during the six weeks hiking trip that follows. Each boy is expected to care for five burros on the trip.

The group packs in with their desert-bred burros. Most burros have to be driven or led individually, but these burros are trained to be strung together like a mule string. They travel well on the trails, following one behind the other. The outfit has never shod their burros, as their hoofs are very hard and strong.

The outfit raises their own burros, and leases a field from the Los Angeles Department of Water and Power for their burros north of Black Rock Springs Road, adjacent to 8-Mile Ranch. At one time, they maintained about seventy head of burros, but now they have downsized to about forty head. During the winter season, the burros graze in a large, sagebrush-covered field, and are fed hay and checked on by Lee and Jen Roeser at 8-Mile Ranch.

The Three Corner Round Outfit, at one time, owned a house, storage shed, and corral in Independence. For years, O. K. Kelley and his son, Jim, of Independence, managed the outfit. When the Hall's owned Hall's Pack Trains at Onion Valley, they leased the property in Independence, and Bud Hall built the barn there.

These pack trips are still offered, but have been affected by the fifteen-person party size limit, restricting the number of youth and leaders, reducing the number of burros per trip, and restricting grazing and campsite destinations through policy changes with the Forest Service and Park Service. They were formerly able to offer this unique experience to a larger group of boys.

Aberdeen Pack Train, owned by Pete Labachotte, was headquartered at Aberdeen, between Independence and Big Pine, in the 1920s. They packed in over Taboose and Sawmill Passes into what is now Kings Canyon National Park. Pete was an old time mustanger, a "wild and wooly cowboy," who had worked for rancher Bill Landers on the Onyx Ranch near Walker Pass.

The Landers ranch was a rangeland outfit, and Landers ran cattle as far south as Victorville. Many years earlier, Landers had turned out eighty Morgan mares with the mustang herds that ran in the Coso Mountains south of Owens Lake. Each year, a crew, including Labachotte, would round up some of these horses and single out three and four-year-old colts that were to be broken for ranch and pack station work. Labachotte also packed for the Wortley Brothers on the 1928 Sierra Club Trip and was considered a top packer.

Stanley Steffen purchased the pack station in about 1927, and invested in much-needed new gear. The Steffen family had homesteaded a ranch near Aberdeen and operated the store located there. Stanley worked for various ranchers at Fort Independence. The Taboose Trail into the Kings River was a treacherous trail at that time. Steffen's packers would untie the mules and lead them one at a time over the dangerous places. Stanley Steffen was still in operation in 1930, with twenty-seven head of stock.

BIG PINE CANYON AND PALISADES GLACIER

Big Pine Canyon is eleven miles west of the town of Big Pine. The parking area at the end of the Big Pine Road is at 7,800 feet elevation, and Palisades Glacier, the southernmost glacier in the Sierra and North America, can be seen from the end of the road. The road has been paved into the canyon, now making access to the lakes and glacier easier. There are seventeen lakes in the region, and the first lake lies at 10,000 feet elevation. The Palisades group of peaks include five peaks that exceed 14,000 feet elevation. Beginning in the 1900s, Big Pine Canyon and Palisades Glacier were very popular vacation areas.

Frank Dusy is credited with the discovery of the Palisades peaks from the westside in 1878. He was a sheepman who grazed his sheep in the summer meadows and explored the western slopes of the Sierra. He organized trips of interested explorers to accompany him. In 1902, Joseph LeConte made the first successful climb of North Palisade Peak at 14,249 feet, the third highest peak in the Sierra. He described his climb in the Sierra Club Bulletin of 1905.

In 1917, Glacier Lodge was built at the end of the road, and was owned by Bertha Hall and her husband. The lodge maintained a few tents on the cliff above Fourth Lake, at 11,000 feet in elevation. During the Great Depression in the 1930s, the Upper Lodge, called Fourth Lake Lodge of Palisade Glacier, was built, replacing the tents. Roy and Maude Steadman operated Glacier Lodge and the Upper Lodge in 1958. This upper lodge had to be torn down after the Wilderness Act was passed in 1964, as it was located in the John Muir Wilderness Area. A fire in 1998 destroyed the historic old Glacier Lodge, and a small store and campground has replaced it.

Early pioneer William A. Baker was a miner and then had a sawmill on Big Pine Creek, homesteading 160 acres there. The little lakes located east of the canyon are named for him. In 1924, a Wm. F. Baker, perhaps a relation, was packing into the Baker Lakes, east of Big Pine Canyon, for a short while.

Logan's Big Pine Pack Outfit was established near the Glacier Lodge by Big Pine Creek in the river canyon, at an elevation of 7,743 feet. Robert "Bob" Logan and his wife operated the station from about 1925 to 1935.

A dam was constructed at the outlet of Second Lake, and Logan packed up all the materials and equipment to the site on mules. The CCC (Civilian Conservation Corps) constructed a dirt road up as far as the second waterfall. The road now ends below the first waterfall, and the Forest Service has closed the old upper portion.

Logan also packed all the materials to construct the Upper Lodge into the site on mules. After construction was completed, his pack outfit packed guests into the lodge, which was a five-and-a-half-mile trip from the pack station. From the Upper Lodge, it was a three-and-a-half-mile hike to the Palisade Glacier.

Beginning in 1929 and continuing for the next thirty years, Robert Clunie, a well-known landscape painter of the region, packed into the Fourth Lake area and established his camp there for the summer. He was a prolific landscape oil painter and loved the region. Norman Clyde, the noted mountain climber, camped a short distance from Clunie and acted as a mountain guide. Long term camps were permitted then.

The pack station packed into the lakes of Big Pine Canyon, Baker Lakes,

Coyote Valley, and Palisades Glacier. Many mountain climbers and glacier observers packed to the upper lakes and glaciers. Mountain climbers love the high, challenging peaks of the Palisades. Horseback riders can ride ten miles from the pack station to within a half-mile of the glacier.

Bob Logan died in 1934, and Mrs. Logan, assisted by Harold Gill, operated that year. Wallace H. Partridge and his two sons, Wilfred and Kenneth, purchased the pack outfit in 1935 and changed the name to **Glacier Pack Train**. Wallace Partridge was a rancher in Big Pine and also ran cattle for the Southern Sierra Power Company at the former Cain Ranch near Mono Lake.

The Partridges had the lease on McMurry Meadow and built a set of corrals there. Pack trips over Taboose Pass began from the meadow. Guests packed into the Kings River on traveling trips. The pack station also utilized Sawmill Pass to pack into the Kings River in Kings Canyon National Park.

The Partridges sold to two brothers from Wyoming by the name of Johnson in 1946. Ed Sargent, a friend of the Johnsons, ran the station the next year and bought out the Johnsons. Sargent ran the pack station until 1954, and sold to Oliver George "Jake" Zediker and his wife, LaVerne.

After the Partridges sold the outfit, Wilfred Partridge and his wife, Doris, continued as cattle ranchers in Big Pine and raised many good quarter horses. Wilfred was the Inyo County Brand Inspector, inspecting the authenticity of brands for livestock sales, for many years. His brother, Kenneth, and his family ranched in Bishop for many years. Both Wilfred and Kenneth were in the ranching business in Big Pine and Bishop throughout their lives. Wilfred Partridge was one of the original organizers of Mule Days, and the first planning meeting was held at his home. He was the first arena show announcer during the early years, and the Mule Days Committee selected him as Most Honored Packer. In his later years, he still enjoyed packing, and packed for the Mammoth Lakes Pack Outfit. He particularly enjoyed all-expense trips, and his stories around the campfire—all true—were greatly remembered by guests.

Jake Zediker had originally come to the eastern Sierra to work for the Forest Service, and he packed for Chrysler and Cook, as had Ed Sargent in previous times. LaVerne was the daughter of Fred Reynolds, a cattle rancher located at Manzanar. As a girl growing up, she spent summers at Templeton Meadow, where her family summered their cattle. Zediker ran about forty head of pack and saddle stock at Glacier Pack Train, was an excellent finish carpenter, and managed the Reynolds cattle ranch in Big Pine.

Hugh and Ivadell Carpenter were the next owners of the outfit, with forty-three head of horses and mules, beginning in 1961 until 1965. Hugh died, and Ivadell sold the business to Murt Stewart.

Murton A. "Murt" Stewart purchased the pack station in 1965, along with thirty-five head of stock, and he and his wife, Jean, operated the station. Stewart had packed for Mt. Whitney Pack Trains on the large Sierra Club trips in the 1940s. He worked in the winters for the California Snow Surveys, skiing into the mountains to measure the snow depth, and was on crews that built the stone snow survey cabins in the region. His son, "Young Murt," took over operation of Glacier Pack Train, and is still operating the pack station.

In 1981, older Murt Stewart purchased the Tunnel Meadows Pack Station, and operated the resort until it closed due to the area being included in the new Golden Trout Wilderness Area around 1983.

BISHOP CREEK

Bishop Creek Canyon is a large, glacially carved canyon with three major forks: the South Fork, Middle Fork, and North Fork. Soaring, glaciated granite peaks surround the basin, located about twenty miles west of Bishop. South Lake is a large lake with an earthen dam at its northern outlet. It is at 9,755 feet elevation and is surrounded by a number of 13,000+ foot peaks, including Mt. Agassiz at 13,882 feet. The South Fork of Bishop Creek flows down the canyon to several power generating plants. Good deer hunting is found on nearby Coyote Flat.

Lake Sabrina is located in the basin of the Middle Fork of Bishop Creek at 9,132 feet, and the basin is ringed with lofty 13,000-foot peaks. Lake Sabrina is a large natural lake with a dam at the lower end, making it even larger. A lovely glacial basin above the lake contains many small alpine lakes.

North Lake is a small lake at 9,280 feet elevation with a dam at the lower end, near the trailhead of the Piute Pass Trail. Piute Pass, at 11,423 feet, is an eleven-mile, relatively easy climb, and accesses the timberline Humphries Basin and Desolation Lakes. Years ago, sheep and cattle grazed in the backcountry over Piute Pass.

SOUTH FORK OF BISHOP CREEK

From South Lake, it is five and a half miles to Bishop Pass, lying at 11,972 feet elevation. It is thirteen miles from South Lake to the Kings River in Kings Canyon National Park. There are numerous lakes on the north side of the pass. Over the pass lies Dusy Basin, with its many timberline lakes. The trail switchbacks from there down LeConte Canyon, meeting the John Muir Trail on the Middle Fork of the Kings River. Destinations from here are Grouse Meadow, Palisades Canyon, and Mather Pass. Little Pete Meadow and Muir Pass lie to the north on the John Muir Trail.

Located just below South Lake is Parcher's Rainbow Camp, built in the 1920s, with a lodge, nineteen cabins, and a boat landing at South Lake open during the summer season. The Rainbow Pack Outfit is located almost adjoining the busy resort.

Andrews Camp, owned by F. K. Andrews, was a 145-acre alfalfa ranch at the present site of the Four Jeffrey Campground, and was located near where Bishop Creek Lodge is now. William Coats settled it and built a log cabin in 1885. He plowed the meadow and planted crops, so the location was called Coats Meadow originally. The camp was at an elevation of 8,500 feet. Andrews offered cabins and tent cabins, campsites, lodge rooms with guest accommodations, meals, and pack trips with Cruse Pack Trains. Advertising brochures outlined long traveling trips from Bishop Creek to Red's Meadow near Mammoth Lakes. Since Andrews Camp was located on private property, Andrews didn't have Forest Service or Park Service permits for pack trips at that time.

Andrews sold his resort and property in 1918 to the R. J. Schober family, who owned the Circle S Ranch in Round Valley. The Schobers called the resort **Schobers' Mountain Ranch, Lodge and Pack Outfit**. In the 1930s, the lodge also operated a store that included fresh milk and butter from

Schobers' Mountain Ranch Dairy. They also sold gas and oil for automobiles now driving to the resorts and campgrounds. The Schobers were still operating the resort in 1941. This is now the Bishop Creek Lodge.

Prior to 1925, there were three pack outfits on the South Fork of Bishop Creek. These three outfits packed over Bishop Pass into the Kings Canyon and the Middle Fork of the Kings River. Trips accessed the lakes below the pass on the north side, and Dusy Basin on the south side of the pass.

Those three outfits were **Sanford Bros. Pack Train, Cruse Pack Trains**, and **Clark's Pack Station**. Up to 1924, Sanford Bros. Pack Train was operated by the three Sanford brothers, Albert "Ab," Stephen H. "Steve," and Harry. They operated from the old ranger cabin where Parcher's Camp is now located. W. D. "Bill" Cruse packed in guests from the Andrews Camp over Bishop Pass until 1924. Frank W. "Bill" Clark also ran pack trips in the same area, calling his outfit Clark's Pack Station.

In 1923, the Forest Service determined that there were too many pack stations operating in the same area, and there was not enough business for the three of them. A decision was made that two should leave, and the one remaining station would be required to fence the meadows used as pastures, and establish a headquarters there as a permanent facility. None of the three current operators chose to do this.

Harry and Etta Halliday then acquired the packing permit from the Forest Service in 1924. Harry was a blacksmith and had an establishment called Harry Halliday's Shoeing Shop in Bishop. He said he didn't know much about the packing business but he sure knew a lot about horses. The Hallidays owned an outstanding Morgan stallion named Redman, as well as some good Morgan mares, and they raised some of their own horses. At that time, ranchers in the Owens Valley were selling out to the Los Angeles Department of Water and Power. Automobiles were becoming more popular and common, so the blacksmith and horseshoeing business was dropping off. However, tourism was increasing and was being promoted by local towns and the City of Los Angeles.

The Halliday family established their pack station on the Green Creek tributary that flowed into Bishop Creek, just north of Parcher's Camp. The elevation at the pack station is 9,200 feet. The Hallidays called their station **Hallidays' Rainbow Pack Outfit**. They lived in a tent while building the first log cabin. The cook cabin was finished that fall of 1924. A sawmill, located above South Lake, supplied the logs. They built corrals and a packing shed and began the job of fencing the meadows for pasture. Halliday bought horses and mules from the Sanford brothers, Cruse, and Clark (the three previous outfits), accumulating thirty head. His daughter, Ruth, was married to Albert "Ab" Sanford.

The first summer was not very busy, and Halliday commented that he could have operated with half the number of stock. By 1934, however, the Hallidays had increased their stock to sixty head and were very busy. They built more needed facilities for their operation. The following year, Harry sold the station to his son, Warren, and his wife, Nedra, and they ran the outfit until 1945. Warren then sold to Alfred and Esther Shelley from Bishop, who operated it for five summers. Alfred Shelley was a beekeeper and a butcher from Bishop.

Rainbow Pack Outfit was next owned by a partnership of Dudley and Alice

Boothe and Orville and Jackie Houghton. They purchased the outfit in 1950 from the Shelleys. Orville was Alice Boothe's brother, and their father was Cad Houghton, a rancher said to be "the best horse trader in the country." Orville was a long time packer, having packed on many Sierra Club trips, and was an excellent team roper. Dudley's father was Roy Boothe, former supervisor of the Inyo National Forest. As young children, Dudley and his sister had accompanied their parents on a pack trip to the Kings River and Grouse Meadow, riding in pack bags on either side of their trusty mule.

The Boothes leased a ranch at the south end of Bishop, where they lived, ran cattle, and pastured their stock in the winter. The Houghtons lived at the pack station in 1950, and both families lived there in 1951. In 1952, the Boothes bought out the Houghtons' interest. The Boothes' four children grew up at the pack station, where John and Roy learned to be packers at a young age. The station had fifty head of stock—thirty horses and twenty mules. There were still Halliday-bred-and-raised Morgan horses in the horse remuda when my husband and I were at Rainbow Pack Outfit in 1955 and 1956 with our very young son, Lee.

The California Snow Survey built a new stone snow survey hut near the foot of Bishop Pass in the summer of 1956. My husband, Lou Roeser, and the Boothes' son, John, spent a good deal of time that summer packing many difficult and unusual loads to the construction site. The pack station packed in all the materials and the camp for the builders. A stout, gentle horse pulled a stone boat sled and dragged local granite to the site for the building. Cement and lumber had to be packed up to the site. Bed springs and mattresses were tricky to pack up the narrow, rocky switchbacks. A heavy steel door and a cumbersome stove took some packing savvy to get the mules to carry them to the site above Bishop Lake, at over 11,000 feet elevation. During the winter, snow surveyors would ski up to the cabin and check on the depth of the snow in the area.

In 1966, Ralph and George Talbot purchased the station and operated it for perhaps two years before the Boothes had it back again. John Boothe married Jill Kinmont, a well-known local ski racer, in 1976. A book about her life and romance with John was a bestseller, and was followed by a movie in two parts. The book and the movie were titled, *The Other Side of the Mountain.* The sequel, *The Other Side of the Mountain Part II*, was partly filmed at the pack station.

The new owners of Parcher's Camp, Dave and Gloria Jacobson, subleased the station, operating it for one summer. Jim and Donna Howell next purchased the pack station and operated it for five years, from 1975 to 1980. The Howells also purchased Sequoia Kings Pack Trains in Onion Valley.

In 1980, Dale Berry and his son, Mark, became the new owners of both stations, calling them the **Bishop Creek Outfit Rainbow Packers, Inc**. Mark Berry was the operating manager. Rainbow Pack Outfit participated annually in Mule Days, with their packers wearing rainbow colored shirts and suspenders, and Mark ran the arena packing competitions. Mark's brother, John, was also involved in packing at several Sierra stations, including Rainbow, and has packed in the Grand Canyon on different mountain trails. John Berry now manages the Grand Canyon mule ride concession.

Mark Berry and his wife, Robin, took over the stable operations at Furnace

Creek Ranch in Death Valley shortly after purchasing the pack station. He, Robin, and their family spent many winters there. Today, their daughter and son-in-law, Samantha and Luis Moya, manage the stables.

In 1991, Dale Berry, Mark's father, wished to sell the outfit, so the Berrys sold to Mike McMillion, who called the station the **Shooting Star Pack Station,** for two years.

During the following summer months, when Death Valley simmered in heat, Mark and Robin Berry continued working at various pack stations with their five children. Their children all learned the packing trade and packed for various outfits. In the winter, they were back in Death Valley.

After taking the station back, Dale Berry sold it again in 1993 to Bill and Dawn Draves, who named it **Rainbow Pack Station**. Bill was a horseshoer by trade and owned the Sierra Shoeing School in Bishop.

Greg and Mike Allen own Sierra Saddlery in Bishop, a very successful outdoor, western, and feed store in Bishop. In 2000, Greg and Ruby Allen, along with their four young daughters, became the new owners of the outfit. They call the station **Rainbow Pack Outfitters** and still operate today.

Greg and Ruby are very interested in the history of the pack station and in preserving the historical buildings, having them listed as a historic site. The buildings were all constructed during the Halliday tenure. The Allens try to make sure improvements to the site keep with the historical character of the pack station and promote traditional skills. Greg and Ruby have been active with the Eastern High Sierra Packers' Association. Their four girls have grown up at the pack station, guiding rides and pack trips. During the winter, the Allens live on their alfalfa ranch in Benton.

MIDDLE AND NORTH FORK OF BISHOP CREEK

On the North Fork of Bishop Creek, the **Tobe Way Pack Outfit**, owned by Roy "Tobe" Way, was in operation by 1923. The original site of the pack station was at the Cardinal Mine, and it later moved to Aspendell. Tobe was involved with the Sanford brothers in packing operations early in the 1920s. He broke horses and trained colts in the Owens Valley. His sister, Bertha Hall, owned Glacier Lodge, and his brother, Guy Way, was a forest ranger in the Inyo National Forest.

Way packed parties over Piute Pass to the Desolation Lakes Basin, Humphreys Basin, Hutchinson's Meadow, Evolution Valley, and French Canyon. The pack station also packed trips into the Lake Sabrina Basin on the Middle Fork of Bishop Creek and its many glacial lakes.

In 1932, Tobe Way was accidentally and tragically shot and killed at the pack station. Tobe's widow sold the outfit in 1933 to Rudolph John Schober, a former teamster and owner of the Schober Resort on the South Fork of Bishop Creek. R. J. Schober purchased the pack station for his sons, Art and John, for $2,900. Art and John called the pack station **Schober Pack Train**, and they operated with thirty-five head of stock in 1934. Art Schober had first packed over Piute Pass with his father in 1921.

By 1939, John was no longer a partner. Art married Lou Schober in 1940. The pack station was relocated to North Lake after the road was built up to the lake. The logs for the corrals were cut from an area south of the pack station. Avalanches have been a reoccurring hazard, destroying some of the facilities.

Headquarters and a residence are located at Aspendell below North Lake, and are accessible all year.

By 1954, Art and Lou Schober had increased their stock to sixty head—thirty horses and thirty mules. They also furnished burros to hiking parties, and the station still had burros available in 1981. Art owned a cattle ranch in Round Valley, where he pastured their stock during the winter months.

In 1977, Art retired, and their son, Walter, joined them and took over running the pack station. Lou Schober always enlivened the Packers' Association meetings with her pithy and humorous comments. Walter was later president of the Packers' Association. He ran the pack station until 1994, when he sold and retired to the ranch in Round Valley.

In 1994, the station was sold to Mike and TessAnne Morgan. Morgan is the grandson of Bruce Morgan and the son of Charles Morgan of Mt. Whitney Pack Trains. Mike has also packed for Frontier Pack Station at Silver Lake. Mike Morgan renamed the pack station **Bishop Pack Outfitters** and still operates it in 2020.

Packers mounting riders for a pack trip up the Bishop Pass trail.
(Boothe Family Collection)

PINE CREEK

Pine Creek Canyon is located to the southwest of Round Valley, north of Bishop. The Sierra displays a warp in the main crest beginning at Coyote Flat, trending more east/west than north/south in this area. Pine Creek Canyon is a classic U-shaped glacial valley. At the headwall of the canyon, three glaciers met to form one huge glacier that carved out the deep canyon that opens into Round Valley.

Mt. Tom and the canyon area have been active mining areas for many years. The Union Carbide Pine Creek Tungsten Mine opened in 1916. The tungsten mine is located high up on a canyon wall at almost 11,000 feet elevation, with Mt. Morgan towering above at 13,748 feet. The Union Carbide Processing Plant Mill (now closed) is located on the canyon floor. A very steep road switchbacks up to the mine from the canyon. At the mine, another former road comes in from Morgan Pass via Rock Creek. The original road accessing the mine was built up Rock Creek Canyon, through the Little Lakes Valley, and over Morgan Pass to the mine. In 1953, the old unmaintained road was regrown with vegetation, making a wide, easy trail to ride on.

Later, the present scary, steep road was constructed from the floor of Pine Creek Canyon. The mining company built a town at the mouth of the canyon called Rovana and an upper village in the canyon to house more than 300 mine employees. Buses shuttled the miners back and forth to their jobs at the mine. On July 24th, 1946, a cloudburst high in the mountains caused a flash flood, which washed out the employee housing at the upper village. The nearby pack station was unharmed in that weather event. However, avalanches have wiped out the facilities twice.

During World War II, U.S. Vanadium (later called Union Carbide) was heavily involved in the production of tungsten and other minerals necessary for the war effort. Scheelite ore, a form of tungsten, is a direct additive to the steel melt, and is a component used in making armor plating on tanks. The Pine Creek Mine was the largest tungsten producer in the world, but it ceased operation in 2000 because of competition from China.

Pine Creek Pack Station is located about a hundred yards from the Gable Canyon junction with Pine Creek in Pine Creek Canyon, at 7,400 feet elevation. The pack station packed tourists into the Pine Lakes and French Canyon over 11,000-foot Pine Creek Pass.

George Brown was an Owens Valley Paiute rancher, teamster, and mule man. He was born in Round Valley on the Kinney Ranch. George and his wife, Frances, operated a dairy at Silver Lake in the June Lake Loop in 1926. They drove their dairy cows back and forth from Silver Lake to their ranch in Round Valley in the spring and fall.

After selling their dairy to Slim Tatum, George and Frances began the **Pine Creek Saddle and Pack Train** in 1934 in Pine Creek Canyon along the creek. Their partner was Oma Y. Mankins, a packer at Hume Lake on the west side of the Sierra. George also did much mine packing for the Tungstar Mine on the north side of Mt. Tom.

During World War II, the pack station was closed to tourists, but Brown had mine packing contracts that he continued fulfilling. He also worked as a cowboy for Jess Chance, a Round Valley cattle rancher. Brown was one of the packers on the famous "Generals' Pack Trip" in 1944. That pack trip began at Mammoth Lakes and came out of the backcountry at Pine Creek by way of Lake Italy.

Ernie Kinney operated the pack station at Pine Creek after the war for a short time. Several avalanches destroyed facilities, and the pack station was closed for a number of years. Spray Kinney, Ernie's father, was a highly respected teamster and freighter, and in 1924, headed the packing operation at the Champion Sparkplug Mine in the White Mountains, north of Bishop. The mine was developed and owned by a dental surgeon, Dr. Joseph A. Jeffrey, and operated from 1921 through 1945. It produced sillimanite/andalusite needed for the porcelain coating around spark plugs, hence the name of the mine. Jeffrey purchased a ranch in the Hamill Valley below the mine location, where he established the mine headquarters. The ranch grew hay and provisions for the mine, as well as raising livestock.

Because of the very steep location, mules were used to haul the ore from the mine over a four-and-a-half-mile trail to a platform, where it was sacked into 100-pound bags and trucked out to the railroad station and settlement at Laws. There were sixteen mules and two packers. They made two round trips each day (year round) with ore sacks packed one or two on each side. These were very heavy loads, but it was a short trip, all downhill. Aparejo pack saddles were used on the mules. The mule corral was located at the bottom of the trail. In later years, Spray's son, Ernie Kinney, packed in supplies and packed out ore until he went in the Navy during WWII. The mine closed in 1945, near the end of the war.

A number of well-regarded early packers, who also worked at various Sierra pack stations, packed at the Sparkplug Mine, including George Brown, Johnny Bacoch, and Ferris Heedick. Ancilito Torres was a noted aparejo packer who worked for Kinney at the mine until it closed, and many early packers learned those historical skills from him. Torres, an arrierro, had arrived from Mexico with five mules. After the mine closed, Torres then went to work for Arch Mahan at Red's Meadow Pack Station, where he remained a packer until he died in his nineties.

In the heavy winter of 1951-52, an avalanche destroyed part of the facilities at Pine Creek, and in 1954, there was only a shed still standing. In 1955, John "Slim" and Dorothy Nivens were offered the special use permit from the Forest Service. Slim rebuilt the pack station, including a bunkhouse, packing sheds, and corrals, and called it Pine Creek Saddle and Pack Train. Slim had thirty head of stock and ran burros. The burros were rented to hiking parties and many Sierra Club trips. In 1959, Nivens and his family ran the stables in Death Valley during the winter, along with Lona and Gene Burkhart.

In 1971, Arnold and Carol Cole of Independence purchased the pack station from the Nivens family. Arnold died in 1976, and Carol and their children continued to operate the outfit. Carol was secretary of the Packers' Association for several years, and was chosen Most Honored Packer at Mule Days. At the end of the season in 1982, Carol Cole sold to Brian and Danica Berner, who called it **Pine Creek Pack Station**. Another avalanche occurred during the record-setting winter of 1982-83, damaging some of the facilities.

The Berners had previously packed at Hilton Creek Pack Station, owned by

Brian's father, Carl Berner. In 1993, the Berners purchased Sequoia Kings Pack Station at Onion Valley from the Berry family and operated both stations. Brian has been president of the Packers' Association, and Danica has been secretary. They are still in operation.

Rainbow Pack Outfit barn and yard in the 1950s. (Boothe Family Collection)

**Corrals at Rainbow Pack Outfit on Green Creek in the 1950s.
(Boothe Family Collection)**

ROCK CREEK

Rock Creek is a long canyon geographically situated at the top of the Sherwin Grade, north of Bishop, where the Sierra batholith bends to the west. The long north-south trending mountain mass throughout the Owens Valley warps to an east -west trend here. Rock Creek Lake is located nine miles up Rock Creek Canyon from Highway 395 at Tom's Place. Rock Creek Canyon includes more than forty lakes within a half-day's ride or hike. Mosquito Flat is the highest road end in the Sierra at 10,250 feet elevation. The trailhead there accesses the Little Lakes Basin, which lies above Mosquito Flat. The basin, dominated by Bear Creek Spire, provides many lakes as the name implies.

The trail traverses through this basin, then up over Morgan Pass below Mt. Morgan at 13,748 feet, and down into Pine Creek Canyon. That trail follows the old road built to access the Pine Creek Tungsten Mine. This early mining road crossed Morgan Pass at 11,104 feet elevation to the rich mine. Although longer in miles, it followed more gradual terrain than the precipitous, steep-sided Pine Creek Canyon. After a new, direct road was built from Pine Creek Canyon, the old road gradually reverted back to a wide trail.

The Mono Pass Trail climbs steeply for three miles to cross Mono Pass at 12,000 feet, into Pioneer Basin and the Recesses, canyons which lie to the southwest of the pass in the Mono Creek Basin. Mono Pass was an important early Native American trail through the Sierra, and later, livestock men used the trail to access summer grazing lands. Bishop area ranchers grazed livestock in the Mono Creek drainage in the early days of settlement. From the Owens Valley, they drove their herds up the Sherwin Grade to Rock Creek, and then over high Mono Pass to country that provided lush summer grazing for their herds.

At the mouth of Rock Creek on the summit of the Sherwin Grade, Hans Lof built a cookhouse and a gas station to service people now driving their automobiles to the eastern Sierra in 1917. He added a store, and then, in 1919, added corrals and stock, and began packing people up the canyon for backcountry trips. By 1924, he operated with about twenty-four head of stock. In 1922, a rough road was built up the canyon. Lof sold his business to Tom Yerby in 1924, and the resort became known as Tom's Place. Yerby did not continue the packing operation, as a corral now operated near Rock Creek Lake. Tom's Place is still in operation today, and is known for its good food.

As the road was built up Rock Creek Canyon, a lodge and pack station were built near Rock Creek Lake. Arthur C. Frost and Mintzer owned the **Broken Bar Pack Outfit** corral at Rock Creek Lakes Resort. The station had two locations: the headquarters corral (now called the Lower Corral) at Rock Creek Lodge, and the Upper Corral at the end of the road above Rock Creek Lake. The station packed tourists over Mono Pass into Mono Creek, as well as into the Little Lakes Basin. Frost also had a stable at June Lake, where he ran day trips and short rides around the lakes.

Frost had acquired some horses that came from around Mono Lake, and they would sometimes escape the pack station and trail back to Mono Lake. A one-eyed gray mare was the leader of the little herd of "bunch quitters." Frost paid young Ken Partridge of the Partridge family, who had owned Glacier Pack Trains at Big Pine, a dollar per animal to ride and lead them back to Tom's Place, where Frost would pick them up. Wallace Partridge, Ken's dad, ran the power company ranch in the Parker Meadows near Mono Lake at that time. Frost wintered his stock along the Owens River on a ranch owned by Daniel G. McComber.

In 1932, Daniel McComber purchased the station, along with forty-two head of stock, and continued to call it the Broken Bar Pack Outfit. In his brochure, he advertised that extended trips were their specialty, and they conducted 100 Mile Circle Trips that took from one to two weeks. In 1935, McComber purchased the nearby Camp Nelson outfit. That same year, he was president of the Western High Sierra Packers' Association. In 1938, he also owned the Broken Bar Pack Outfit at Quaking Aspen on the west slope of the Sierra. McComber sold the Rock Creek Lake pack station to Wendell and Carrie Gill in 1940.

Wendell Gill was from a long-time packing family. His father, Dee, was a well-known packer on the Kern Plateau, and had packed salt from the Saline Valley salt mines to the livestock herds grazing there. Wendell and his brother, Harold, packed on many Sierra Club trips for Allie Robinson, and rounded up wild horses on the desert mustang ranges. Carrie Gill, Wendell's wife, was the sister of Henry Olivas, and from a long-time packing family in the Lone Pine area. Gill renamed the pack station **Rock Creek Pack Station** and operated it for five years. The station then went to Frank Freeland for a brief tenure from 1945 to 1946.

In 1947, a partnership of Herb and Marge London, Chuck and Dorothy Hovey, and Paul Streckewald purchased the outfit from Freeland. Herb and Marge London and Paul Streckewald worked together in the Los Angeles Flight Dispatch office of American Airlines for a number of years. During World War II, they enjoyed spending vacation time in the Sierras when gasoline ration stamps were available. In 1947, Frank Freeland offered the pack station for sale in the Los Angeles Times. They answered the ad, and together, along with Chuck Hovey, purchased the station with forty-five head of stock.

Herb London became the general manager, Paul the assistant manager, and Chuck a general partner. Early on, London wanted to concentrate on providing longer, all-expense trips in the Mono Creek drainage, and on conducting traveling trips through the Sierra. Russ and Anne Johnson, who later owned McGee Creek Pack Station, worked at Rock Creek from 1948 to 1950, specializing in conducting the all-expense traveling trips.

The owners lived at the Lower Corral, where their stock was pastured. In 1948, Rock Creek Pack Station expanded to the Upper Corral location two miles above the Lower Corral as a base for the longer pack trips. They needed a large building at the Upper Corral, so the office cabin from the Lower Corral was moved. Paul and Russ cut the cabin in half, and Paul hauled the two sections on his truck up to the new site on the hill above the Rock Creek Lakes Store. Herb wanted the building larger, so a ten-foot addition was made between the two halves of the cabin.

The partners looked for a means to use the stock and equipment on a more year-round basis. They signed an agreement with G. Putnam, owner of

Stovepipe Wells Hotel in Death Valley. Herb and Marge London, along with Paul Streckewald, ran the stables the winter of 1947-48. Saddle horses were provided for hour and day rides, and for cookouts where customers rode to and from the dinner site. Paul and Herb built a corral there out of railroad ties that they picked up from an abandoned railroad. The following winter, Russ and Anne Johnson ran the stables at Stovepipe Wells for Rock Creek, and Russ also did mine packing for the Gold Hill Dredging Company. The Johnsons packed for Rock Creek Pack Station for three years before purchasing McGee Creek Pack Station.

In 1952, London bought out his two partners, and by 1965, he operated with sixty-five head of stock. Herb was president of the Eastern High Sierra Packers' Association, and was elected a Supervisor of Inyo County for twelve years.

Rock Creek pastured their stock during the winter at the Pool Field north of Independence, along with Mammoth Lakes Pack Outfit and Red's Meadow Pack Station. In the fall, the horses and mules were driven from the pack station down the canyon and past Tom's Place, then hauled to winter pasture in stock trucks. In the late 1960s, the station began conducting spring horse drives with guests from the Pool Field to the pack station.

In 1972, Herb London and Bob Tanner of Red's Meadow arranged with Ike Livermore to form a partnership with Tommy Jefferson and acquire Mt. Whitney Pack Trains. Mt. Whitney Pack Trains could no longer operate horses and mules on the Mt. Whitney Trail, but was issued Forest Service pack permits to other Owens Valley trailheads. This enlarged the backcountry areas that could be visited by Rock Creek's large traveling trips.

Herb's son, Craig, graduated from the University of California, Davis, as a veterinarian, and joined Herb in the operation of the business. Craig had grown up at the pack station, and learned to ride and pack at a very early age. Rock Creek specialized in all-expense traveling trips; many were through various universities, and offered college credits to the participants. This type of business was very successful for them.

In 1981, Dave Dohnel, along with his grandfather, Chuck Hovey, visited Rock Creek Pack Station. Dave liked the station and the area so much that, in 1982, he bought out his grandfather's partnership interest. In 1992, Dohnel sold his interest in the station back to Herb and Craig London, and, with his brother, Kent, purchased Frontier Pack Station at Silver Lake. Craig London continues owning and managing the pack station today, along with Cottonwood Pack Station and Virginia Lakes Pack Station.

HILTON LAKES

Hilton Lakes lie in a high, glacial granite basin, which holds ten beautiful lakes fairly close to each other. Other than the first lake, Davis Lake, they are all called by numbers rather than proper names. The Hilton Lakes Basin can be accessed by trail from Hilton Creek near Crowley Lake, McGee Creek Pack Station in McGee Canyon, and from Rock Creek Canyon, north of the Rock Creek Lakes Store. In the 1940s, a mining road was cut to the Hilton Creek Tungsten Mine, but the old mine no longer operates, and the road has naturalized.

Today, McGee Creek Pack Station and Rock Creek Pack Station service this basin of lakes. The trail up Hilton Creek has an access branch trailing over a low glacial moraine from McGee Canyon. The trail then continues past the two lower lakes, and passes over a divide into Rock Creek Canyon.

Hilton Lakes Camp and Pack Station was established in 1921 by Brown. The log cabin lodge, dining room, housekeeping cabins, tent cabins, rental boats, and dock were located at Davis Lake, the first and largest of the lakes. The pack station headquarters at Hilton Creek in Long Valley were at 7,200 feet elevation. Pack strings and riders climbed five miles to Davis Lake at 9,801 feet. The trail climbs over a sagebrush moraine for 2,600 feet to the glacially carved canyon. It was a two-and-a-half-hour ride to the camp at Davis Lake. Guests rode into the backcountry camp or were packed into the ten lakes of Hilton Lakes Basin for fishing, hunting, and recreation.

At the end of the season in 1946, Brown sold to Clyde Pearson, who called it **Pearson's Hilton Lakes Camp**. Pearson increased the number of stock to twenty-three head. In 1959, the resort was purchased by Ed and Lil Kyte and called **Kyte's Hilton Lakes Pack Station.** After the passage of the 1964 Wilderness Act, the resort at Davis Lake had to be removed, as no permanent structures are permitted in wilderness areas. With the resort no longer in operation, the demand for packing services decreased. Short saddle rides were available for a while.

Thomas L. Williams purchased the pack station from the Kytes. He sold it in 1978 to Carl Berner and his wife, Faye, along with their two sons, Brian and Bruce, who called it **Hilton Lakes Camp and Pack Station**. The Berners advertised housekeeping cabins and dormitory accommodations at the headquarters overlooking Crowley Lake in Long Valley and pack trips to the Hilton Lakes Basin. They pastured their stock on nearby meadows leased from the Department of Water and Power. The Berners operated the pack station until the Forest Service permit was not renewed when it expired. Brian and Danica Berner purchased Pine Creek Pack Station and Sequoia Kings Pack Trains, and continue to operate Pine Creek in 2020.

McGEE CREEK AND CONVICT LAKE

McGEE CREEK

McGee Canyon is a colorful glaciated canyon with a surprising riot of various colored strata and twisted rock layers. The McGee Canyon Road from Highway 395 to the pack station travels up over a large, well-defined glacial moraine. The views of Long Valley and Crowley Lake are spectacular.

The first section of the trail up the canyon from the road end was a mining road to Baldwin Canyon, where the turnoff went up to the Scheelore Tungsten Mine, which operated in the 1940s and 1950s. From that junction, the trail continues up the main canyon to the many other lakes and McGee Pass. The old mining road has naturalized.

McGee Pass is 11,900 feet elevation, where alpine sky pilot (*Polemonium eximium*) flowers flourish. It is surprising to find clusters of these glorious, fragrant blue flowers growing profusely among the red rocks above the tree line on a high, windswept, and rocky pass. The trail is a gateway to Upper Fish Creek, a tributary and headwaters of the San Joaquin River. From the top of McGee Pass, it is a fairly easy scramble to the top of Red Slate Mountain at 13,163 feet elevation, lying just to the west. The north side of the great mountain drops in sheer cliffs to the meadows of the Convict Lake basin. The McGee Pass trail continues to Tully's Hole, where it intersects the John Muir Trail.

In 1872, brothers Alney and Bart McGee homesteaded a cattle ranch on McGee Creek in Long Valley and opened a stage station. Their Long Valley ranch pastured many head of cattle during the summer months. Early sheep and cattle ranchers established livestock trails over McGee and Hopkins Passes, crossing the main crest of the Sierra. In the 1930s, a CCC Camp was located at Big McGee Lake, and the men worked on McGee and Hopkins Passes.

The California Department of Fish and Game planted golden trout above the first falls in McGee Canyon in 1919, and later in Baldwin Lake. In the early 1950s, Phil Pister, Cliff Brunk, and Russ Johnson packed golden fingerlings by mule, then scrambled through shifting talus, carrying the fish cans on their backs.

In the late 1920s, Cecil R. Thorington began a pack station at McGee Creek, calling it **McGee Pack Train**. The station was located at the foot of the McGee Hill along McGee Creek.

Thorington's father, William Thorington, who had been born in Genoa, Nevada, had purchased the Old's Ranch in Round Valley, west of Bishop, and raised goats. In 1927, his son, Cecil, married Beatrice "Sis" May, a granddaughter of Alney McGee, early owner of the McGee Ranch in Long Valley. Cecil was a packer/foreman for Mammoth Pack Outfit, owned by Charlie Summers, for some years, and then created a new station called McGee Pack Train at McGee Creek. By 1930, Thorington, along with Lee Summers, was packing fingerling trout into the backcountry lakes with mule strings for the Fish and Game Department. Thorington and Summers planted Lee and Cecil Lakes—named after the two men—along with Upper Fish Creek. In 1934, the McGee Pack Train operated with thirty head of horses and mules.

In 1938, Thorington was a constable of the Mammoth Township and ran for Sheriff of Mono County. He was elected and served for twenty-eight years. "Big Cec," as he was called, was a large man, and it was said that he never had to use a "persuader." Coley Ward managed the pack station for Thorington, as he was now busy with his sheriff duties at the county seat in Bridgeport.

The U.S. Public Roads Administration built McGee Canyon Road in 1944 as a mining access road up to the Scheelore Tungsten Mine in Baldwin Canyon. The active mine was high on the south slopes of Mt. Baldwin at 11,000 to 11,600 feet elevation. A locked gate was placed at the wilderness line of the High Sierra Primitive Area to prevent vehicles other than mine trucks from accessing the wilderness.

In June of 1944, Thorington sold the pack station to Alton and Ted Birmingham. The sale included two cabins along McGee Creek on DWP land, ten horses, five mules, eleven riding saddles, and seven packsaddles, along with other gear. Birmingham called the station **McGee Creek Pack Station**, and it was relocated to a new site up the canyon, shortly below the primitive area boundary, at 7,700 feet elevation. Whether the buildings were moved to the new site or built there is unclear. William P. Powell owned the pack station briefly in 1945 and 1946, and he probably built the main house, where my husband, Lou, and I lived when we worked there in 1953 and '54. Charles "Chuck" and Helen Lumpkin purchased the pack station in 1947, and their sixteen-year-old son, Bob, packed for them. They were from Bishop and wintered their stock in Round Valley. Helen Lumpkin baked pies and bread, and served fresh churned butter for customers and fishermen along the creek. Her lunches became quite popular with summer visitors.

A beaver pond often occupies the meadow about three miles—or a two-hour ride—up the canyon, providing excellent fishing. McGee Creek is a popular fishing stream for brown trout. In the backcountry, the lakes in McGee Canyon were known for their excellent fishing.

In 1951, Russ and Anne Johnson purchased the pack station from the Lumpkins. During World War II, Russ worked in the San Diego defense industries as a tool and die designer. Because of gas rationing, Russ and Anne rode a Greyhound bus to Mammoth Lakes for their first pack trip into the Sierra with Mammoth Lakes Pack Outfit. They were from western Colorado and loved the high mountains. After several pack trip vacations, they decided to work at a pack station, and were employed by Herb London at Rock Creek Pack Station in 1948. Russ and Anne conducted their all-expense traveling trips

At McGee Creek, Russ was very innovative and made many improvements around the station. They built a rental tent cabin and bunkhouse room, and served meals to their customers, as well as the fishermen camping on McGee Creek or staying in the nearby campgrounds. Russ built a new saddle shed that was state-of-the-art among pack stations.

A fenced pasture lease to the north of the facilities, adjoining the corrals, is part of the pack station permit, where stock graze when not being used. When we worked there, in 1953 and 1954, the animals were turned out to graze at night, and early in the morning, the packer would wrangle them into the corrals for a little hay and grain. The Johnsons did not have a stock truck or trailer in the early days, so the stock was trucked commercially from winter pasture in Round Valley to the bottom of the McGee moraine, where the animals were unloaded and driven up the hill to the pack station. Later, Russ and Anne purchased 8-Mile Ranch north of Independence, and the stock wintered there. Their stock was branded with the Circle Dot brand of the ranch. They lived at the ranch during the winter.

The Johnsons visited area resorts, advertising their day fishing trips to Grass and Round Lakes. Anne was an expert fishing guide, and the day fishing trips became very popular with visitors. Russ added a little store counter in the main house and sold fishing tackle and rods. Anne sent out a weekly fishing report to sports reporters and sporting goods stores throughout Southern California.

Russ and Anne were very active in the Eastern High Sierra Packers' Association, and Russ served as secretary and president of the organization. They rewrote and printed the association's bylaws booklet and produced the advertising brochures for many years. During the winters, they worked at Chalfant Press in Bishop. They also worked with the Sport Shows in Southern California. Russ became active as an area photographer and, with Anne, wrote many articles on packing. They published a guidebook and a book on the ghost town of Bodie.

In 1968, Russ and Anne sold the pack station to Dave McRoberts who, with his wife, ran the station for ten years and wintered at 8-Mile Ranch. In 1978, McRoberts sold to John and Suzy Ketcham and their daughter, Jennifer. The 8-Mile Ranch became the Ketchams' winter headquarters. John continued to grow top quality alfalfa hay, and Suzy raised Morgan horses that they used in their dude string.

Suzy and Jennifer ran the pack station with an almost all-girl packing crew. This was a great opportunity for young women who wanted the opportunity to work as packers or wranglers. At Mule Days in 1984, McGee Creek Pack Station competed in the arena packing competitions with a women's team, against the men's teams, and did very well. In 1985, there was a women's packing team category that the McGee Creek girls won.

In 1980, the McGee Creek Road was paved from the old highway up to the Forest Service campground that had been rebuilt and improved. In 1992, the Forest Service moved the trailhead back down the canyon to its present location above the pack station, and built an improved, paved trailhead parking and rest area at the new end of the road.

In the heavy winter of 1982-83, an avalanche destroyed the main house, bunkhouse, and rental cabin. The corrals and packing facilities were not damaged. In August, a new combination house and bunkhouse was completed, but the Ketchams did not replace the rental cabin.

After Suzy died in 1985, John and Jennifer ran the pack station. John was president of the Eastern High Sierra Packers' Association, and Jennifer was secretary for many years. They also ran the Sports Show booth for the association for many years.

In 1988, Jennifer Ketcham married our son, Lee Roeser. They bought out John Ketcham's interest in the pack station. John continued farming the alfalfa field at 8-Mile Ranch until he retired, selling the hay ranch interest to the Roesers. Lee and Jennifer maintain their headquarters and live at

8-Mile Ranch in the winter, where Lee built his saddle shop. Lee built all-new saddles for their dude string and new pack gear. They built an arena for training young horses and mules.

Until Lou and I sold the Mammoth Lakes Pack Outfit, Lee and Jen combined their stock with ours on the spring and fall horse drives from Independence winter pastures to the mountains for the busy summer packing season and back again.

Lee has been vice president and president of the Packers' Association, and Jennifer became the association's Washington D.C. legislative and public relations representative during the decade-long lawsuit by environmentalists against the Forest Service and the pack stations. She testified before the U.S. Congress subcommittee on National Parks, Recreation, and Public Lands. Lee packs for the Forest Service, and Jennifer continues to manage the pack station.

In 2010, the Mule Days Celebration selected Lee and Jennifer as Most Honored Packers and honored Jennifer as Packer of the Decade. Both Lee and Jennifer are second generation Most Honored Packers, as Lou and I were selected for that honor in 1982, and John Ketcham was honored in 1989. In 1919, Lee was honored to be selected for the Mule Days Hall of Fame. The Roesers' twenty mule Range of Light Pack String of large, matched black mules perform beautifully in the opening of each Mule Days show in the arena.

The pack station packs parties into the lakes of McGee Canyon in the John Muir Wilderness Area. The McGee Pass Trail goes over the almost 12,000-foot pass and drops into Upper Fish Creek, Horse Heaven, and Tully's Hole, where it connects with the John Muir Trail. The pack station also has an active day ride schedule of one-hour, two-hour, and half-day trail rides. During the wildflower season, scenic wildflower rides are very popular. They also provide pack trips into the Hilton Lakes Basin as well as the Convict Lakes Basin, accessed by the Laurel Pass Trail.

CONVICT LAKE

Convict Lake, at 7,583 feet elevation, is a moraine-impounded glacial lake. The last large glacier left a dam of glacial material across the colorful basin of twisted red and gray metamorphic rocks. Mt. Morrison (12,268 feet) and Laurel Mountain (11,818 feet) tower over the large, spectacular lake. Fossils of crinoids and graptolites are discovered in the lakes basin. Lake Mildred, at 9,760 feet elevation, is a five mile trip from the trailhead, and is the first lake up the canyon. It is located at the north end of a long meadow, dominated by 13,163 foot Red Slate Mountain at the upper end. There are nine lakes in the upper basin, and no trail pass breaches the precipitous crest to allow access to the southward Fish Creek Basin.

Lloyd Summers of Mammoth Pack Outfit owned most of the mining claims in Laurel Creek upward to Laurel and Bloody Mountains, as well as mines in Convict Canyon, with two other partners. In 1932, his mining company was called the S. S. and K. Mining Company. Lloyd Summers also owned the King Creek group of mines in the Ritter Range.

Bausch and Lomb Company owned a calcite mine high on the side of Mount Baldwin. The calcite crystals from the mine were used for lenses in the sights for bombers during World War II, and also were used for binocular lenses. A miner carefully packed the fragile, well-padded calcite ore on a gentle mule and led it down the steep canyon on foot. However, new processes soon made calcite obsolete for this purpose.

The seven-mile-long Laurel Pass Trail begins at the Laurel Creek trailhead on the Sherwin Creek Road. It follows a steep, unmaintained mining road over the Laurel Creek Moraine, gaining about 2,000 feet. This road was built in 1955 to access a tungsten mine near Bloody Mountain above. Cattle graze a large meadow in a hanging valley at the top of this moraine. Above the meadow are the Laurel Lakes. The nearby fish hatchery at Hot Creek experimented using those lakes for rearing golden trout and capturing their eggs, but the venture was not very successful and was eventually abandoned. The trail from Laurel Meadow then switchbacks up over a saddle (Laurel Pass) between Bloody Mountain and Laurel Mountain, and eventually drops into Genevieve Lake. The views from this lunar-like, treeless basin are quite stunning, looking directly down on Convict Lake, 3,000 feet below, and distant Crowley Lake. From Genevieve Lake, the other lakes in the basin can be easily accessed.

In 1919, the Forest Service studied Convict Lake, with ideas and proposals for a permittee to build a summer camp there with cabins and a boat dock. Fred Raymer was granted a permit to establish a camp by the lake. From 1927 to 1933, Fred and Edith Raymer operated a camp at Convict Lake with a small number of stock for trips up the canyon. In 1933, William J. and Dolly Garner purchased the camp from the Raymers, calling it **Bill Garner's Camp and Pack Outfit.** The Garners had previously managed the Arcularius Fishing Ranch on the Owens River for Frank Arcularius. They constructed facilities and cabins on the property, and advertised horses with guides to the upper lakes.

In March of 1949, the Garners sold the resort to Ivan and Marguerite White, along with Paul and Fern Martin. The sale included thirteen horses, four mules, a stable and corrals, saddles, and equipment, in addition to the store, restaurant, and cabins. The **Convict Lake Pack Station** as the station was now called, primarily provided day rides to the upper lakes, one-hour rides, and a few pack trips. McGee Creek Pack Station also provided pack trips to the upper lakes using the canyon trail. The trail up the narrow canyon to the lakes basin had a good number of switchbacks, but was passable and a fairly good riding trail at this time.

Ed Thistlethwaite, a well-known old-time packer and Western artist, was the wrangler at the station for several years. He was from England and spoke with a very proper English accent but stuttered. Lou and I have a fond memory of Ed Thistlethwaite on one particular day. I had accompanied Lou as a helper on a resupply for the U.S. Fish and Wildlife research camp at Clover Lake. On the return trip, we caught up with Russ Johnson, who was packing out a couple from Bishop who had been camped at Genevieve Lake, and we fell in behind them. As we passed Lake Mildred and started down the Canyon Trail, we were behind Ed Thistlethwaite and his day riders. The couple Russ was packing out were anxious to reach Convict Lake and their car, and to return to home in Bishop. They became increasingly irritated with the slower pace of Ed and his day party. The views of Convict Lake are spectacular, but the couple ignored them. At one view stop, the woman impatiently called out to Ed in a loud voice, "Can't you ride a little faster? We want to get home before dark!" Ed slowly turned and looked up the hill at her and stated haltingly, as he stuttered, "Madame, the essence of packing is not haste." With that said, he slowly continued down the trail in his dignified manner.

Russ Johnson at McGee Creek Pack Station had a contract with the U.S. Fish and Wildlife Service to supply their research camps at the upper lakes. The agency maintained a research station on Lower Convict Creek and studied fish in the lakes of the basin for a number of years. McGee Creek Pack Station also handled some pack trips. There was a dim trail from McGee Canyon around McGee Mountain that dropped into Convict Creek just below Convict Lake. The McGee Creek packer would trail the necessary stock from McGee Creek Pack Station around to Convict Lake via this trail. It was usually dark when the packer and mules would reach Convict Lake. During the two years we were at McGee Creek, Lou's assignment was the weekly resupply, and sometimes moving a camp to another lake.

In 1957, Convict Lake Pack Station and Resort was sold to Gordon Dolan with thirty-five head of stock. Dolan then sold it to Dick Meyers in 1960.

The following year, 1961, Meyers sold Convict Lakes resort to J. Robert "Bob" and Dorothy Wenger. By 1963, the Wenger family had thirty-nine head of horses and mules. Their two children, Jeff and Joanie, worked with them in the business. The Wengers established the outstanding restaurant at the resort that is still renowned in the area for fine dining.

In the heavy winter of 1969, the Convict Creek crossing three miles up the creek in the narrow upper canyon washed out. The Forest Service installed two or three different steel bridges at the difficult stream crossing, each in various years, and the bridges continued to wash out. The stream crossing had not been difficult for stock without a bridge, but hikers had difficulty crossing the creek early in the year with high water. The Convict Creek trail is no longer used by commercial stock.

Another trail into the upper basin travels over Laurel Pass from Laurel Creek to Genevieve Lake and then accesses the other lakes. Our pack station, Mammoth Lakes Pack Outfit, packed over this trail to the upper lakes after Convict Lake Resort ceased using the Convict Creek trail. We trucked stock from Mammoth Lakes to the Laurel Pass trailhead on the Sherwin Creek Road.

The Wengers sold the resort and pack station to a corporation in 1982, and Dan Dinsmore managed the resort. In 1983 and '84, Lou and I subleased the Convict Lake Stables and called it Convict Lake Pack Station. We conducted one and two-hour guided trail rides around the lake. We advertised packing to the upper lakes basin and day rides in the Mule Days Program. After we did not renew the sub-lease, the corporation managers resumed offering a schedule of rides around the lake. The current owners of the resort are bringing fresh, new thinking to the facilities, and a love of the area, while still honoring the historical setting of the resort. The stables offer two-hour scenic horseback rides around the lake during the summer season.

Later, Lee and Jennifer Roeser at McGee Creek Pack Station started conducting pack trips to the beautiful Upper Convict Basin Lakes over Laurel Pass and continue to provide this service today.

MAMMOTH LAKES

At Mammoth Lakes, there occurs a wide opening in the Sierra Nevada front that is dominated by Mammoth Mountain, a dormant volcano rising abruptly from the western edge of the Long Valley Caldera. The caldera exhibits fumaroles and hot springs, and has frequent seismic activity. A gap in the Sierra allows storms from an opposite gap in the Coast Range to flow across, bringing more snow and moisture. This additional moisture creates a Jeffrey pine forest extending toward the White Mountains, the largest Jeffrey pine forest in the country. Mammoth Mountain receives the benefit of this moisture in snowfall, providing a long season for the ski slopes of Mammoth Mountain Ski Area.

The Mammoth Lakes Basin is broad and dotted with lakes, bounded on the west by the precipitous Mammoth Crest or Rim, and on the north by Mammoth Mountain. Thousands of years ago, the waters from this basin drained into the San Joaquin River, but subsequent glaciations changed the course of the drainage to the east side of the range. Mammoth Creek drains into the Upper Owens River system.

Lodges, resorts, and the pack station are located here, as well as one of the country's largest ski resorts on Mammoth Mountain. Trails leading out of the basin and intersecting with the John Muir Trail are the Duck Pass, the Mammoth Rim, and the Mammoth Pass Trails.

Gold was discovered on Red Mountain in the 1870s, and several gold mining towns were established along the creeks. Mammoth City was the largest, followed by Pine City, Mineral Park, and Mill City. The region was named after the Mammoth Mining Company Incorporated in 1878. Travel to the new boomtown from the west crossed the Sierra over the French Trail (Fresno Flats Trail).

Cattle ranchers had been grazing the Mammoth Meadows and Long Valley during the summer season since 1861. Many of them drove their cattle up into the mountains for high meadow grazing. Tom Williams had a ranch in the meadows and drove his cattle over Mammoth Pass to Deer Creek for summer grazing. Tom Rickey, the largest rancher in the eastern Sierra, drove his cattle from Long Valley over various passes into the Fish Creek Basin. The large drainage of Fish Creek is a tributary to the Middle Fork of the San Joaquin River. Early settlers in the area called Fish Creek the South Fork of the San Joaquin River, not realizing at first that there was another South Fork.

MAMMOTH MEADOWS

Mammoth Camp Pack Outfit was located in the Mammoth Meadows, called Big Windy Flat by the early settlers, below Red Mountain and Mammoth Rock. There were ranches in the meadows and a hotel and summer cabins along the creek.

Charles Summers and his brother John were cattle ranchers in the area. Charlie established his ranch headquarters at Laurel Creek, while John had his spread on Mammoth Creek near Casa Diablo Hot Springs. In 1915 or earlier, Charlie Summers began packing in tourists from Mammoth Camp to the backcountry. The large barn and corrals across the road from the Wildasinn

Hotel were the headquarters for Mammoth Camp Pack Outfit for a time.

In 1917, Summers purchased the Wildasinn Hotel and, in 1918, added a large, new hotel built with logs cut in the Mammoth Lakes Basin. Guests for pack trips stayed at the hotel or cabins before and after their trip. Some camped along the creek. More summer cabins were built along Mammoth Creek. The Summers family operated a hotel, store, sawmill, and dairy in the meadows. The post office was in a corner of the general store, where Charlie's son, Lloyd Summers, was the postmaster. Packers trailed the stock up the old mining road to Lake Mary in the Mammoth Lakes Basin, often the night before a trip departure. Sometimes, twenty to thirty head of stock were led or driven up to Lake Mary. Pack trips went over Duck Pass into the huge canyon of Fish Creek, with dozens of lake basins, or over Mammoth Pass to the Middle Fork of the San Joaquin River.

In 1919, the Forest Service announced plans to improve the old mining wagon road to Pine City in the Mammoth Lakes Basin the following summer. They assured the public that the road from Mammoth Camp to Pine City would have no more than a ten percent grade. After the improved road to the lakes basin was completed in 1919, lodges and cabins were established and built by the lakes. Tamarack Lodge at Twin Lakes, Wildyrie Lodge at Lake Mamie, and Crystal Crag Lodge at Lake Mary were the first. That year, Charlie and Lloyd Summers fenced in a meadow and put up a corral on the south side of Lake Mary. Pack trips from the **Mammoth Pack Outfit**, as it was now named, departed from there.

LAKE MARY

The site of old Pine City is located just north of Lake Mary, between Lake Mary and Twin Lakes in the Mammoth Lakes Basin. During the mining boom, Pine City was a thriving little town. The trail to the west side of the Sierra, variously called Fresno Flats Trail, French Trail, or Mammoth Pass Trail, from Mammoth Lakes to Fresno Flats (the present town of Oakhurst) passed through Pine City. The camp was situated by a small creek, opposite from the gold mines on Red Mountain. Lake Mary, called Summit Lake then, was a popular location for Sunday picnics. There was even a dance platform on the lake. Prior to being dammed, the lake was much smaller.

Beginning in 1872, the Pine City Feed and Livery Stable made regular trips with tourists and freight across the Sierra using the Fresno Flats Trail. The terminus was at Fresno Flats, or Oakhurst. After the mines failed, Charlie Albright, a prospector and miner, occupied one of the old cabins in 1883. He cut hay in the little nearby meadow for his two burros and continued to work his claims.

Tourists packed in over Mammoth Pass to the Middle Fork of the San Joaquin River and the Ritter Range. Another trail went over Duck Pass to Duck Lake and deep Fish Creek Basin. In 1920, Clark Keely, a summer resident of Mammoth Camp, went on a pack trip to Purple and Virginia Lakes over the old Duck Pass Trail. The trail went from Emerald Lake to Woods Lakes and over the top of the crest, to the east of the current pass route. The packer was Dave Jackson, a long time Paiute packer from the Owens Valley. Jackson Lake (now called Grassy Lake) and Jackson Meadow on Minnow Creek were named for him. In 1921, Keely described a pack trip to the San

Joaquin River for ten days.

The Keely family camped at Soda Springs, near the Devils Postpile, each summer for an extended stay. His mother, Mrs. Keely, strongly believed in the health benefits of camping out in the mountains during the summer. The family began summering at Mammoth Camp, first staying at the Summers' Mammoth Hotel. They later bought land from the Summers, building a beautiful log cabin along Mammoth Creek for their summer residence.

By 1933, with a better road into the Mammoth Lakes Basin, the Mammoth Pack Outfit operated from a facility across the road from the Lake Mary Pack Station, owned by Don McGuffin. Lloyd Summers' sons, Lee and Verne, packed for him. Cecil Thorington, Fred Hamer, Sabert Brown, Slim Tatum, George Brown, Howard Rodgers, and Dave Jackson were packers there in the 1920s. Other Mammoth Pack Outfit packers in the '20s and '30s were Shannon LeBarge, Rosachi, Leland Arigoni, and Lawson DeChambeau.

In 1932, Lloyd and Sybil Summers officially established their Mammoth Pack Outfit at Red's Meadow. The outfit had been packing into Red's Meadow and the San Joaquin River since 1915 and had a corral there. Lloyd's brother, "Young Charlie" Summers, and his family managed the Mammoth Pack Outfit at Agnew Meadows, built after a road was cut over Minaret Summit down to Agnew Meadows. In 1933, Lloyd Summers advertised pack station locations at Mammoth Camp, Lake Mary, Red's Meadow, and Agnew Meadows. At the end of the season in 1935, Summers sold the outfit at Red's Meadow to Archie and Gladys Mahan, while continuing to operate the other three outfits.

In 1923, there were still a dozen or so cabins standing in the old mining town of Pine City. The old site of the Pine City Feed and Livery was part of the community. C. A. "Charlie" Roberts began his pack station operation, called **Roberts Pack Train**, on this site and ran about twenty head of stock. He also had a corral at Pumice Flat on the Middle Fork of the San Joaquin River and packed in tourists to the region over the Mammoth Pass Trail. He also kept a pack of hound dogs and hunted lions. Slim Tatum packed for Roberts in 1924, and long-time packer Chet Squires packed for him as well.

In 1930, Roberts sold the pack station to a partnership of Donald Edward McGuffin, Ernie Smith, and Edward W. Brown. They called the station **Lake Mary Pack Station**. In 1933, McGuffin bought out his two partners. Included in the sale were fifty-eight horses and mules, forty-five saddles and tack, thirty packsaddles and tack, and other packing and horse equipment. The horses were branded with the Bar H on the left stifle. McGuffin worked at the Santa Anita Race Track in Southern California during the winters.

Don McGuffin moved several ranch buildings from the Bishop area in sections and put them back together again at the site. These were old ranch buildings that the Los Angeles Department of Water and Power were planning to burn. As the City purchased ranches for their water rights, they often removed or destroyed the houses and barns, as they chose not to become landlords. The kitchen/dining room and big saddle shed were two buildings that McGuffin moved to Lake Mary. The buildings were located on the west side of the Lake Mary Road and across the little creek. Don's office was on the east side of the creek near the road. In 1934, he had forty-five head of horses and mules.

McGuffin pioneered day ride trails to the top of Mammoth Mountain and the top of Red Mountain, where guests from the nearby lodges could ride horseback and admire the stunning views. This was long before there was a ski lift at Mammoth Mountain.

By 1933, the Hayden Map of the area, an advertising map produced by Emmett Hayden, showed that there were two pack stations across the road from each other. Lloyd Summers and his Mammoth Pack Outfit had established their pack station with cabins and corrals on the east side of the Lake Mary Road on the mining claim. Don McGuffins's Lake Mary Pack Station was on the west side of the road.

In 1937, a new highway location was established, with the road completed by 1939. The new road bypassed the original Mammoth Road (now called the Old Mammoth Road) that climbed up to the lakes basin from the Mammoth Meadows, and isolated the little community of Mammoth Camp along Mammoth Creek. The village and resort businesses moved their establishments north to the newly constructed and paved road. Lloyd Summers, the postmaster, moved a cabin from the pack station to house the post office in the new town. It served for many years, and when the new post office was constructed in 1948, the old building was moved again and became the bunkhouse at the pack station, where it still stands today.

In 1939, Lloyd Summers purchased the Lake Mary Pack Station from McGuffin for $1,850, with $900 down. The bill of sale included twenty-one horses and mules, two cows, thirty-five saddles and tack, twenty packsaddles and tack, one corral, and three cabins, one of which was the barn. There were also water rights to Lake Mary and Coldwater Creek. Summers merged the two stations into one under the **Mammoth Lakes Pack Outfit** name, and moved buildings to the west side of the road and the little creek, along with the existing Lake Mary Pack Station buildings. This is still the present location of the Mammoth Lakes Pack Outfit.

In 1940, Lloyd Summers advertised Mammoth Pack Outfit at Lake Mary and Mammoth Pack Outfit at Agnew Meadows. "Young Charlie" Summers and his family still ran the pack outfit at Agnew Meadows, and Lloyd, Sybil, and their three sons were at the Lake Mary outfit.

In 1943, former owner Don McGuffin, married Alice Austin of Tamarack Lodge at Twin Lakes, and together they ran that lodge and cabins for many years, until selling it to Bob Stanford in 1959. The McGuffins loved square dancing, and Don was an accomplished caller for their weekly dances. Lou and I enjoyed the square dances in 1952, while we were dating that summer.

During World War II, Lloyd's two older sons enlisted in the Service. Lee was stationed in Alaska, and Verne was in the South Pacific. Lloyd and Sybil ran the pack station. On a busy August morning in 1945, as Lloyd was opening the dude horse corral gate, he suffered a fatal heart attack. This was a difficult time for Sybil, but she took over the management of the station. She was also the postmaster for the community. Lee eventually returned from Alaska and took over operation of the pack station.

Packers during these years included Don Douglas, Dave Jackson, Dutch Spaethe, Lawrence and Lester Cline, and Jim Nicol. Lee married Don Douglas's daughter, Dorothy, in 1946. Lee's son, Don, grew up at the pack station. John Summers, Lee and Dorothy's son, was born in 1950, and went to the pack station when he was two months old.

In 1952, Lou Roeser, a young Arizona cowboy, arrived at the pack station and was hired by Lee Summers to pack for the summer. Lou met me when I was Program Director and Assistant Manager at Camp High Sierra during summers while attending UCLA. As one of my duties, I guided the Camp High Sierra trail rides out of the pack station. We were married the following March of 1953. Between 1953-1956, Lou and I worked at McGee Creek Pack Station and Rainbow Pack Outfit.

In 1954, Lee Summers acquired a third interest in the Independence pasture lease called the Pool Field or the Thibault Lakes Field. The stock of three pack stations wintered there: Mammoth Lakes Pack Outfit, Red's Meadow Pack Station, and Rock Creek Pack Station. Mammoth Lakes Pack Outfit had eighty head of stock in 1957.

In 1960, Lee Summers sold the pack station to me and Lou, along with Louis "Louie" and Dorothy Russell Fitzhugh, my brother-in-law and sister. Lou was the managing partner. The Independence pasture lease was included in the sale. Beginning in 1960, we expanded the day ride schedule and pack trip offerings. In 1971, Lou and I purchased the Fitzhughs' interest in the pack outfit.

From 1964 to 1968, Mammoth Lakes Pack Outfit operated a stable at the Mammoth Mountain Inn. Short horseback rides and dinner rides to Minaret Summit were provided to guests at the inn.

Our son, Lee Roeser, had been packing mules since he was a boy, and he and our daughters, Kerry, Maryl, and Leslie, were active working members of the pack station team. As the pack station grew with more activities, the siblings assumed management roles. Lee managed packing operations and pack station logistics; Kerry and Leslie ran the day ride corral, and assisted with the kitchen, backcountry cooking, and office operations. I handled the reservation bookings, correspondence, and bookkeeping for the business, besides managing the pack station kitchen and backcountry cooking operation for the all-inclusive trips.

As the business expanded, more cabins, packing sheds and packing docks, and corrals were added, and cabins were remodeled. A new office and day ride corrals were added on the east side of the little creek.

In 1968, we were granted a Forest Service permit for a new horse operation and resort, eventually called Sierra Meadows, in Old Mammoth. Lou began building the new resort in the Mammoth Meadows on the Sherwin Creek Road. It began as a summer operation, with horse boarding, hayrides, and short guided rides. In January of 1971, the first lodge building burned to the ground, and Lou had to begin all over again rebuilding the lodge. Arnie Metcalf, along with his wife Susan, became a partner and the manager at Sierra Meadows in 1976. Sierra Meadows was then expanded to a winter operation as well, with a cross-country ski center. The new resort business was named **Sierra Meadows Equestrian and Ski Touring Center.** Due to health reasons, in 1981, the Metcalfs left the partnership, and we resumed management.

Lou had long wanted to add sleigh rides to the winter activities, so in 1982, he built a winterized barn, and remodeled the dining rooms and kitchen. We purchased two sleighs and five new Percheron draft horses. We added sleigh rides and dinners to the recreation Sierra Meadows provided. Our next business acquisition was Mammoth Snowmobile Rentals, and we added guided snowmobile tours to the winter ski activities offered. Many employees worked both summers and winters for the outfit. In 1987-1989, Sierra Meadows put on Old West Days in conjunction with the town, and created and put on the Carriage Show and carriage lunch ride over the Fourth of July weekend.

In 1976, the pack outfit resumed old-time horse drives from the Mammoth Lakes headquarters to our winter pasture in Independence—this time including customers. The guests were a working part of the crew, driving loose horses and mules a hundred miles. Spring and fall horse drives have continued at the outfit each year since. The five-day drives were an important tradition and event that our whole family and crew participated in, with all the working aspects of planning and implementing the large mobile event with fifty clients. It was a fast moving adventure, with a new camp set up each night along the way and three delicious meals prepared each day for the hungry wranglers. These drives almost immediately became extremely popular, with many guests returning year after year.

Three and four-day trail rides, outside of the wilderness areas where quotas were imposed, were also very popular with customers. We rode to Bodie, the Sweetwater Mountains, the Inyo Mountains, and the Glass Mountains. On these trips, staff-driven vehicles hauled the riders and horses to the beginning of the ride, with the wrangler crew, including Lou and I, guiding the riders to our next camp. Staff went on ahead to set up camp and prepare the meals. The stock and guests were then transported back to the pack station at the end of the ride. In addition to these trips, cattle drives and a mustang viewing were added to trip offerings.

For a few years beginning in 1977, we also ran the Bridgeport Pack Trains out of the Bridgeport and Devil's Gate areas.

In 1983-84, we sub-leased the Convict Lake Stables and ran their short rides. Bob Morgan, grandson of Bruce Morgan, was the guide. Mammoth Lakes Pack Outfit continued conducting pack trips over Laurel Pass to the upper lakes in Convict Basin.

By 1980, we were running 120 head of stock. In 1982, we were chosen Most Honored Packers at Mule Days. Lou continued to be active in the Packers' Association, serving as president and vice president, and was on the board of directors many times. He and I were also active with the National Forest Recreation Association and were on their board of directors for a number of years.

Our son, Lee, married Jennifer Ketcham of McGee Creek Pack Station in 1988. Sons-in-law Matt Engelhart and Mike Elam worked at the business enterprises as well. It had always been a family operation. In 1991, we sold Mammoth Snowmobiles, and in 1992, we sold Sierra Meadows Equestrian and Ski Touring Center.

In 1998, we sold Mammoth Lakes Pack Outfit to John L. Summers, the son of Lee and Dorothy Summers, from whom we had purchased the pack station in 1960. John's great grandfather, Charlie Summers, had begun the packing operations so many years before. John, a building contractor, remodeled many of the buildings, but sadly, the historic cookhouse burned. The Summers family continues to own and operate the pack station. To this day, the pack station has only been operated by two families—the Summers and the Roesers.

RED'S MEADOW

The Middle Fork of the San Joaquin River is located fifteen miles west of Mammoth Lakes near the Devil's Postpile National Monument. It lies in Madera County, but is only accessed by the Minaret Summit Road (9,176 feet elevation) that is located in Mono County, out of Mammoth Lakes. The valley of the Middle Fork of the San Joaquin River is located in the Sierra National Forest, but in 1965, the Inyo National Forest took over management due to sole road access from Mono County on the east side of the range. Sierra National Forest has access to the area only by trail. The Devil's Postpile National Monument is located near Red's Meadow and Rainbow Falls. There are a number of popular Forest Service campgrounds in the valley, and fishing in the San Joaquin River is celebrated.

The John Muir and Pacific Crest Trails pass through the valley of the Middle Fork of the San Joaquin River. The Pacific Crest Trail from Mexico to Canada is 2,620 miles long and joins the John Muir Trail through much of the Sierra. The Mammoth Pass Trail (also called the Fresno Flats Trail or the Old French Trail) crosses through Red's Meadow on its journey between Oakhurst and Mammoth Lakes.

The Ritter Range is a secondary crest in the Sierra with spectacular glaciated peaks and many beautiful lakes. Mt. Ritter is the highest peak, at 13,156 feet, and Banner Peak, just to the north, is next at 12,957 feet. The Minarets, to the south of Mt. Ritter, are popular with mountain climbers. A section of this range, including Mounts Ritter and Banner and the Minarets, can be seen from Long Valley on Highway 395 and rivals the Grand Tetons in beauty. Several small glaciers are found in favorable situations on the mountains, but indications in 1932 showed that the remnant glaciers were gradually disappearing. A systematic geological study of the region was not undertaken prior to 1930. Geologists did fieldwork and mapping during the summer seasons of 1930 and 1931.

Red Sotcher, also spelled Satcher, was a large, red-bearded sheepherder who arrived in Red's Meadow in 1879, herding sheep. He established a small farm and grew vegetables there for the residents of the mining towns in Mammoth Lakes. It is doubtful that he ever homesteaded his meadow area. Early owners of mining claims in the area, John Beck, Tom Beasore, Jack Maloney, and Johnnie Shaw, who knew Sotcher, stated that he also sold beef to the miners. The local legend claims that he stole cattle and horses from the westside ranchers and from the eastside ranchers. He pastured these stolen animals in the meadow and changed the brands before selling to the opposite side, and was never caught.

In 1890, the Minaret region was included in Yosemite National Park, with much controversy. There were a number of mining claims located in the Ritter Range. From 1890 to 1905, the U.S. Cavalry patrolled the area, primarily to control the sheep herds. On February 7, 1905, the park boundaries were changed to exclude the region, placing it in the Sierra National Forest. Since the withdrawal, proposed bills to place the Ritter Range back in Yosemite National Park, advocated for by interested groups such as the Sierra Club, have been unsuccessfully pursued in Congress. The Devil's Postpile was declared a National Monument in 1911.

After withdrawal from the park, prospecting and mining in the region was

226

actively renewed. Some of these early claims were the Iron Mountain Group in 1905 and the Nidiver Group in 1909-1912. Tom Agnew, C. John Beck, Tom Beasore, Jim Sullenger, and Dave Nidiver were early locators of claims. By 1932, there was a network of good trails built by the Forest Service and mining interests. Garnet Lake was named for the garnet crystals located in the area.

The Minaret Consolidated Mines Company had thirty-four claims in the upper Minaret Creek Basin on a tributary fork known as Johnston Creek, named for an early prospector. A number of ores were found including lead, silver, zinc, and copper, but no gold. In 1930 to 1933, the company was actively prospecting, and considerable work was done at the various mine sites, including construction of a few mine buildings. Before the road was built, the mines depended on pack mule strings to handle their supplies and equipment, and pack ore out.

During two winter seasons, from about 1928 to 1930, Tex Cushion of Mammoth Lakes, with his husky dog teams, freighted supplies, mail, and equipment to the Minaret Mine over Minaret Summit. Lloyd Summers owned two claims in the Minaret Mining District at Lake Superior on King Creek, showing copper ore, and he was a partner in a mining venture with Joseph Kennedy in 1932.

In 1922, **Minaret Summit Pack Station** was located at Minaret Summit and operated until 1926, when the Minaret Road was cut by the mining company. The station was nestled in a hollow to the right of the current Forest Service Minaret Vista location. Asa and Lola Cline, along with their sons, Vasey, Wilfred, and Lester, operated the pack station, packing trips into the Middle Fork of the San Joaquin River and surrounding lakes. After the road was built, they moved their pack station to Deadman and Glass Creeks, packing over Deadman Pass into the Middle Fork.

The Minaret Consolidated Mines Co. built a road from Minaret Summit to Red's Meadow in 1926, on the site of the old Starkweather toll road. It was a one-lane dirt road with very few pullouts. A spur off this new road was graded into Agnew Meadows. A tractor road was built by the company up Minaret Creek to the mine on Volcanic Ridge, at 10,000 feet elevation.

The **Shawhawk Pack Station** was located at Minaret Summit and owned by W. H. Patten from 1928-30. He may have purchased the Minaret Summit Pack Station from the Cline Family and changed the name. Patton sold the Shawhawk Pack Station to Overton and Offut at the end of his last season.

From 1915 to 1934, the Mammoth Pack Outfit, owned by Charlie and Lloyd Summers, packed tourists into the Middle Fork of the San Joaquin River from Lake Mary and the Mammoth Meadows. This was still backcountry then with no roads, and many tourists packed into the river and the lakes. They were packed in over Mammoth Pass, and many stayed for several weeks. Recreation trips packed into Shadow Lake, Garnet Lake, Thousand Island Lakes, Beck Lakes, Lower Fish Creek, Island Crossing, the Margaret Lakes, and Silver Creek.

Summers maintained corrals at Pumice Flat, along the San Joaquin River, and Red's Meadow. Charlie Roberts from Lake Mary also had a corral at the San Joaquin River and packed in tourist parties. In 1932, Lloyd Summers operated a pack station there, called the **Mammoth Pack Outfit at Red's Meadow.** "Young Charlie" Summers, Lloyd's younger brother, oversaw it.

227

Arch G. Mahan Jr., a former football player at Stanford University from Southern California, was a partner, along with his father, A. G. Mahan, in the Mammoth Consolidated Mining Company in Mammoth Lakes. Arch came to Mammoth in the fall of 1926, and in the spring of 1927, his father and a group of men purchased seven mining claims on Red Mountain above Lake Mary. They also leased the Old Mammoth Mine. With men working all summer, they had opened the Number 3 tunnel of the old mine by fall. After a severe earthquake covered up the tunnel again, they gave up that option and began developing the Lake Mary claims they had purchased.

The Mammoth Consolidated Mining Co. functioned year round, with sometimes as many as twenty employees, from 1924 through 1932. Arch skied in and out to the mine buildings twice a month during the wintertime to take in payroll and and pick up supplies, leaving a car at Highway 395 near the Sherwin Grade for use. When Mammoth Lakes was snowed in, Bill Lewis's and Tex Cushion's dog teams carried in the supplies to the miners at the cabins. There was an exceptionally heavy winter in 1932. After 1932, the mines were idle, although Mahan planned to install flotation equipment and reopen. In 1935, a fire burned the large engine and compressor plant. The mine didn't reopen. The Forest Service now maintains the mine location as a walk-through historic site called the Mammoth Consolidated Gold Mine.

In 1934, after the mine closed, Arch Mahan looked around the area for another business venture. Mahan and his wife, Gladys, purchased the **Red's Meadow Pack Train** from Lloyd Summers. In 1935, he built a store with living quarters attached, and gradually added cabins, packing facilities, stock, and more amenities at the site, creating **Red's Meadow Resort.** Some buildings were partially constructed during the winter and hauled into the valley when the road opened up in the summer.

The Mahans ran forty head of horses and twenty-five head of mules. The resort also rented boats on Sotcher Lake for fishermen. By 1954, the Mahans had increased their stock to seventy-five head. The store was rebuilt in 1958, and the stock increased to eighty-five head. The Minaret Summit Road, although still a dirt road, was widened and improved. By 1946, the road into Red's Meadow was in the present location, but it was still dirt and mostly one-lane.

Herb Carls began packing for Arch in 1947, and was a packer for fourteen years before becoming a partner in 1960. Prior to packing at Red's Meadow, Carls, who was from Idaho, had been in World War II and had parachuted behind German lines in the Normandy Invasion.

From 1944 until 1969, Anecleto Torres, an arriero or mulatero (mule packer), packed for Red's Meadow Pack Station, and was one of the few packers who still knew how to fit and pack an aparejo packsaddle. He had previously packed for the Spark Plug Mine in the White Mountains until it ceased operation.

Arch and Gladys purchased the Agnew Meadows Pack Train from Jack Summers in December of 1950, and operated the station as part of their Red's Meadow Resort.

Bob Tanner worked for Mahan in 1958 and 1959, living at the Agnew Meadows station with his wife, Jean, and their small daughter, Suzanne. Tanner, a college student from Redlands, had arrived in Mammoth Lakes in the summer of 1949 to work for the Forest Service on their trail crew. While working for the Forest Service, he packed for Russ and Anne Johnson at McGee Creek Pack Station on days off. He also met his future wife, Jean, the summer of 1952. Jean was a UCLA sorority sister of me and my sister, Dorothy Russell Fitzhugh, and worked at Camp High Sierra in Mammoth Lakes during her summer vacations in 1952 and 1953. After serving two years in the Navy, Bob returned to pack at McGee Creek Pack Station in 1956. He then packed for Arch Mahan, running the Agnew Meadows corrals. Bob and Jean's son, Bobby, was born at the end of the season in 1959.

In 1958, Arch Mahan was appointed a Mono County Supervisor to fill an unexpired term and remained in that position until he retired in 1979. Mahan became state president of the Association of California Counties and vice president of the Association of Counties of the Thirteen Western States. With his new Mono County duties, Arch took in two partners in 1960 to run the busy resort business, Herb Carls and Bob Tanner.

Bob and Jean Tanner taught school at Bishop High School during the winters. Herb Carls and his wife, Betty, ran a small ski lodge in Mammoth Lakes in the winter. In 1965, the Tanners bought out Herb Carls' interest in the stations, both **Red's Meadow Resort and Pack Station** and Agnew Meadows Pack Station. Carls went to work for the Forest Service, running their packing operations in the Mammoth area, and built the tack room and corrals for the Forest Service on the Sherwin Creek Road. These facilities were located across the road from Sierra Meadows Equestrian Center. Carls and Lee Summers worked together for a number of years, from the mid-sixties into the eighties.

The Mule House Café was constructed in the 1960s, serving meals to the public, with a separate dining room for their large crew. More rental cabins were built, and the number of stock for the two stations was increased to 110 head. Red's Meadow pastured their stock in the Pool Field during the winter, along with Mammoth Lakes and Rock Creek pack stations.

Bob Tanner, Herb London, and Tommy Jefferson formed a partnership in 1972 to acquire Ike Livermore's interest in Mt. Whitney Pack Trains. This additional permit gave Red's Meadow's traveling pack trips access to the southern Sierra region. Mt. Whitney had permits for the southern Sierra passes into the Sequoia and Kings Canyon National Parks' many lakes and streams.

Bob's son, Bobby, grew up at the pack station and was active with his father. Bob became very interested in the Death Valley Borax wagons and Twenty Mule Teams, and began putting together a team of red pack mules and harnesses. Assisting Bob and Bobby in harnessing and training the mules to pull the huge wagons was Henry Olivas, a retired Lone Pine packer. In recent years, Bobby switched the color of the Twenty Mule Team from red mules to black mules. He was able to borrow the Death Valley Borax wagons for the Mule Days Parades, but realized that replicas of those wagons needed to be built for use in parades and events.

Working with the Death Valley Conservancy, money was raised to have beautiful replicas built by a wagon builder in Montana. A special mule barn was built at the Laws Museum in Bishop to house these superb wagons. Except when the wagons are at parades, the public can see them at the Laws Museum. The mules are at the pack station in the summer, packing gear and supplies to destination lakes for the vacationing public. The Twenty Mule Team and new wagons have appeared at the Rose Parade on New Year's Day and at the Washington D.C. 4th of July Parade, 2017. Bobby and Lee Roeser ride the wheel horses, gentle saddle draft horses, and handle the jerkline that connects all the mules, ending with the lead team.

Bobby Tanner purchased Rock Creek Lodge in Rock Creek and began remodeling and adding more cabins. The lodge stays open during the winter, and cabins needed to be winterized. After Bob passed away, Bobby and his wife, Claudia, took over the Red's Meadow Resort and Pack Station, owning and operating the station today.

AGNEW MEADOWS

In 1870, Tom Agnew, a local miner, built a mining cabin in the meadow. He located a number of claims northwest of Agnew Meadows. Agnew served as a guide for U.S. Cavalry troops who patrolled the area when it was part of Yosemite Park. In 1926, a road was constructed from Minaret Summit to Red's Meadow by the Minaret Consolidated Mining Company. A branch road was extended from this road to the meadows. The Agnew Meadows Mining Corporation owned twelve claims on the east side of Agnew Meadows. In 1932, they sunk a shaft and cut a cross cut tunnel to connect to the shaft. The Minaret Mining Company, with Mr. Starkweather of Los Angeles as president, owned claims from Minaret Summit down to Agnew Meadows. In 1932, this company had also sunk a shaft and had made many surface cuts searching for ore outcrops.

Agnew Meadows Pack Station is located at the foot of the Minaret Summit Road, eight and a half miles west of Mammoth Lakes along the Middle Fork of the San Joaquin River. Lloyd Summers opened a pack station at Agnew Meadows with his brother, Charlie, and Althea Summers, operating the station after the 1926 road was built. The station was called **Mammoth Pack Outfit at Agnew Meadows**, and they also used the corral at Pumice Flat near Red's Meadow. Eventually it became **Agnew Meadows Pack Train**. Pack trips started from Agnew Meadows and went into Shadow, Ediza, Garnet, and Thousand Island Lakes. Their stock grazed in the meadows. Agnew Meadows was also the starting point for trips into the Tuolumne Meadows area of Yosemite National Park.

In 1947, Jack R. Summers, Charlie's son, ran the pack station. Glenn McNinch, who operated the Death Valley Stables at Furnace Creek, purchased the pack station. But apparently, Jack took it back after a year or so, and sold the outfit at the end of the season in 1950. Arch and Gladys Mahan purchased the station and combined it with their Red's Meadow Resort. At the time of the purchase, there were thirty-three head of horses, ten mules, saddles and packsaddles, a tack shed and corrals, and one living cabin. Bob Tanner and Herb Carls became partners with Arch Mahan in 1960, with Tanner later buying Mahan out.

Tanner had several new buildings constructed in the 1960s and 1970s to accommodate their increasingly busy operations. Agnew Meadows Pack Station has continued as part of Red's Meadow Resort, and Bobby and Claudia Tanner operate the resort and pack station.

JUNE LAKES LOOP

CRESTVIEW

Highway 395 continues on north from the Mammoth Lakes turn-off toward the intersection to the June Lakes Loop. Midway between them is an area known as Crestview, just north of Deadman Creek and nine miles north of the Mammoth 203 junction. In 1927, Clarence Wilson built Crestview Lodge, which included a dining room, bar, store, and dance floor, as well as guest cabins. It was located on the west side of the highway until it was sadly razed in 1977. The State Highway maintenance station known now as the Caltrans Maintenance Station at Crestview is across the road on the east side.

This small area is unique in that it is geologically located in the Long Valley caldera at the foot of the northwest wall of the caldera. The highway quickly and steeply climbs up the wall to a large basin beyond called the Mono Lake Basin.

After the Minaret Summit Road was built in 1926, Asa and Lola Cline, with their sons—Vasey, Wilfred, and Lester—moved their operation, Minaret Summit Pack Station, to Glass and Deadman Creeks. The new name was **Glass Creek Pack Station**. They packed over Deadman Pass to access the Middle Fork of the San Joaquin River Basin, with many beautiful lakes.

Wilfred Cline became a well-known rodeo stock contractor in the eastern Sierra. The Cline family organized two-day rodeos all over the area. Lester Cline was a well-known saddle bronc rider and rodeo performer. He also established a pack station at the Crestview Lodge with a partner. The Cline family participated in the pack station activities.

Center Pack Train was located with a corral and office at Crestview Lodge on Highway 395. There was also an upper corral at the head of Deadman Creek, to the west of Crestview Lodge. Wilfred Cline and M. D. King, III, owned the station. The trail went up Glass Creek. They packed parties over Deadman's Pass into the San Joaquin River, the Clark Lakes, the Ritter Range, and Rush Creek. Their stock grazed at Big Springs, the headwaters of the Upper Owens River.

Besides fishing and deer hunting, they also arranged lion and bear hunts, as well as a wild horse chase, or a mustang hunt. Cowboys chased and roped mustangs and attempted to domesticate and train them. The station advertised airplane passenger service to a landing field at the lower corral by Crestview Lodge. In addition, they offered a month-long Western vacation at their Crestview Lodge field headquarters location, that allowed guests to "learn to ride, shoot, pack, campfire cook, rope, fish, and hunt." This stay included "your own horse and saddle, bed, grub, and cowboy dances." This was quite popular.

JUNE LAKES LOOP

A fourteen-mile detour off Highway 395 to June, Gull, Silver, and Grant Lakes, along with Rush Creek, leads visitors through this beautiful area. The location and beautiful setting draws many vacationers and fishermen to the area each summer. Alger Lake, Thousand Island Lake, and the Clark Lakes are popular backcountry destinations. June Lake was an early resort mecca and attracted early filmmakers from Hollywood. The Silver Lake Pines area was subdivided for summer cabins.

The California Electric Power Company built dams at Agnew, Gem, and Waugh Lakes, with a generating station below on Rush Creek. The Power House, as it is known, was constructed in 1915, and the Gem Lake Dam was built in 1916.

Roy Carson, and later his son, worked for the power company at the Power House. After World War I, the Carson Family built the Carson Camp at Silver Lake, operated by Roy and Nancy Carson. The Carsons built a log cabin and gradually added to it. They arranged pack trips and horseback riding for their guests, calling the business **Sierra Saddle Camp Livery**. Pack trips packed into Rush Creek above Gem Lake in 1929.

Leonard L. "Slim" Tatum arrived in Bishop from Texas in 1923 and worked for the Hillside Cattle Company. In 1924, he packed for Charlie Roberts at Lake Mary. Slim then worked for Bill Symons, who grazed cows in the June Lakes Basin during the summer. Slim and Frank "Bill" Clark formed a partnership to purchase the Broken Bar Pack Outfit at June Lake from Art Frost. The station was located on the June Lake Loop Road. The Broken Bar Pack Outfit, owned by Art Frost, was advertised as operating from Rock Creek Lake and Carson Camp at Silver Lake in 1924. Clark formerly had operated a pack station on the South Fork of Bishop Creek prior to 1924.

In 1926, George Brown operated the dairy at Silver Lake. He and his wife bottled and delivered milk in the summertime. In the winter, Brown drove his cows back to the ranch in Round Valley. The next year, he sold the dairy to Slim Tatum and started the pack station at Pine Creek.

Slim married Hazel Schober, sister of Art and John Schober, in 1925. The Tatums called their dairy the Pine Cone Dairy, with Hazel accomplishing the milking and Slim handling the milk deliveries.

Prior to 1920, Wilfred Dixon Sr. began a pack station called **Frontier Pack Train** on the north side of Silver Lake. In 1934, Dixon sold his station to Slim Tatum.

In 1936, Tatum operated the station with fifty-two head of stock. Lester Cline, of the large Cline family, packed at the station in the 1930s. Gem Lake Lodge was a backcountry camp, and Frontier Pack Train packed guests and supplies up to the lodge. From the pack station, pack trips trailed up the Angels Flight Trail to Gem, Agnew, and Waugh Lakes, and over Donahue Pass into Yosemite National Park.

Tatum became a favorite character with the Hollywood film crews who were filming in the June Lake area. He instituted popular weekly campfires with music, songs, and colorful stories told by Slim himself. Pack station stock was rented to these movie companies, as well as to Russ Spainhower, movie stock supplier in Lone Pine.

The Tatums owned a ranch in Round Valley, where they raised cattle and quarter horses. Slim's stud was a well-bred quarter horse from the King Ranch in Texas. The Schober family owned a neighboring cattle ranch, along with Schober Pack Train on the North Fork of Bishop Creek. The two family ranches are still operated by their children. Tatum was president of the Eastern Sierra Packers' Association and was selected as the first Grand Marshall of the Mule Days Parade in 1970.

After World War II in 1945, Tatum sold the pack station to Elmer C. Jensen. By this time, the station ran ninety-eight head of stock. Jensen operated two corrals, the headquarters at Silver Lake and a corral at June Lake. He was the Most Honored Packer at Mule Days in 1975. In 1958, along with sixty head of stock, Jensen sold to Richard L. and Dorothy Kelsey, who operated the station for a short time. The Kelseys then sold the station to Clair "Bob" Vinnedge in 1960.

Vinnedge, with his son, Ken, owned the Hansen Dam Stables in Chatsworth in the San Fernando Valley, along with Cottonwood Pack Station. By 1963, Frontier Pack Train had one location and thirty head of stock. The station had been located on the east side of the road north of Silver Lake. The Forest Service required the pack station to move to a new location on the west side of the road, where the station is now located. A Forest Service campground is now on the old pack station site. Packers assisting Bob were his son, Ken "Sonny" Vinnedge, and his son-in-law, Sonny Merk.

In 1966, both Bob's son and son-in-law died tragically just a few weeks apart in separate accidents, and Bob was very ill with cancer. He sold to David "Babe" Jay, who had packed for him previously. Jay operated the station until 1974, when it was sold to Dink Getty.

Dink Getty made many major facility improvements to the outfit and added more stock. Getty added very successful horse drives and mustang trail rides to his menu of activities. He also purchased and enlarged a boarding stable facility at Mill Pond in Round Valley, where he resided in the winter. They sold the Mill Pond Boarding Stable, which also does lessons and horse training.

In 1977, the power company needed to do major work resurfacing the dam at Waugh Lake. Since the dam is located in the Minaret Wilderness Area, the Forest Service determined that sand and cement for the repairs could not be flown in by helicopter. Materials would have to be hauled in by pack strings of mules. Six pack stations were involved in the sand packing effort: Frontier Pack Station, Leavitt Meadows Pack Station, Mammoth Lakes Pack Outfit, McGee Creek Pack Station, Red's Meadow Resort, and Rock Creek Pack Station. The sand packing occurred from the Silver Lake site and from Agnew Meadows Pack Station.

Getty sold to the Dohnel brothers, Dave and Kent, in 1992. Dave Dohnel had been a partner of Herb London's Rock Creek Pack Station since 1982, and sold his interest there in order to purchase Frontier Pack Train with his brother, Kent. Their grandfather, Chuck Hovey, had been an original partner with Herb London at Rock Creek.

The Dohnels increased the schedule of planned trips at the outfit. Frontier Pack Station participated in the New Year's Day Rose Parade in Pasadena with pack strings and riders for several years. Dave supplied stock and wranglers, along with riding and directing, for the Reno Rodeo Cattle Drive that arrived at the Fairgrounds for the opening of the Reno Rodeo for a number of years. The station conducts biannual horse drives to and from their winter pasture, along with mustang viewing trips. On the fall trip, they drive their stock to the winter pasture at Black Lake near Adobe Meadows. Kent Dohnel has a Department of Water and Power lease in Bishop that is the winter headquarters for the pack station operation. Dave Dohnel has now retired, and Kent Dohnel manages the pack station today with his son, Justin.

In 1946, Allie Robinson ran a corral at June Lake on the June Lake Loop Road called **Robinson's June Lake Saddle Livery**. This business was established after he sold his Independence operations and before he purchased the Leavitt Meadows Pack Station. He advertised excursions around the June Lakes Loop and to the upper lakes.

233

LUNDY AND VIRGINIA LAKES AND BRIDGEPORT VALLEY

LUNDY CANYON

Lundy Canyon, with Lundy Lake at the mouth, lies just north of Mono Lake and south of the Conway Summit. The canyon, with its lovely waterfalls, heads up to Yosemite and the high plateau north of Saddlebag Lake. A favorite hike that necessitates two vehicles begins at Saddlebag Lake, with a boat ride across the lake, a hike crossing the plateau, and then a descent of Lundy Canyon to the canyon floor, where the second vehicle awaits. There are no longer any packing services to the lakes and streams in this area.

Mines were established on the south wall of Lundy Canyon, about two miles upstream from Lundy Lake. Other mines, notably the May Lundy Mine, were located in Lake Canyon, high on the slopes of Mt. Scowden. Beginning in 1880, the town of Lundy grew at the upper end of Lundy Lake. In Lundy Canyon, in 1894, the **Lundy Livery and Feed Stables** supplied packing services to the towns of Lundy and Lee Vining, along with the nearby mines. In 1908, A. Taylor had operated The Taylor House Hotel for eight years. He operated an extensive livery business with many saddle and pack animals. The route from the town of Lundy to Yosemite Valley was reported in a 1908 Mono County tourist brochure as being easily traveled and a favorite way for visitors to journey to Yosemite from this area. It is presumed that the route was the pack trail from Lake Canyon to Bennettville at the Tioga Hill mining community.

Lundy Lake provided good fishing for trout during the mining days as it does today. The trout are thought to have been Lahontan cutthroat trout originally planted from Virginia Creek.

VIRGINIA LAKES

The Virginia Lakes basin is located nineteen miles south of Bridgeport, west of the top of Conway Summit, at 9,770 feet elevation. The extensive aspen meadows leading up to the high lakes are dominated by 12,374-foot Dunderberg Peak, which was first called Castle Peak. In the fall, the region is a blaze of yellow and orange. There are ten lakes in the basin, and the three lower lakes can be reached by road. The first lake, Trumbull Lake was named after an early homesteader.

In 1924, there was no road into the lakes, but a road had previously been built to the Dunderberg mines. Walter and Anita Foster and their friends, Charles and Louise Fostler, all from Los Angeles, constructed a road from the mine road into the basin in 1924. They were assisted by a miner, J. P. Cooney. They planned to build a fishing camp, and received a permit from the Forest Service for this purpose on completion of the road. The Virginia Lakes Camp on Little Virginia Lake was built in 1924 by Walter and Anita Foster on the north side of the lake. It was open for business on June 21, 1924. The Fosters and Cooney then constructed another road from the fishing camp to Highway 395 at Conway Summit the following summer. Walter Foster worked for film companies in Hollywood, and many directors and actors were among their guests.

The three lower lakes in the basin, Little Virginia Lake, Big Virginia Lake, and Trumbull Lake, had been stocked with cutthroat trout in 1899 by pack train. Two other lakes were stocked by the Fosters. Then, in the fall of around 1928, Walter Foster arranged to stock four of the five upper lakes with fingerling trout obtained from the hatchery on Fern Creek, near June Lake. Walter backpacked fingerlings to these high lakes.

Today, the Virginia Lakes Resort comprises twenty housekeeping cabins, a café, store, and rental boat landing, and is host to many guests each season. There are ten timberline lakes within a short distance from the resort, and trails lead to the Green Lakes basin and into Yosemite National Park. Horseback rides are quite popular with guests of the resort and campers in the campgrounds.

Virginia Lakes Pack Station is located on Virginia Creek, a half mile below the Virginia Lakes Resort located at Little Virginia Lake, at 9,770 feet elevation.

During the 1930s, Richie Conway and the Dondero family did some packing at Virginia Creek and Green Creek. Conway had grazing leases for cattle and sheep along the creeks.

Shortly after the road was completed in 1924, the pack station was established by Willard Ahrens, who was packing in the Bridgeport Valley. He established the pack camp there, where the fishing camp, including a lodge and cabins, was being built by the Fosters. In 1927, the **Virginia Lakes Saddle and Pack Outfit** was packing into Summit Lake and the northern regions of Yosemite National Park. After the Fosters constructed another more direct road into the lakes basin, Ahrens built a service station, lunch counter, and several rental rooms at the top of Conway Summit. In 1927, he sold the Conway Summit business to Bob Bivens, a friend of the Fosters.

In 1929, Gordon Barks bought the **Virginia Lakes Pack Outfit**, along with twenty-two saddle and pack stock, from Ahrens. **Gordon's Saddle Livery** packed tourist trips into the backcountry. Barks was sixty-six years old, and the following summer, he was bucked off a horse and sadly died. Jack and Kay Lynn, a young couple in their twenties, were working for him, and since Barks had no heirs, they continued operating the pack station. Jack Lynn continued to own Virginia Lakes Pack Outfit until 1949. Boats were packed into the upper lakes by mule.

In 1950, Dick Sawyer and Jay Pearce owned **Virginia Lakes Pack Station**. Colonel Beale purchased the station in 1954, and sold it back to Sawyer in 1958. In 1960, Sawyer operated Virginia and Buckeye Pack Stations with twenty head of stock. The Buckeye Station was a deer hunting location, with trips into Rickey and Eagle Peaks, along with Buckeye Canyon. Sawyer's brother in law, Harold Moore, became a partner in 1963. Sawyer was having health problems with the high altitude, so Harold Moore took over, owning and operating the station until 1978.

That year, Virginia Lakes Pack Station was sold to Tom Roberts and Bart Cranney at an auction on the Courthouse steps in Bridgeport. They obtained the Dressler pasture lease, with a corral and cabin, at Devil's Gate, and operated hunting and fishing trips into the Little Walker area. Roberts bought out Cranney's interest in the station the following year, and operated it until 2002. The pack outfit specialized in all-expense trips, including gourmet meals, into the northern section of Yosemite National Park and the Hoover Wilderness Area. They advertised a second pack station location as Devil's Gate Pack Station for hunting trips in Molybdenite, Burt Canyon, and other adjoining areas in the fall.

In 2003, Matt and Billie Taylor, along with Steve Ybarra, purchased Virginia Lakes Pack Station. Taylor had packed for Mineral King Pack Station, Red's Meadow Pack Station, and Yosemite Park and Curry Company Stables in Yosemite. Steve Ybarra was a packer for Curry Company, where he met Matt Taylor. He also packed for the Park Service packing services in Yosemite National Park. The new partners made many improvements to the infrastructure at the pack station.

The station packs visitors into the lakes above Virginia Lake and passes by Summit Lake into the lightly-traveled northeastern section of Yosemite National Park and the Hoover Wilderness Area. Traveling trips visit Benson and Tilden Lakes and Virginia Canyon. A side access trail crosses to the Green Lakes Basin. The pack station provides access to the Green Lakes Basin and Buckeye Canyon, as there are presently no pack stations in operation between Virginia Lakes and Leavitt Meadows. In addition to pack trips, two-hour, four-hour, and all-day horseback trips are available.

Craig London of Rock Creek Pack Station purchased Virginia Lakes Pack Station and continues the same program, accessing the beautiful backcountry of Virginia Lakes, the Green Lakes Basin, and Yosemite National Park.

GREEN LAKES

The Green Lakes Basin contains many beautiful lakes. The trail continues past Summit Lake into the northeast boundary of Yosemite National Park, and down Virginia Canyon. The basin can be accessed from the Green Lakes Road south of Bridgeport, or from the Virginia Lakes Road on Conway Summit.

Jay Pearce Pack Stations, owned by Jay Pearce, were located in several locations at various times. He had corrals and facilities at Virginia Lakes, Green Lakes, Devil's Gate, and Little Walker River. He advertised packing into the Hoover Primitive Area, Eastern Yosemite, Desert Creek, Flatiron Ridge, Molybdenite Creek, Little Walker River, as well as Anna, Emma, and MacMillion Lakes. He ran fifty head of stock between the stations he packed out of Green Lakes Resort, with a lodge and guest cabins located along the creek, was the headquarters for the pack station. From there, Pearce packed into the Green Lakes Basin and Yosemite National Park. He operated from 1946 to 1960. Curly Wilson, who later operated Buckeye Pack Station, and his brother, packed for him, as well as for the Hunewills.

In 1960, Pearce sold to Merlin and Jean Williamson, who called it **Green Creek Pack Station,** along with sixty head of stock. They operated Devil's Gate Pack Station as well. However, by 1963, Pearce had the resort and stations back again. He then sold, with three locations, to Dr. Ralph Hughes in 1964. Claude Hunewill, of the Hunewill ranching family in the Bridgeport Valley, was the manager for some years. In 1967, Chad J. Palmer, with his wife, Bea, replaced Dr. Hughes in the Packers' Association as an owner of **Green Lakes Resort and Pack Stations**. In 1970, Hughes was again the sole owner. In 1974, there was a brief partnership for a couple of years with Devil's Bedstead Ranch and North American Adventures, with George May,

Johnny Lundy, and others. The Green Lakes Resort and Pack Station are no longer in operation, and facilities are no longer present.

TWIN LAKES

The Hoover Primitive Area was established in 1931 within the Inyo and Humboldt-Toiyabe National Forests. In 1957, it was called Hoover Wild Area, and in 1964, it became the Hoover Wilderness Area. Originally, it encompassed 48,601 acres, and presently, has increased to 128,421 acres. It ranges approximately from Tioga Pass to Sonora Pass, east of Yosemite National Park. Cattle and sheep grazing continue, as those activities preceded wilderness designation.

Lower and Upper Twin Lakes are located up above the lush Bridgeport Valley, at an elevation of about 7,000 feet. Matterhorn Peak and the Sawtooth Ridge of the Sierra Nevada glaciated fault scarp, created by fault-block uplifting followed by glaciated carving, make a dramatic backdrop for the two large, beautiful lakes. Matterhorn Peak, at 12,264 feet elevation, dominates the viewshed, and a number of high alpine lakes are cradled in the glaciated montane scenery. Trails access the Hoover Wilderness Area and the northeastern section of Yosemite National Park. On the Robison Creek Trail, Barney and Crown Lakes are popular stops on the trail to Rock Island or Mule Passes, or Peeler Lake, located on the crest, all leading into Yosemite's backcountry. To the north, in the next canyon, is another popular trail at Buckeye Creek, leading over Buckeye Pass into the park.

George Byron "By" Day, an early rancher, purchased land around Upper and Lower Twin Lakes in the 1860s and ran sheep and cattle there in the summer months. In 1936, the family leased land to Hal Maltby for a resort. Maltby first built his cabins between the two lakes, then moved to the upper end of the upper lake. Maltby ran the resort there from 1937 to 1950, when he gave up the lease because of his health. In 1952, "By" Day's granddaughter, Alpha, and her husband, Norman Annett, took over. Norman and Alpha Annett renamed the resort Annett's Mono Village, and they added many new facilities. There was a pack station operation already there. In 1959, Bob Hetherington began running the horse operation for several years, calling it **Twin Lakes Pack Station.** From 1972-74, Emmet Merritt ran the **Mono Village Pack Station** at Upper Twin Lakes, and was a member of the Eastern Sierra Packers' Association. After this period, the Annetts ceased the horse operations at the resort. Mono Village resort is currently a thriving operation with a rental boat landing, store, restaurant, cocktail lounge, motel, cabins, and a campground.

Bridgeport Pack Stations operated from several locations over the years. Locations were at Robinson Creek along Twin Lakes Road (a cabin there is still called "the pack station") and Buckeye Canyon. Trips were packed into areas in the Hoover Wilderness Area, including Hunewill and Barney Lakes, as well as Buckeye Canyon and Eagle Peak, and into Yosemite National Park.

In 1941, A. J. "Jack" and Lucille E. Hunewill Bogard began a pack station at Buckeye Canyon along the creek, mainly for hunting trips. There was a corral at Buckeye Creek, but no permanent buildings there. In 1942, Jack and Lucille opened their resort cabins, campsites, and corral along Robinson Creek, calling it **Bogard's Camp**. They advertised spot trips, day and hour trips, pack trips to Peeler Lake and Yosemite National Park, and excellent deer hunting. They operated Bogard's Camp from 1942 to 1958, and had twenty head of stock.

In 1958, the Bogards subleased their resort to H. Lynn and Lois E. Nearpass, and in 1959, sold it to the Nearpasses, who called the resort **Doc and Al's Camp**. They ran ten horses and advertised corrals and pasture available; guests just needed to "bring your own horse." In 1964, they dropped out of the Packers' Association, as they were no longer packing into the backcountry. They ran the camp until 1970, when it was operated by Harry and Yvonne Adie. The horse operation had previously been discontinued.

Intermittently from 1946 to 1975, Claude Hunewill operated the **Buckeye Pack Station**. He was a nephew of Lucille Bogard. In 1952, Jay Pearce and Curly Wilson operated it, and in 1953 and 1954, Curly Wilson operated the station on his own. In 1960, Claude Hunewill operated the **Bridgeport Pack Stations** with two locations—Twin Lakes and Buckeye Canyon. From 1960 to 1962, Dick Sawyer ran the pack station. Then Claude and Florence Hunewill ran the station until 1975, when Claude sold his stock and ceased operations. The Hunewill Family Corporation owned the land and the Forest Service leases. They were involved with all of the pack station operations to some extent. Curly Wilson worked for them and managed the pack stations for many years.

The Hunewill Guest Ranch in the Bridgeport Valley provides ranch vacations with saddle horses and trips for their guests. The ranch has been in the family for over one hundred and fifty years, passed down to Stan and Jan Hunewill, and now their three children—Jeff, Betsy, and Megan—along with their spouses and families, who are all involved in the operation of the ranch. They conduct a very popular cattle drive each fall when their cattle are moved back to Smith Valley in Nevada for the winter. Since it can be quite cold at that time of year, guests enjoy going back to the guest ranch each night for a hot shower and comfortable bed.

Mules loafing in the corral at Frontier Pack Station, on the June Lake Loop.

SONORA PASS REGION AND ANTELOPE VALLEY

The region includes the Little Walker River area off the Little Walker Road and Leavitt Meadows on the Sonora Pass Highway 108. Paved, narrow Sonora Pass, at 9,624 feet in elevation, is the next trans-Sierra Nevada road north of Tioga Pass. The West Walker River runs through the extensive Leavitt and Pickle Meadows, at 7,000 feet elevation. In 1943, for the movie, For Whom the Bell Tolls, the scenic locations for the guerilla band's hideout in Spain were filmed on the pass.

The Bidwell-Bartleson emigrant party in 1841 pioneered the Walker River route across the Sierra. They had abandoned their wagons in eastern Nevada and packed their horses and mules the rest of the way to California. The party crossed the summit to the south of the current pass. In 1859, there was a trans-Sierra pack trail called the Sierra-Mono Trail. It was used extensively by pack trains accessing the mining booms east of the Sierra in 1859. Monoville, Bodie, Aurora, and Virginia City were destinations for merchandise and provisions from Sonora and the Central Valley. Sol Carter had pack trains working out of Sonora that ran regular packing services. Terrence Brodigan owned Sonora House and Livery Stable, and he also provided pack trains to Monoville, Aurora, and Bodie. A new road was begun in 1861 and became a toll wagon road called the Sonora-Mono Wagon Road. It was, of course, closed in winter.

Cattle ranchers homesteaded land in the meadows many years ago, and a stage stop hotel was located near the extensive meadows. In 1863, Hiram Leavitt built a stage stop and inn along the river adjacent to the meadows to service the traffic of pack trains and later wagons between the town of Sonora and the mining camp of Aurora. Cattle and sheep are still grazed during the summer months throughout this area, but not in Yosemite Park.

DEVIL'S GATE AND LITTLE WALKER

Cooney Lewis, at Devil's Gate along Highway 395, between Bridgeport and Coleville, began **Cooney Lewis Pack Train** in 1907. He packed into the Little Walker area, as well as Emma and Anna Lakes. In 1933, he advertised twenty-six years in this district and promoted three backcountry cabins that he packed tourists into for fishing and hunting. One of them was a Rickey ranch line cabin, a cow camp located on summer grazing range. In 1939, Lewis displayed a limit of ten golden trout caught at Anna Lake, fourteen miles west of his camp, at the general store in Bridgeport.

Devil's Gate and Little Walker Pack Stations were locations used by Jay Pearce Pack Stations. From there, they accessed the Little Walker River, Burt Canyon, and Molybdenite Canyon.

In the early '60s, Merlin Williamson operated out of Devil's Gate, as well as the Green Creek Pack Station.

In 1963, Dr. Ralph Hughes bought the Green Lakes Resort and Pack Stations that included this area. In 1967-69, Chad and Bea Palmer were partners in the operation and owned Little Walker Pack Station in Burt Canyon. Chad Palmer had purchased one acre of private land in Burt Canyon and operated the Little Walker Pack Station from there. Palmer leased adjoining Forest Service land as well. My husband, Lou Roeser, and I purchased the Little Walker Pack Station site, located in Burt Canyon at Willow Flat, from Bea Palmer in 1976, after the pack station no longer operated there.

Also in 1976, we applied for a permit and ran a packing operation in the Bridgeport and Devil's Gate areas, calling it **Bridgeport Pack Trains**. From 1976 to 1981, we leased the Devil's Gate Pack Station site, the Dressler Ranch on Highway 395, and ran pack trips from that location, especially during hunting season. We had a Forest Service Outfitter-Guide packing permit to also run pack trips out of Buckeye Canyon, Green Creek, Devil's Gate, Little Walker River, Burt Canyon, Molybdenite Canyon, and the Sweetwater Mountains. After these years, we made a business decision to terminate the permit and packing service in this area, although we continued to enjoy our property in Burt Canyon.

In 1982, Tom Roberts, who had purchased Virginia Lakes Pack Station, acquired the lease for the Dressler Ranch, using it to pasture his stock in the spring and fall, along with running hunting trips out of the area.

LEAVITT MEADOWS

Beautiful Leavitt Meadows are located on Highway 108, the Sonora Pass Road, about seven miles west of Highway 395. Pack trips originate here and pack into the headwaters of the West Walker River including Fremont Lake, lakes along the west fork of the West Walker River, and Piute Meadows in the Hoover Wilderness Area, and into northeastern Yosemite National Park over Dorothy Pass. Visitors to the area from the San Francisco Bay and the Central Valley use Sonora Pass to access this popular eastside location.

The U.S. Marine Corps Mountain Warfare Training Center is located at Pickel Meadows, four miles east of Highway 395 on the Sonora Pass Highway 108, just to the north of Leavitt Meadows. The military base in the Humboldt-Toiyabe National Forest was established in 1951 during the Korean War. The base trains military units in mountain warfare and survival, both winter and summer. As part of their training procedures and maneuvers, the Marine Corps purchased pack mules and horses and originally sent chosen marines to local pack stations for training in packing methods. The Horsemanship and Animal Packing Division maintains pack mules, and recently added burros, as donkeys are more common in the Middle East and other parts of the world. This has been particularly important to troops serving in the high mountains of Afghanistan. The base offers training in packing techniques and advanced horsemanship. The base also offers training for troops in other branches of the Service. Many of the horses used are mustangs obtained from the Bureau of Land Management, which trains them and offers them for sale in Carson City, Nevada.

Norman Dickson and Alvin Andrews began the **Leavitt Meadows Pack Station** in 1935 or earlier. Andrews owned a homestead in Slinkard Valley, and his log cabin is still standing. Dickson owned a mine in Risue Canyon on the west side of the road in the Sweetwater Mountains. Mrs. Evelyn "Lynn" Llewellen owned an interest in the packing operation, and then sold to Tom Kurisky in 1937. After her death in 1940, Perry Bush operated Leavitt Meadows Pack Station and ran the business for seven years. The Llewellen family sued Kurisky in 1942 for non-payment.

In 1947, Bush sold the pack station to Allie and Doris Robinson, who called it **Leavitt Meadows Pack Train**. Allie had previously sold his pack stations in the Owens Valley, and was briefly packing out of June Lake. In 1952, the Robinsons operated the station with forty horses and twenty mules. At the end of the season in 1956, the Robinsons sold the pack station to Howard Black, who was involved with wrangling for the movie industry. Black's HB Bar brand is still used by the station today.

Three years later, in 1959, Black sold to Ariel O. "Slim" and Edith Cranney and Kent Bunn, with fifty head of stock. They called it **Leavitt Meadows Pack Station**. Slim Cranney owned a riding and boarding stable in Montebello, in Southern California, and did some recreational packing in Nine Mile Canyon in the southern Sierra. Their children and grandchildren grew up working at the station. Slim later bought out his partner, Kent Bunn.

In 1972, when Slim retired, Bart Cranney, his son, took over running the station with a partner, Dr. Will Grishaw. Dr. Grishaw's son, Don, was a packer at the station from 1972-1987. Dr. Grishaw died in 1999. Bart's wife, Shirley, was the Mono County tax collector for a number of years, and Bart was president of the Eastern High Sierra Packers' Association and active in Mule Days. He was selected to be the Most Honored Packer at the 2004 Mule Days, and rode in the parade with his proud grandson, Travis. Bart died in 2007 after a long illness, and his memorial service was held at the pack station.

Craig Randall, who worked for Bart and his family, now operates the pack station with his family, offering the same full-service packing services that the Cranney family provided for so many years.

COLEVILLE AND LITTLE ANTELOPE VALLEY

The rural Antelope Valley lies partly in California, with the northeastern part over the state line in Nevada. The small town of Coleville is located near the middle of the valley on the west side. Topaz Lake, at the north end of the valley, is divided between California and Nevada. Little Antelope Valley lies west of the larger Antelope Valley and slightly above in elevation. This smaller valley was formerly a large cattle ranch, but is now owned by the California Department of Fish and Wildlife as a winter deer refuge, along with nearby Slinkard Valley.

In 1984, as part of the California Wilderness Act of 1984, the Carson-Iceberg Wilderness Area was established, with 161,181 acres extending from Ebbetts Pass to Sonora Pass. The Pacific Crest Trail runs across it for twenty-six miles. The wilderness includes the headwaters of the Carson River, which flows to the east, ending in the Carson Sink east of Carson City. Much of this area was prospected during the silver mining booms of the 1860s, and several mining towns were located here. Early ranchers homesteaded the valleys, and the large meadows provided lush grazing for cattle and sheep. Livestock allotments still continue in this area.

This wilderness is a land of few lakes, but many deep river canyons. Pack trips travel into Corral Valley, Coyote Valley, Poison Lake, Bagley Valley, Silver King Creek drainage, Snodgrass Creek, Tamarack Creek, and the East Fork of the Carson River in the Carson-Iceberg Wilderness Area.

Silver King Creek is home to the Paiute trout, a subspecies of the native Lahontan cutthroat trout and a very colorful fish. The unique, rare fish has a similar evolutionary history as the golden trout, but with a more limited home. The fish are found above Llewellyn Falls, which provides an impassable barrier.

Little Antelope Pack Station was first located on the Mill Creek Road, then on the Golden Gate Mine Road below Rodriguez Flat in Little Antelope Valley. The early headquarters were near the Slinkard Valley Road entrance to Slinkard Valley, on a flat on the south side of the road. The pack station was later moved up on top of the bench near Rodriquez Flat, and is located in Alpine County, California. From this higher elevation, the trail to Silver King Creek and Snodgrass Creek drainages is downhill from the station.

The pack station began operation in the early 1940s, or probably earlier. H. D. Winkle owned the station for some years prior to 1952. He sold it to Charles "Chet" and Irene Roberts, who also owned the Golden Gate Mine. Irene Roberts was the postmaster for Coleville for a number of years. In 1959, Chet Roberts sold the station to Robert G. "Bob" Hetherington, who had been a packer at Red's Meadow Pack Station, and had also operated Twin Lakes Pack Station. Hetherington had thirty head of stock.

At the end of the season in 1961, Bob sold the station to Ted and Mabel Birmingham. Birmingham had twenty-four head of stock in 1963. This same year, Birmingham purchased Coleville Pack Station from Bob Tracy and combined it with Little Antelope Pack Station. The following year, in October of 1964, Birmingham sold the merged pack stations, as Little Antelope Pack Station, to Bob Vinnedge of June Lake.

Bob Vinnedge also owned Frontier Pack Station. His son, Ken Vinnedge, his daughter, and son-in-law, Sonny Merk, worked at the station. Sonny Merk managed the pack station until he tragically died in the fall of 1965, followed by the accidental death of Bob's son, Ken.

Bob Vinnedge then sold the pack station to Ray and Judy Holmgren in 1966. Holmgren was a horse dealer and trader from Southern California, and owned a well-bred quarter horse stallion, Ranchero Reed. He had the new lodge built by a local Coleville builder, Bob Thomas, and moved the station up on top of the bench, at an elevation of 7,690 feet. The lodge and corrals are now located at Rodriguez Flat, up the steep Golden Gate Road.

In 1967, six of the northern pack stations decided to withdraw from the Eastern High Sierra Packers' Association, and possibly form their own group. They held that their business interests were different from the southern and central Sierra packers. Meetings were some distance away, often in the Owens Valley. However, Little Antelope Pack Station decided to remain in the association. In 1970, Ray Holmgren was on the Board of Directors.

In 1973, Larry Mitchell and Mike Mandichak purchased the station. Larry and Marilyn Mitchell operated the station and ran a children's summer camp there. At the end of the season in 1980, Vic Bergstrom and his sons, Mark and Ray, purchased the station from Larry Mitchell. The Bergstroms leased it to a vacation corporation for a while, before having it back again.

After being closed for several years, Vic Bergstrom sold the station to Joe Cereghino, and Joe reopened the station for the 2005 season. He offered all types of packing operations. The pack station services the Carson-Iceberg Wilderness Area. Cereghino also operates the Wolf Creek packing operation on the east Carson River.

Bob Tracy owned the **Coleville Pack Station**, and had office and reservation headquarters in the Tracy's Bar building on Highway 395, across the road from the schools in Coleville. The Bob Tracy family was an early pioneer family in the Antelope Valley. Bob Tracy owned the pack station for a number of years prior to 1952. Trips began in Little Antelope, where the stock was then trailed to Rodriguez Flat on the ridge above the valley. Tracy also had corrals in Silver King Canyon, about three quarters of a mile downhill from Rodriguez Flat. In 1956, Bob and Florena Tracy, along with their son, Lynn, operated the station with twenty head of stock. They packed into Corral and Coyote Valleys, Fish Valley, Snodgrass Canyon, and the headwaters of the East Carson River. In the fall, they packed in hunting trips.

In 1963, the Tracys sold the stock and permit to Ted Birmingham, who combined the packing operation with his Little Antelope Pack Station. Bob Tracy moved to the Central Valley, where he died in 1970. Chiseled on his tombstone in the Coleville cemetery is an illustration depicting a packer leading a mule.

McKay's Pack Station was owned by Marvin McKay for some years before 1952. He ran his packing services from his home and cattle ranch on Highway 395 at Topaz Lane. In 1954, McKay ran twenty-five head of stock and packed into Mill Canyon, Slinkard Valley, and the Sweetwater Mountains, mostly for deer hunting. The McKays also had cattle leases in the Sweetwater Mountains. By 1964, he only had eight head of stock, and shortly thereafter, went out of business.

A pack trip travels the high country in the John Muir Wilderness.

Eastern High Sierra Packers' Assoc. Map, showing pack station locations along Hwy. 395 (El Camino Sierra).

244

Looking down on McGee Creek Pack Station in the 1950s. (Russ and Anne Johnson)

The packing shed at McGee Creek Pack Station in the 1950s.
(Russ and Anne Johnson)

245

Forrest Newman and Lee Roeser packing in front of the old MLPO packing barn.

Lee Roeser & Bobby Tanner with the 20 Mule Team & Borax Wagons, Death Valley.
(Lee and Jen Roeser Collection)

At the inlet of Virginia Lake on the JMT, packer Lee Roeser waters his mule string.

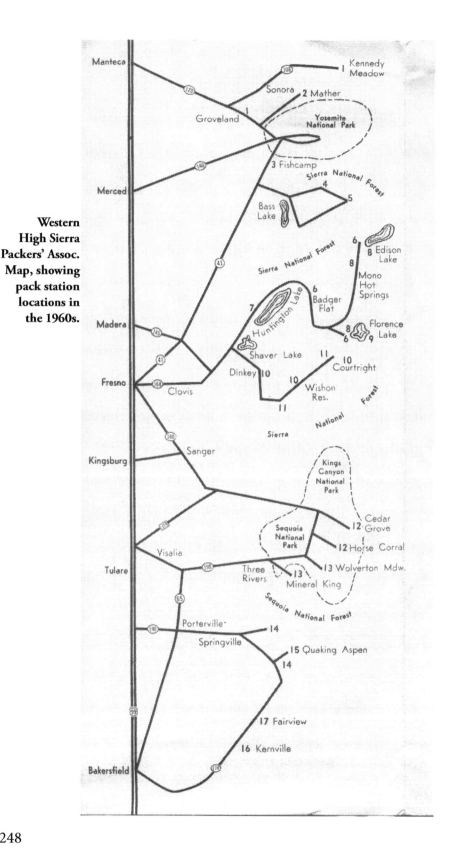

Western High Sierra Packers' Assoc. Map, showing pack station locations in the 1960s.

WESTERN HIGH SIERRA PACK STATIONS

The more gradual slope of the country on the western side of the Sierra is quite different from the abrupt eastern side. The gradual climb toward the high peaks is heavily forested and the home of giant sequoia trees. Pack stations extended from the southern tip of the Sierra at Kernville in a south to north line on both sides of the range. For this study, the southern stations begin at the Kern River in the Walker Pass area, and the northernmost station, on the western slope, ends at Kennedy Meadows on the Sonora Pass Road.

KERN RIVER AND KERNVILLE

The Kern River is the highest elevation river of its size in the United States and originates in the high country near Mt. Whitney. It then flows through the largest glacial trench in America to Lake Isabella in the Kern River Valley. There are many tributaries joining the Kern River as it flows southwest. Walker Pass, in the lower valley, provides a road route across the southern Sierra. The North Fork of the Kern River (also called Main Fork) is seventy-eight miles long. Only the lower seventeen miles are accessible by road. Over twenty-one miles of the river are located in wilderness areas that are mostly in a precipitous canyon. The South Fork of the Kern River flows through forty-one miles in wilderness areas.

The Sherman Pass Road now accesses the Kern Plateau from Blackrock near Kennedy Meadows, winding in a northeast direction, and thence to Highway 395. In 1936, the CCC extended the Kern River Road to Johnsondale, a logging center. The road crosses the river at the Johnsondale Bridge, then becomes the Johnsondale Road and connects to Quaking Aspen.

The Kern River, above Kernville, is a major hydroelectric power generation area. In 1910, the Southern California Edison Company set up work Camp No. 8 for their workmen, as their uppermost camp, at Road's End, on the North Fork of the Kern River. The Fairview Dam is fifteen miles upstream from the Edison Hydroelectric Powerhouse No. 3, and both were completed in 1921.

From the 1920s to the 1940s, many Western movies were filmed in the Kern River Valley. Packers in the area, along with their horses and mules, were in constant demand from the film companies. Irvin Wofford, an early rancher and packer on the North Fork of the Kern, had steady employment supplying the film companies.

In the early 1950s, when the Lake Isabella Dam was built, the resulting lake covered the old town of Kernville. The townspeople had to look for a new site to relocate their town, and the spot chosen for this new Kernville was the old Burlando Ranch. The present day town moved to higher ground west of the new lake, along the North Fork of the Kern River, closely enclosed by mountains. River rafts and kayaks now replace pack mule strings.

There were several pack stations located along the North Fork of the Kern River, north of Kernville. All these stations packed trips into the Kern Plateau area, the Little Kern River area (the waters of the beautiful golden trout), and eventually to Mt. Whitney. The stations were in fairly close proximity to each other in the narrow river canyon. In the early part of the century, the pack stations in the southern Sierra had very busy packing schedules, as they were closer to metropolitan centers in Southern California. Deer hunting was especially good on the Kern Plateau at that time. Trails are steep and brushy, and in the lower canyons, it is quite warm in the summer. As roads were further cut into the backcountry, accessing this region, trail usage lessened.

J. C. Howe was the first to settle on the North Fork of the Kern River. In 1910, he built a cabin above Fairview. The name Fairview applied to a two-mile section along the river. The area was part of a ranch cow camp used by Stony Rhymes and Lucien Barbeau. The old cow camp was below Fairview Pack Station.

The SQF Complex Fire of September/October 2020 has been devastating to the Kern River watershed and Plateau of the southern Sierra, accessed from both sides of the range, burning 150,000 plus acres at the time of writing, and threatening historic structures.

Matt Burlando packed mules, was a blacksmith for the Southern California Edison Company, and lived at Camp No. 8. Later, Matt moved back down the river and established Fairview Lodge, where he served meals to Edison Company employees and tourists. The lodge was operating in 1915. Burlando acquired a string of burros and began packing in tourists, calling the station **Fairview Pack Station**. In 1916, the Burlandos left Fairview to ranch in Kernville and sold the resort to Symes. Symes' partner was Frank A. Garbut, who was a founder of the Los Angeles Athletic Club. In 1941, Frank Garbut was a member of the High Sierra Packers' Association. A number of people leased the resort from Garbut during the years he owned it. Tom Allred was one who leased it in the early days.

In 1928, Garbut leased the resort to Kenneth and Chester Wortley, who operated it until about 1934 and called it **Fairview Pack Outfit**.

The Wortley Brothers first built a pack station at Nine Mile Canyon on the eastside of the Sierra, north of Mojave. In 1925, they moved their headquarters location to the Bloomfield Ranch on the South Fork of the Kern River. Since this location could be accessed from the Walker Pass Road, they could now make a one-day trip instead of a two-day trip to the Kern River. Chet and Ken built a trail up the west side of the river.

The Wortleys then established a summer camp for boys on the Kern River by Manter Creek. In 1925, they bought twenty-five small saddles to pack in the boys' camp. It was a short distance from Fairview.

The brothers packed in the Carl Curtis Boys' School from Los Angeles/ Beverly Hills on a two-day trip of hard riding from Fairview to reach the cabin and camp each summer. The Carl Curtis Boys' School later moved the camp to the Kern River near Kernville, where they operated for a number of years. The facilities are still there.

Many Hollywood celebrities sent their boys to the private school and summer camp. Boys included Jackie Coogan, child movie star, Loren Grey, son of very popular and prolific Western fiction writer Zane Grey, Jimmy Rogers, son of Will Rogers, and a son of Cecil B. DeMille. On their first trip in, over one hundred head of horses and mules were required. A summer in the wilderness was an adventure these boys remembered all their lives.

The family of Jackie Coogan loved the area so much, they built Coogan's Cabin on Tea Flat, at the junction of the South Fork of the Kern River and Manter Creek in 1923.

The Wortley brothers packed for a while up the North Fork of the Kern River from Fairview as well as from the Bloomfield Ranch location. They contracted to pack in some of the large Sierra Club Outing trips.

In 1928, the Wortley brothers packed the Sierra Club from Fairview Pack Outfit to Mount Whitney and back. There were up to a hundred and fifty head of stock and sixteen packers. Packers on that large trip included Gerry and Lauren Mack, Owens Valley brothers who packed for Allie Robinson, and Pete Labachotte, who owned a pack outfit in Big Pine.

The Wortleys had achieved an excellent reputation for well-run pack trips, and they packed in many notable people from Hollywood and Los Angeles. Ken and Chester were the main characters in a Zane Grey novel and spent sixteen winters with Zane Grey. Ken Wortley acted in several western films. He was selected as a Most Honored Packer at Mule Days in 1989.

Clifford and Trudy Cross leased Fairview in 1937, and continued for five years. Cliff had previously packed for Tom Allred. In about 1942, John McNally Sr. and his son, Johnny McNally Jr., leased the resort, calling it McNally's Fairview Lodge. John E. McNally Jr. and Pauline McNally eventually purchased the resort and called the pack station **John's Horse Camp** or **Fairview Pack Station**, running fifty head of stock. The station was located below Camp Pascoe and Kern River Pack Train, fifteen plus miles up the Kern River from Kernville. McNally Jr. supplied horses and cattle for movies. He became a rodeo stock contractor, producing rodeos around California and Nevada until the mid 1950s. Pauline, Johnny's wife, was considered an excellent packer. His headquarters were at Bodfish, Lake Isabella.

In the late 1940s, the McNallys opened the steakhouse restaurant at Fairview that became very popular. The old Fairview Lodge became a part of this steakhouse dining room. In 1961, McNally's daughter and son-in-law, Mary Anne and Bill Cole, took over and increased the dining room size to seat 150 people. Their younger daughter, Joan, operated the High Sierra School of Western Horsemanship at Lake Isabella. The McNallys were still operating in 1969. After retiring, Johnny McNally became a deputy sheriff for Tulare Country for many years. The resort is still thriving, with a renowned restaurant, and was untouched by the McNally Fire, although it reportedly began there from a campfire that went out of control.

Clarence Pascoe moved to Kernville from the Glennville area in 1902. In 1913, he packed tourist parties into Sequoia National Forest from Kernville. He was a teamster, blacksmith, and constable in the area, and first packed out of old Kernville. His two sons, Cecil J. and Earl V. Pascoe, helped their father with pack trips, and the boys began packing at a very young age. Earl had his own pack string by the age of fourteen, and his first pack animals were burros. Wild burros roamed the valley in the early days. When the two boys were older, they each formed their own pack stations in the Kernville area, and packed trips into the Kern River and the Kern Plateau. Both boys were considered vaqueros, top hands, and exceptionally good ropers.

Cecil was a well-respected horse trainer, " a big, fine looking man" who operated his **Bar 53 Pack Outfit** from his ranch in Caldwell Canyon, at Camp Pascoe. He also packed out of Road's End at Pascoe's Lodge and Pack Station, his brother Earl's outfit. He ran about forty head of stock in the 1920s and 1930s. His son, Dick, became a prominent rodeo cowboy.

Earl V. Pascoe was also "a big, fine looking man," and he established his pack station twenty miles up the Kern River from Kernville at Road's End. Earl married Lucille Calkins. Her father was Harold "Bill" Calkins, who lived above them at Camp Durrwood. In 1922, Earl Pascoe located his corral at the end of the road on the North Fork of the Kern River and called it **Pascoe's Lodge and Pack Station.** In 1922, he ran only about ten head of stock. In 1926, he moved in three cabins from the Southern California Edison Co. that the company was discarding, and later built a lodge there. In 1927, Earl and Lucille lived at Road's End year round.

By 1934, they had added a store, cottages, and a dining room, calling it **Camp Pascoe.** In 1934, Earl Pascoe operated with sixty-five head of stock. In 1935, he was a charter member of the newly organized High Sierra Packers' Association. His daughter, Carolyn Pascoe, was an excellent hand, packer, and rider. Earl Pascoe owned the station for forty years. According to the plaque at Road's End, he had as many as a hundred and fifty head of horses and mules at one time, and employed twelve to thirteen packers working for the station. Pascoe retired from active management in 1952 and sold the resort to Mildred and Skeets Byers.

In 1962, it was sold to Bob King, and the resort continued to cater to visitors, but with the intrusion of roads, packing was no longer continued. In 1973, Al and Frank Keegan bought the resort and added a restaurant. Mike and Marcia Burford next owned it. In 2002, the huge McNally Fire burned the resort to the ground, and only a stone marker remains.

In the 1920s and 1930s, the **Kern River Pack Train**, owned by Bob Welch, was located at Belleview on the Kern River, about halfway between Road's End and Fairview. Welch ran twenty-five head of stock, and his pack station was a quarter mile below Camp Pascoe and Road's End. He complained that there was a price war going on between the pack stations. He rented stock from J. C. Howe and Howe's partner, Monroe George, and then became a partner with Howe. Howe and Monroe, who were lion hunters and trappers, were happy to have Welch handle the packing business. J. C. Howe had climbed Mt. Whitney in the winter while on a trapping expedition. In 1929 Welch bought out Howe and Monroe, and eventually had up to seventy-five head of stock. He went out of business in 1959.

Durrwood on the Kern or **Durrwood's Pack Outfit** was located on the Kern River Road, about four miles above Fairview and a half mile up river from Road's End. From the mouth of Durrwood Creek, a trail ascends the Kern River to Lloyd Meadow. There is a Lower Durrwood and an Upper Durrwood Creek that are still not accessed by road. Tourists were packed into the Kern River and Mt. Whitney, and the upper reaches of the Kern River. William "Bill" Durrwood was an early cattle rancher near Weldon, and established a ranch in the valley. Durrwood came into the country in 1879 as

252

a cowboy, became a ranch foreman, then owned his own ranch. Durrwood Creek is named after him.

Beginning in 1921, Harold M. "Bill" Calkins established a backcountry resort where Durrwood Creek empties into the North Fork of the Kern River. Calkins was a charter member of the High Sierra Packers' Association. He and his wife, Lou, built a lodge and cabins for guests. In 1934, the station ran fifteen head of stock. Their daughter, Lucille, married Earl Pascoe of Road's End. As the road pushed up river, Calkins moved his lower camp up across the river, to what became known as Lower Durrwood. In 1944, the Calkins sold their resort and retired.

In 1962, Al Reid owned the station and called it **Durrwood Pack Station and Resort**. It was still in operation in 1972. Lower Durrwood is now a bed and breakfast near South Creek Falls, called Durrwood Creek Bed and Breakfast.

Gregory, Pat, and Peter Brady, and I. L. Wofford were other early Kern Valley packers. In the 1920s and 1930s, Bill Peyton packed from Kernville. Hobbs and Frank Burton operated out of Posey in 1934. In the 1920s, Ed Snider ran a station at California Hot Springs.

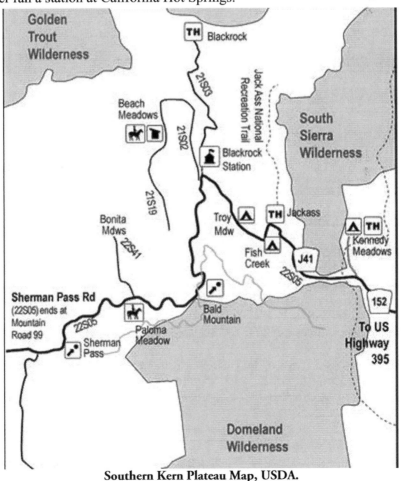

Southern Kern Plateau Map, USDA.

253

CAMP NELSON, CAMP WISHON, QUAKING ASPEN MEADOW, LEWIS CAMP, AND BALCH PARK

This region is at the junction of the North Fork and the Middle Fork of the Tule River. Located in this area are Camp Nelson, Quaking Aspen Meadow, and Balch Park. There are fourteen named groves of giant sequoias on the many forks of the Tule River. Porterville is the access town for the area.

CAMP NELSON

Camp Nelson, at 4,670 feet elevation, is on the Middle Fork of the Tule River, and is along Highway 190, forty-five minutes east of Porterville. John Milton Nelson homesteaded property and built a resort hotel catering to tourists in the 1890s. From 1922 to 1934, Charles Smith, his son-in-law, owned the resort. In 1934, his grandson, Nelson Smith, took over the operation. The **Camp Nelson Stables and Pack Train** ran ninety head of stock. Hank Houghton, a packer from Bishop, on the eastside, packed at Camp Nelson while attending college in Porterville from 1935 to 1937. He was the brother of Alice Houghton Boothe, who owned Rainbow Pack Outfit out of Bishop.

In 1935, Daniel G. McComber owned the pack station and was the first president of the new High Sierra Packers' Association. McComber also owned Broken Bar Pack Outfit at Rock Creek Lake on the east side of the range in 1932. He applied this title to both of his holdings. Woody Hannam began operating Camp Nelson Stables in 1962.

CAMP WISHON AND QUAKING ASPEN MEADOW

Camp Wishon is on the East Fork of the Tule River on Highway 190, about thirty miles from Porterville, and about two miles from Quaking Aspen Meadow. There is a store, a restaurant, cabins, and a trailer park there today. Various outfits packed from here, packing into the Great Western Divide Country and Sequoia National Park and Forest. Early pack station operators were Malvin Duncan, Jim MacDonald, and Walley Rutherford.

Highway 190 ends at Quaking Aspen Meadow, about forty-five minutes east of Porterville. There were two busy pack stations located beyond the Quaking Aspen Campground, across the road from each other. Trips from here pack into the Sequoia National Park, and Sequoia National Forest, along with the Upper Kern River backcountry and Big and Little Kern River Canyons. Native golden trout abound in the Kern River area.

Quaking Aspen Meadow Pack Station was owned by Walter Greigg in 1935. He ran about thirty head of stock and packed into Lloyd Meadow. In 1938, he sold to Daniel "Mac" McComber, who owned Camp Nelson Stables and called his outfits **Broken Bar Pack Trains**.

In 1946, Fred Cypert owned the pack station. By 1952, Vernie T. Pace owned the station, calling it **Aspen Meadow Pack Station**, until he sold it to Robert "Bob" and Darlene Garrison in 1960, along with forty-two head of stock. In 1964, the Garrisons sold to Clark Wicks, who kept the name Aspen Meadow Pack Station, also calling it **Wicks Pack Train**. Dan Shew began his packing career as a packer for Wicks in 1969, soon after he moved to Porterville.

In 1978, Dan Shew purchased Aspen Meadow Pack Station and called it **Golden Trout Wilderness Pack Trains**. He moved the station buildings six miles down the road after the road was extended, near Lewis Camp trailhead. Shew consolidated Woody's Pack Station with his Golden Trout Wilderness Pack Trains. The facilities and services included a lodge, cabins, meals available for pack station guests, and boarding for private horses. In addition to day rides and pack trips, the pack station offered cattle drives. Shew and his wife, Kelly, and their family operated the station for over twenty-five years.

The station sold again in 2005 to Steve Day and his wife, Rinda, who continue the same services, calling it **Golden Trout Pack Station**. Early in the season, Golden Trout Pack Station packs rafts, kayaks, and supplies for several rafting companies who guide white water trips from the Forks of the Kern. This packing is conducted out of their Lloyd Meadow pack station site on the Lloyd Meadow Road. The trail is several very steep miles down to the river from the pack station.

The Lewis Camp Trailhead is eight miles north of Quaking Aspen Meadow, just beyond the Golden Trout Pack Station. From the trailhead, the Little Kern River can be accessed from the Lewis Camp/Jordan Trail.

Rutherford Pack Station was established around 1910 by Kenneth Rutherford, with thirty head of stock. In 1941, during World War II, while his son, Owen, was in the service, Rutherford leased the station to Chet Ainsworth, who had been packing out of Dillonwood. Dan Farris, Chet Ainsworth's grandson, packed at the station while his grandfather was running it. Farris was a professional packer all of his adult life, and packed for the Mammoth Lakes Pack Outfit for over thirty years. After that station sold, he packed at McGee Creek Pack Station for Jennifer and Lee Roeser until retiring.

In 1945, after the war, Owen Rutherford took over the operation, calling it Rutherford Pack Station. He had nice-looking black mules and decorated their tack with silver discs. In 1952, he had thirty-five horses and thirty mules.

In 1960, Rutherford sold the station to Robert Sherwood "Woody" Hannam, with sixty head of stock. Hannam called the station **Woody's Pack Station**. He had packed for one season while in college at Hall's Pack Trains in Onion Valley. He married Betty in the early '60s, and they raised their three children at the pack station, wintering at Camp Nelson. Betty cooked for crew and guests, as well as cooking on backcountry trips and guiding guests on trail rides. In 1962, Hannam operated from two locations—Quaking Aspen Meadow and Camp Nelson Stables. By 1968, Hannam ran about eighty head of stock.

LEWIS CAMP

Lewis Camp, or Camp Lewis, at 6,500 feet elevation, is located on the west bank of the Kern River Canyon on the Hockett Trail near Coyote Creek on the west, and Golden Trout Creek on the east. Golden Trout Creek cascades in a series of falls over the canyon wall directly opposite Lewis Camp. Access to the area began with the building of the Hockett Trail in 1861, connecting Visalia and Lone Pine, and crossing the legendary Kern River twelve miles below Lewis Camp. Situated in the southeast corner of Sequoia National Park, the area consists of natural lush meadows and exciting small stream fishing, as well as good, dependable lake fishing in Kern Lake, Little Kern Lake, Little Lake, and Big Lake, making this area a fisherman's paradise. The beautiful Kern River rainbow trout are a localized, endemic subspecies found in the main Kern River and a few tributaries. The upper reaches of Golden Trout Creek are the home of the colorful California golden trout.

When Camp Lewis was in operation, guests would ride or hike in from Lone Pine, thirty miles eastward, Mineral King, twenty-four miles, or Quaking Aspen, twenty-eight miles to the west, making this the most remote resort in the region. After the creation of the Tunnel Meadow landing strip and air camp, visitors could fly in from the Lone Pine airfield. Then, it was only a nine mile hike or horseback ride to Camp Lewis.

By 1875, Dick Runkel from Lone Pine had a pasture and operated a small store. He filed on 160 acres in 1889, and it was referred to as Runkel's Place. After he died in 1891, the property went to E. H. Edwards, who owned a ranch and general store in Lone Pine, and who leased the camp to various people. In 1898, he sold it to John Lewis of Fort Independence, who was a lawyer and a brother-in-law of Edwards. Lewis began a backcountry camp with meals and accommodations for trail riders, and called the little resort Camp Lewis or Lewis Camp. The old sign at the camp read "Camp Lewis," and John Lewis operated it until 1912.

In 1903, the Sierra Club chose to make this area a campsite stop on their Third Annual Sierra Club Outing Trip. A work party traveled into Camp Lewis early to seek and prepare for their 200-plus party of "Sierra Clubbers." John Lewis assisted them in selecting and preparing a campsite area adjacent to Camp Lewis. The horse crossing was about a mile up Coyote Creek, and a temporary footbridge was constructed just below it. In honor of one of the Founding Board members of the Sierra Club, Warren Olney, the campsite was called Camp Olney.

From 1912 to 1944, the Lewis Camp was first operated, then purchased by Jules and Mae Conterno from Lone Pine. First, they purchased the equipment in 1916, then the land in 1926. Jules was a graduate of Annapolis, an engineer, and Mae was the daughter of Albert Johnson, who was in the party of fishermen who made the first ascent to the top of Mt. Whitney. Conterno made many improvements, building a sawmill from which he milled boards for his store and tent cabin bases, along with a swinging bridge. A stock bridge across the Kern River was there from 1923 to 1954, and pack stock had to cross it slowly, one animal at a time. In the 1930s, the camp provided accommodations for large traveling pack excursions. There were six tent cabins, a tent top dining room, a plank-covered log cabin store, and a kitchen. Mrs. Conterno cooked delicious home cooked meals, and tents could be rented.

The upper canyon was transferred from the Forest Service into Sequoia National Park in 1926. Two years later, the Park Service bought that part of Lewis Camp, on the west side of the river, from the Conternos, with the Sierra Club contributing $1,000 toward the purchase. The backcountry Kern Canyon Ranger Station was built the same year on the Lewis Camp property, and was located on the Kern River and Coyote Creek. Around 1940, the Forest and

Park Services constructed a steel suspension bridge a half-mile downstream. The Conternos had a lifetime tenancy on the property, and when they died in 1942 and 1943, the camp reverted to the Park Service.

Ray Buckman of Mineral King Packing Company leased the camp for six years, beginning in 1938, with a well-supplied camp manager and a cook, and used it for pack trips from his pack station. Mrs. William Neelands and her son, Bill, managed the resort for some time. In 1951, the resort closed, and after 1953, the Park Service gradually razed the buildings. The balance of the thirty acres on the east side of the Kern River, in the Inyo National Forest, were purchased by Ben Fish, an active Sierra Club member, and his family, including his nephew Henry Brown, a Sierra historian, and are still held in private ownership.

BALCH PARK/ SHAKE CAMP

Balch Park is located twenty-six miles from Springville in the Mountain Home State Forest, at 6,500 feet elevation, among giant sequoias. It is located on the North Fork of the Middle Fork of the Tule River.

Between 1885 and 1905, the surrounding forests were heavily logged. The Summer Home area was located in what is now Balch Park, and Mountain Home was a mile north. Residents of the San Joaquin Valley were attracted to the pleasant summer climate, where they could escape the summer heat of the valley. Tulare County residents vacationed at Summer Home, and Visalia residents summered at Mountain Home.

Balch Park is owned by the Parks and Recreation Department of Tulare County, and is in the midst of the state forest that was a gift to the county from A. C. Balch in 1923. There are over 4,000 sequoia trees in the 4,590-acre park that was acquired by the state in 1945.

From 1910 to 1940, George Dillon operated **Balch Park Pack Trains**. He was the father-in-law of Owen Rutherford. In 1935, he had twenty-five head of stock. His station was near Shake Camp, a previous logging center.

From 1910 to the 1940s, the **Mountain Home Pack Station** at Shake Camp was owned by Frank Negis. In the 1940s, Frank's son, Roy C. Negis, took over the pack station. He had already acquired Balch Park Pack Trains from George Dillon, and called the station by that name. Negis ran fourteen horses and fourteen mules. In 1960, he sold to Clark Wicks, who called his operation **Balch Park Pack Station**.

In 1964, Wicks purchased Aspen Meadow Pack Station from Bob Garrison and now ran two outfits. He ran about thirty-five head of stock.

In 1971, he sold to Dan Shew, who kept the name Balch Park Pack Station. In 1983, Dan Shew sold the station to his brother, Tim Shew, and his wife, Dianne. In 2020, the pack station has been family-owned by the Shews for over forty-five years. The station offers a variety of pack trips and guided horseback rides.

In 1930, Art Griswold operated a station in Balch Park. He constructed over fifty switchbacks on the trail that is now called the Griswold Trail. In 1935, he was operating at Shake Camp at the end of the road, with forty head of stock. He also worked out of Camp Wishon. In 1935, the newly organized High Sierra Packers' Association elected him temporary president.

Another pack station in the Tule River area was established by Otis Lawson.

In Springville, Charles A. Spangler and Murdock operated an outfitting business in 1935 to beyond 1941. Spangler was a member of the High Sierra Packers' Association.

The beautiful, historic mule barn at the Yosemite Stables, has seen many years of saddle trips.

THREE RIVERS AND MINERAL KING

THREE RIVERS

The town of Three Rivers is located in a mountain valley at the junction of three forks of the Kaweah River, and at the junction of present Highways 198 and 180. In 1880, the town had a population of 150. In 1903, the government extended the Colony Mill Road eight miles further to Giant Forest. This remained the main entrance to Sequoia Park for many years.

A number of packers operated out of the town area in the early years, packing up to Mineral King and Giant Forest for trips. In 1874, Bert Smith packed in the area. In 1924, he sold his outfit to Lawrence Davis, who had the **Davis Corrals**. Lawrence Davis had been a packer and guide in that area since 1912, and was part of the pioneer Davis family. Orlin "Ord" Loverin was operating with twenty-five head in 1935. His brothers and later his sons worked with him. Other Three Rivers packers in the 1930s were Tom Carroll, Frank Eggers, and Metzger.

MINERAL KING

The Mineral King Valley, a high, pristine alpine valley surrounded by 11,000-foot peaks, is twenty-five miles east of Three Rivers, and is at 7,500 feet elevation. The long, narrow, and deep glacially-carved valley is at the headwaters of the East Fork of the Kaweah River.

Silver was discovered there in 1872. Jack Meadows, along with the Mineral King Wagon and Toll Road Company, originally built a trail called the Meadows Trail in 1873. The trail was improved to handle wagons in 1879 and renamed the Mineral King Road. The present road is almost the same as the original road and is only partially paved, located along the canyon wall with precipitous drop-offs. It is winding and narrow, with 698 hair-raising curves on the road, and is twenty-five miles long, requiring two hours to travel it today. There is still no electricity in the valley.

In 1965, the Forest Service released a prospectus for a new ski area in Mineral King Valley. Walt Disney was an avid skier, and in 1969, the Disney Corporation launched an ambitious proposal to create a huge ski resort complex in Mineral King Valley. Construction of a new, all-weather road to enter the valley from Sequoia National Park was a stumbling block. The one-lane dirt road that currently accessed the valley was not adequate for the planned first class ski resort. The Sierra Club originally supported the ski resort proposal, but when the massive size of the planned resort became known (nearly six times the size of Squaw Valley), the Club vigorously opposed the road and the development plan. The development called for facilities to service two million annual visitors. The Sierra Club eventually went to court over the proposal, and because of the negative publicity that soon evolved, Disney withdrew their proposal.

The valley was originally located within the Sequoia National Forest. After the controversial Disney winter resort proposition was withdrawn, the valley was quietly added to the boundaries of Sequoia National Park in 1978. The valley had not been included in Sequoia National Park originally because of the mining activity. The Park Service had long coveted the beautiful valley.

In 1850, Thomas Davis homesteaded a cattle ranch in Woodlake, but his passion was hunting and fishing in the Sierra. In 1904, Davis bought the Mineral King Butcher Store, and he and his family began spending summers up in the mountain valley. As **Mineral King Packing Company**, they also provided packing services to visitors to the area. Before 1917, there was no organized commercial packing in the valley. Jeff Davis, the son of Thomas, and his four sons began expanding their "side business" of packing tourists as soon as demand increased, around 1917.

The Davis company packed tourists across the Sierra to Mt. Whitney, where visitors could ride horses to the crest and look down on Lone Pine thousands of feet below. "High country touring" had become a fad with some urban visitors, and these trips often lasted for a month. Mt. Whitney is twenty miles east of Mineral King as the crow flies, and was a magnet for many early pack trips.

In 1917, Phil Buckman went to Mineral King, spending time with the Davis family and enjoying the carefree summer lifestyle of the family. Phil's cousin, Ray Buckman, had previously worked for Broder and Hopping, packers at Three Rivers and Giant Forest, when he was a boy. Phil, along with the Davis brothers, attended Occidental College in Eagle Rock, a suburb of Los Angeles.

In 1920, Phil Davis became the leading packer in the family business. The pack station was the largest and most successful in Mineral King. His three brothers, Roy, Gene, and Lawrence, were associated with Phil in the packing business. Phil Buckman became Phil Davis's assistant in 1927, and his partner in 1929. Also in 1929, a young high school graduate, Ike Livermore, went to work at the pack station. He was eighteen and had just graduated from Thacher School in Ojai, a private, horse-oriented high school.

After a long dispute with the Forest Service, Phil Davis lost his packing permit at the end of the 1929 season. The Davis brothers continued packing out of Three Rivers, with corrals in Mineral King to the south, above the summer cabins. Their pack outfit was near the trailhead to Farewell Trail. Lawrence Davis was still operating in 1941 in the Upper Kern River Canyon, and was a member of the High Sierra Packers' Association.

In 1930, Phil Buckman obtained the Mineral King Packing Company permit from the Forest Service. Ike Livermore packed for Buckman that season. By 1933, Phil's cousin, Ray, and his wife, Gem, had joined the outfit. They maintained a large packing operation, cabins, post office, a dining room, and a store, and were located closest to the trailheads. In 1935, a partnership of Phil and Ray Buckman owned the resort. In 1937, Ike Livermore joined the partnership, and it was a very well-run business enterprise. In 1938, Phil Buckman retired from active packing to become a football coach. The new partnership was called **Mineral King Pack Trains and Resort.**

In 1940, Ray Buckman purchased the Ross Brothers Pack Station, located just down the road from them, and merged it with his outfit. Jack and Barbara Hansen, Ray's daughter and son-in-law, ran the store, and Gem ran the dining room.

Livermore enlisted in the U.S. Navy during World War II, and in 1946, after returning from the war, he sold his interest in Mineral King to put together his own outfit on the east side of the Sierra, Mt. Whitney Pack Trains.

In 1954, Lee Maloy purchased Mineral King Pack Trains from Ray Buckman, and continued to operate his outfit at Wolverton Meadow by Giant Forest, under Maloy Pack Trains. Maloy also purchased the Silver City Pack Station from Walter Wells, and operated it along with Mineral King. Buckman kept the store and resort, calling it Mineral King Resort.

In 1958, Maloy sold **Mineral King Pack Station** to William E. "Bill" and Marilyn DeCarteret. Lee Maloy continued to operate Maloy Pack Trains at Wolverton Meadow. The DeCarterets also acquired the Silver City Pack Station corrals and operated them until 1960, when Silver City and Mineral King were consolidated into **DeCarteret Pack Trains**. In 1960, DeCarteret operated with sixty head of stock. From 1962 to 1966, Bill and Marilyn DeCarteret leased and operated the Mineral King Store, dining room, and cabins from Ray Buckman. Marilyn was the postmaster of the little post office. Ray Buckman sold the resort, believing in the proposed Disney ski resort.

In 1965, DeCarteret purchased the Maloy Pack Trains at Wolverton Meadows from Lee and Blanche Maloy, who retired and purchased a saddle shop in Reno. In 1969, DeCarteret was president of the Westside High Sierra Packers' Association and also president of the National Forest Recreation Association.

In 1973, Don and Phyllis Bedell purchased Mineral King Pack Station at the end of the season. The DeCarterets kept Wolverton Meadow Pack Station. After retirement from busy pack station operations, DeCarteret began constructing and supplying packing gear, not only for commercial pack stations, but also the Forest Service and Park Service packing operations. In 1988, Bill and Marilyn DeCarteret were selected Most Honored Packers by the Mule Days Committee.

Don Bedell was raised in Lone Pine, where his father had packed for Chrysler and Cook and Rock Creek Pack Stations. Don was in the cattle business after college for a number of years, but he liked packing so much that, in 1965, he and Phyllis worked for Bill DeCarteret, managing Wolverton Meadow Pack Station. Later, Kerry and Robin Bedell, their daughters, worked as trail guides at Wolverton when they were in high school.

The Bedell's four children, Jeff, Kerry, Robin, and David, were actively associated with their parents, packing and guiding in the summers, and were participants at Mule Days for many years. Their Mule Days packing team won a championship one year. The Bedells were also active with the Western High Sierra Packers' Association.

Don Bedell took over Kennedy Meadows Pack Station from the Quinns in 1990. From there, he conducted hunting trips and horse drives. Between the two stations, they covered almost all of the Kern River backcountry.

Mineral King Pack Station was originally under a twenty-year Forest Service permit, but when Mineral King Valley was added to Sequoia National Park, the pack station became a Park Service concessionaire. Pack station permits issued by the Park Service are quite different from the Forest Service permits. The Sequoia and Kings Canyon National Parks decreed that the permit holder had to bid on his own permit against other bidders, even though he already owned the facilities. Permits were for five years. This is a different concept concerning permittees than the Forest Service has. The Forest Service has issued long-term resort permits, and usually renews a permit when it expires. The permit holder owns the buildings, facilities, and infrastructure, such as water lines, etc. The long term resort permit procedure encourages permittees to invest in the infrastructure of their pack station. The Park Service prefers to negotiate with large corporations rather than individual, family businesses as their concessionaires.

In 1996, Bedell's Park Service packing permit at Mineral King expired, and the Park Service put the permit out to public bid. The new permit was awarded to Jerry Page from Arizona, who chose not to purchase the facilities. Since the Pages did not purchase Mineral King Pack Station, only the permit, they had no facilities, stock and equipment, or headquarters, only a permit to operate. Bedell was required by the Park Service to tear down all their buildings and facilities and haul them off at his expense. The Park Service then allowed Page to operate out of the Park Service corrals in Mineral King for a time.

Jerry Page was also awarded the Wolverton Pack Station permit at Giant Forest after Sandy Vincent's permit expired and she had to bid for her own station that she had owned for many years. Again, Page did not purchase that pack station, and Sandy Vincent was required by the Park Service to remove the facilities. The operation of these two pack stations by Jerry Page proved to be unsuccessful. Those two permits have closed—Wolverton in 2002 and Mineral King in 2003. The visiting general public in need of stock-supported trips no longer have access to the backcountry from Mineral King or Wolverton. These former national park pack stations had also provided horseback trail trips for one and two hours that were looked forward to and enjoyed by visitors staying in resorts and campgrounds as part of their summer vacation.

Don Bedell continued packing operations at Kennedy Meadows until 1998. After closing his corral, he packed for other packers, Tim Loverin at Cedar Grove and Lee and Jennifer Roeser at McGee Creek. In 2005, Don and Phyllis were selected Most Honored Packers at Mule Days.

In 1918, Tom Phipps owned a pack station at Mineral King, down the road from Mineral King Pack Station. The location was near the old dumpsite at the base of Timber Gap. Phipps sold a half interest in his pack station to Roland S. Ross. At the station, they also had a store and post office. They called the outfit **Phipps and Ross Pack Station**.

In 1927, Roland bought out Phipps' interest, and Bart Ross, Roland's younger brother, began packing for him. The station became known as **Ross Brothers Pack Station at Mineral King**. In 1935, they ran sixty head of stock. In 1937, Roland sold a half interest in the pack station to Bart Ross and continued as a silent partner, having another job in the lower valley. Bart married Helen that year, and they ran the pack station, store, and post office together. 1939 was their last summer in operation, and at the end of the year, Bart and Roland Ross sold to Ray Buckman of Mineral King Packing Company. Bart Ross was selected Most Honored Packer at Mule Days in 1987, and rode in the parade in a mule-drawn surrey driven by my husband, Lou.

Two packers who worked for the Ross outfit for a long time were Frank Mires and George Hinkel. Bart Ross thought they were two of the best mountain packers in the Sierra. George was taught by and had begun packing for Allie Robinson when he graduated from high school.

Silver City Pack Station and Resort was six miles down the road from Mineral King Valley. Silver City was established in 1872, when silver was discovered and the Mineral King Mining District was established. Later, it became a resort, and in the 1920s and '30s, popular dances were held every Saturday night.

From 1929 to 1949, Craig Thorne owned the pack station. In 1945 and '46, Murray Hall leased the station from Thorne. Hall had worked for the Sequoia Park Service for three years previously as head packer. Hall began his own pack station, Hall's Pack Train, at Kennedy Meadows in 1946.

In 1949, Onis Imus Brown and his wife, Mabel, purchased the Silver City Pack Station from Craig Thorne. Brown, a long time packer, had been packing in the area since 1915, and was one of three persons to make the first ascent of Black Kaweah Peak in 1920.

In 1952, Walter Wells was the owner, and in 1954, he sold to Lee Maloy, who operated it until 1957, when it was sold, along with Mineral King Pack Station, to Bill DeCarteret. The DeCarterets ran the corrals, and in 1960, merged the station with Mineral King.

Today, the pack station is no longer in operation, but the resort is still very popular. It is called the Silver City Mountain Resort and is owned by Connie and Norm Pillsbury. They operate on private property and have a restaurant, store, bakery, cabins, and the only gas station in Mineral King.

For a few years, E. L. Burchell operated a pack station in Mineral King called **Burchell's Pack Station** and ran with fifty head of stock. The station was closed in 1968.

Yosemite Valley Stables in operation in 2011.

SEQUOIA AND KINGS CANYON NATIONAL PARKS

Sequoia National Park was established in 1890 and encompasses more than 631 square miles. Kings Canyon National Park was established fifty years later in 1940 and encompasses 722 square miles. The two parks have been jointly administered since 1943. They have a combined size of 1,353 square miles, and are located east of Fresno. The Generals Highway runs about fifty miles from Sequoia's southern approach at Ash Mountain Entrance, traveling north through Giant Forest to Grant Grove in Kings Canyon. Giant Forest, named by John Muir, is 1,880 acres and contains some of the largest sequoia trees, including the General Sherman Tree, largest known tree in volume.

The U.S. Cavalry patrolled the park lands until the establishment of the National Park Service in 1915. The first cavalry troops arrived from the Presidio in San Francisco by railroad and brought with them sixty horses and twenty mules.

GIANT FOREST AND WOLVERTON MEADOWS IN SEQUOIA NATIONAL PARK

Giant Forest and adjacent Wolverton Meadows are accessed from the Ash Mountain Entrance on Highway 198. There were a number of "squatters" living at Giant Forest early on. James Wolverton had a cabin and gardens there in 1891. When he died in 1893, the park took over his land. The intense summer heat of the central valleys drove resident families to the high country, where they camped for the summer, sometimes for two months or more.

In 1898, John Broder and his partner, Ralph Hopping, both had cattle ranches in Lower Kaweah River canyon. Hopping's ranch was located in Redstone Park on the North Fork of the Kaweah River. They began a tourist packing business called **Broder and Hopping** in 1898, operating from the Redstone ranch, where they put up a tent hotel. The Army was in the process of rehabilitating the rough Old Colony Mill Road to Sequoia National Park. Broder and Hopping established the first stage line into Sequoia National Park, using the Old Colony Mill Road.

In Giant Forest at Round Mountain, they opened Camp Sierra with tent cabins. In 1900, they owned eighty-five head of stock, ten tents, and a cookhouse. Guests boarded the stage, then rode horseback for four miles to Giant Forest to vacation at Camp Sierra. Hopping and his wife operated Camp Sierra, and Broder ran the stage business and packing operations from Redstone.

The packing business at Three Rivers and Giant Forest, called Broder and Hopping, was soon established. They were stock contractors, and conducted trips from Mineral King across the Sierra to Mt. Whitney. In 1902, they took in a partner, Jim Griffin, who had been packing for them.

In 1903, they brokered the horses and mules for the 1903 Third Annual Sierra Club Outing Trip. Over 200 club "trippers," plus crew, traveled from Mineral King across the Sierra to Mt. Whitney and back again. It took many mules and packers to move the camp through the mountains. One of their packers on that trip was Orlin "Ord" Loverin, then seventeen years of age, who would later own a pack station in Giant Forest.

Ralph Hopping and his family had come to the Kaweah area from New York to join a socialist utopian cooperative, the Kaweah Colony, in 1891. Ralph was an amateur entomologist, and in 1905, was a ranger in Sequoia Park. He discovered a new beetle in Giant Forest that was named for him in 1906, and he later became a government entomologist.

In 1907, John Broder suddenly died, and in 1908, Hopping and Griffin were forced to sell because of financial problems. They sold to Chester Wright, who operated until 1917 with sixty head of stock. In 1917, Wright sold to **Kings River Park Company**, which operated with about sixty head of saddle and pack stock until 1924. This company was a concessionaire company of Sequoia National Park and General Grant National Park, and was also a subsidiary of the Yosemite Park and Curry Company.

Stephen Mather, head of the National Park Service, pressured his friend Howard Hays to form a new company called Sequoia and General Grant National Parks Company. In 1926, the new concessionaire company was in charge of all trail transportation in Sequoia and General Grant National Parks. Hays brought in his brother-in-law, George Mauger, as manager, and Hays and Mauger ran the company for the next forty years.

Worth Ryder and Fred Askins packed in Giant Forest and General Grant Grove. They had also sold out to the Kings River Park Company by 1924. They had purchased Camp Kanawyer at Copper Creek from Poley Kanawyer in 1918, and then sold the Camp to Yosemite Park and Curry Company in 1920. The Kings River Park Company was not satisfied with their concessionaire operations.

In 1924, the company awarded a twenty-year contract for **Giant Forest Pack Station** to Orlin "Ord" Loverin. Loverin owned twenty head of stock and purchased sixty more. He had begun his own packing business in 1916 in Three Rivers, was a well-respected packer, and was highly recommended. Ben and Bob Loverin, his brothers, packed with him.

After a "honeymoon" period, the concession company again became dissatisfied with the operation of the station and Ord Loverin. The Park Service superintendent defended Loverin, but, after much dissension, the company awarded the pack station contract to Earl A. and Edna B. McKee in 1934.

Ord kept thirty-five head of stock and operated out of Three Rivers for a few large groups, including assisting McKee with big trips.

In 1947, his brother, Ben, ran his packing business for a time. Ben was the Park Service trail crew boss for many years and became well-known as a "mountain man" character. He used quantities of dynamite for blowing up rocks, trees across the trails, and everything that could be removed with an explosion. Packers who worked for him related sitting on boxes around the campfire that turned out to be dynamite boxes.

Ord's grandson is Tim Loverin, current owner of Cedar Grove and Grant Grove pack stations.

Earl McKee had begun packing in 1909, and reportedly, had his first string of mules when he was nine years old. His brother, Ernest, was also a packer. The McKees operated the Giant Forest Pack Station at Wolverton Meadow after 1934.

In 1946, McKee died suddenly while on a pack trip in Kings Canyon. His widow, Edna, his eldest daughter, Blanche, and her husband, Lee Maloy, took over operation and called the station **Maloy Pack Trains**. Lee and Blanche's sons, Leroy and Bill Maloy, helped in the business and were considered very good packers. Blanche's brother, Earl McKee Jr., also packed in the family business. McKee packed for the Sequoia and Kings Canyon Park Service trail crew from 1957 to 1962, and packed in the materials for seven steel bridges installed in the park. Packing bridge materials is quite a challenge.

The Fuller family, of Fuller Paint Company, packed in with the McKee/Maloy operation for thirty years (from approximately 1929 to 1961). Their trips were month-long traveling vacations, and they traveled all over the Sierra. In 1950, the party came out at Yosemite National Park. Mr. Fuller was crippled from polio, but could ride a horse, and he eagerly looked forward to his yearly pack trip. The party was always a large group with family and friends, and required thirty-five to forty-five head of stock with at least ten crewmembers. Jim O'Brien, Fuller's attorney, went in with the trip every year, and after Mr. Fuller died, he purchased the Fuller Paint Company. Maloy also packed in the Crocker and Schilling families each summer for many years. These were also large catered family traveling trips. In 1960, Maloy Pack Trains ran seventy-five head of stock and was set up to handle these large traveling trips.

In 1965, the Maloys sold the Giant Forest station to Bill and Marilyn De-Carteret. The DeCarterets renamed the station **Wolverton Meadow Pack Station**. They also operated the Mineral King Pack Station, running the pack stations under the name **DeCarteret Pack Trains**. In 1977, The DeCarterets sold Mineral King Pack Station, but retained Wolverton Pack Station at Giant Forest.

In 1982, they sold Wolverton Pack Station to John and Sandy Vincent of Woodlake. The Vincents also owned Horse Corral Pack Station, twelve miles east of the Generals Highway between Kings Canyon and Sequoia National Parks.

After the Vincents were divorced, Sandy Vincent continued to run the Wolverton Pack Station until the permit expired in 1996. She was required to bid on her own station for a permit renewal. Her bid submitted to the Sequoia and Kings Canyon National Park Service was not accepted. Instead of renewing her permit, the Park Service awarded a new permit to Jerry Page from Arizona, who had also been awarded the permit for Mineral King. Page did not purchase the stock and facilities, so Vincent was required to remove all the buildings and corrals at her own expense.

Page's five-year permit ran out in 2001, was temporarily reissued for one year, and was canceled in 2002. The operation of the station was not very successful. The Park Service was in the process of removing all commercial buildings at Giant Forest, and determined that the station was too close to the new parking lot at the General Sherman Tree. Horsemen's groups opposed and requested relocation for the pack station, but in 2006, the pack station remained closed. The Park Service announced they were accepting concession bids to open a station, but to date, a stable or pack station business has not been opened. For many visitors, a horseback ride in the park is an essential part of their vacation, as not all mountain visitors are ardent hikers.

GRANT GROVE IN KINGS CANYON NATIONAL PARK

The Grant Grove section of Kings Canyon National Park is fifty-four miles by road from Fresno on Highway 180. Grant Grove is located just beyond the Big Stump Entrance. General Grant Grove Park was established in 1890, a week after Sequoia National Park was designated. Grant Grove was a separate national park, but combined with Kings Canyon in 1940.

The first crossing made through the high country to the eastside was in 1858, when J. H. Johnson and five friends traveled from the Kings River and over Kearsarge Pass to the east.

In 1925, Richard "Dick" Wilson operated a pack station at Grant Grove, called **Grant Grove Stables,** with twenty-five head of stock. By 1941, he also had a station at Cedar Grove, **Wilson Pack Trains**, where he ran fifty-five horses and forty-five mules. In 1955, he sold the Cedar Grove pack station to Sam Davis and kept the Grant Grove Stables. In 1991, Dick Wilson Jr., his son, operated the Grant Grove Stables.

Around 1991, Tim, grandson of Ord Loverin, and Patti Loverin purchased the Grant Grove Stables. By 2004, Loverin had both stations, Grant Grove Stables and Cedar Grove Pack Station. The Loverins also provide pack trips in the Mineral King backcountry. They offer a variety of horseback rides and pack trips from their locations.

In 2000, Tim Loverin was awarded the contract to supply the Bearpaw High Sierra Camp at Bearpaw Meadow by mule string. Guests hike in eleven and a half miles from Grant Grove to the camp, which was established in 1934. Lodging is in tent cabins, delicious meals are served in a large cook tent, and hot showers are furnished at the camp.

Other early packers in the area included R. T. Coker, a packer at Big Meadows in 1935. Also, W. Orval Dean's Pack Train operated at Barton Flats in 1952, and ran twenty-five horses and twenty-five mules.

HUME LAKE, HORSE CORRAL MEADOW, CEDAR GROVE, KINGS CANYON NATIONAL PARK

The Kings Canyon Scenic Byway, Highway 180, is fifty miles long. It starts at the Hume Lake Ranger District west of Kings Canyon, outside the park, and winds down into Kings Canyon to Cedar Grove. The drive from Grant Grove into the valley of Kings Canyon to Cedar Grove/Zumwalt Meadows at Road's End is about thirty miles.

The road that became Highway 180 was built from 1929 to 1939. Hume Lake, at 5,200 feet elevation, is a dammed reservoir constructed in 1908. It is located in Sequoia National Forest on Tenmile Creek, a tributary to the Kings River, twenty-six miles from Cedar Grove, and four miles off the highway.

Spectacular Kings Canyon, in Kings Canyon National Park, is deeper than the Grand Canyon or Hell's Canyon. John Muir once called it "a rival to Yosemite." Its deepest point is 8,200 feet from the canyon floor to the peaks above. The elevation at Horse Corral Meadow is 7,500 feet, while the elevation of Cedar Grove is 4,500 feet, making summers there warm. Lush Zumwalt Meadows are located in a spectacular setting, surrounded by high granite walls lying deep in the canyon. Packers of the area pack into Kings Canyon National Park.

In the 1890s, John Fox owned a pack station and provided guide service in Cedar Grove, even to John Muir. In 1896, he built a hotel at Cedar Grove.

Peter Apoleon "Pole" Kanawyer (1849-1908) was a miner who prospected in Kings Canyon in the 1880s. In 1896, Kanawyer homesteaded property on the Kings River between Copper Creek and the South Fork of the Kings River, where he had a copper mining claim. This was forty years before the road was extended to Cedar Grove. He established a camp that gradually expanded into Camp Kanawyer, which catered to the Sierra Club and other tourists. Kanawyer operated a small pack station called **Kanawyer Pack Station**. His wife, Viola, cooked for these groups and was known for her pies, attested to even by John Muir. She was also an expert fisherman.

"Pole" was the first ranger for the area under the Sierra Forest Reserve. Pole and Viola ran the camp and pack station for twelve years before Pole's death in 1908. His son, Ione "Poley" Napoleon Kanawyer also packed for his father, as did their other son, Tom. "Poley" Kanawyer took over after his father died.

In 1902, William Colby of the Sierra Club had made the decision to conduct the Second Outing Trip to Kings Canyon. He persuaded Poley Kanawyer to purchase more pack stock in order to pack supplies in, as this trip would be the first one using all pack stock. On the previous trip, wagons had transported the camp supplies to Yosemite Valley and Tuolumne Meadows. There were 200 Sierra Clubbers plus crew and packers on this historic trip, and 25,000 pounds of baggage. Fifty of the participants climbed Mt. Brewer. In the early years, the Sierra Club alternated the Outing Trips between Yosemite National Park, the Kings River Canyon, and Mineral King or the Kern River.

In 1917, Kanawyer Pack Station was located at Cedar Grove and Hume Lake. In 1918, Poley Kanawyer sold Camp Kanawyer to Worth Ryder. After only two years, Ryder sold it to the Yosemite Park and Curry Company (the parent company of Kings River Park Company) in 1920. In 1926, Camp Kanawyer was closed, and in 1927, the buildings were torn down. Kanawyer continued to operate the pack station at Cedar Grove.

In 1935, Poley Kanawyer sold Kanawyer Pack Station at Cedar Grove to Hugh and Nellie Traweek of Hume Lake. Hugh Traweek had packed for the Kanawyers in 1917. In 1918, while working for the Yosemite Park and Curry Company, he packed for the Sierra Club Outing Trip in Yosemite National Park. Hugh Traweek had been packing from Hume Lake as the **Bar Seven Pack Train**. He made his headquarters at Cedar Grove and operated a corral at Horse Corral, running pack stations from 1927 to 1945.

In 1945, Traweek sold the Cedar Grove station to Sam B. and Janet Davis, and the name Bar Seven Pack Train was then applied to the Davis's stations. After selling, Traweek free-lanced for a number of years, helping out other packers with stock and equipment that he had kept. In 1958, Traweek applied for a packing permit to reopen a packing business in Kings Canyon. He was a popular and able packer; however, the Park Service determined that it would undermine the established pack station that was in successful operation.

Packers in the Hume Lake area, besides Hugh Traweek in the early years, were Oma Y. Mankins in 1943 and H. Wacaser in 1946.

In 1952, Sam Davis had twenty-five horses, twenty mules, and fifteen burros at the Bar Seven Pack Train at Cedar Grove. Sam Davis and his wife Janet were from the East Coast. Sam was a graduate of Princeton University and had a master's degree from Harvard. He taught school at a private preparatory high school and conducted canoe trips for young people during the summers. He thought outfitting pack trips would be akin to outfitting canoe trips in the wilderness. He was a good listener and learned the packing business by asking questions and then by doing. Sam and Janet's three sons packed at the stations for their parents.

In 1955, Davis purchased the Cedar Grove pack station from Dick Wilson. Davis also purchased the Horse Corral Pack Station from Ernest Cecil. In 1960, Davis ran 100 head of stock under Bar Seven Pack Train and was active in the Packers' Association. Davis and Ike Livermore became good friends.

In 1923, J. A. "Don" Cecil began the **Cecil Pack Train** at Eshom Creek. His brand was C-C. He took Hal Clark in as a partner. In 1925, the pack station moved to Big Meadow, and Clark sold out his interest to Cecil in 1927. Ernest E. Cecil, Don's eldest son, and his wife, Dena, took over the Cecil Pack Train in Big Meadow, where they also operated a store and service station.

The Forest Service cut a road seven miles further into Horse Corral Meadow in 1940. The meadow is twelve miles east of the Generals Highway between Kings Canyon and Sequoia National Parks, inside Giant Sequoia National Monument in Sequoia National Forest.

Ernest Cecil then built a new pack station at Horse Corral Meadow called **Horse Corral Pack Station**. The store and cabins at Big Meadow were removed and reassembled later at Horse Corral Meadow, and a frame house was built. A service station to accommodate automobiles was added.

In 1940, the road was completed to Cedar Grove, and the Cecils built a second pack station there. When the **Cedar Grove Pack Station** opened, the Cecil family lived there for three years in tent cabins. Then they moved back to Horse Corral Pack Station, established it as their headquarters, and hired managers for Cedar Grove. The Cecils built a second cabin at Horse Corral with a larger kitchen. They operated with 100 head of stock from Memorial Day to the end of deer season in October.

The trail from Horse Corral to Cedar Grove is now called the Don Cecil Trail. The Cecils' daughter, Darl, became camp cook at the age of fifteen. Gene Rector packed for the Cecils and later married Darl. Betty Cecil Goins, Ernest's sister, and her husband had a cow camp at Horse Corral Meadow, two miles from the pack station. Their family still runs cattle there, three generations later.

In 1940, when Kings Canyon National Park was created, parts of the forest that had been good deer hunting were now within the new park boundaries with no hunting permitted. This cut down on the demands of stock for deer season. Cecil sent extra stock and packers to help out Owen Rutherford at Quaking Aspen, who had a large deer season.

In 1945, Cecil sold the Cedar Grove Pack Station to Sam B. Davis and kept the Horse Corral Pack Station (Cecil Pack Train). In 1952, the Cecils had thirty horses and twenty-five mules. In 1955, Cecil sold Horse Corral Pack Station to Sam Davis, who merged it with his Cedar Grove Pack Station and continued to call his outfit Bar Seven Pack Train. Sam Davis had around thirty-five burros by the time he sold out.

In 1962, Sam and Janet Davis sold both pack stations to Allen R. "Bob" Simmons. Simmons had been associated with Cunningham's outfit at Mono Hot Springs. After selling, Davis moved to Santa Barbara to run a private school and raise avocados and lemons.

Bob Simmons called the businesses **Kings Canyon Pack Station** and Bar

Seven Pack Train, and he operated with 100 head of stock. In the early 1970s, Bob's son, Jack, and his wife, Joanne, bought Horse Corral Pack Station from Bob. They had been operating big game hunting camps in the Rocky Mountains.

In the 1980s, Jack Simmons sold Horse Corral Pack Station to Dave Wilson, who operated it for several years. Dave Wilson was an early competitor at Mule Days and a colorful performer. By 1991, Horse Corral Pack Station was owned by John and Sandy Vincent. Ten years later, it was sold to Gayl "Jonesy" and Nancy Jones.

In 2000, Charley and Judy Mills purchased the station and changed the name to **Horse Corral Packers**. They currently provide complete packing services as well as short daily horseback rides. They also offer boarding for private horses. They run seventy-five head of horses and mules during the season and winter them in Three Rivers. Pack trips pack in over historic Elizabeth Pass.

Bob Simmons sold Cedar Grove Pack Station to Tracy and Ann Terzian. They sold the station to Tim Loverin, a grandson of Ord Loverin, and a third generation packer. Loverin continues to operate both **Cedar Grove Pack Station** and Grant Grove Stables as a Park Services Concessioner.

Tuolumne Stables supplies the Yosemite High Sierra Camps.

COOLIDGE MEADOW,
WISHON AND COURTWRIGHT RESERVOIRS,
AND DINKEY CREEK

This area is reached from the Huntington Lake Road, Highway 168, south of Shaver Lake. Dinkey Creek is sixty-five miles northeast of Fresno. The Pacific Gas and Electric Company built two dams in the area for their hydroelectric projects. A dam was built on the North Fork of the Kings River, and Coolidge Meadows was flooded to form Wishon Reservoir. Helms Creek Fork was dammed, and Sand Meadows flooded to form Courtright Reservoir.

There were a number of packers in the area in the early days. They packed into Crown Valley and the Middle Fork of the Kings River region, LeConte Divide, Black Cap Basin Lakes, and Dinkey Lakes. There is abundant grazing and numerous campsites. Hell for Sure Pass, at the top of the LeConte Divide, is 11,300 feet elevation, and Kings Canyon National Park is on the other side of the pass. The South Fork of the San Joaquin River country is beyond.

COOLIDGE MEADOWS

In 1935, the Crabtree brothers owned the **Arrow Heart Pack Train**, and they packed out of Coolidge Meadows. Rae Crabtreee was one of the charter members of the High Sierra Packers' Association. In 1952, Rae called the pack station **High Sierra Packer**, or **Rae Crabtree Pack Stations**, with headquarters at Dinkey Creek. He also had a cattle and dude ranch. In 1954, Rae had forty-five horses and forty-five mules. In 1964, he and his wife, Beth, had sixty-five head of stock.

Other packers in Coolidge Meadows in the 1930s were William "Bill" Bash and Jay Robinson.

WISHON AND COURTWRIGHT RESERVOIRS

The Wishon Dam, which created Wishon Reservoir, was constructed in 1958 by the Pacific Gas and Electric Company. Wishon Dam and its companion, Courtright Dam/Reservoir five miles to the north, are part of PG & E's Haas-Kings River Project. Coolidge Meadows are near Wishon Reservoir.

Gerald "Jerry" Miller purchased the stations at Wishon and Courtwright Reservoirs, calling his business **Gerald Miller Pack Stations**. In 1969, he sold the business to Stephen and Bea Wright, who then called the business **Wishon Lake Pack Station**. In 1984, Bea and her daughter, Stephanie Wright, were operating the station. In 1982, Stephanie, a top hand, won some ladies' packing events at Mule Days.

The Wright family sold the stations to Dr. Allen Clyde and his wife, Deborah, of Clovis, who changed the name to **Clyde Pack Outfitters**. By 2003, the Clyde Pack Outfitters were located on Highway 168 with five locations: the Dinkey Creek Station; headquarters at Pole Corral Creek near Buck Meadow; Woodchuck Trailhead Spike Station near Wishon Lake; Maxson Trailhead Spike Station at Courtright Reservoir; and Cliff Lake Spike Station. The outfit eventually acquired all the stations in this area. Currently, Clyde Pack Outfitters is offering horseback rides and pack trips out of Wishon Reservoir and Dinkey Creek Station into the Dinkey Lakes Wilderness and John Muir Wilderness above Courtwright and Wishon Reservoirs.

Allen Clyde operates with about sixty horses, many of them raised by the Clydes. He does not use mules, as he maintains horses are cheaper than mules, and he can buy three horses for the price of one mule. The horses are wintered on their ranch near Auberry. They also run 200 head of cattle on a 10,000-acre grazing permit in the John Muir Wilderness east of Shaver Lake. Their historic grazing permit is from the 1880s.

DINKEY CREEK

Dinkey Creek, a tributary to the North Fork Kings River, is almost thirty miles long. It empties into the North Fork Kings River near Balch Park. From the junction on Highway 168 to Shaver Lake, it's located about twelve miles to the southeast.

In 1935, John Dale operated the **Diamond X Pack Train** at Dinkey Creek. Dale Lake was named for him after he planted fish there, as well as in Diamond X Lake. He was a member of the Packers' Association in 1941. He still owned the station in 1947, but by 1952, had sold it to Walter R. Bunn and Cecil Phipps. They ran twenty-five horses and fifteen mules. Bunn owned the Diamond X Pack Train in 1954.

In 1935, Ted and Elsie Anderson also packed out Dinkey Creek. They were active in the Packers' Association in 1941. The family owned and operated the **Dinkey Creek Inn and Pack Station** for many years. Their two daughters, Virginia and Betty, along with another girl, drove the sixty head of horses and mules from their ranch in Auberry to the pack station at Dinkey Creek, a distance of thirty-one miles. Ted stocked many lakes in the area, and one lake was named after Virginia.

Clyde Johnson was the owner of the **Crown Valley Pack Station** in 1935, and packed into Crown Valley from Dinkey Creek. Crown Valley is at 8,400 feet elevation. In 1964, Clyde W. Johnson III and Edwin A. Johnson, Clyde's sons, owned the pack station. They operated as a dude ranch and ran thirty-five head of stock. The Johnson family were cattle ranchers in the area and still own private ranch land in Crown Valley.

In 1949, Al Avila packed out of the area. The **Sleepy 2F Pack Train** was operating at Dinkey Creek under Arnold Bowline in 1952.

In the 1950s, **Dean and Dave's Pack Train**, owned by David J. and Erdeen Fraga, was operating at Dinkey Creek. In 1960, Fraga had sixty head of stock. They packed into the Dinkey Lakes, Black Cap Basin, and the Kings River, and were operating with seventy head of stock in 1964. In 1969, they advertised their business as **Dean-Dave's Pack Train Guest Ranch** at Dinkey Creek. The Fragas were still there in 1971.

SHAVER LAKE, HUNTINGTON LAKE, FLORENCE LAKE, MONO HOT SPRINGS, AND LAKE THOMAS EDISON

In early Sierra history, Native Americans, settlers, livestock herders, miners, and explorers used the old Mono Trail, with their supplies carried by pack stock.

Shaver Lake, a popular recreation area, lies at 5,500 feet elevation, surrounded by the Sierra National Forest, about fifty miles from Fresno on Highway 168. It is a reservoir built in 1927 on Stevenson Creek by the Southern California Edison Company. The massive, devastating Creek Fire burned through this and the Huntington Lake areas in September/October 2020, burning well over 300,000 acres.

Huntington Lake is situated on the edge of the Kaiser Wilderness Area at 7,000 feet elevation, and is sixty-four miles from Fresno and about sixteen miles beyond Shaver Lake. The lake is a reservoir on the site of former Home Camp Meadow in a large valley, and now hosts a multitude of recreational opportunities for visitors. In the winter, the Huntington Lake Road is groomed for cross-country skiing and snowmobile use.

The Big Creek-San Joaquin River hydroelectric project was begun in the early part of the century, and the roads were originally power company roads to build and access the dams. The reservoirs are part of the hydroelectric system of the Southern California Edison Company.

From 1910 to 1913, the Southern California Edison Company constructed three dams to create Huntington Lake Reservoir. Construction was begun at Huntington Lake on the Kaiser Pass Road in 1920, following the old Mono Trail. Mules were used extensively in the construction phase. During the same summer, a road was built along the north shore of Huntington Lake. Two new hydroelectric work camps were located along the newly completed road. These camps were "mini towns" with bunkhouses, commissaries, recreation facilities, and a doctor's office and hospital.

The Kaiser Pass Road was next completed to the small, natural Florence Lake. A new construction camp, known as Camp 63, was built at the intake of the Florence Lake Tunnel. The same kind of town was built there as at Huntington Lake. Florence Lake is twenty-two miles from upper Huntington Lake. In 1925, dam construction at Florence Lake began. Logging occurred in the lake basin to accommodate the new reservoir. All vegetation and trees were removed from the basin, and gravel and soil from the valley site were used to construct the dam. The Southern California Edison Co. completed Florence Lake Dam in 1926. When it was built, it was the largest dam of its type. It is 3,200 feet long with fifty-eight arches. The road was then improved and opened for tourist travel.

Next, the Kaiser Pass Road was extended to Vermillion Valley. The road to Florence and Thomas Edison Lakes lies deep in the mountains, and can be quite harrowing, with one lane and pull-outs.

The reservoir site for the Vermillion Valley Dam was a broad, flat valley in a forest of tall Jeffrey pines, surrounded by high peaks. Red colored bluffs generated the name of the valley, and Mono Creek flowed through it. The Southern California Edison Company constructed a dam across Mono Creek at the lower end of the valley, where glacial moraines caused it to be narrower. Trees were logged, and the valley floor that would be the bottom of the reservoir was scoured by heavy equipment to provide material for building the dam. Work camps were established in the valley. The 167-foot-high Vermillion Valley Dam was completed in the fall of 1954, and the lake that filled the valley was named Lake Thomas Edison. The surface area of the new lake is approximately three square miles, and is at 7,300 feet elevation. A ferry boat takes visitors across the lake to the trailhead leading to the John Muir Trail.

During new dam location and construction in the 1910s to the late 1940s, the Southern California Edison Company maintained large numbers of mules and saddle animals in the lake areas. There were a series of Southern California Edison Company pack stations located around Huntington Lake. In the 1930s, after Huntington Lake was created, the company began selling their no-longer-needed pack animals and equipment to local commercial packing operations.

SHAVER LAKE AND HUNTINGTON LAKE

There is a long, rich packing history at Huntington Lake. In the 1920s, there were two pack stations at the lake. Vaud Cunningham bought out the Southern California Edison pack stations. He owned one, and Glenn Burns owned the second. Both of these outfits used buildings and materials moved from the old construction work camps around the lake.

Prior to 1920, E. H. Barnett operated a pack station out of Lakeshore at Huntington Lake, and Glenn Burns first packed for him in 1921. Glenn T. Burns had begun cattle ranching in the San Joaquin Valley, and hired out as a packer during the hot valley summers. His cattle ranch grew to 2,300 acres, and his wife cared for the ranch while Glenn went packing into the mountains. After six years, Burns purchased the station from Barnett. In 1928, he established another station at Camp 62 (an old SCEC work camp). Burns packed for the Girls Camp at Huntington Lake for some years, calling it **Huntington Lake Stables.**

In 1935, the **Glenn Burns Pack Station** at Huntington Lake bought out E. R. Casner, whose pack station was located near Mono Hot Springs. Casner, who also owned Casner Drug Company in Fresno, had been in operation for some time, and ran forty head of pack and saddle stock. By the 1950s, Burns had built his pack station up to 167 head of horses and mules.

In 1941, Burns was an active member of the High Sierra Packers' Association, with his headquarters near Billy Creek. In 1946, he began packing the Joseph Wampler Trail Trips, six-week-long trips that traveled the entire length of the John Muir Trail, each summer. Some of their customers hiked the distance while others rode horseback.

Burns had been in the packing business for thirty-four years when he sold his station to Dillard and Floyd Fike in 1954, and it became the **D & F Pack Station**. Burns kept some of his stock and continued to pack the Wampler Trips. In 1963, he sold his remaining mules to Red's Meadow Pack Station, and accepted a job packing for the Inyo National Forest for eight years before retiring. He was a partner for many years in the Pick and Shovel Mine at Minnow Creek and Jackson Meadow in the Silver Divide country. He sold that mine interest and cabins to Dr. Jim Fisher of Auburn.

The **Huntington Lake Lodge** was owned and probably built by the Southern California Edison Company. They used their saddle and pack animals at the lodge to transport tourists around the lake and into the backcountry. The **Huntington Lake Hotel** was owned by Anita Walling, and in 1930, she sold her packing business to Vaud Cunningham. The sale included forty-five head of stock, thirty riding saddles, forty-two packsaddle sets, and four camp cooking outfits, plus other items, for $2,500. Cunningham called his outfit **V/C Tourist Packers**, and he employed his two cousins, Tom and John "Shorty" Cunningham as packers. Vaud had been packing since 1922 at Florence Lake. In 1939, the Edison Company sold all of their pack animals and equipment to Cunningham.

In 1941, Vaud Cunningham sold his business to Dillard and Floyd E. Fike, and they renamed the station **D & F Pack Station**. In 1954, Fike purchased Glenn Burns Pack Station, with headquarters near Billy Creek, and merged the two outfits. At that time, there were 130 head of stock used at the corrals. Fike moved four buildings from Billy Creek to their Deer Creek headquarters and the Badger Flat spike station. In 1960, Floyd and Eleanor Fike had 100 head of stock. By 1969, Floyd Fike and Russell Fike, his son, owned the station. Mrs. Fike was secretary of the High Sierra Packers' Association for many years.

In 1980 the Fikes sold to Brad Myers, a former employee of D & F Pack Station, who continued the operation. The headquarters station is located a quarter mile from the Deer Creek Campground. In addition to the main Deer Creek headquarters, D & F Pack Station operated spike stations at Badger Lake and Edison Lake, and the **Shaver Stable**. Myers operated with sixty head of horses and mules. In 2009, Randy and Sue Walker purchased the pack station from Myers, and operate a full service packing business with forty head of pack and saddle animals. The D & F Pack Station operates out of Huntington Lake and Badger Flat, offering different types of pack trips and horseback rides. Trips go into Kaiser, John Muir, Dinkey Lakes, and Ansel Adams Wilderness areas.

Brad Myers kept the Shaver Stable at Shaver Lake after selling D & F Pack Station, and continued operating the stable business on Highway 168. In 2016, he sold the business to Gabrielle Kant, along with her husband and family. They have a schedule of trail rides from one hour to four hours and an evening sunset ride.

In 1935, Jay Robinson operated a station at Shaver Lake, and also operated at Coolidge Meadows and Dinkey Creek. In the 1940s, Jack E. Ducey ran a pack station at Lakeshore called the **Jack Ducey Pack Outfit**. He ran about fifty head of stock and packed into Kings Canyon National Park.

In 1964 the **Lazy A. Pack Station**, owned by Archie L. Frantzich, operated with twenty head of stock. In 1964-69, **Huntington Lake Pack Station** was run by S. Joseph "Joe" and Peg Bridges at Badger Flats, Florence Lake, Lake Thomas Edison, and Lakeshore at Huntington Lake. They had sixty head of stock.

FLORENCE LAKE AND BLAYNEY MEADOWS

Blayney Meadows and Blayney Hot Springs, located in the Sierra National

Forest, were previously called Lost Valley, and, before that, Hidden Valley or Hidden Valley Meadows. The name of the meadow commemorates William Farris Blayney, who grazed sheep there in the 1870s. They are located about five miles east of Florence Lake, on the South Fork of the San Joaquin River.

The meadow was originally homesteaded around 1895, and the original owners were the Shipp family. There are still two other private ranches in the valley. Sheep and cattle grazed in the valley in the earliest years of settlement. The Sally Keys Lakes are named for Sallie Keys Shipp, one of the early residents. The Shipp family operated a guest ranch near Blayney Hot Springs in 1895.

The 200-acre ranch has been in operation catering to guests for over seventy-five years. The ranch is 7,600 feet in elevation, with the San Joaquin River running through it. The John Muir Trail is located adjacent to the ranch. The ranch also adjoins the Lost Valley Camp and Pack Station, owned by the Ross family on another old homestead.

John Shipp sold the ranch to Jack Ducey, who operated a pack station at Huntington Lake, in 1940. Ducey continued to operate it as a guest ranch and renamed it the **Diamond D Guest Ranch.**

In 1946, Nate and Pansy Combs purchased the ranch and began a packing operation. When they sold it, the ranch was divided into three portions. In 1947, Karl Smith was on a backpack trip with Sam Peckinpaw (before Sam became a famous screen director) and first saw the ranch. He became enchanted with the place and was determined to purchase it whenever possible. Meanwhile, he and his wife, Adeline, purchased the Florence Lake Store and Ferry. In 1953, Karl and Adeline purchased a third portion of the original ranch and changed the name to **Muir Trail Ranch**.

Karl and Adeline Smith met at Fresno State, where Adeline earned her teaching degree. Karl was a professional musician and played the horn in the Dallas Symphony Orchestra. During the winters Adeline taught school in Auberry.

At the Muir Trail Ranch, facilities include a lodge, dining room and kitchen, eight log cabins, five tent cabins, and two improved hot springs. The ranch can handle about twenty people at a time, and horses are available for trail riding and pack trips.

In order to reach the ranch after the long winding drive to Florence Lake, guests take the ferryboat across the lake, then ride a horse or hike five and a half miles in, about two hours, to reach the ranch. There is a very rough road where supplies and gear may be hauled from Florence Lake to the ranch by truck.

Karl Smith died in 1981, and Adeline operated the ranch, assisted by her daughter, Karla Hurley, and her husband, Tom. Adeline Smith died in 2008, and Karla Hurley's family still operates both the Florence Lake Store and Ferry and the Muir Trail Ranch. In 2011, Karla's daughter, Hilary, and her husband, Luke Painter, took over management of the guest ranch. Luke is the son of another packing family, Robin and Mark Berry.

Presently, horseback riding and pack trips are available for ranch guests, but no packing services to the general public are offered. The ranch maintains about forty-five head of stock. The stock is driven to the ranch in the spring and remains there until the fall, when the animals are driven back out of the mountains.

With the popularity of hiking the John Muir and Pacific Crest Trails, the ranch now picks up resupply boxes of food and provides hot showers for hikers passing through.

In 1932, Fred Ross established a boys' camp on forty acres of private land purchased from George Smith. In 1935, Ross built the base camp. He also had a pack station corral on the southeastern side of Florence Lake that he built in 1938. The **Lost Valley Boys' Camp** operated until about 1941. Ross had a partner, David McKenzie. From 1932 to 2006, the **Lost Valley Camp** was owned by Fred and Clara Belle Ross, in later years, assisted by their son Richard Ross and his wife, Susie.

Their corrals, **Lost Valley Pack Station**, are on the southeast side of Florence Lake, and they pack into the South Fork of the San Joaquin River. On their private land in the meadow, they constructed four cabins as well as a lodge, kitchen, and dining areas. In 1961, the camp added an A-frame cabin and storage shed to accompany their corral at Florence Lake.

Now, the pack station is operated by Richard Ross and his sister Penny. The camp is located near the Muir Trail Ranch. Formerly, the Lost Valley Pack Station offered many types of pack trips and rented burros. Presently, from their corrals at Florence Lake, they offer dunnage, full service, and resupply trips to walking parties with packers and mule strings. No saddle horses or rental burros are available. The Rosses were the last packers to still rent burros to hiking parties.

A popular program at the camp is the former High Sierra Elderhostel, now called Road Scholar. High Sierra Road Scholar at Blayney Meadows offers two sessions of one week each every summer at the base camp. Campers hike in the four miles to camp after ferrying across Florence Lake. Gear is transported to the camp in a Mercedes "Unimog" truck from the lake.

In 1935, Claude Berryhill owned a pack station in Blayney Meadows and Huntington Lake, with twenty head of stock.

MONO HOT SPRINGS AND LAKE THOMAS EDISON

Mono Hot Springs, at 6,700 feet elevation, lies along the South Fork of the San Joaquin River, and consists of six separate hot springs. The hot springs are located between Florence Lake and Lake Thomas Edison on the Kaiser Pass Road, seventeen miles northeast from Huntington Lake. The historic Mono Hot Springs Resort was built in 1935, a few years after Southern California Edison Company completed the road.

In the 1940s, Bill Stevenson operated **High Sierra Pack Station** at Mono Hot Springs. The station was purchased by brothers Thomas H. and John E. "Shorty" Cunningham in 1948. They had first packed for their cousin, Vaud Cunningham, at Huntington Lake. In 1954, the two brothers ran fifty horses and thirty-five mules, and by 1960, they had increased their stock to 125 head. They were partners for nineteen years. Shorty was president of the Western High Sierra Packers' Association. In 1968, Tom's son, John, bought out his uncle's interest in the station and continued the partnership with his dad.

In 1969, the Forest Service offered them a new site near the newly created Lake Thomas Edison. They built a new facility there, but the record heavy winter of 1968-69 destroyed the building. In 1971, the Cunninghams moved their pack station to another site near the lake and moved the headquarters from Mono Hot Springs to that location. There is little remaining evidence of the old pack station now at the Mono Hot Springs site.

John Cunningham met Jenise on a pack trip, and they were married in 1974. In 1980, John took over the operation from his father. In 2011, they operated with eighty-five head of stock.

Currently, John and Jenise Cunningham operate the pack station with their High Sierra Pack Station headquarters at Lake Thomas Edison. Backcountry trips travel into the John Muir and Ansel Adams Wilderness areas. The Florence Lake station corrals are located at the west end of Florence Lake, and trails rides are offered there. The Cunninghams also provide packing services at Florence Lake with reservations.

John and Jenise were selected Most Honored Packers at Mule Days in 2009. John had competed in the packing events at Mule Days as a young man in the 1970s.

The shoeing shed at Kennedy Meadows is what every horseshoer dreams of.

BASS LAKE, BEASORE MEADOWS, MUGLER, MILLER, AND JACKSASS MEADOW

Bass Lake reservoir, located in Sierra National Forest at 3,415 feet elevation, was built by the Southern California Edison Company and supplied the first hydroelectric generating project to Central California. It is located one hour north of Fresno, and about fifteen miles from the south entrance to Yosemite National Park.

The Beasore Road from Bass Lake to Beasore Meadows was built in 1923. Before the road was built, the area was accessed by the old stock trail. The road leads eventually from Bass Lake to Soldier Meadow on the Granite Creek Fork of the San Joaquin River, where it ends. It passes through Beasore Meadows, Mugler Meadow, and Miller Meadow.

At Soldier Meadow, at 7,000 feet elevation, the Mammoth Pass Trail passes 77 Corral and Sheep Crossing on the historic French Trail from Fresno Flats to Mammoth Lakes on the east side of the range. Miller and Lux Ranch, the largest known ranch in the area, drove sheep from their ranch near Tres Pinos up through the San Joaquin and 77 Corral, then over the Sierra to their West Walker River ranches near Yerington, Nevada.

In the early days, there were three pack stations in the area. One was located at Beasore Meadows, one at Jackass Meadow, and one at Miller Meadow.

BASS LAKE

In 1935, Fred Dupzyk operated out of Bass Lake. From 1935 to 1941, Mr. and Mrs. V. Chubb packed into Yosemite from Bass Lake and Jackass Meadows, contracting with the park concessionaire. They were members of the Western High Sierra Packers' Association. Al Pettit owned the **Bass Lake Stables** in 1952.

BEASORE MEADOWS

Beasore Meadows, on the Beasore Road, is located about twenty miles from Oakhurst, above Bass Lake, and is near the southern Yosemite Park boundary. Located at 6,800 feet elevation, it is a lush meadow landscape with gorgeous wildflower displays, and is adjacent to the historic Jones Store. It was the first stop along a well used cattle trail in the 1800s, and cattle still graze in the area today.

John Beasore began to run cattle in the 1860s, and homesteaded the meadows that were named after him. When John Beasore's son Tom died, John's nephew, Tom Jones, inherited the homestead from him. Tom Jones grew up in that area and began his packing career at Bass Lake.

Jones opened the first backcountry pack station in Madera County. From the early 1920s to 1935, Tom and his wife, Ella Jones, owned the **Beasore Meadows Pack Station**, seven or eight miles below Mugler Meadow and ten miles below Jackass Meadows and Globe Rock. They operated at Beasore Meadows and Mugler Meadow. Tom Jones built the Jones Store on Beasore Road in 1936, when the road was built. Tom Jones's pack station, store, cabins, and campground serviced visitors to the west side of the Minaret Wilderness Area and southern Yosemite National Park. Tom Jones employed many Native

American packers during his tenure. The horses and mules were driven back and forth each spring and fall to a ranch in Coarsegold, to the west in the foot-hills, for winter pasture.

Johnny Alberta was sent to the mountains as a young boy of about eight years old with Obert Bundy, a family friend, because he suffered from asth-ma in Patterson during the hot summer. He continued to go to the mountains every summer. When old enough, he went to live with Tom and Ella Jones at Beasore Meadows, and worked around the resort and pack station each sum-mer. He became an unofficial foster son of Tom and Ella, so he took Jones as his surname. Johnny guided his first pack trip when he was twelve or thirteen years of age. After Ella died, Tom married Hilda and continued operating his pack station, store, and resort. By 1935, Johnny Jones was running the outfit for Tom. He packed for Tom for twenty years before going out on his own in Mugler Meadow.

While working for Tom, Johnny had begun buying some stock and equip-ment of his own. Johnny couldn't afford to buy out the outfit at Beasore Meadows, but in 1953, clients of his helped him purchase Mugler Meadow and begin a pack station there.

From 1952 until 1956, A. L. "Al" Pettitt from Bass Lake leased Tom Jones's pack station. Tom Jones had died, and his second wife, Hilda E. Jones, leased the pack station out. From 1957-1961, Ralph Walton from Bass Lake leased the station, calling it Walton's Pack Station. He ran forty head of stock. In 1962-63, Wayne Tex, packer, leased the store and pack station. The last leasees were Murray and Maggie Ward in 1966-67. After 1970, Hilda Jones closed the pack station.

The Jones Store is still there and has become quite famous for its fresh baked pies, cheeseburgers, and tri-tip beef sandwiches. It is still operated by descendents of Tom Jones.

MUGLER MEADOW

Mugler Meadow is off Beasore Road at 6,000 feet in elevation, and is the headwaters of Chiquito Creek. In 1953, Johnny Jones leased Mugler Mead-ow from Eldon and Nellie Behney of Lemoore for two years, and eventually purchased the forty acres of private land for $1,600. He packed from there, calling his operation **Johnny Jones Pack Station**. The road went through the middle of the meadow, and Jones built his facilities there.

Jones built a two-story main house, barn, corrals, and a pack shed. The pack shed was constructed from split logs erected vertically, with flat side on the inside and log side on the outside. He also had a packing permit at Soldier Meadow where the road ended. The Forest Service only allowed him to build a corral, pack shed, and loading dock there. The crew stayed in tents. Jones had a ranch in Coarsegold where he wintered his stock.

In 1955, he bought twenty-five mules in Phoenix, Arizona. The Tennes-see-raised mules were gentle and could be ridden. Jones also bought mules for Bob Barnett at Yosemite Curry Company Stables. He operated his station with about forty head of stock and two or three other guides that he hired. His older brother, Joe Alberta, with his wife Gloria and their five children, worked with Johnny for many years.

Wayne Tex began working for Johnny when he was twelve years old, much as Johnny had for Tom Jones. In 1968, Wayne Tex managed the station for Johnny until it was sold in 1970. Johnny Jones sold his stock and Forest Service permits to Wes Craven of Miller Meadow, a Fresno County Supervisor, and the pack station was closed. Jones kept the Mugler Meadow home and facilities that were on private property, and concentrated on breeding and training mules.

In 1973, Bob Barnett from the Yosemite Park and Curry Company Stables talked Jones into guiding Governor Ronald Reagan and his family on a family pack trip into the Yosemite Park wilderness. Johnny wasn't told who the VIP was but the stables were furnishing the stock. Ike Livermore and his wife, Dena, were also going on the trip. Ike's son, Sam, who was working for the Curry Company in Yosemite, was to be one of the packers. Ike Livermore was the California State Resources director for Reagan at the time. Later, Jones said he was happy he had agreed to be the guide as it was a wonderful trip.

Jones was a judge at Mule Days for several years. He had three world champion racing mules, the most famous of which was called Rabbit. In 1985, he was Most Honored Packer at the Mule Days Parade. With Dwight Barnes, Jones wrote a book about his packing experiences titled *Following the Bells*.

MILLER MEADOW

To reach Minarets Pack Station, the road follows the north side of Bass Lake to the Beasore Road and continues forty miles to the pack station. It is located at Miller Meadow near Clover Meadow, where there is a ranger station. The pack station serves the west side of the Minaret Wilderness Area, now called Ansel Adams Wilderness Area. They also pack into the southwestern corner of Yosemite National Park. It is the most remote station on the west side of the Sierra.

In 1935, W. F. Dillon ran a pack station called **Miller Meadow Pack Station.** In the 1940s and 1950s, Milton H. Parker of Bass Lake ran the **Sierra Pack Camp.** He also had a corral at Clover Meadow and was a member of the Western High Sierra Packers' Association. The pack station packed into the southern area of Yosemite National Park, the headwaters of the San Joaquin River on the North Fork, and the western side of the Ritter Range. In 1960, he operated with sixty head of stock. Parker sold the Sierra Pack Camp station to Milton Herschfelt in 1962.

Milt Herschfelt changed the name of the station to **Minarets Pack Station**. The resort also offered lodging and meals. Herschfelt sold to Wes Craven in 1969. Craven was a Fresno County Supervisor, who had bought out the packing permit and stock of Johnny Jones's outfit at Mugler Meadow in 1970. In 1972, Wes and his son, Brad Craven, operated both outfits and the permit at Soldier Meadow. From 1970 to 1981, Bern and Claudia Box of North Fork managed the resort for Wes Craven. John Andrews, Ric Rasmussen, and Bill Seney formed a group and purchased the Minarets Pack Station from Craven.

Two years later, Watson Moore bought out Rasmussen's interests. In 1984, Moore was president of the Western High Sierra Packers' Association. After selling his interest in the pack station, Watson Moore became an insurance agent, handling liability insurance for most of the Sierra pack stations. In 1986, John Andrews formed a group of associates who owned the pack station. Besides Andrews, associates included Bob Lovelace and Bruce Negri, who managed the outfit.

In 1991, Miller Meadow Inc. purchased the operation from John Andrews, Lovelace, and other partners. Members of the corporation included manager Bart Topping, Jerry Hansen, and Tom Walters. Bart Topping and his wife, Cindy Topping, have continued the ownership of the Minarets Pack Station. In 2008, they were assisted by their son, Owen, and his wife, Tracy. Tracy Harris Topping, formerly of Bishop, packed for Red's Meadow Pack Station for many years prior to her marriage. Daughter Jessica and her husband, Scott Jones, also assist in the family-run business.

The Topping family has been attending Mule Days for many years and competing in the various events. The two younger couples have been on a world champion pack team. The Minarets Pack Station pack team won the World Championship Pack Team three straight years. Bart Topping was selected Most Honored Packer in 2008.

The facilities include a lodge, store, cafe, and a fifteen-site campground on seventeen private acres. Their campground has accommodations for visitors camping with private stock and parking for horse trailers or live-in horse trailers. They operate their packing services with seventy head of stock. The Toppings have cattle grazing permits near the station that have been in the family for three generations, and use the Soldier Meadow pasture.

JACKASS MEADOW

Just past the turnoff to Minarets Pack Station on the Beasore Road is Jackass Meadow at 7,000 feet elevation, one of the largest meadow complexes in the central Sierra.

In the 1930s, Newton Jasper Phillips of Fish Camp moved his pack station to Jackass Meadow. In 1935, Billy Brown owned **Billy Brown's Pack Outfit** at Jackass Meadow. Mr. and Mrs. Chubb also ran trips out of the meadow. In the 1940s, William Stathem and the Leap Brothers operated in the area. In the 1950s, Bill Baker ran a pack station, and in 1964, the pack station had fifteen head of stock. Miller Meadow, Inc. bought out the pack station at Jackass Meadow.

In 1952, the Mammoth Pack Outfit, on their legendary spring horse drive from Coarsegold to Mammoth Lakes, spent the night at Milton Parker's Sierra Pack Camp corrals at Jackass Meadow. The Drive crossed the Sierra on the old French or Fresno Flats Trail. Lee Summers, owner of the station, led the horses, mules, and crew over the difficult drive. The previous fall, the crew had driven the horses and mules over the mountains to winter on a ranch in Coarsegold.

FISH CAMP AND CHERRY VALLEY

FISH CAMP

Fish Camp, at 5,062 feet elevation, is located just off of Highway 41, two miles outside of the southern boundary of Yosemite National Park near Wawona. It was formerly known as Happy Camp and Berry's Fish Camp. Charles Berry homesteaded land in Fish Camp in around 1900.

In 1900, Newt Jasper Phillips moved from Santa Barbara and homesteaded land at Bootjack, southeast of Mariposa, and in the same year, he began packing tourists into Yosemite. There was a large demand for guides and saddle and pack stock. He operated from Fish Camp until the 1930s, when he moved to Jackass Meadow. From 1910 to 1935, there was a pack station at Jerseydale, about nine miles south-southeast of El Portal, owned by Lloyd and Newt. J. Phillips, which packed into the southern area of Yosemite National Park. The Phillips may have been the first packers in the area.

Fred Wass worked as a packer and guide from 1916 to 1921 in Yosemite for the Yosemite Park and Curry Company. For the next ten years, he worked for the Forest Service and managed a cattle ranch. In 1930, he went to work for the Curry Company again at Wawona. In 1934, he and his wife, Beryl, started the **Fred Wass Pack Outfit** at Fish Camp on land that they rented from Charlie Berry, the owner of Fish Camp. This was on land previously leased by the Phillips. Wass operated with ten head of stock in 1935, gradually building up to thirty head.

In 1937, Wass obtained a Forest Service special use permit on twenty acres at Skidder Camp, an abandoned logging camp of the Sugar Pine Lumber Company. Wass was the first Forest Service permitted packer in the area. Other packers worked off of private land to get around having to obtain a Forest Service permit. The land was about two miles in on the Big Sandy Road, and he built the pack station there. The station is still located at that site. In 1943, Wass had a permit to operate in Yosemite National Park and was a member of the High Sierra Packers' Association, Western Unit. He never had more than one other packer beside himself during his operation of the station, as he liked to give his customers personal service.

By 1950, much of the Forest Service land that Wass packed into was being logged. Jeeps were using the logging roads to drive in, pushing the wilderness back further from his station. Melvin Wass, Fred's nephew, had worked for Fred off and on, and in the fall of 1958, before deer season, Fred sold the pack station to Melvin and Alfred Wass, along with Joe Silva. In 1962, they called the station **Fish Camp Pack Station**. After selling out to his nephew, Fred continued to spend summers around Edison Lake, looking after cattle for rancher Lester Bissett.

Melvin Wass sold the station to Troy and Lorene Henry, along with twenty head of stock. Troy Henry was a well-known horse trainer in the Fresno area. Troy ran an extensive horse operation, including horse boarding, rental and lease horses, lesson horses, training horses, a tack store, wagon rides, and a pony ring, to which he added the pack station. He was a mentor of well-known horse trainer Pat Parelli, who worked for Henry for some time. Troy Henry sold the station to Michael Knapp in October of 1965.

Michael and his wife Sherry changed the name of the station to **Yosemite Trails Pack Station,** under their Lazy K Ranches. Now, they have shortened the name to **Yosemite Trails**. The station headquarters are on the Jackson Road near Fish Camp, on 7.7 acres, just two miles from the southern boundary of Yosemite National Park. By 1986, their son, Larry, was involved with the pack station, and is the general manager today in 2020. The Knapp family operate with about a hundred head of stock, and supply horses to nearby summer camps. Most of their saddle horses are raised from their Quarter Horse mares, and are known for their gentle, friendly manners.

A nearby large hotel, Tenaya Lodge, owned by the concessionaire at Yosemite National Park, provides customers with day trips and horse activities at Yosemite Trails. The station also conducts dinner rides where guests can either ride a horse or ride in a wagon, and they provide magical sleigh rides in the winter season. The half-day trail ride to the Mariposa Redwood Grove inside the park is very popular with visitors.

The Knapps own a large cattle and horse ranch near Chowchilla with 40,000 acres of summer grazing up into the High Sierra near Yosemite Park, called the Lazy K Ranches. They have several registered Quarter Horse stallions and a band of outstanding mountain-raised mares. Their registered colts are in demand each year at their annual "Pick a Colt" sale. My grandson, Rial Engelhart, owns two of their horses and used one as his college rodeo horse while attending Fresno State College. His horse, Vaquero, was chosen as Horse of the Year by the Western Region of the National Intercollegiate Rodeo Association. Now, he uses him on the professional rodeo circuit as well as for ranch work.

Floyd Branscom, a rancher, operated a pack station out of Mariposa with sixteen head of stock. In 1935, George Hamby at Koontz Meadows and Fish Camp operated with ten head of stock. He was a cattle rancher in the area.

CHERRY VALLEY

The road to Cherry Lake Reservoir turns off the Big Oak Flat Road. Cherry Valley Reservoir was created when a 315 foot high rock dam was completed on Cherry Creek in 1956. The area is at 4,700 feet elevation, near the Yosemite Park boundary, and is quite warm in the summer. Lake Eleanor is another reservoir nearby, and both are part of the San Francisco City and County water projects.

Cherry Valley Packers was a pack station established by Murat Brummette in Cherry Valley before the dam and reservoir were built. Construction on the dam began in 1953. In 1954, Jack Cagianut then purchased the station, calling it **Cherry Valley Pack Station**, and still owned it in 1962. Joe Barnett then purchased it from Cagianut and sold it to George Tennant. Tennant ran twenty head of stock. In 1969, Reno Sardella purchased the station and called it **Kerrick Corral.** Sardella operated a large packing operation from two locations: Kerrick Corral and Kennedy Meadows. Pack trips traveled into the north part of Yosemite National Park and the Emigrant Wilderness.

In 1971, Sardella sold the station to Marvin and Kay DeVotee, along with sixty head of stock. They called it **Cherry Valley Pack Station**. Marvin died suddenly at the pack station, and in 1975, Kay operated it with Bill Rutherford. In 1989, Kay DeVotee continued to operate the pack station. The Forest

Service directed her to move the station to a new location that they had selected, but she had permanent buildings at the current site and refused to move. Around 2000, when the permit expired, the Forest Service took over and bulldozed the buildings. There is no pack station located at Cherry Lake now, and no outfitter services for the public.

Horse and mule barns at Yosemite Valley Stables, formerly providing spectacular guided rides.

Tuolumne Stables pack string crossing the Tuolumne River in Yosemite, 2018. (Kerry Roeser)

285

WAWONA, YOSEMITE VALLEY, TUOLUMNE MEADOWS, AND HETCH HETCHY RESERVOIR IN YOSEMITE NATIONAL PARK

The Army managed and patrolled Yosemite from 1892 until the Park Service was created in 1916, when the Park Service administration took over. When the Army patrolled the park, their headquarters were located near the campground, where they had built the large, now historic barn. The hotel and stables were purchased by Yosemite National Park in 1932.

All of the horse and mule operations in Yosemite National Park are now under lease to the current concessioner, who has a contract with the Park Service to supply visitor services.

WAWONA

Wawona, located east of Mariposa on Wawona Road, Highway 41, is twenty-seven miles from Yosemite Valley. Wawona was a Sierra Miwok camping area and given the name meaning "big tree" for the massive sequoias in the Mariposa Grove. The beautiful meadows and forest are at 3,999 feet elevation.

Clark's Station at Wawona, at the southern entrance to Yosemite, was a stage stop for travelers to Yosemite Valley beginning in 1856. It was owned by Galen Clark, who had preempted or homesteaded 160 acres of land. Travelers on the stages spent the night at the rough hotel before continuing on for the eight-hour stagecoach ride to Yosemite Valley. Clark took in Edwin Moore as a partner in 1869, and Moore and his wife managed it. It was then called Clark's and Moore's Station.

Henry Washburn was a livery stable owner in Mariposa. Washburn, William F. Coffman, and E. W. Chapman purchased Clark's Station from Clark and Moore in 1874. This partnership had already been established and was operating a livery and stage business in the area. Washburn and his two brothers then bought out Coffman and Chapman. Henry's wife renamed the resort Wawona, after a Miwok name. The Washburn brothers rebuilt the main building of the hotel in 1879 after a fire the year before. The brothers and their family operated the stables, stages, and resort until 1932.

In 1932, Yosemite National Park purchased the resort from the Washburn family. Donald Tresidder of Yosemite Park and Curry Company then took over management of the Wawona resort facilities. The current concessioner manages all visitor facilities.

Today, the **Wawona Stables** conduct two-hour and day horse and mule rides into areas of southern Yosemite National Park. This is the only park stable still offering horseback riding in Yosemite National Park for the visiting public.

Thornton Jackson owned a pack station at Wawona and packed into the southern end of Yosemite National Park. In 1922, James Fulmer purchased this station and packed fishing parties into the park. During hunting season, he packed into the Mt. Raymond and Cold Springs area, as no hunting is permitted in the park. His stock wintered at the ranch of Floyd Branscom in Mariposa. Fulmer, a former rancher himself, worked for a logging mill in Wawona and trapped during the winter. He operated until the late 1920s, when Wawona became part of the park, and the Park Service stopped outside packers from packing into the park. After discontinuing packing, he worked for the Park

Service on trails and roads before returning to the cattle business. Malcolm Fulmer, James's son, packed for the Curry Company while attending college, and for some period later.

YOSEMITE VALLEY

The incomparable Yosemite Valley, located east of the San Joaquin Valley, lies in a deep, narrow, glaciated valley at 4,000 feet elevation. It is seven miles long and one to two miles wide. The towering cliffs and domes rise 3,000 to 4,000 feet above the valley, with spectacular waterfalls tumbling down. The Merced River meanders east to west through the valley.

In 1866, James Hutchings began the first saddle train business in Yosemite Valley in connection with his Hutchings House hotel business. He provided a livery service for visitors and met stages before a road reached the valley. He personally acted as a guide, and, when John Muir worked for Hutchings, he also performed guide services.

Fred Brightman started another saddle train business in competition with Hutchings in 1870. He took in George W. Kenney as a partner. When they ran into financial deficits, they took in another partner, Aaron Harris. Brightman then left the partnership.

William F. Coffman purchased the **Hutchings' Stables** stock, equipment, and business in 1878, and began his saddle train business. In 1885, Coffman merged his saddle train with George Kenney, and together they bought out Harris. They called the new business **Coffman and Kenney Yosemite Stables**. The location was near the present Ahwahnee Hotel and was locally referred to as Kenneyville. Coffman died in 1898, but the business continued on, with Coffman and Kenney remaining the name of the stables, until the Park Service organized a new concessionaire policy.

Stephen Mather had determined there should only be one concessionaire for the tourist businesses in the valley. The contract was awarded to D. J. "Joe" Desmond and was called the **Yosemite National Park Company**. Desmond bought out Coffman and Kenney's Yosemite Stables. Desmond built the first High Sierra Camps in 1916, but went bankrupt two years later. The company was then merged with the Curry Camping Company, becoming the **Yosemite Park and Curry Company** in 1925.

David and Jennie Curry opened Camp Curry in 1899 at the base of Glacier Point. The camp was a village of tent cabins with a kitchen and dining room. It was an instant success and expanded rapidly. After David died in 1917, Jennie Curry, with the help of her three children, took over and ran it. She had turned over management of the camp to her son-in-law, Dr. Donald Tresidder, when, in 1925, Curry Camping Company merged with the Yosemite National Park Company to form the Yosemite Park and Curry Company, managed by Tresidder. The company was called Curry Company for short. Prior to 1935, the Curry Company ran 150 head of horses and mules. The company was sold in 1970 to Music Corporation of America.

Stables had been established at the park in the following locations: Yosemite Valley Stables, Wawona Stables, Tuolumne Meadows Stables, and White Wolf Stables. The current concessionaire operates all the visitor services in the valley and park.

Yosemite Valley Stables was the headquarters of one of the largest horse rental operations in the United States. The day rides offered trips to some of the most scenic areas of the park. The elevation of the valley stables is 4,000 feet. The historic Yosemite Valley Stables are now closed, and trail rides are presently only offered in the park at the Wawona Stables.

TUOLUMNE MEADOWS AND WHITE WOLF

Tuolumne Meadows Stables are located at Tuolumne Meadows, a high country meadow at 8,600 feet in elevation. There are numerous trails and many directions in which to travel, including Lyell Canyon and Donahue Pass to the south, the Tuolumne River and Virginia Canyon to the north, Cathedral Pass to the southwest, and Mono Pass to the southeast.

The Tuolumne Meadows Stables pack supplies and services to the five High Sierra Camps: Glen Aulin, May Lake, Sunrise, Vogelsang, and Merced Lake. Visitors may backpack or ride mules, while their personal items are packed by mules to a comfortable base camp. The camps provide tent cabins with beds and bedding, meals in a central dining hall, and best of all, hot showers! There are four-day and six-day circle trips that are very popular. The trips are so popular that the reservations are obtained through a drawing or lottery system.

White Wolf Lodge and Stables was located at White Wolf Meadow, near the Middle Fork of the Tuolumne River off the Tioga Pass Road, at 8,000 feet elevation. John Meyers homesteaded the meadows in the 1870s. The Meyers family eventually enlarged their cattle ranch into a guest lodge in 1926, and added two duplexes during the same period. In the 1930s, they added cabins. In addition to day rides, the stables offered spot and extended pack trips in the park. In the 1950s, White Wolf was sold to the National Park Service. The stables were closed, but the lodges and cabins remained in operation. The current concessioner began rehabilitation in 2014, and the lodge offers twenty-four tent cabins and four traditional cabins, plus rooms in the central lodge.

Robert "Bob" Bright owned **Aspen Valley Lodge and Stables** on the Old Tioga Road, which was located on private land within the park boundaries. He refused to sub-contract with the concessionaire company, as he believed he was entitled to a direct permit from the National Park Service. In 1940, the new Tioga Road was constructed and isolated Aspen Valley. He eventually sold to the Park Service.

HETCH HETCHY RESERVOIR

Hetch Hetchy Valley became the site of a dam and reservoir after a bitter battle to provide water for the City of San Francisco. The valley was similar to, and many claimed as beautiful as Yosemite Valley, with many waterfalls on the Tuolumne River. After a long battle led by John Muir against construction, Congress approved the dam project in 1913. O'Shaughnessy Dam was constructed on the Tuolumne River to create Hetch Hetchy Reservoir from 1914 to 1920. The reservoir is at 3,814 feet in elevation.

Camp Mather was established to house the many workers needed to build the dam. Later, it became a camp for visitors to the area. Joe Barnes, a young Arizona cowboy, worked for a pack outfit in the area, and when that outfit withdrew, Joe purchased the location. He began the **Mather Saddle and Pack Station** at Camp Mather in 1929. It is located one mile outside of Yosemite National Park on the 360-acre resort owned by the City of San Francisco. The corrals are located near the Evergreen Lodge on the Evergreen Road. Joe Barnes's son, Jay, grew up in the business, looking forward to going to the mountains each summer. In 1980, Jay Barnes and his wife, Elizabeth, took over the business and raised two sons at the pack station, growing up there as Jay had grown up.

In 2011, the station ran pack trips into the remote northwestern Yosemite National Park and conducted day rides around Hetch Hetchy Reservoir. The station also offered hayrides, breakfast, and sunset rides for guests at Camp Mather. The Barnes family has celebrated eighty-three years in the business, and winter at their cattle ranch east of Oakdale. Jay Barnes was selected Most Honored Packer by Mule Days in 2011. The huge Rim Fire that started on August 20, 2013, burned through the camp, although the buildings were saved. In 2016, the Barnes family retired and closed the station.

Mather Saddle Horses and Pack Station at Camp Mather is a new operation, and is offering short rides by Chaparral Ranch.

Kennedy Meadows Lodge and Pack Station is located off of the Sonora Pass Highway.

SONORA PASS REGION

PINECREST LAKE

A short distance off State Highway 108 is Pinecrest Lake, owned by Pacific Gas and Electric. In 1856, a dam was constructed on the Stanislaus River, and the ensuing reservoir was called Strawberry Lake. In 1916, a larger, 143-foot dam was created, and sometime later, the lake was renamed Pinecrest Lake. The elevation of the reservoir is about 5,600 feet. The resort community and Dodge Ridge Ski Area are located nearby.

In 1929, **Strawberry Stables** was located in the meadow on Old Strawberry Road. In 1954, Hart "Cappy" Cook operated the stables. In the 1950s, Reno Sardella purchased the station, and he moved it to a location off Highway 108 near Pinecrest.

Renato "Reno" Sardella was a long time rancher in the Sonora area. For over fifty years, Sardella had pack stations, resorts, and stables in the region. He worked as a movie extra and stunt man, drove stage coaches, and supplied stock for many movies filmed in the area. He had begun his packing career at the Dardanelles resort area in 1929, with his first pack station located on the Middle Fork of the Stanislaus River, about two miles west of the current location of Dardanelles Resort Lodge.

Sardella called his operation **Sardella's Pack Station**, and it grew to over 200 head of stock. He and his wife, Geraldine "Jerry," operated the pack station for many years. In 1953, the station moved to Bell Meadows, then to Kerrick Corral Meadow in 1958. In 1960, Sardella bought the packing and stable operations at Pinecrest, and then again moved the pack station further down the road. He purchased Aspen Meadow, where the station has remained, near Pinecrest Lake and Dodge Ridge Ski Area. As roads were cut into the Sierra backcountry, many pack stations moved their facilities to the end of the road. Many of the early pack stations had few facilities attached.

In 1962, Reno and Geraldine purchased the Kennedy Meadows Resort, and then purchased Cherry Valley Pack Station, operating under the name of **Kerrick Corral**. Sardella operated the three locations for several years and ran between 100 and 200 head of horses and mules. In 1970, Sardella sold Kennedy Meadows Resort to Willy Ritts and partner, Jay Gilbert.

Then, in 1971, he sold Cherry Valley Pack Station to Marvin and Kay DeVotee. Sardella, along with his daughter and son-in-law, Laverne and Jack Litteral, continued to operate Sardella's Pack Station at Aspen Meadow near Pinecrest or Kerrick Corral. Sardella was still the owner, and Laverne was the manager. Jack Litteral, his son-in-law, was a former sheriff in the area, as was Reno's brother. Sardella was selected Most Honored Packer at Mule Days in 1986.

In 1999, after Sardella had died, Laverne sold the pack station to Josh and Amanda Bloom. The Blooms were longtime residents of the Sonora area. Josh is the brother of Matt Bloom, owner of Kennedy Meadows Pack Station. The station was renamed **Aspen Meadow Pack Station**. The Blooms ran sixty head of horses and mules. The pack station offered trips and packing services into the Emigrant Wilderness Area and the Stanislaus National Forest. Their stock wintered on an 800-acre ranch in the Sonora foothill area.

In 2016, the Blooms sold the station to Seth and Caitie Diemel and Doug

Morgan, who worked for the outfit. They run over 100 head of stock and are the youngest pack station owners in the Sierra. In addition to complete pack trip services, they offer one-hour, two-hour, half-day, and full-day trail rides.

In 1962, **Pinecrest Stables** packed into the Emigrant Wilderness Area and parts of the northern section of Yosemite National Park. The pack station was established by Oddie Albertson. The **Trout Creek Pack Station**, owned by Jack Milford in Sonora, packed into the Emigrant Basin. In 1964, Jim and Russell Farr owned the **Dodge Meadows Pack Station** and packed into the Emigrant Wilderness Area.

KENNEDY MEADOWS AND SONORA PASS

Highway 108 parallels the South Fork of the Stanislaus River in an east/northeast direction. Kennedy Meadows, on the Stanislaus River and in the Stanislaus National Forest, is about sixty miles from the town of Sonora. The elevation of the resort is 6,335 feet.

From near Kennedy Meadows to the top of Sonora Pass, at 9,623 feet, the highway climbs 4,000 feet in fifteen miles, crossing the Pacific Crest Trail at the summit. Sonora Pass is the second highest road pass in the Sierra Nevada Range. Highway 108 continues on to meet Highway 395 on the east side of the Sierra.

Beginning during the California Gold Rush, Sonora Pass was a major trans-Sierra route for wagon trains and pack trains. It was originally called the Emigrant Pass Route, as the earliest emigrant pack train, the Bartleson/Bidwell party, attempted to take wagons over the pass in 1841. The wagons were abandoned before reaching the High Sierra, and the lumber was used to make pack saddles for their animals. They crossed the pass using pack mules.

In 1886, Andrew Thomas Kennedy and J. F. Kennedy homesteaded about 600 acres in the area, and they operated this ranch for many years. Cattle grazing has continued in the area around the meadows and Kennedy Lake.

The Tuolumne County Water and Electrical Power Company created the Relief Dam and Reservoir on the Middle Fork of the Stanislaus River in 1906. Mule strings were used to haul in supplies and equipment to build the dam. In 1921, the Sierra and San Francisco Power Company enlarged the Relief Dam and Reservoir. Pacific Gas and Electric Company then purchased the dam. There are also other small check dams at other lakes in the area.

Charlie Ledshaw established a hunting camp in Kennedy Meadows near the Middle Fork of the Stanislaus River. He was paid to eradicate mountain lions. In 1917, Ledshaw and his partner, Edwards, added a gas station, store, and pack station, calling it **Kennedy Meadows Resort and Pack Station.** In 1929, they sold their business to Frank and Irene Kurzi. The original hotel was built in the 1930s by the Kurzis, but burned down in the winter of 1940-41. It was rebuilt by July of 1941, as that summer, the movie *For Whom the Bell Tolls* was scheduled to be filmed there. The film starred Gary Cooper and Ingrid Bergman, and filming began in the fall and continued until December 7, 1941, on the set at Kennedy Meadows. In 1945, Kurzi sold to Lou Bitner.

Two or three years later, Bitner sold the resort to Clifton "Cliff" and Rose Mitchell. Mitchell's father, Mills, had been ranching in the area since the late 1800s, and held a cattle grazing permit at Kennedy Lake. He sold beef to the power company to feed their crew building the Relief Reservoir. In 1958, when Cliff and Rose divorced, Rose received the resort and ran it for three years. Cliff kept the grazing lease and ran cattle there every summer. The cattle were trucked to corrals below Douglas Resort, and then the cowboys drove them to the summer grazing near Kennedy Lake.

In 1961, Reno and Geraldine "Jerry" Sardella, along with area rancher Sanguinetti, purchased the Kennedy Meadows Resort from Rose Mitchell. Willie Ritts began his packing career as a packer for Sardella in the 1960s, while attending college. In 1970, Ritts and Jay Gilbert, from Oakdale, purchased the station from Sardella. Willie Ritts bought out his partner, Gilbert, in 1977.

In 1997, Ritts partnered with Matt Bloom, and then, in 2000, he sold the Kennedy Meadows Resort and Pack Station to Matt and Leslie Bloom and their family. Matt is the brother of Josh Bloom, owner of Aspen Meadow Pack Station. Ritts continued with the cattle grazing operation at Kennedy Lake until he retired and Bloom acquired the lease.

In the fall of 2007, the lodge buildings and seven cabins burned down in a fast moving fire that began in the lodge. The Blooms rebuilt the lodge, keeping with the charm of the old buildings, but with new conveniences and modern construction practices. The resort reopened in April of 2008, and the lodge, including the store and dining room, was completed by June of that year. New cabins were built during the summer. The resort continues to provide excellent vacation services for the public. In 2018, the Donnell Fire, a fast burning fire in the Carson-Iceberg Wilderness Area, threatened the resort, but was stopped near it.

In 2016, Matt Bloom and his family ran about 150 head of stock. They operate a very busy resort, consisting of a restaurant, store, bar, cabins, and a pack station. The facilities are on a 244-acre site on private property leased from Pacific Gas and Electric Power Company.

Pack trips access the Emigrant Wilderness Area and the headwaters of the Stanislaus River, as well as the northern part of Yosemite National Park. Stock is also trucked to trailheads in the Carson-Iceberg Wilderness Area for trips. The Pacific Crest Trail is accessed from the top of nearby Sonora Pass. The resort also does resupply for through hikers on the Pacific Crest Trail.

The pack station has a reputation for beginning their pack trips very early in the morning to avoid summer heat. Clients are asked to have their gear at the packing docks by 6 a.m., but the packers often begin on busy mornings at 3 a.m. Their shoeing building is probably one of the most complete and user-friendly shoeing facilities at any Sierra pack station.

The land is currently being turned over from Pacific Gas and Electric to Tuolumne County.

REFERENCES

Albright, Horace Marden and Marian Albright Schneck. *The Mather Mountain Party of 1915: A Full Account of the Adventures of Stephen T. Mather and His Friends in the High Sierra Of California.* Three Rivers, Sequoia Natural History Association, 1990.

Austin, Mary. *The Land of Little Rain.* Boston, Houghton Mifflin, 1903.

---. *The Flock.* Boston, Houghton Mifflin, 1906.

Babb, Dave. "Eastern Sierra's Fish planting offers 'insiders' look." *Chalfant Press Fishing and Vacation Guide,* Bishop, Ca., Chalfant Press, 1990.

---. "Fish Planting in the Eastern Sierra." *The Album 2*, no. 4. Bishop, Ca., Chalflant Press, 1989.

Back Country Horsemen of America. BCHA and BCHC newspaper and website publications.

---. "1999 Congress on Recreation and Resource Capacity, Back Country and Wilderness Recreation Using Saddle and Pack Stock." BCHC.

---. "BCHA Position Statement on Wilderness Purity." Steve Didier, Public Lands Officer, BCHA, 2005.

---. "A Position Statement on: 'Stock Free' Wilderness Recreation Opportunities." Dennis Dailey, Wilderness Consultant, BCHA, n. d.

---. "A Strategy For Addressing the 'Stock Free' Issue," BCHA, n. d.

---. "History of the Mt. Whitney Trail and Shelter." Ann Lange, Wilderness Committee Chair, n.d.

---."Mission Statement," BCHA, n. d.

---. "Mules and Packing," BCHA, Jan. 1996.

---. "John Muir & Norman B. 'Ike' Livermore." BCHC, Winter 2004.

Bade, William Frederic. "On the Trail With the Sierra Club." *Sierra Club Bulletin 5* (1904-1905).

Barrett, Bob. *Yosemite: Where Mules Wear Diamonds.* Oakhurst, Ca., Ponderosa Printing, 2nd ed., 1989.

Bingaman, John W. (Retired District Park Ranger 1896-1987). *Guardians of the Yosemite, A Story of the First Rangers.* Desert Printers, 1961.

Bowman, Ezra. *The High Sierra*. Time-Life Book, Time Inc., 1972.

Breck, Vivian. *High Trail*. N.Y., DoubleDay & Co. Inc., 1948.

---. *Hoofbeats on the Trail*. N.Y., DoubleDay & Co. Inc., 1950.

Brewer, William H., *Up and Down California in 1860–1864*. Edited by Francis P. Farquhar, Berkeley, University of Calif. Press, 2003. First published 1930 Yale University Press.

Bristow, Gwen. *Calico Palace*. New York, Thomas Y. Crowell Co., 1970.

---. *Jubilee Trail*. New York, Thomas Y. Crowell Co., 1950.

Brower, David R. "Are Mules Necessary?" *Sierra Club Bulletin 33*. March, 1948.

---. "Wilderness Outing." 1947.

Brown, Henry McLauren. *Mineral King Country*. Fresno, Ca., Pioneer Publishing Co., 1988.

---. "The Heyday of Packing." *The Californians*. Sept./Oct. Issue, 1990.

---. "Lewis Camp." *Los Tulares,* Mar. Issue, 1969.

Browne, J. Ross. *Mining Adventures: California and Nevada 1863 to1865*. Balboa Island, Ca., Paisano Press, 1961.

Browning, Peter. *Place Names of the Sierra Nevada*. Berkeley, Wilderness Press, 1986.

Cain, Ella M. *The Story of Early Mono County*. Fearon Publishers, 1961.

Caldwell, Gary. *Mammoth Gold: The Ghost Towns of Lake District*. Mammoth Lakes, Ca., Genny Smith Books, 1990.

Caughey, John Walton. *Gold is the Cornerstone*. Berkeley, University of Calif. Press, 1948.

Chalfant, W. A. *The Story of Inyo*. Reprinted by Warren Chalfant Clarke, Bishop, Ca., Chalfant Press Inc., 1975.

Cleland, Robert Glass. *This Reckless Breed of Men: The Trappers and Fur Traders of the Southwest*. New York, Alfred A. Knopf & Publisher, 1963.

Clingan, Helen and Forest. *Oak to Pine to Timberline*. Fresno, Ca., Pioneer Publishing Co., 1985.

Colby, Josephine. "Kern River Canyon: The Sierra Club's Expedition - 1903." *Overland Monthly.* Jan., 1904.

Cunningham, John and Jenise (High Sierra Pack Station). "People and Personalities: Horse Pack Supported Partners." *Trail Crew Field Notes, A Newsletter of the Non-profit High Sierra Volunteer Trail Crew.* Interviewed by Emmy Duxbury, 2011.

Daly, H. W. (Chief Pack Master of the U. S. Cavalry). *Manual of Pack Transportation* (1908). Government Printing Office, 1917. Reprinted by The Long Riders' Guild Press.

DeCarteret, Bill. *Mountains, Mules and Memories.* USA, CreateSpace, 2016.

Eldredge, Ward. *In the Summer of 1903, Colonel Charles Young and the Buffalo Soldiers in Sequoia National Park.* Three Rivers, Ca., Sequoia Natural History Assoc., 2003.

Essin, Emmett M. *Shavetails and Bell Sharps, The History of the U.S. Army Mule.* Lincoln, University of Nebraska Press, 1997.

Evermann, Barton Warren. *The Golden Trout of the Southern High Sierras.* Bulletin of the Bureau of Fisheries 25. Washington D. C., 1906.

Farquhar, Francis P. *History of the Sierra Nevada.* Berkeley, University of Calif. Press, 1965.

Fisher, Jack. *Stopping the Road: The Campaign Against Another Trans-Sierra Highway.* The Sager Group, LLC, 2014.

Fisher, Jane. *The Album, Times and Tales of Inyo-Mono.* Bishop, Ca., Chalfant Press Inc., 1987-1993.

Fletcher, Thomas C. *Paiute, Prospector, Pioneer.* Artemisia Press, 1987.

Garriques, George L. "Aparejo." First published in *Western Horsemen.* Oct., 1978.

Giacomazzi, Sharon. "Romancing the Sierra: Mono Pass and Bloody Canyon." *High Sierra Weekend.* Aug. 20, 1992.

Gilbert, Bil. *Westering Man: The Life of Joseph Walker.* New York, Atheneum, 1983.

"Governor Reagan Takes to the Saddle." *Fresno Bee.* June 29, 1972.

Greenwald, John A. *Saddleback Sightseeing in California.* Baldwin Park, Ca., Gem Guides Book Co., 1992.

Halliday, Warren J., and Phyllis Skaggs. " A Packer Reminisces." *The Album*. Bishop, Ca., Chalfant Press, Summer 1994.

Hill, Mary. *Geology of the Sierra Nevada*. Berkeley, University of Calif. Press, 1975.

"History of Jordan Hot Springs." *Inyo National Forest, Mt. Whitney Ranger District*. n. d.

Holland, Dave. *On Location in Lone Pine*. Lone Pine, The Holland House, 1990.

Holliday, J. S. *The World Rushed In: The California Gold Rush Experience*. Edited by J. S. Holliday, New York, Simon & Schuster, 1981.

Howard, Thomas Frederick. *Sierra Crossing: First Roads to California*. Berkeley, University of Calif. Press, 1998.

Huggins, Ellie. *All Roads Lead to Yosemite*. Coldstream Press, 1999.

Hutchings, James. "Packing in the Mountains of Calif.." *Hutchings' California Magazine* Vol. 1, no. 6. Dec. 1856.

---. *In the Heart of the Sierras*. N. A., 1886.

Inyo Anno Domini 1912, Beautiful Owens Valley. The Inyo Register, Bishop, Ca., Chalfant Press, 1983.

Irwin, Sue. *California's Eastern Sierra*. Cachuma Press, 1991.

Jackson, Louise A. *The Mule Men*. Missoula, Mountain Press Publishing Co., 2004.

Jepson, Willis Lynn. "Mt. Whitney, Whitney Creek and the Poison Meadow Trail." *Sierra Club Bulletin 4*, 1903.

---. "Mules and Men." *Sierra Club Bulletin 32*, 1947.

"John Broder of Three Rivers Was First Packer Into Giant Forest." *Visalia Times-Delta Vacation and Progress Edition*. n. d.

Johnson, Russ and Anne. *Your High Sierra Wilderness Guide*, Bishop, Ca., Russ and Anne Johnson, 1963.

Johnson, Shelton (Yosemite National Park Ranger). "A History Remembered" (Sierra Buffalo Soldiers). *Yosemite Guide*. Vol. XXXII No. 1, Summer/Fall 2003.

Johnston, Anna Mills. "A Trip to Mt. Whitney in 1878." *Mt. Whitney Club Journal 1*. May 1902.

Jones, Johnny. *Following the Bells: Traveling High Sierra Wilderness Trails.* As told to Dwight H. Barnes, Oakhurst, Ca., Dwight Barnes, 1994.

Kay, Jane. "'Ike' Livermore - environmentalist from Gold Rush family." *San Francisco Chronicle*. Dec. 8, 2006.

Kimball, H. Stewart (Chairman 1951-1972). *History of the Sierra Club Outing Committee, 1901–1972*. 1990.

King, Clarence. *Mountaineering in the Sierra Nevada*. Lincoln, University of Nebraska Press, 1970. First published in1872 by James R. Osgood Co., Boston.

Leadabrand, Russ. *Exploring California Byways V: Historical Sites*. Ward Ritchie Press, 1971.

---. *Exploring California Byways: From Kings Canyon to the Mexican Border.* Ward Ritchie Press, 1969.

LeConte, Joseph. *A Journal of Ramblings Through the High Sierra of California.* N. A., 1870.

LeConte, Joseph N. "Among the Sources of the South Fork of the King's River." *Sierra Club Bulletin 4*. June, 1903.

Leitritze, Earl. *A History of Calif. Fish Hatcheries (1870-1960)*. State of Calif. Fish and Game, 1970.

Lewis, Oscar. *High Sierra Country*. Boston, Little, Brown and Co. in association with Duell, Loan & Pearce Inc., 1955.

Lilbourne, Winchell. *History of Fresno County and the San Joaquin Valley*. 1933.

Livermore, Jr., Norman B. (Ike)."A One-Man Diamond Hitch: With Suggestions on Saddling and Loading a Pack Animal." *Sierra Club Bulletin 21*. Feb., 1936.

---. "A West Side Packer on A High Trip." *Sierra Club Bulletin 24*. June, 1939.

---. "Sierra Packing and Wilderness Policy." *Sierra Club Bulletin 32*. May, 1947.

---. "Oh! For the Life of a Packer!" *Sierra Club Bulletin 34*. June, 1949.

---. "Packing 50 Years Ago." *The Album: Times and Tales of Inyo-Mono*

County. Bishop, Ca., Chalfant Press, July, 1990.

Matthes, Francois E. *The Incomparable Valley, A Geological Interpretation of the Yosemite*. Berkeley, University of California Press, 1950.

McDermand, Charles. *Waters of the Golden Trout Country*. New York, G. P. Putnam's Sons, 1946.

Mono County. Mono Co., Ca., Nov., 1908.

Morgan, Wallace M. *History of Kern County, California*. Apple Manor Press, 2016.

Mosher, Jo. "Betty Hannam: Frontier Wife." *California Living, Los Angeles Herald-Examiner*. Sept. 8, 1968.

Muench, Joyce and Josef. *Along Sierra Trails: Kings Canyon National Park*. Hastings House, 1947.

Muir, John. *The Mountains of California*. First published by Century, New York and Fisher Unwin, 1894.

---. *My First Summer in the Sierra*. First published by Houghton Mifflin Co., Boston and Constable, London, 1911.

---. *The Yosemite*. First published by The Century Co., New York, 1912.

Mule Days Programs/Magazines. Various publishers, 1972-2019.

Old Spanish Trail, The. Printed courtesy of Dan O'Laurie Museum. Published by Utah's Canyonlands, in cooperation with the Bureau of Land Management, Moab District, n. d.

Olivas, Ethel and Henry. "The Olivas Family." As told by Ethel and Henry Olivas to B. C. Dawson. *Saga of Inyo County*. Bishop, Ca., So. Inyo American Assoc. of Retired Persons, 1977.

Otter, Floyd L. *The Men of Mammoth Forest: A Hundred-Year History of a Sequoia Forest and Its People in Tulare Co., Calif.* Visalia, Edward Brothers Inc., 1963.

Perkins, Peter. *Cowboys of the High Sierra*. Flagstaff, Northland Press, 1980.

Powers, Bob. *Hot Springs Country*. Arthur H. Clark Co., 1989.

---. *North Fork Country*. Arthur H. Clark Co., 1989.

---. *South Fork Country*. Arthur H. Clark Co., 1988.

Reed, Adelle. *Old Mammoth*. Edited by Genny Smith, Palo Alto, Ca., Genny Smith Books, 1982.

---. "Cattlemen of Inyo-Mono." Pioneer Days, *Mono Herald, Chronicle-Union*. Thur. Feb. 7, 1980.

Reed, Lester. *Old-Timers of Southeastern California*. Redlands, Ca., Lester Reed, 1967.

Rojas, Arnold R. *These Were the Vaqueros*. Collected Works of Arnold R. Rojas. 1974.

Roeser, Marye. "2007 Most Honored Packer, Ike Livermore." *Mule Days Magazine*, 2007.

Rose, Gene. "Packer Not Ready To Pack It In." *The Fresno Bee*. April 22, 19??, (Glenn Burns at 76).

Roth, Hal. *Pathway to the Sky: The Story of the John Muir Trail*. Howell-North Books, 1965.

Russell, Carl P. *One Hundred Years in Yosemite*. Berkeley, University of Calif. Press, 1931.

Sanborn, Margaret. *Yosemite*. Yosemite, Ca., Yosemite Assoc., 1989.

Sanderson, Charlotte. "With the Sierra Club in King's River Canyon." *Sierra Club Bulletin 4* (1902-1903).

Sargent, Shirley. *Wawona's Yesterdays*. Yosemite, Ca., Yosemite Natural History Association, 1961.

Savory, Theodore H. *The Mule*. Scientific American Offprint, Dec. 1970.

Schaffer, Jeffrey P. and Thomas Winnett. *Tuolumne Meadows, High Sierra Hiking Guide #4*. Berkeley, Wilderness Press, 1970.

Sheridan, Michael F. *Guidebook to the Quaternary Geology of the East-Central Sierra Nevada*. Phoenix, Michael F. Sheridan, Lebeau Printing Co., 1971.

Sherwin, Ray. "Mammoth Pass Road Newsletter." Feb. 21, 1963.

---. "Minaret Summit to North Fork: Wilderness or Trans-Sierra Highway." Genny Smith Papers, Bancroft Library, Berkeley, University of Calif., 1966.

Sierra Club Bulletin (Many articles). San Francisco, Sierra Club.

---. "Trails." 1940.

Sierra Club Wilderness Outings. Brochure text by Genny Schumacher Smith. San Francisco, Sierra Club, 1965.

Smith, Genny Schumacher. *Deepest Valley*. San Francisco, Sierra Club, 1962.

---. *Sierra East, Edge of the Great Basin*. Berkeley, University of Calif. Press, 2000.

Smith, David A. (Historian). "The Military and Yosemite: The Cavalry Years." The Burdick Military History Project, San Jose University, n. d.

Sowaal, Marguerite. *Naming the Eastern Sierra: Dirty Sock to Bloody Canyon*. Bishop, Ca., Chalfant Press, 1985.

Starr, Jr., Walter A. *Starr's Guide, Guide to the John Muir Trail and the High Sierra Region*. San Francisco, Sierra Club, 1967.

Swain, William. "Diary of William Swain." *The World Rushed In: The Calif. Gold Rush Experience*. Edited by. J. S. Holliday, New York, Simon and Schuster, 1981. First published 1849.

Taylor, Ron. "Mule Train: Memories." *The Fresno Bee*. Mon. Oct. 25, 1976.

Thomann, Jane A. *The Zig Zag Post Office and its Neighbors: Little Lake, Inyo Co. Calif. 1885-1971*. Historical Society of the Upper Mojave Desert Press. n. d.

Thompson, David. *The Tennessee Letters – 1857-1860*. Compiled by David Thompson, Reno, Nev., The Grace Dangberg Foundation Inc., Printed by A. Carlisle and Co., 1983.

Vargo, Cecile Page. "Hauling It In and Hauling It Out, Anecdotes of the Old Time Packers." *Explore California History*. Sept. 2014 Issue.

Wadsworth, Ginger. *John Muir: Wilderness Protector*. Lerner Publishing Group, 1992.

Wampler, Joseph and Weldon F. Heald, Charles McDermand. *High Sierra Mountain Wonderland*. Berkeley, Ca., 1960.

Webster, Beverly. "The Whitney Survey Party in the Sierra Nevada." *The Album*. Bishop, Ca., Chalfant Press, 1993 Annual Edition.

White, Stuart Edward. *The Mountains*, New York, Grosset & Dunlap Publishing, 1904.

---. *The Pass*, First published in Outing Magazine, New York, The Outing Publishing Co., 1906 (Farquhar No. 20).

Wiltsee, Ernest A. *The Pioneer Miner and the Pack Mule Express*. San Francisco, Calif. Historical Society, 1931.

Winnett, Thomas and Karl Schwenke. *Sierra South*. Berkeley, Wilderness Press, 1968.

Winnett, Thomas and Jason Winnett. *Sierra North*. Berkeley, Wilderness Press, 1985.

Woo, Elaine. "Norman Livermore Jr., 95; advised Gov. Reagan on environmental issues." *Los Angeles Times*. Dec. 9, 2006.

Wyman, Alisha. "Pack, saddle business still thrives." (Jay Barnes), *The Union Democrat*. Tues. Oct. 19, 2004

MANUSCRIPTS, DOCUMENTS, LETTERS, AND INTERVIEWS

Bedell, Don and Phyllis. Conversations/interviews.

Booth, Roy. "I Remember - The Forest Service Hosts Two 4-Star Generals." Oct. 10, 1944.

Burkhart, Lona. Phone conversations to update and edit packing history outline, n. d.

Cecil, Dena. "History of Cecil Pack Train." Jan. 21, 1985.

Clyde, Dr. Allen. Letter response to packing history outline, n. d.

Cook, Deborah (niece of Ted Cook). Personal letter and documents regarding Chrysler and Cook Mt. Whitney Pack Trains, Aug. 22, 2005.

Davis, Janet. Additional westside packing history, letter Aug. 6, 2003, emails Sept. 13, 2003 and Feb. 20, 2004.

DeCarteret, Bill and Marilyn. Response and edits to email packing history outline of Mar. 28, 2004, letter response and edits, April 3, 2005.

Dohnel, Dave. Letter response and edits to packing history outline, n. d.

Hall, Bud. Personal packing history letter n. d., phone calls/interviews.

Johnson, Anne. "McGee Creek Pack Station, a Short Historical Story." n. d.

---. Email response and edits to the packing history manuscript, June 10, 2005, conversations/interviews.

Keely, C. Clarke. "Recollections." Jan. 12, 1985.

Langdon (Vincent), Mardi. Personal letter regarding working for Kennedy Meadows Pack Trains, 1981-82.

Lange, Ann (BCHC). Conversations/interviews.

Lewis, Sam. "History of Sam Lewis's Packing Experiences." Oct. 14, 1968.

Livermore, Jr., Norman B. (Ike). *The Tourist Packing Business of the High Sierra Region* Ross, Ca., Feb. 1935. (Thesis for Master's Program at Stanford).

---. Personal letter and phone call with edits to packing history outline and manuscript, April 25, 2005, conversations/interviews.

Mack, Gerald. "1932 Sierra Club Outing." Written in the 1970s-80s and documented by Arlene Pearce, Bishop, Ca.

Moore, Sharon. Email response to packing history outline, Jan. 15, 2004.

Morgan, Charles. "Mt. Whitney Pack Trains 1946 to 1971."

---. "Mule Packers and the Sierra Club." n. d.

Rector, Darl (Ernest and Dena Cecil's daughter). Letter response to packing history outline, Sept. 9, 2003, email response Feb.28, 2004.

Roeser, Jennifer A. Testimony Before the Sub-committee on National Parks, Recreation and Public Lands, Committee on Resources, House of Representatives, Hearing on HR "Right to Ride Livestock on Public Lands" Act of 2003. Sept. 30, 2003.

Ross, Bart. Personal packing history letter, 1987, conversations/interviews.

Schober, Walt. Email of the Schober packing history, Oct. 4, 2000.

Sears, Barney. "Biographical Sketch of Barney Sears Mule Skinner." Letter addressed to Neal M. Rahm, Forest Supervisor of Inyo National Forest, Feb. 8, 1949.

Topping, Bart and Cindy. Letter response with edits to packing history outline, n. d.

U.S. Forest Service. "Commercial Pack Stock Use Authorizations for the Ansel Adams and John Muir Wildernesses." Cumulative Effects Analysis, Proposed Action, Inyo and Sierra National Forests, June, 2004.

---. "Trail Management Plan for the John Muir, Ansel Adams, and Dinkey Lakes Wildernesses." Proposed Action, Inyo and Sierra National Forests, June, 2004
---. Wilderness Act of 1964.

---. John Muir Wilderness Plan, 1974.

Wass, Forrest. Personal letter with short packing history of his father, Fred Wass, Aug. 9, 2005.

Womack, J. C. (State Highway Engineer). "Feasibility of, including F. H. 100 (Forest Highway 100), in the State Highway System, a Trans-Sierra Highway from Interstate 5 near Los Banos to California Nevada Stateline near Benton Station." Issued by Calif. Dept. of Public Works, Mar. 4, 1966.

PUBLIC LIBRARIES AND COLLECTIONS

Eastern California Museum, Independence, Ca.

Inyo Co. Library and Archives, Bishop, Ca.

Kern Valley Museum, Kernville, Ca.

Laws Museum and Library, Bishop, Ca.

Mono Co. Library and Archives, Bridgeport, Ca.

MISC. SOURCES

Eastern High Sierra Packers' Association

Western High Sierra Packers' Association

U. S. Forest Service- Inyo National Forest

American Mule Museum, Bishop, Calif.

Back Country Horsemen of California

Owens Valley History website, Ray DeLea

Fifty plus years of accumulated knowledge from being in the packing business: my husband, Lou Roeser, sharing the business and working together, (Mammoth Lakes Pack Outfit), my sister and brother-in-law, Dorothy and Louie, and niece Laurie Fitzhugh, Jack and Adrienne Hastings, our children– Lee and Jennifer Roeser, (McGee Creek Pack Station), Kerry and Mike Elam, Leslie and Matt Engelhart, and Maryl Roeser–, my brother-in-law and sister-in-law, Bud and Betty Palmer.

Extensive conversations with pack station owners/packers, over many years including:
Eastside packers: Greg and Ruby Allen, Brian and Danica Berner, Mark and Robin Berry, Dudley, Alice, and John Booth, Gene and Lona Burkhart, Herb

Carls, Bart Cranney, Bud and Dave Hall, Ray Holmgren, Claude Hunewill, Stan and Jan Hunewill, Tommy Jefferson, Kathy Jefferson Bancroft, Russ and Anne Johnson, John and Suzy Ketcham, Sam Lewis, Jr, Ike Livermore, Herb, Marge, and Craig London, Arch Mahan, Don McGuffin, Slim Nivens, Harold Moore, Charlie and Mike Morgan, Chad Palmer, Wilfred and Kenneth Partridge, Allie Robinson, Lee and Jennifer Roeser, Art and Walt Schober, Lee, John, Sybil, and Verne Summers, Murt Stewart, Bob, Jean, and Bobby Tanner, Slim Tatum, Bob Vinnedge, Bob Wenger, Dennis Winchester.

Westside packers: Jay Barnes, Don and Phyllis Bedell, Josh and Matt Bloom, Glenn Burns, John and Jenise Cunningham, Janet and Bo Davis, Bill and Marilyn DeCarteret, Lee Maloy, Earl McKee Jr., Watson Moore, Brad Myers, Luke and Hilary Painter, Bart Ross, Adeline Smith, Cindy and Bart Topping.

Forest Service packers: Herb Carls, Michael Morse, Leo Porterfield, Lee Roeser, Henry Thorne.

Countless packers, many of whom worked for us as well as other pack stations, and many who became our extended family: Red Altum, Steve and Laura Barger, Sharon and Jerry Blanks, Barney Chapman, Gene Cooper, Matt Durham, Rene Duykaerts, Dan Farris, Max Fly, Jim Heavens, Frank Hunter, Carl James, Sallie Joseph, Butch Lee, Scott Lee, Ed Leos, Larry Maurice, Forrest Newman, Rob Pearce, Dan Price, Kent Reeves, Hank Simpson, Dave Stamey, Frank Twitchell, Gabe Williams, Rob Willis, Bryan "Butch" and Carol Willmon, Brad Witman, musicians Pete Watercott, Derik Olson and so many, many more! These folks worked with us at the pack station, horse drives, Sierra Meadows, and Lou's commercial film work, and knew our business well.

"Learning the Ropes." (Leslie Roeser Engelhart)

Dorothy Fitzhugh on her horse Mickey at Grassy Lake on the cover
of a MLPO brochure. (Hugh Avery)

Lou Roeser with a string of mules at Squaw Lake by Lake of the Lone Indian. (Steve Lucasik)

Lou Roeser and mules on the crest of Hopkins Pass make a remarkable silhouette.
(Steve Lucasik)

Lou Roeser and pack trip party on Hopkins Pass headed down to Big McGee Lake.

Marye Roeser on her horse, Copper, on the top of McGee Pass in 1954.
(Steve Lucasik)

**Marye and Lou Roeser on their horses on the MLPO Horse Drive. Happy Trails!
(William Shepley Collection)**

**Front Cover Illustration: "Top of the Pass." Watercolor by Marye Roeser
Back Cover Illustration: "Sierra Mule Pack String." Watercolor by Marye Roeser**